ADULT SEQUELS

compiled by
Mandy Hicken

CAREER DEVELOPMENT GROUP

(GROUP OF CILIP, THE CHARTERED INSTITUTE OF LIBRARY
AND INFORMATION PROFESSIONALS)

THE CDG acknowledge the assistance of
REMPLOY LIMITED
in the production of this publication
2004

REMPLOY

The Career Development Group 2004

016·80883

1st edition 1922 by Thomas Aldred
2nd edition 1928 by W. H. Parker
3rd edition 1947 by F. M. Gardner
4th edition 1955 by F. M. Gardner
5th edition 1967 by F. M. Gardner
6th edition 1974 by F. M. Gardner
7th edition 1982 by M. E. Hicken
8th edition 1986 by M. E. Hicken
9th edition 1986 by M. E. Hicken
10th edition 1991 by M. E. Hicken
11th edition 1995 by M. E. Hicken
12th edition 1998 by M. E. Hicken

British Library Cataloguing-in-Publication Data.

A catalogue record for this book is available from the British Library.

ISBN 1-901353-09-5

Jacket design by Origin Studios, Stoke-on-Trent
Printed by and bound by Page Bros, Norwich

PREFACE TO THE THIRTEENTH EDITION

For this, the thirteenth edition of 'Sequels', I had accumulated a whole catalogue drawer full of new entries. I decided, therefore, to do a bit of weeding, and have taken out a lot of the very long series of detective stories published in the 1940s and 50s, long out of print, and unlikely to be remembered by many readers. I have, of course, kept in the series by authors like Agatha Christie and Ngaio Marsh, who have never gone out of print or fashion. The older material can still be accessed by consulting an earlier volume of 'Sequels'.

There has been a large number of new series, many of which look like running for the foreseeable future, as new writers, particularly of thrillers, emerge, and established authors continue to add new series to their output

The overall pattern of the book remains the same, and includes
- a) novels in which the same characters appear
- b) sequences of books connected by a theme
- c) sequences with an historical or geographical connection
- d) non-fiction, particularly autobiography, intended to be read in sequence

As far as paperback fantasy novels are concerned, I have only listed the ones that are direct sequels (many of them are written as trilogies within a series). Otherwise, 'Star Trek' novels would occupy about ten pages of the book. A full list of titles in the series is usually printed in each of the books.

My thanks go to all the people who have taken the trouble to write to me with corrections and additions to the book – I appreciate your help, and am delighted that so many library users find 'Sequels' valuable in choosing their reading material. Thanks also to colleagues in the profession for their advice, and the occasional use of their databases.

Special thanks to Holt Jackson, who continue to supply me with their weekly lists of forthcoming titles. Because of this advance information, I have been able, for the first time, to list titles up to June 2004 which will give a bit more currency to 'Sequels'.

Mandy Hicken   January 2004

AB HUGH, D.
DOOM
1 Endgame
2 Infernal sky

AB HUGH, D.
WAR LORD
1 Arthur, war lord (1994)
2 Far beyond the wave (1994)

ABBEY, L.
UNICORN AND DRAGON
1 Unicorn
2 Dragon
3 The green man

ABBEY, L.
ULTIMA SAGA
1 The forge of virtue
2 The temper of wisdom

ABBOTT, J.
WHIT MOSLEY
1 Cut and run (2004)
2 A kiss gone bad (2004)
3 Black Jack point (2004)

ABRAHAM, C
THE ONEDIN LINE
1 The shipmaster (1973)
2 The iron ships (1974)
3 The high seas (1976)
4 Trade winds (1977)
5 The white ships (1979)
6 Turning tide (1980)

ABSE, D.
1 Ash on a young man's sleeve
2 There was a young man from Cardiff
   (1991)
3 A poet in the family (1974)

ACHEBE, C.
AFRICAN TRILOGY
1 Things fall apart (1958)
2 No longer at ease (1960)
3 Arrow of gold (1964)

ACTON, H.
1 Memoirs of an aesthete (1948)
2 More memoirs of an aesthete (1970)

ADAM, P.
MIKE MCLEAN
1 A nasty dose of death (1993)

2 An exceptional corpse (1994)
3 Toxin (1995)

ADAMS, D.
DIRK GENTLY
1 Dirk Gently's Holistic Detective Agency
   (1987)
2 The long dark teatime of the soul (1988)

ADAMS, D.
HITCH-HIKER''S GUIDE TO THE
GALAXY
1 The hitch-hikers guide to the Galaxy
   (1979)
2 The restaurant at the end of the Universe
   (1980)
3 Life, the Universe and everything (1982)
4 So long, and thanks for all the fish (1984)
5 Mostly harmless (1992)

ADAMS, JANE
DET. INSPECTOR MIKE CROFT
1 The Greenway (1995)
2 Cast the first stone (1996)
3 Fade to grey (1998)
4 Final frame (1999)

ADAMS, JANE
RAY FLOWERS
1 Angel gateway (2000)
2 Like angels falling (2001)
3 Angel eyes (2002)

ADAMS, R.
1 Shardik (1974)
2 Maia (1984)

ADAMS, R.
WATERSHIP DOWN
1 Watership Down (1978)
2 Tales from Watership Down (1996)

ADAMS, ROBERT
HORSECLANS
1 The coming of the Horseclans (1985)
2 The swords of the Horseclans (1985)
3 The revenge of the Horseclans
5 The savage mountains (1985)
6 The patrimony (1985)
7 Horseclans odyssey (1985)
8 The death of a legend (1985)
9 The witchgoddess (1985)
10 Bili the axe (1985)
11 Champion of the last battle (1985)
12 A woman of the Horseclans (1985)

ADAMSON, JOY
1 Born free (1960)
2 Living free (1961)
3 Forever free (1962)
4 Elsa and her cubs (1965)

ADDIS, FAITH
1 The year of the cornflake (1983)
2 Green behind the ears (1984)
3 Buttered side down (1985)
4 Down to earth (1987)
5 Taking the biscuit (1989)
   NF Country life

AGRY, E.
O'REILLY
1 Assault Force O
2 O'Reilly:blowtorch (1982)

AHERN, J.
THE SURVIVALIST
1 Total war
2 The nightmare begins
3 The quest
4 The doomsayer
5 The web
6 The savage horde
7 The prophet
8 The end is coming
9 Earth fire
11 The reprisal
12 The rebellion
13 Pursuit
14 The terror
15 Overlord
16 The arsenal
17 The ordeal
18 The struggle
19 Final rain

AIKMAN, A.
BOYET RHODES
1 The caves of Segonda (1985)
2 The eye of Itza (1986)
3 The brokers of doom (1987)

AIRD, C.
INSPECTOR C. D. SLOAN
1 The religious body (1966)
2 A most contagious crime (1967)
3 Henrietta who? (1968)
4 The complete steel (1969)
5 A late phoenix (1970)
6 His burial too (1973)
7 Slight mourning (1975)
8 Parting breath (1977)
9 Some die eloquent (1979)

10 Passing strange (1980)
11 Last respects (1982)
12 Harm's way (1984)
13 A dead liberty (1986)
14 The body politic (1990)
15 A going concern (1993)
16 Injury time:short stories (1994)
17 After effects (1996)
18 Stiff news (1998)
19 Little knell (2000)
20 Amendment of life (2002)
21 Chapter and hearse: short stories (2003)

AIRTH, R.
DET. INSPECTOR MADDEN
1 River of darkness (1999)
2 The blood-rimmed tide (2001)

ALBANY, J.
S.A.S.
1 Warrior caste (1982)
2 Mailed fist (1983)
3 Deacon's dagger
4 Close combat (1983)
5 Marching fire (1984)
6 Last bastion (1984)
7 Borneo story (1985)

ALBERT, M.
PETE SAWYER
1 Stone angel (1986)
2 Back in the real world (1987)
3 Get off at Babylon (1988)
4 Long teeth (1988)
5 The midnight sister (1989)
6 Bimbo heaven (1990)
7 The last smile (1989)
8 The zig-zag man (1991)
9 The Riviera contract (1992)

ALDERMAN, G.
1 The memory palace
2 Lilith's castle

ALDING, P.
CID ROOM
1 The C.I.D. room (1967)
2 Circle of danger (1968)
3 Murder among thieves (1969)
5 Despite the evidence (1971)
6 Call back to crime (1972)
7 Field of fire (1973)
8 The murder line (1974)
9 Six days to death (1975)
10 Murder is suspected (1977)
11 Ransom town (1979)
12 A man condemned (1981)

13 Betrayal by death (1982)
14 One man's justice (1983)

ALDISS, B.
1 The hand-reared boy (1970)
2 A soldier erect (1971)
3 A rude awakening (1978)

ALDISS, B.
HELLICONIA TRILOGY
1 Helliconia Spring (1982)
2 Helliconia Summer (1983)
3 Helliconia Winter (1985)

ALEICHEM, S.
TEVYE
1 The old country (1966)
2 Tevye's daughters (1973)

ALEXANDER, B.
SIR JOHN FIELDING
1 Blind justice (1995)
2 Murder in Grub Street (1996)
3 Watery grave (1997)

ALEXANDER, D.
PHOENIX
1 Dark Messiah
2 Ground zero

ALEXANDER, L.
CHRONICLES OF PRYDAIN
1 The book of three
2 The black cauldron
3 Castle of Llyr
4 Taran wanderer
5 The High King

ALEXANDER, M.
THE WELS OF YTHAN
1 Ancient dreams
2 Magic casements
3 Shadow realm

ALEXANDER, S.
MICHELANGELO BUONAROTTI
1 Michelangelo, the Florentine (1957)
2 The hand of Michelangelo (1965)
3 Nicodemus (1985)

ALIENS
1 The labyrinth, by S.Perry (1996)
2 Alien harvest, by R.Sheckley (1996)
3 Rogue, by R.Sheckley (1997)
4 Music of the spears, by Y.Navarro (1997)
5 Hunter's planet, by D.Bischoff (1998)

ALLBEURY, T.
TAD ANDERS
1 Snowball (1974)
2 The Judas factor (1984)

ALLDRITT, K.
BLACK COUNTRY SERIES
1 The good pit man (1976)
2 The lover next door (1978)
3 Elgar on the journey to Hanley (1979)

ALLEGRETTO, M.
JACOB LOMAX
1 Death on the rocks (1988)
2 Blood stone (1989)
3 Dead of winter (1990)

ALLEN, C. V.
1 Leftover dreams (1992)
2 Chasing rainbows (1993)

ALLEN, CONRAD
GEORGE PORTER DILMAN
1 Murder on the Lusitania
2 Murder on the Mauretania
3 Murder on the Minnesota

ALLEN, R. B.
VENERA
1 The torch of honour
2 Rogue powers

ALLEN, R. M.
1 Caliban (1993)
2 Isaac Asimov's inferno (1994)

ALLEN, S.
GHOSTS
1 Reluctant ghost
2 Meddlesome ghost
3 Helpful ghost

ALLINGHAM, M.
ALBERT CAMPION
1 The crime at Black Dudley (1929)
2 Mystery mile (1929)
3 Look to the lady (1931)
4 Police at the funeral (1931)
5 Sweet danger (1933)
6 Death of a ghost (1934)
7 Flowers for the judge (1936)
8 The case of the late pig (1937)
9 Dancers in mourning (1937)
10 The fashion in shrouds (1938)
11 Mr. Campion and others (1939)
12 Black plumes (1940)

13 Traitor's purse (1941)
14 Coroner's pidgin (1945)
15 More work for the undertaker (1948)
16 Tiger in the smoke (1952)
17 The beckoning lady (1955)
18 Hide my eyes (1958)
19 The china governess (1963)
20 The mind readers (1965)
21 Cargo of eagles (1967)
22 Mr. Campion's farthing (1968)
23 Mr. Campion's falcon (1969)
24 Mr. Campion's lucky day and other stories (1973)

ALLISON-WILLIAMS, J.
THE TABARD INN
1 Mistress of 'The Tabard' (1983)
2 Simon of 'The Tabard' (1984)

ALMEDINGEN, E. M.
THORNGOLD FAMILY
1 Fair haven (1959)
2 Dark splendour (1961)

AMBLER, E.
ARTHUR ABDEL SIMPSON
1 Light of day (1962)
2 Dirty story (1967)

AMBLER, E.
CHARLES LATIMER
1 The mask of Dimitrios (1939)
2 The intercom conspiracy (1970)

AMES, D.
SGT. JUAN LLORCA
1 The man in the tricorn hat (1962)
2 The man with three Jaguars (1963)
3 The man with three chins (1964)
4 The man with three passports (1967)

AMIS, K.
PATRICK STANDISH
1 Take a girl like you (1960)
2 Difficulties with girls (1988)

ANAND, V.
NORMAN TRILOGY
1 Gildenford (1979)
2 The Norman pretender (1980)
3 Disputed crown (1982)

ANAND, V.
BRIDGES OVER TIME
1 The proud villeins (1990)
2 The ruthless yeoman (1991)

3 Women of Ashdon (1992)
4 The faithful lovers (1993)
5 The cherished wives (1994)

ANDERSON, K. J.
THE SAGA OF SEVEN SUNS
1 Hidden empires (2002)
2 A forest of stars (2003)

ANDERSON, J. R. L.
PIET DEVENTER
1 A sprig of sea lavender (1978)
2 Festival (1979)
3 Late delivery (1982)

ANDERSON, P.
THE KING OF YS
1 Roma mater
2 Gallicenae
3 Dahut
4 The dog and the wolf

ANDERSON, P.
POLESOTECHNIC LEAGUE
1 The Earthbook of Stormgate
2 The trouble twisters
3 War of the wingmen
4 Trader to the stars
5 Satan's world
6 Mirkheim

ANDERSON, P.
FLANDRY
1 Ensign Flandry (1977)
2 A circus of hells (1978)
3 The rebel worlds
4 Tiger by the tail
5 Honourable enemies
6 Flandry of Terra
7 Commander Flandry (1979)
8 A handful of stars
9 Knight Flandry (1980)
10 A stone in Heaven (1981)
11 The game of Empire (1994)

ANDERSON, P.
ANSON GUTHRIE
1 Harvest of stars
2 The fleet of stars

ANDERSON, V.
1 Spam tomorrow (1956)
2 Our Square (1957)
3 Beware of children (1958)
4 Daughters of divinity (1959)
5 The Flo affair (1963)

6 The Northrepps grandchildren (1968)
7 Scrambled eggs for Christmas (1970)

ANDREWS, L.
THE GARDEN
1 One night in London (1980)
2 Weekend in the Garden (1981)
3 In an Edinburgh drawing room (1983)
4 The phoenix syndrome (1987)

ANDREWS, L.
ST. MARTHA'S HOSPITAL
1 The light in the ward (1984)
2 The healing time (1986)
3 Front line, 1940 (1990)

ANDREWS, V.
DOLLENGAGER FAMILY
1 Garden of shadows (1987)
2 Petals on the wind (1980)
3 If there be thorns (1981)
4 Seeds of yesterday (1984)
5 Flowers in the attic (1980)

ANDREWS, V.
CASTEEL FAMILY
1 Heaven (1986)
2 Dark angel (1987)
3 Fallen hearts (1989)
4 Gates of paradise (1989)
5 Web of dreams (1990)

ANDREWS, V.
CUTLER FAMILY
1 Dawn (1990)
2 Secrets of the morning (1991)
3 Twilight's child (1992)
4 Midnight whispers (1992)
5 Darkest hour (1993)

ANDREWS, V.
LOGAN FAMILY
1 Melody (1997)
2 Heart song (1997)
3 Unfinished symphony (1997)
4 Music in the night (1998)
5 Olivia (1999)

ANDREWS, V.
LANDRY FAMILY
1 Tarnished gold (1996)
2 Ruby (1994)
3 Pearl in the mist (1994)
4 All that glitters (1995)
5 Hidden jewel (1996)

ANDREWS, V.
HUDSON FAMILY
1 Rain (2000)
2 Lightning strikes (2001)
3 Eye of the storm (2001)
4 End of the rainbow (2002)

ANDREWS, V.
ORPHANS
1 Butterfly (1998)
2 The runaways (1999)
3 Brooke (2000)

ANDREWS, V.
WILLOW DE BEERS
1 Willow (2002)
2 Wicked forest (2003)
3 Twisted roots (2004)

ANGELOU, M.
1 I know why the caged bird sings (1984)
2 Gather together in my name (1985)
3 Singin' and swingin' and makin' merry like Christmas (1985)
4 The heart of a woman (1986)
5 All God's children need travelling shoes (1987)
6 Wouldn't take nothing for my journey now (1995)
7 A song flung up to heaven (2002)
NF Autobiography

ANGOFF, C.
POLONSKY FAMILY
1 Journey to the dawn (1951)
2 In the morning light (1952)
3 The sun at dawn (1955)
4 Between day and dark (1959)
5 The bitter spring (1961)
6 Summer storm (1963)
7 Memory of autumn (1968)
8 Winter twilight (1970)
9 Season of mists (1971)
10 Mid-century (1974)
11 Toward the horizon (1980)

ANSA, T. M.
1 Baby of the family (1995)
2 The hand that I fan with (1997)

ANTHONY, E.
DAVINA GRAHAM
1 The defector (1980)
2 Avenue of the dead (1981)
3 Albatross (1982)
4 The company of saints (1983)

ANTHONY, E.
AUSTRIAN SERIES
1 Imperial Highness (1953)
2 Curse not the King (1954)
3 Far fly the eagles (1955)

ANTHONY, M.
THE LAST RUNE
1 Beyond the pale
2 The keep of fire
3 The dark remains
4 Blood of mystery (2002)

ANTHONY, M. D.
CANTERBURY MYSTERIES
1 The Becket factor (1996)
2 Dark provenance (1997)
3 Midnight come (1998)

ANTHONY, P.
1 Chthon (1967)
2 Phthor (1970)

ANTHONY, P.
BATTLE CIRCLE
1 Sos the rope (1968)
2 Var the stick (1971)
3 Neq the sword (1971)

ANTHONY, P.
CLUSTER
1 Vicinity (1979)
2 Chaining the lady (1979)
3 Kirlian quest (1979)
4 Thousandstar
5 Viscous circle (1981)

ANTHONY, P.
TAROT TRILOGY
1 God of Tarot
2 Vision of Tarot
3 Faith of Tarot

ANTHONY, P.
THE APPRENTICE ADEPT
1 Split infinity (1981)
2 Blue adept (1981)
3 Juxtaposition (1983)
4 Out of phaze (1988)
5 Phaze doubt (1991)

ANTHONY, P.
THE MAGIC OF XANTH
1 A spell for the chameleon (1977)
2 A source of magic (1979)
3 Castle Roogna (1979)

4 Centaur Isle (1982)
5 Ogre, Ogre (1982)
6 Night mare (1983)
7 Dragon on a pedestal (1985)
8 Crewel Lye (1988)
9 Golem in the gears
10 Vale of the vole (1988)
11 Heaven cent (1989)
12 Robot adept (1989)
13 The man from Mundania (1990)
14 Unicorn point (1990)
15 Isle of view (1991)
16 Question quest (1992)
17 Harpy thyme (1993)
18 Geis of the gargoyle (1994)
18 The colour of her panties (1992)
19 Roc and a hard place (1995)
19 Demons don't dream (1993)
20 Yon ill wind (1996)

ANTHONY, P.
MODE
1 Virtual mode (1991)
2 Fractual mode (1992)
3 Chaos mode (1994)

ANTHONY, P.
OF MAN AND MANTA
1 Omnivore
2 Orn
3 Ox

ANTHONY, P.
BIO OF A SPACE TYRANT
1 Refugee
2 Mercenary
3 Politician
4 Executive
5 Statesman

ANTHONY, P.
INCARNATIONS OF IMMORTALITY
1 On a pale horse (1986)
2 Bearing an hour glass (1986)
3 With a tangled skein (1987)
4 Wielding a red sword (1987)
5 Being a green mother (1988)
6 For love of evil (1990)
7 And eternity (1990)

ANTHONY, P. & MARGROFF, R. E.
MINERALS
1 Dragon's gold (1991)
2 Serpent's silver (1992)
3 Chimaera's copper (1993)
4 Orc's opal (1993)
5 Mouvar's magic (1994)

APPIAH, A.
SIR PATRICK SCOTT
1 Avenging angel (1990)
2 Nobody likes Letitia (1994)
3 Another death in Venice (1995)

APPIGNANESI, R.
ITALIA PERVERSA
1 Stalin
2 The mosque (1985)
3 Destroying America (1987)

ARCHER, F.
1 The distant scene (1967)
2 Under the parish lantern (1969)
3 Hawthorn hedge country (1970)
4 Secrets of Bredon Hill (1971)
5 A lad of Evesham Vale (1972)
6 Muddy boots and Sunday suits (1973)
7 Golden sheaves, black horses (1974)
8 When village bells were silent (1975)
9 Poacher's pie (1976)
10 By hook and by crook (1978)
11 When Adam was a boy (1979)
12 Fred Archer, farmer's son (1986)
13 The village of my childhood (1989)
    NF Country life in the Cotswolds

ARCHER, J.
1 Kane and Abel (1980)
2 The prodigal daughter (1982)

ARDEN, T.
THE OROKON
1 The harlequin's dance (1997)
2 The king and queen of swords (1998)
3 Sultan of moon and stars (1999)
4 Sisterhood of the blue storm (2001)

ARDIN, W.
CHARLES RAMSAY
1 Plain dealer (1992)
2 Some dark antiquities (1994)
3 Light at midnight (1995)
4 The Mary medallion (1996)

ARLEN, L.
THE BORODINS
1 Love and honour (1984)
2 War and passion (1984)

ARMITAGE, A.
HAWKSMOOR
1 Hawksmoor (1981)
2 Hunter's moon (1985)
3 Touchstone (1987)

4 Hawkrise (1988)
5 The dark arches (1996)

ARMITAGE, A.
EVA BOWER
1 Chapter of innocence (1988)
2 Chapter of echoes (1989)
3 Chapter of shadows (1990)

ARMSTRONG, C.
DET. FRANK PAGAN
1 Jig (1987)
2 Mazurka (1988)
3 Mambo (1990)
4 Jigsaw (1994)
5 Heat (1996)

ARMSTRONG, D.
DET. INSPECTOR FRANK KAVANAGH
1 Until dawn tomorrow (1996)
2 Thought for the day (1997)
3 Small vices (2002)

ARMSTRONG, S.
CLACHAN
1 A croft in Clachan (1976)
2 Clachan days (1977)
3 A hotel by Clachan (1978)
4 The electrics come to Clachan (1979)
5 Jamie in Clachan (1980)
    NF Life in the Scottish Highlands

ARMSTRONG, T.
THE CROWTHER CHRONICLES
1 The Crowthers of Bankdam (1940)
2 Pilling always pays (1954)
3 Sue Crowther's marriage (1961)
4 Our London office (1966)

ARMSTRONG, V.
DET. SGT. JUDITH PULLEN & RALPH
ARNOTT
1 Sleight of hand (1991)
2 The honey trap (1992)
3 Close call (1994)
4 Beyond the pale (2002)

ARNOLD, B.
COPPINGER TETRALOGY
1 A singer at the wedding (1979)
2 The song of the nightingale (1980)
3 The muted swan (1981)
4 Running to Paradise (1983)

ARNOLD, R.
1 A very quiet war (1962)
2 Orange Street and Brickhole Lane (1963)
  NF Autobiography

ARNOTHY, C.
1 I am fifteen and I do not want to die
  (1963)
2 It is not so easy to live (1965)

ASARO, C.
SAGA OF THE SKOLIAN EMPIRE
1 Primary inversion (1998)
2 The radiant seas (1999)

ASH, S.
THE TEARS OF ARTAMON
1 Drakhaoul (2003)
2 Prisoner of Ironsea Tower (2004)

ASHTON, H.
WILCHESTER CHRONICLES
1 Tadpole Hall (1941)
2 Joanna at Littlefold (1945)
3 Yeoman's Hospital (1949)
4 The Captain comes home (1950)
5 Half-crown house (1956)

ASHWORTH, S.
1 A matter of fat (1992)
2 Personal growth (1993)

ASIMOV, I.
FOUNDATION
1 Prelude to Foundation (1988)
2 Foundation and Empire (1952)
3 Second foundation (1953)
4 Foundation's edge (1983)
5 Foundation (1951)
6 Foundation and Earth (1986)
7 Forward the Foundation (1993)

ASIMOV, I.
ELIJAH BALEY
1 The caves of steel (1954)
2 The naked sun (1958)
3 The robots of dawn (1983)
4 Robots and Empire (1985)

ASIMOV, I.
FANTASTIC VOYAGE
1 Fantastic voyage (1966)
2 Destination brain (1987)

ASIMOV, I.
BLACK WIDOWERS DINING CLUB
1 Tales of the Black Widowers (1975)
2 More tales of the Black Widowers (1977)
3 Casebook of the Black Widowers (1980)
4 Puzzles of the Black Widowers (1990)

ASIMOV, I.
ROBOTS
1 I, Robot (1950)
2 The rest of the robots (1967)
3 The positronic man, with R.Silverberg
  (1992)
4 Caliban, by R.M.Allen (1993)

ASIMOV, I.
DAVID STARR - SPACE RANGER
1 Space ranger (1972)
2 Pirates of the asteroids (1972)
3 The big sun of Mercury (1972)
4 The oceans of Venus (1972)
5 The rings of Saturn (1973)
6 The moon of Jupiter (1973)

ASPLER, T.
EZRA BRANT
1 Blood is thicker than Beaujolais (1995)
2 The beast of Barbaresco (1996)
3 Death on the Douro (1997)

ASPRIN, R.
SANCTUARY
1 Thieves world
2 Tales from the vulgar unicorn
3 Shadows of Sanctuary
4 Storm season
5 The face of chaos

ASPRIN, R.
MYTH
1 Mythnomers and imperfections
2 Another fine myth
3 Myth directions
4 Hit or myth
5 Myth conceptions
6 Myth-ing persons
7 Little myth marker
8 M.Y.T.H. INC. link
9 Myth Inc. in action

ASPRIN, R.
PHULE
1 Phule's company
2 Phule's paradise

ASTLEY, J.
1 Fall of Midas (1976)
2 Copsi Castle (1978)

ASTOR, BROOKE
1 Patchwork child
2 Footprints (1986)

ATKINS, E.
1 We bought an island (1976)
2 Tales from our Cornish island (1986)

ATKINS, M. E.
IRIS SERIES
1 By the north door
2 Palimpsest (1981)
3 Samain (1977)
4 Tangle (1988)

ATTANASIO, A.
RADIX
1 In other worlds
2 Radix

ATTANASIO, A.
THE DOMINIONS OF IRTH
1 The dark shore (1997)
2 The shadow eater (1998)
3 Octoberland (1998)

ATTANASIO, A.
ARTHURIAN SERIES
1 Arthor (1994)
2 The dragon and the unicorn (1995)
3 The eagle and the sword (1997)
4 The wolf and the crown (1998)

AUDEMARS, P.
M. PINAUD
1 The two imposters (1959)
2 The fire and the clay (1960)
3 The turns of time (1961)
4 The crown of night (1962)
5 The dream and the dead (1963)
6 The wings of darkness (1963)
7 Fair maids missing (1964)
8 Dead with sorrow (1965)
9 Time of temptation (1966)
10 A thorn in the dust (1966)
11 The veins of compassion (1967)
12 The white leaves of death (1968)
13 The flame in the mist (1969)
14 A host for dying (1970)
15 Stolen like magic away (1971)
16 The delicate dust of death (1973)
17 No tears for the dead (1974)

18 Nightmare in rust (1975)
19 And one for the dead (1975)
20 Healing hands of death (1977)
21 Now dead is any man (1977)
22 A sad and savage dying (1978)
23 Slay me a sinner (1979)
24 Gone to her death (1981)
25 The bitter path of death (1982)
26 The red rust of death (1983)
27 A small slain body (1985)

AUEL, J.
EARTH'S CHILDREN
1 Clan of the cave bear (1980)
2 The valley of horses (1983)
3 The mammoth hunters (1985)
4 Plains of passage (1990)
5 The shelters of stone (2002)

AUSTEN, J.
MANSFIELD PARK
1 Mansfield Park (1814)
3 Mansfield revisited, by Joan Aiken (1984)
4 Mrs. Rushworth, by V.Gordon (1989)
5 The reluctant baronet, by J.Gillespie (1998)

AUSTEN, J.
PRIDE AND PREJUDICE
1 Pride and prejudice (1813)
2 Pemberley shades, by D.Bonavia-Hunt (1970)
3 Teverton Hall, by J.Gillespie (1983)
4 Pemberley, by E.Tennant (1993)
5 Presumption, by J.Barrett (1994)
6 The unequal marriage, by E.Tennant (1994)
7 Deborah, by J.Gillespie (1995)
8 The confession of Fitzwilliam Darcy, by M.Street (1999)

AUSTEN, J.
EMMA
1 Emma (1815)
2 The journal of Miss Jane Fairfax, by C.Grey (1984)
3 Jane Fairfax, by Joan Aiken (1990)
4 Perfect happiness, by Rachel Billington (1996)
5 Emma in love, by Emma Tennant (1996)

AUSTEN, J.
NORTHANGER ABBEY
1 Northanger Abbey (1816)
2 Uninvited guests, by Jane Gillespie (1992)

AUSTEN, J.
PERSUASION
1 Persuasion (1818)
2 Sir Willy, by Jane Fairfax (1992)

AUSTEN, J.
SENSE AND SENSIBILITY
1 Sense and sensibility (1811)
2 Margaret Dashwood, by F.Brown
3 Susan Price, by F.Brown
4 Brightsea, by Jane Gillespie (1987)
5 Eliza's daughter, by Joan Aiken (1994)
6 Elinor and Marianne, by Emma Tennant (1996)

AUSTER, P.
NEW YORK TRILOGY
1 City of glass (1986)
2 Ghosts (1986)
3 The locked room (1986)

AUSTIN, DEE.
1 Reckless heart
2 Wild prairie sky

AUSTWICK, J.
1 Murder in the Borough Library (1959)
2 The County Library murders (1962)
3 The Mobile Library murders (1963)
4 The Borough Council murders (1965)

AVERY, V.
1 London morning (1980)
2 London shadows (1981)
3 London spring (1982)
   NF Autobiography

AWLINSON, R.
AVATAR TRILOGY
1 Shadowdale
2 Tantras
3 Waterdeep

AYER, A. J.
1 Part of my life (1977)
2 More of my life (1984)
   NF Autobiography

AYLETT, S.
BEERLIGHT
1 The crime studio (1994)
2 Bigot Hall (1995)
3 Atom (2000)
4 Toxicology (2001)

AYLETT, S.
ACCOMPLICE
1 Dummyland (2002)
2 The velocity gospel (2002)
3 Karloff's circus (2004)

BABSON, M.
1 A trail of ashes (1983)
2 Death swap (1984)

BABSON, M.
TRIXIE DOLAN
1 Reel murder (1986)
2 Encore murder (1989)
3 Shadows in their blood (1991)
4 Even yuppies die (1993)
5 Break a leg, darling (1995)

BABSON, M.
PERKINS & TATE LTD.
1 Cover up story (1970)
2 Murder on show (1972)

BACCHELLI, R.
1 Mill on the Po (1952)
2 Nothing new under the sun (1956)

BACHMANN, D.
SARNIA SAGA
1 A sound like thunder (1966)
2 An elusive freedom (1997)
3 Winds of change (1998)

BACHMANN, L. P.
BEN CLANCY
1 The legend of Joseph Nokato (1971)
2 The ultimate act (1972)

BADDOCK, J.
CORMACK & WOODWARD
1 The radar job (1986)
2 Emerald (1987)

BAGBY, G.
INSPECTOR SCHMIDT
1 Bachelor's widow (1935)
2 Murder at the piano (1936)
3 Murder half-baked (1938)
4 Murder on the nose (1939)
5 Bird walking weather (1940)
6 Corpse with the purple thighs (1941)
7 The corpse wore a wig (1942)
8 Here comes the corpse (1943)
9 Red is for killing (1944)
10 Original carcase (1946)
11 Dead drunk (1954)

12 The body in the basket (1956)
13 Murder in wonderland (1965)
14 Corpse candle (1967)
15 Another day another death (1969)
16 Honest reliable corpse (1970)
17 Killer boy was here (1971)
18 Two in the bush (1976)
19 My dead body (1976)
20 Innocent bystander (1977)
21 The tough get going (1978)
22 Better dead (1978)
23 Guaranteed to fade (1979)
24 I could have died (1979)
25 Mugger's day (1980)
26 Country and fatal (1981)
27 A question of quarry (1981)
28 The sitting duck (1982)
29 The golden creep (1982)
30 The most wanted (1984)

BAGLEY, D.
CURTIS AND HARDIN
1 Flyaway (1978)
2 Windfall (1982)

BAGLEY, D.
SLADE
1 Running blind (1970)
2 The freedom trap (1971)

BAGNOLD, E.
VELVET BROWN
1 National Velvet (1939)
2 International Velvet, by Bryan Forbes (1978)

BAILEY, A.
1 America lost and found (1980)
2 England first and last (1985)
   NF Autobiography

BAILEY, HILARY.
1 Polly put the kettle on (1975)
2 As time goes by (1988)

BAILEY, M.
MATILDA HAYCASTLE
1 Dreadful lies (1994)
2 The cuckoo case (1995)

BAILEY, PAUL
1 Gabriel's lament (1986)
2 Sugar cane (1993)

BAILEY, R.
BROTHERS OF THE DRAGON
1 Brothers of the dragon
2 Straight on til mourning

BAKER, D.VAL
1 The sea's in the kitchen (1963)
2 The door is always open (1965)
3 We'll go round the world tomorrow (1966)
4 To sea with "Sanu" (1968)
5 Life up the creek (1971)
6 The petrified mariner (1972)
7 Old mill by the stream (1973)
8 Spring at Land's End (1974)
9 Sunset over the Scillies (1975)
10 A view from the valley (1976)
11 A long way to Land's End (1977)
12 The wind blows from the West (1978)
13 All this and Cornwall too (1979)
14 A family for all seasons (1979)
15 As the stream flows by (1980)
16 Upstream at the mill (1981)
17 A family at sea (1981)
18 Summer at the mill (1982)
19 Down a Cornish lane (1983)
20 Family circles (1984)
21 When Cornish skies are smiling (1984)
22 My Cornish world (1985)
23 The waterwheel turns (1983)
24 The mill in the valley (1984)
25 Cornish prelude (1985)
   NF Life in Cornwall

BAKER, DONNA
GLASSMAKERS SAGA
1 Crystal (1987)
2 Black cameo (1988)
3 Chalice (1989)

BAKER, DONNA
WEAVERS
1 The weaver's daughter (1991)
2 The weaver's dream (1991)
3 The weaver's glory (1992)

BAKER, H.
1 All the gods are dead (1984)
2 Alive to the burning (1985)

BAKER, JOHN
SAM TURNER
1 Poet in the gutter (1995)
2 Death minus zero (1996)
3 King of the streets (1998)
4 Walking with ghosts (1999)

5 Shooting in the dark (2001)
6 The meanest flood (2002)

BAKER, S.
ASHLU CYCLE
1 Drink the fire from the flames
2 Firedance

BALDWIN, A.
MEN AT WAR
1 The last heroes (1986)
2 The secret warriors (1987)
3 The soldier spies (1988)
4 The fighting agents (1988)

BALDWIN, J.
1 Notes of a native son (1955)
2 Nobody knows my name (1961)

BALDWIN, M.
PATRICK MATSON & THE COMMITTEE
1 Exit wounds (1988)
2 Holofernes (1989)

BALL, J.
JACK TALLON
1 Police chief (1982)
2 Trouble for Tallon (1982)

BALL, J.
VIRGIL TIBBS
1 In the heat of the night (1966)
2 The cool cottontail (1967)
3 Johnny get your gun (1970)
4 Five pieces of jade (1972)
5 The eyes of the Buddha (1976)
6 Then came violence (1980)

BALLARD, J. G.
1 Empire of the sun (1984)
2 The kindness of women (1991)

BANKS, I. M.
THE CULTURE
1 Consider Phlebas (1987)
2 The player of games (1988)
3 The use of weapons (1990)
4 The state of the art (1991)
5 Against a dark background (1993)
6 Feersome Endjinn (1994)
7 Excession (1996)
8 Inversions (1998)
9 Look to windward (2000)

BANKS, L. R.
1 The L-shaped room (1968)

2 The backward shadow (1970)
3 Two is lonely (1974)

BANKS, L. R.
THE BRONTES
1 Dark quartet (1976)
2 Path to the silent country (1977)

BANKS, O.
AMOS HATCHER
1 The Rembrandt panel (1984)
2 The Caravaggio obsession (1985)

BANNERMAN, B.
DAVE WOOLF
1 Orbach's judgement
2 The judge's song
3 Controlling interest
4 The last Wednesday

BANNISTER, JO
DET. CHIEF INSPECTOR FRANK
SHAPIRO
1 A bleeding of innocents (1993)
2 Sins of the heart (1994)
3 Burning desires (1995)
4 No birds sing (1996)
5 Broken lines (1998)
6 The hireling's tale (1999)
7 Changelings (2000)

BANNISTER, JO
BRODIE FARRELL
1 Echoes of lies (2001)
2 Reflections (2003)
3 The depths of solitude (2004)

BANVILLE, J.
1 Dr. Copernicus
2 Kepler
3 The Newton letter
4 Mefisto (1986)

BARCLAY, J.
CHRONICLES OF THE RAVEN
1 Dawn thief (1999)
2 Noonshade (2000)
3 Nightchild (2001)

BARCLAY, J.
LEGENDS OF THE RAVEN
1 Elfsorrow (2002)
2 Shadowheart (2003)
3 Demonstorm (2004)

BARCLAY, T.
CRAIGALLAN FAMILY
1 A sower went forth (1980)
2 The stony places (1981)
3 Harvest of thorns (1983)
4 The good ground (1984)

BARCLAY, T.
TRAMONT SERIES
1 The wine widow (1985)
2 The champagne girls (1986)
3 The last heiress (1987)

BARCLAY, T.
CORVILL FAMILY
1 Web of dreams (1988)
2 Broken threads (1989)
3 The final pattern (1990)

BARD, M.
1 The doctor wears three faces (1949)
2 Forty odd (1952)
3 Just be yourself (1957)
   NF Autobiography

BARKE, J.
ROBERT BURNS
1 The wind that shakes the barley (1946)
2 The song in the green thorn tree (1947)
3 The wonder of all the gay world (1949)
4 The crest of the broken wave (1953)
5 The well of the silent harp (1954)
6 Bonnie Jean (1958)

BARKER, C.
BOOK OF THE ART
1 The great and secret show (1989)
2 Everville (1994)

BARKER, P.
THE REGENERATION TRILOGY
1 Regeneration (1991)
2 The eye in the door (1993)
3 The ghost road (1995)

BARLING, T.
CHARLIE DANCE
1 The smoke (1986)
2 Smoke dragon (1988)
3 Smoke dance (1991)

BARNARD, R.
SUPT. PERRY TRETHOWAN
1 Sheer torture (1981)
2 Death and the princess (1982)
3 The missing Bronte (1983)

4 Bodies (1986)
5 Death in purple prose (1987)

BARNARD, R.
DET. CONSTABLE CHARLIE PEACE
1 Death and the chaste apprentice (1989)
2 A fatal attachment (1992)
3 A hovering of vultures (1994)
4 The bad samaritan (1996)
5 No place of safety (1997)
6 The corpse at the Haworth Tandoori (1998)
7 The bones in the attic (2001)
8 Mistress of Alderley (2003)

BARNES, JOHN
1 A million open doors (1997)
2 Earth made of glass (1998)

BARNES, JULIAN
1 Talking it over (1991)
2 Love, etc. (2000)

BARNES, L.
MICHAEL SPRAGUE
1 Bitter finish (1983)
2 Dead heat (1984)
3 Cities of the dead (1986)

BARNES, LINDA
CARLOTTA CARLYLE
1 A trouble of fools (1988)
2 The snake tattoo (1989)
3 Coyote (1991)
4 Steel guitar (1992)
5 Snapshot (1993)
6 Hardware (1995)
7 Cold case (1997)
8 The big dig (2003)

BARNES, T.
DET. SUPT. BLANCHE HAMPTON
1 A midsummer killing (1990)
2 Dead meat (1991)
3 Taped (1992)

BARNETT, J.
SUPT. OWEN SMITH
1 Marked for destruction (1982)
2 Diminished responsibility (1984)

BARNETT, P,
THE STRIDER CHRONICLES
1 Strider's galaxy
2 Strider's universe

BARNWELL, W.
BLESSING TRILOGY
1 The Blessing papers (1981)
2 The Sigma curve (1982)

BARR, P.
ALICE GREENWOOD
1 Chinese Alice (1981)
2 Uncut Jade (1983)

BARR, P.
JAPAN
1 The coming of the barbarians (1967)
2 The deer cry pavilion (1968)

BARRON, S.
JANE AUSTEN MYSTERIES
1 Jane and the unpleasantness at
   Scargrave Manor (1996)
2 Jane and the man of the cloth (1997)
3 Jane and the wandering eye (1998)
4 Jane and the genius of the place (1998)

BARRON, T. A.
THE LOST YEARS OF MERLIN
1 The lost years of Merlin (1996)
2 The seven songs of Merlin (1997)
3 The fires of Merlin (1998)

BARSTOW, S.
ELLA LINDLEY
1 Just you wait and see (1987)
2 Give us this day (1989)
3 Next of kin (1991)

BARSTOW, S.
VIC BROWN
1 A kind of loving (1962)
2 The watchers on the shore (1965)
3 The right true end (1976)

BARTH, R.
MARGARET BINTON
1 The rag bag clan (1983)
2 One dollar death (1985)
3 A ragged plot (1984)
4 The co-op kill (1986)

BARTON, A.
1 Two lamps in our street (1965)
2 The penny world (1969)
3 School for love (1976)
   NF Autobiography

BARTON, J.
WASTEWORLD
1 Aftermath
2 Resurrection
3 Angels
4 My way

BASTABLE, B.
MR. MOZART
1 Dead, Mr. Mozart (1994)
2 Too many notes, Mr. Mozart (1995)

BATEMAN, C.
DAN STARKEY
1 Divorcing Jack (1994)
2 Of wee sweetie mice and men (1996)
3 The horse with my name (2002)

BATES, H. E.
UNCLE SILAS
1 My Uncle Silas (1953)
2 Sugar for the horse (1957)

BATES, H. E.
THE LARKINS
1 The darling buds of May (1958)
2 A breath of French air (1959)
3 When the green woods laugh (1961)
4 Oh! to be in England (1963)
5 A little of what you fancy (1970)

BATES, H. E.
AUTOBIOGRAPHY
1 The vanished world (1969)
2 The blossoming world (1971)
3 The world in ripeness (1972)

BATTISON, B.
DET. CHIEF INSPECTOR JIM
ASHWORTH
1 The Christmas bow murder (1994)
2 Fool's ransom (1994)
3 Crisis of conscience (1995)
4 The witch's familiar (1996)
5 Truths not told (1996)
6 Poetic justice (1997)
7 Jeopardy's child (1997)
8 Mirror image (1998)

BATTLETECH
1 Way of the clans, by R.N.Charrette
2 Bloodname, by R.N.Charrette
3 Falcon guard by R.Thurston
4 Wolf pack, by R.N.Charrette
5 Natural selection, by M.Stackpole
6 Mercenary's son, by W.H.Keith

7 The price of glory, by W.H.Keith
8 Decision at Thunder Rift, by W.H.Keith
9 Ideal war, by C.Kubasik
10 Main event, by J.D.Long
11 Blood of heroes, by A.Keith
12 Assumption of risk, by M.A Stackpole
13 Far country, by P.Rice
14 D.R.T., by J.D.Long
16 Close quarters, by V.Milan
16 Bred for war, by M.A.Stackpole
17 I am Jade Falcon, by J.D.Long
18 Highland gambit, by B.L.Pardoe
19 Star lord, by D.G.Phillips
20 Malicious intent, by M.A.Stackpole
21 Wolves on the border, by R.N.Charette
22 Tactics of duty, by W.H.Keith
23 Blood legacy, by M.A.Stackpole
24 Blood of Kerensky, by M.A.Stackpole
25 Sword and fire, by T.S.Gressman
26 Freebirth, by R.Thurston

BAUMAN, J.
1 Winter in the morning (1986)
2 A dream of belonging (1988)
   NF Autobiography of a Polish girl

BAXTER, S.
XEELEE SEQUENCE
1 Raft (1991)
2 Time like infinity (1992)
3 Flux (1993)
4 Ring (1994)
5 Vacuum diagrams (1997)

BAXTER, S.
MAMMOTH TRILOGY
1 Mammoths (1999)
2 Longtusk (2000)
3 Icebones (2001)

BAXTER, S.
MANIFOLD
1 Time (1999)
2 Space (2000)
3 Origin (2001)

BAYER, W.
LT. FRANK JANEK
1 Switch (1985)
2 Wallflower (1992)
3 Mirror maze (1994)

BAYLEY, B. J.
JASPERODUS
1 The soul of the robot (1974)
2 The rod of light (1984)

BAYLEY, B. J.
CHRONOS
1 Collision with Chronos
2 The fall of Chronopolis
3 The knights of the limits

BAYLEY, JOHN
1 Alice (1994)
2 The queer captain (1995)
3 George's lair (1996)

BEAR, G.
1 Infinity concerto (1988)
2 The serpent mage (1988)

BEAR, G.
EARTH
1 Eon (1988)
2 Eternity (1989)
3 Legacy (1995)

BEAR, G. & BRIN, D.
2ND FOUNDATION TRILOGY
1 Foundation and chaos (1998)
2 Foundation's triumph (1999)

BEATON, C.
1 The wandering years, 1922-39 (1964)
2 The years between 1939-44 (1966)
3 The happy years, 1944-48 (1972)
4 The strenuous years, 1948-55 (1973)
5 The restless years, 1955-63 (1976)
6 The parting years, 1963-74 (1978)
   NF Diaries

BEATON, M. C.
HAMISH MACBETH
1 Death of a gossip (1989)
2 Death of a cad (1990)
3 Death of an outsider (1995)
4 Death of a perfect wife (1995)
5 Death of a glutton (1996)

BEATON, M. C.
AGATHA RAISIN
1 Agatha Raisin and the quiche of doom (2002)
2 Agatha Raisin and the vicious vet (2002)
3 Agatha Raisin and the potted gardener (2003)
4 Agatha Raisin and the walkers of Dembley (2004)

BEAUMAN, S.
GINI HUNTER
1 Lovers and liars (1994)
2 Danger zones (1996)

BEAUVOIR, S. DE
1 Memoirs of a dutiful daughter (1959)
2 The prime of life (1963)
3 Force of circumstances (1965)
4 All said and done (1974)
   NF Autobiography

BECKER, S.
1 The Chinese bandit (1975)
2 The last mandarin (1979)
3 The blue-eyed Shan (1982)

BECKWITH, L.
BRUACH
1 About my father's business (1971)
2 The hills is lonely (1959)
3 The sea for breakfast (1961)
4 The loud halo (1964)
5 A rope in case (1968)
6 Lightly poached (1973)
7 Beautiful just (1975)
8 Bruach blend (1978)
9 The bay of strangers (1988)

BEDFORD, W.
1 Happiland (1990)
2 All shook up (1992)

BEEBEE, C.
THE HUB
1 The hub (1987)
2 The main event (1989)

BEECHAM, R.
AMANDA VALENTINE
1 The garbage dump murders (1994)
2 Second guess (1995)

BEERE, P.
TRAUMA (2020)
1 Urban prey
2 The crucifixion squad

BELL, P.
D.C.I. BROWNE & D.S. BENNY
MITCHELL
1 The dead do not praise (1990)
2 Feast into mourning (1991)
3 No pleasure in death (1992)
4 The way of a serpent (1993)
5 Downhill to death (1994)

6 Sleeping partners (1995)
7 A multitude of sins (1997)
8 Blood ties (1998)
9 Stalker (2000)
10 Reasonable death (2001)

BELLE, P.
HERON FAMILY
1 The moon in the water (1984)
2 The chains of fate (1984)
3 Alathea 1985 (pb) 1989 (hb)

BELLE, P.
WINTERCOMBE
1 Wintercombe (1988)
2 Herald of joy (1989)
3 A falling star (1990)
4 Treason's gift (1992)

BELLE, P.
THE CITY
1 The silver city (1994)
2 The wolf within (1995)
3 Blood imperial (1996)

BENFORD, G.
FOUNDATION TRILOGY
1 Matter's end (1996)
2 Foundation's fear (1997)

BENFORD, G.
GALACTIC CENTRE
1 Great sky river (1987)
2 Tides of light (1989)
3 Furious gulf (1994)
4 Sailing bright eternity (1995)

BENISON, C. C.
HER MAJESTY
1 Death at Buckingham Palace (1996)
2 Death at Sandringham House (1997)

BENNETT, FRANCIS
1 Making enemies (1998)
2 Secret kingdom (1999)

BENNETT, M.
MABEL COURT
1 A child's voice calling (2002)
2 A child at the door (2002)

BENSON, E. F.
LUCIA
1 Queen Lucia (1922)
2 Miss Mapp (1922)
3 Lucia in London (1927)

4 Mapp and Lucia (1935)
5 Lucia's progress (1935)
6 Trouble for Lucia (1939)
7 Lucia in wartime, by Tom Holt (1985)
8 Lucia triumphant, by Tom Holt (1986)

BENTLEY, J.
1 Proud Riley's daughter (1988)
2 Sing me a new song (1990)

BENTLEY, P.
TALES OF THE WEST RIDING
1 Panorama (1952)
2 Take courage (1940)
3 Manhold (1941)
4 The House of Moreys (1953)
5 Inheritance (1932)
6 Carr (1929)
7 Life story (1952)
8 The spinner of the years (1928)
9 A modern tragedy (1934)
10 Sleep in peace (1938)
11 The rise of Henry Morcar (1946)
12 Quorum (1950)
13 Noble in reason (1955)
14 Love and money (1957)
15 Crescendo (1958)
16 Kith and kin (1960)
17 Tales of the West Riding (1965)
18 A man of his times (1966)
19 Ring in the new (1969)
20 More tales of the West Riding (1975)

BENZONI, J.
CATHERINE
1 One love is enough (1963)
2 Catherine (1963)
3 Belle Catherine (1966)
4 Catherine and Arnaud (1967)
5 Catherine and a time for love (1968)
6 A snare for Catherine (1974)

BENZONI, J.
FALCON
1 Lure of the falcon (1978)
2 The devil's diamonds (1980)

BENZONI, J.
MARIANNE
1 Marianne (1969)
2 Marianne and the masked prince (1971)
3 Marianne and the privateer (1972)
4 Marianne and the rebels (1973)
5 Marianne and the Lords of the East (1975)
6 Marianne and the crown of fire (1976)

BERENSON, L.
MELANIE TRAVIS
1 A pedigree to die for (1995)
2 Dog eat dog (1996)
3 Hair of the dog (1997)
4 Watchdog (1998)
5 Hush puppy (1999)
6 Unleashed (2000)
7 Once bitten (2001)
8 Hot dog (2002)
9 Best in show (2004)

BERG, C.
THE RAI-KIRAH
1 Transformation
2 Revelation
3 Restoration

BERGER, J.
REINHART
1 Crazy in Berlin (1958)
2 Reinhart in love (1963)
3 Vital parts (1971)
4 Reinhart's women (1982)

BERGER, J.
INTO THEIR LABOURS
1 Pig earth (1979)
2 Once in Europa (1987)
3 Lilac and Flag

BERNIERES, L.DE
MACONDO
1 The war of Don Emmanual's nether parts (1990)
2 Senor Vivo and the Coca lord (1991)
3 The troublesome offspring of Cardinal Guzman (1992)

BIBBY, J.
RONAN
1 Ronan the barbarian (1995)
2 Ronan's rescue (1996)
3 Ronan's revenge (1998)

BICKERS, R. T.
DAEDALUS QUARTET
1 The gifts of Jove (1983)
2 A time for haste (1984)
3 Too late the morrow (1984)
4 The sure recompense (1985)

BIDERMAN, B.
JOSEPH RUDKIN
1 The Genesis files (1988)
2 Judgement of death (1989)

BIELENBERG, C.
1 The past is myself (1984)
2 The road ahead (1992)
NF Autobiography

BIGGINS, J.
OTTO PROHASKA
1 A sailor of Austria (1991)
2 The Emperor's coloured coat (1992)
3 The two-headed eagle (1993)
4 Tomorrow the world (1994)

BIGGLE, L. J.
JAN DARZEK
1 This darkening universe (1979)
2 All the colours of darkness (1964)
3 Watchers of the dark (1968)
4 Silence is deadly (1980)

BINCHY, D.
BRULAGH
1 The last Madonna (1991)
2 The last resort (1992)
3 Fireballs (1993)

BINGHAM, C.
1 Belgravia (1983)
2 Country life (1985)
3 At home (1986)

BINGHAM, C.
NIGHTINGALES
1 To hear a nightingale (1989)
2 The nightingale sings (1996)

BINGHAM, J.
SUPT. BROCK
1 Brock (1981)
2 Brock and the defector (1982)

BIRDSALL, J.
1 The boys and the butterflies (1988)
2 Moths in the memory (1990)
NF Autobiography

BIRMINGHAM, S.
1 Our crowd (1968)
2 The rest of us (1985)

BISCHOFF, D.
SPACE PRECINCT
1 The deity father (1995)
2 Demon wing (1995)
3 Alien island (1996)

BISHOP, S. P.
TRACK
1 Track
2 Partners in death
3 Apache gold

BLACK, L.
KATE THEOBALD
1 The penny murders (1979)
2 The eve of the wedding (1980)
3 The Rumanian circle (1981)

BLACK, V.
SISTER JOAN
1 A vow of silence (1992)
2 A vow of chastity (1992)
3 A vow of sanctity (1993)
4 A vow of obedience (1993)
5 Vow of penance (1994)
6 Vow of devotion (1994)
7 Vow of fidelity (1995)
8 Vow of poverty (1996)
9 Vow of adoration (1996)
10 Vow of compassion (1997)

BLADE RUNNER
ANDROIDS
1 Do androids dream of electric sheep?, by
  P.K.Dick (1972)
2 The edge of human, by K.W.Jeter (1995)
3 Replicant night, by K.W.Jeter (1996)

BLAIR, E.
FLOWER OF SCOTLAND
1 Flower of Scotland (1997)
2 Goodnight sweet prince (1999)

BLAISDELL, A. [E. LININGTON]
SGT. IVOR MADDOX & WILCOX ST.
PRECINCT
1 Greenmask (1965)
2 No evil angel (1966)
3 Date with death (1967)
4 Something wrong (1968)
5 Policeman's lot (1969)
6 Practice to deceive (1971)
7 Crime by chance (1974)
8 Perchance of death (1978)
9 No villain need be (1979)
10 Consequence of death (1981)
11 Skeleton in the closet (1983)
12 Felony report (1985)
13 Strange felony (1986)

BLAKE, M. G.
AYESTHORPE SERIES
1 The Peterloo weaver (1981)

2 The Peterloo inheritance (1981)
3 Bitter legacy (1982)

BLAKE, M. G.
BLAKE'S SEVEN
1 Blake's seven, by T. Nation (1980)
2 Project Avalon, by T.Hoyle (1981)
3 Scorpio attack, by T.Hoyle (1981)
4 Afterlife (1984)

BLATTY, W.
1 The exorcist (1971)
2 Legion (1983)

BLEASDALE, A.
SCULLY
1 Scully (1975)
2 Who's been sleeping in my bed? (1977)

BLISH, J.
AFTER SUCH KNOWLEDGE
1 A case of conscience (1959)
2 Dr. Mirabilis (1962)
3 Black Easter (1969)
4 The day after judgment (1972)

BLISH, J.
CITIES IN FLIGHT
1 They shall have stars
2 A life for the stars
3 Earthman come home
4 A clash of cymbals

BLISHEN, E.
RECYCLING MY MEMORIES
1 Roaring boys (1964)
2 This right soft lot (1969)
3 A cack-handed war (1972)
4 Uncommon entrance (1974)
5 Sorry, Dad (1977)
6 A nest of teachers (1980)
7 Shaky relations (1981)
8 Lizzie Pye (1982)
9 Donkey work (1983)
10 A second skin (1984)
11 Outside contributor (1986)
12 The disturbance fee (1988)
13 The penny world (1990)

BLOCH, R.
1 Psycho (1960)
2 Psycho 2 (1986)
3 Psycho house (1995)

BLOCK, L.
AFFAIRS OF CHIP HARRISON
1 No score
2 Chip Harrison scores again
3 Make out with murder
4 The topless tulip caper
5 Five little rich girls (1984)

BLOCK, L.
BERNIE RHODENBARR
1 Burglars can't be choosers (1979)
2 The burglar in the closet (1980)
3 The burglar who liked to quote Kipling (1981)
4 The burglar who studied Spinoza (1982)
5 The burglar who painted like Mondrian (1984)
6 The burglar who traded Ted Williams (1994)
7 The burglar who thought he was Bogart (1995)
8 The burglar in the library (1997)
9 The burglar in the rye (1999)
10 The burglar on the prowl (2004)

BLOCK, L.
MATTHEW SCUDDER
1 Sins of the fathers (1978)
2 Time to murder and create (1979)
3 In the midst of death (1980)
4 A stab in the dark (1982)
5 Eight million ways to die (1983)
6 When the sacred ginmill closes (1987)
7 Out on the cutting edge (1988)
8 A ticket to the boneyard (1990)
9 A dance at the slaughterhouse (1991)
10 A walk among the tombstones (1992)
11 The devil knows you're dead (1994)
12 A long line of dead men (1995)
13 Even the wicked (1996)
14 Everybody dies (1998)
15 Hope to die (2001)

BLOCK, L.
EVAN TANNER
1 The thief who couldn't sleep
2 The cancelled Czech
3 Tanner's twelve swingers (1999)
4 Two for Tanner
5 Tanner's tiger (1968)
6 Here comes a hero
7 Me Tanner, you Jane
8 Tanner on ice (1999)

BLUNT, B.
1 Treacherous moon

2 Deep ran the river (1986)
3 Star sapphire (1988)

BLUNT, W.
1 Married to the single life (1983)
2 Slow on the feather (1986)
NF Autobiography

BOAST, P.
1 London's child (1987)
2 The millionaire (1989)
3 London's daughter (1992)

BOGARDE, D.
1 A postillion struck by lightning (1977)
2 Snakes and ladders (1978)
3 An orderly man (1983)
4 Backcloth (1986)
5 A particular friendship (1989)
6 A short walk from Harrod's (1993)
NF Autobiography

BOGART, S. H.
R.J.BROOKS
1 Play it again (1995)
2 As time goes by (1996)

BOGGIS, D.
1 Killer instinct (1980)
2 A time to betray (1981)

BOISSARD, J.
MOREAU FAMILY
1 A matter of feeling (1979)
2 Christmas lessons (1984)
3 A time to choose (1986)

BOLITHO, J.
DET. CHIEF INSP. IAN ROPER
1 Kindness can kill (1993)
2 Ripe for revenge (1994)
3 Motive for murder (1994)
4 Dangerous deceit (1995)
5 Finger of fate (1996)
6 Sequence of shame (1996)
7 An absence of angels (1997)
8 Exposure of evil (1998)
9 Victims of violence (1999)
10 Baptised in blood (2000)
11 Lessons in logic (2002)

BOLITHO, J.
ROSE TREVELYAN
1 Snapped in Cornwall (1997)
2 Framed in Cornwall (1998)
3 Exposed in Cornwall (1998)

4 Buried in Cornwall (1999)
5 Betrayed in Cornwall (2000)
6 Plotted in Cornwall (2001)
7 Killed in Cornwall (2002)
8 Caught out in Cornwall (2003)

BOLTON, M.
LAWSON OF SPECIAL BRANCH
1 The softener (1986)
2 The testing (1987)

BOND, M.
M. PAMPLEMOUSSE
1 Monsieur Pamplemousse (1983)
2 Monsieur Pamplemousse and the secret mission (1985)
3 Monsieur Pamplemousse on the spot (1986)
4 Monsieur Pamplemousse takes the cure (1987)
5 Monsieur Pamplemousse aloft (1988)
6 Monsieur Pamplemousse investigates (1990)
7 Monsieur Pamplemousse rests his case (1991)
8 Monsieur Pamplemousse on location (1992)
9 Monsieur Pamplemousse takes the train (1993)
10 Monsieur Pamplemousse on vacation (2002)
11 Monsieur Pamplemousse hits the headlines (2003)

BONFIGLIOLI, K.
CHARLIE MORTDECAI
1 Don't point that thing at me (1974)
2 Something nasty in the woodshed (1977)
3 After you with the pistol (1979)
4 The great Mortdecai moustache mystery (1999)
5 The Mortdecai ABC (2001)

BOONE, J. C.
REMINGTON
1 Lawman's justice (1988)
2 Showdown at Comanche Butte (1988)
3 West of the Pecos (1989)
5 Wyoming blood trail (1990)

BOOTH, S.
DET. CONSTABLE BEN COOPER
1 Black dog (2000)
2 Dancing with the virgins (2001)
3 Blood on the tongue (2002)
4 Blind to the bones (2003)

BORGEN, J.
WILFRED SAGEN
1 Lillelord (1955)
2 The dark springs (1956)
3 We've got him now (1957)

BORGES, J. L.
1 Six problems for Don Isidro Parodi (1981)
2 Chronicles of Bustos Domecq (1982)

BOSSE, M.
ASIAN SAGA
1 The warlord (1984)
2 Fire in Heaven (1986)

BOVA, B.
ORION
1 Orion (1984)
2 Vengeance of Orion (1988)
3 Orion in the dying time (1991)

BOVA, B.
KINSMAN SAGA
1 Kinsman (1965)
2 Millenium (1976)
3 Colony (1979)

BOVA, B.
VOYAGERS
1 Voyagers (1986)
2 The alien within (1987)
3 Star brothers (1990)

BOVA, B.
RED PLANET
1 Mars (1993)
2 Return to Mars (1999)

BOVA, B.
MOONBASE SAGA
1 Moonrise (1996)
2 Moonwar (1997)

BOVA, B.
THE ASTEROID WARS
1 The precipice (2001)
2 The rock rats (2002)

BOWEN, G.
JOANNE KILBOURN
1 Deadly appearances (1990)
2 Murder at the Mendes (1991)
3 The wandering soul murders (1993)
4 A colder kind of death (1995)
5 A killing spring (1997)

BOWERS, E.
MEG LACEY
1 Ladies night (1990)
2 No forwarding address (1993)

BOWIE, J.
1 Penny buff (1975)
2 Penny boss (1976)
3 Penny change (1977)
   NF Autobiography of a teacher

BOWKER, D.
CHIEF SUPT. VERNON LAVERNE
1 The death prayer (1995)
2 The butcher of Glastonbury (1997)

BOWLES, C.
MIKE HAZZARD
1 Flying blind (1986)
2 Flying Hazzard (1987)

BOWLING, H.
1 Gaslight in Page Street (1991)
2 The girl from Cotton Lane (1992)

BOWRING, M.
1 The animals came first (1976)
2 Animals before breakfast (1978)
3 Animals round the clock (1981)
   NF Autobiography

BOYER, E. H.
WORLD OF THE ALFAR
1 The sword and the satchel
2 The elves and the otterskin
3 The thrall and the dragon's heart
4 The wizard and the warlord
5 The troll's grindstone
6 The curse of Slagfid

BOYER, R.
DOC ADAMS
1 Billingsgate shoal (1985)
2 Penny Ferry (1985)
3 Moscow metal (1988)

BOYLAN, C.
1 Home rule (1992)
2 Holy pictures (1989)

BOYLAN, J. F.
1 The planets (1991)
2 The constellations (1995)

BOYLE, J.
1 A sense of freedom (1977)
2 The pain of confinement (1984)
NF Prison diaries

BOYLE, T.
DET. FRANCIS DE SALES
1 Only the dead know Brooklyn (1987)
2 Post-mortem effects (1988)
3 Brooklyn three (1991)

BRADFORD, B. T.
EMMA HARTE
1 A woman of substance (1979)
2 Hold the dream (1985)
3 To be the best (1988)
4 Emma's secret (2003)

BRADLEY, H.
1 And Miss Carter wore pink (1971)
2 Miss Carter came with us (1973)
3 In the beginning, said Great Aunt Jane (1975)
4 The Queen who came to tea (1978)
NF Reminiscences of Edwardian life

BRADLEY, J.
BATTLESQUAD
1 Alamein attack (1982)
2 Slaughter in Sicily (1983)
3 Killer winter (1983)
4 Bloody bridgehead (1984)

BRADLEY, M. Z.
DARKOVER SERIES
1 Darkover landfall
2 The spell sword (1990)
3 Star of danger (1993)
4 Shattered chain
5 The winds of Darkover
6 The bloody sun
7 Sword of Aldones
8 Heritage of Hastur
9 The planet savers
10 The world wreckers (1989)
11 Hunters of the red moon
12 The forbidden tower
13 Stormqueen (1989)
14 Two to conquer
15 Sharra
16 Thendara House
17 City of sorcery (1990)
18 The heirs of Hammerfell (1991)

BRADLEY, M. Z.
AVALON
1 The forest house (1993)

2 The mists of Avalon (1984)
3 Lady of Avalon (1997)
4 Priestess of Avalon (2000)

BRADLEY, R. J.
1 Lady in Gil
2 Scion's lady

BRADSHAW, G.
ARTHUR AND GAWAIN
1 Hawk of May (1981)
2 Kingdom of summer (1982)
3 In winter's shadow (1982)

BRADY, J.
MATT MINOGUE
1 A stone of the heart (1988)
2 Unholy ground (1989)
3 Kaddish in Dublin (1990)

BRAGG, M.
THE TALLENTIRE FAMILY
1 The hired man (1968)
2 A place in England (1970)
3 Kingdom come (1980)

BRAGG, M.
SAM RICHARDSON
1 A son of war (1999)
2 The soldier's return (2000)
3 Crossing the lines (2003)

BRAINE, J.
1 One and last love (1981)
2 These golden days (1985)

BRAINE, J.
CLIVE AND ROBIN LENDRICK
1 Stay with me till morning (1970)
2 The two of us (1984)
3 My one true love (1985)

BRAINE, J.
JOE LAMPTON
1 Room at the top (1959)
2 Life at the top (1962)

BRAINE, J.
XAVIER FLYNN
1 The pious agent (1975)
2 Finger of fire (1977)

BRAITHWAITE, R.
A YORKSHIRE TRILOGY
1 Martha (1983)

2 Ben (1984)
3 The house in Kingston Square (1985)
NF History of a Bridlington family

BRANDNER, G.
THE HOWLING
1 The howling
2 The return
3 Echoes

BRANDON, R.
ANDREW TAGGART
1 Mind out (1991)
2 The gorgon's smile (1992)

BRASON, J.
SECRET ARMY
1 Secret army (1978)
2 Secret army dossier (1979)
3 End of the line (1980)

BRASON, J.
HOWARD'S WAY
1 Howard's way (1986)
2 Howard's way 2 (1987)
3 Howard's way 3 (1988)

BRATA, S.
1 My god died young (1968)
2 Confessions of an Indian woman-eater (1971)
3 A traitor to India (1976)

BRAUN, L. J.
QWILLERAN AND KOKO SERIES
1 The cat who could read backwards (1966)
2 The cat who ate Danish modern (1967)
3 The cat who turned on and off (1968)
4 The cat who played Brahms (1970)
5 The cat who played Post Office (1987)
6 The cat who knew Shakespeare (1989)
7 The cat who saw red (1990)
8 The cat who sniffed glue (1990)
9 The cat who had 14 tales (1990)
10 The cat who went underground (1990)
11 The cat who talked to ghosts (1990)
12 The cat who lived high (1991)
13 The cat who knew a Cardinal (1991)
14 The cat who moved a mountain (1992)
15 The cat who wasn't there (1993)
16 The cat who went into the closet (1993)
17 The cat who came to breakfast (1994)
18 The cat who blew the whistle (1995)
19 The cat who said cheese (1996)
20 The cat who tailed a thief (1997)
21 The cat who sang for the birds (1998)
22 The cat who saw stars (1999)
23 The cat who robbed a bank (2000)
24 The cat who smelled a rat (2001)
25 The cat who went up the creek (2001)
26 The cat who brought the house down (2003)
27 The cat who talked turkey (2004)

BRAUN, M.
LUKE STARBUCK
1 Hangman
2 Jury of six
3 The spoilers
4 Tombstone
5 Manhunter
6 Deadwood
7 The Judas tree

BRAY, D.
CAPTAIN DAVY
1 Between two shores (1984)
2 The captain

BREAM, F.
REV. JABAL JARRETT
1 The Vicar done it (1982)
2 The Vicar investigates (1983)
3 Sealed and despatched (1984)
4 With murder in mind (1985)
5 The problem at Piha (1986)

BREEN, J.
JERRY BROGAN
1 Vicar's roses (1984)
2 The gathering place (1984)
3 Triple crown (1985)
4 Loose lips (1990)

BREESE, A.
1 Setting out (1981)
2 A loving imprint (1982)

BRENCHLEY, C.
BEN MACALLAN
1 Dead of light (1995)
2 Light errant (1997)

BRENNAN, C. M.
INVADERS OF CHARON
1 The genesis web
2 Nomads of the sky

BRENNAN, C. M.
MARTIAN WARS TRILOGY
1 Rebellion 2456

2 Hammer of Mars
3 Armageddon of Vesta

BRENNAN, C. M.
INNER PLANETS TRILOGY
1 First power play
2 Two prime squared
3 Matrix cubed

BRENNAN, J. H.
DEMONSPAWN
1 Firewolf
2 Crypts of terror

BRETT, S.
CHARLES PARIS SERIES
1 Cast in order of disappearance (1975)
2 So much blood (1976)
3 Star trap (1977)
4 An amateur corpse (1978)
5 A comedian dies (1979)
6 Dead side of the mike (1980)
7 Situation tragedy (1981)
8 Murder unprompted (1982)
9 Murder in the title (1983)
10 Not dead only resting (1984)
11 Dead giveaway (1985)
12 What bloody man is that? (1987)
13 A series of murders (1989)
14 Corporate bodies (1991)
15 A reconstructed corpse (1993)
16 Sicken and so die (1995)
17 Dead room farce (1997)

BRETT, S.
MRS. PARGETER SERIES
1 A nice class of corpse (1986)
2 Mrs. , presumed dead (1988)
3 Mrs. Pargeter's package (1990)
4 Mrs. Pargeter's pound of flesh (1992)
5 Mrs. Pargeter's plot (1996)
6 Mrs. Pargeter's point of honour (1999)

BRETT, S.
THE FETHERING MYSTERIES
1 The body on the beach (2000)
2 Death on the Downs (2001)
3 The torso in the town (2002)
4 Murder in the museum (2003)
5 The hanging in the hotel (2004)

BRETTON, B.
1 Somewhere in time (1996)
2 Tomorrow and always (1996)
3 Destiny's child (1996)

BRIDGE, A.
JULIA PROBYN
1 The lighthearted quest (1956)
2 The Portuguese quest (1956)
3 The numbered account (1960)
4 The dangerous islands (1964)
5 Emergency in the Pyrenees (1965)
6 The episode at Toledo (1967)
7 The malady in Madeira (1969)

BRIDGWOOD, C.
STEINS OF GRAYLINGS
1 This wicked generation (1987)
2 The dew of heaven (1989)

BRIERLEY, D.
CODY
1 Cold war (1979)
2 Blood group O (1980)
3 Skorpion's death (1985)
4 Snowline (1986)
5 Death & Co. (1999)

BRIERLEY, D.
THE VELVET REVOLUTION
1 On leaving a Prague window (1995)
2 Horizontal woman (1996)
3 The cloak-and-dagger girl (1998)

BRIGGS, V.
THE WAY AHEAD
1 Sacred ground (1975)
2 Reap the harvest (1976)
3 Yours is the earth (1977)

BRIN, D.
1 Startide rising
2 The uplift war

BRIN, D.
UPLIFT TRILOGY
1 Brightness reef (1996)
2 Infinity's shore (1997)
3 Heaven's reach (1998)

BRINDLEY, L.
1 They must have seen me coming (1980)
2 There's one born every minute (1982)
3 Vicky and I (1984)

BRINDLEY, L.
TANQUILLAN
1 Tanquillan (1986)
2 The tender leaves of hope (1987)
3 Our summer faces (1988)

BRITTAIN, V.
DIARIES
1 Chronicle of youth (1984)
2 Chronicle of friendship (1986)
3 Wartime chronicle (1989)

BROCH, H.
THE SLEEPWALKERS
1 The romantic (1888)
2 The anarchist (1903)
3 The realist (1918)

BROD, D. C.
QUINT MCCAULEY
1 Murder in store (1990)
2 Error in judgement (1991)
3 Masquerade in blue (1992)

BROMIGE, I.
THE RAINWOOD FAMILY
1 The quiet hills (1966)
2 The stepdaughter (1967)
3 An April girl (1969)
4 The tangled wood (1969)
5 A sheltering tree (1970)
6 A magic place (1971)
7 A bend in the river (1975)
8 The distant song (1977)
9 The happy fortress (1978)
10 The years between (1991)

BRONTE, C.
JANE EYRE
1 Jane Eyre
2 The quiet stranger, by R.Kydd (1991)

BRONTE, E.
WUTHERING HEIGHTS
1 Wuthering Heights
2 Heathcliff, by l.Haire-Sargeant (1992)
3 Return to Wuthering Heights, by N. Thorne (1996)

BROOKE, J.
ORCHID TRILOGY
1 The military orchid
2 A mine of serpents
3 The goose cathedral

BROOKE, K.
EXPATRIA
1 Expatria (1991)
2 Expatria incorporated (1992)

BROOKE-ROSE, C.
JIB AND JAB
1 Xorandor (1986)
2 Verbivore (1990)

BROOKMYRE, C.
ANGELIQUE DE XAVIA
1 A big boy did it and ran away (2001)
2 The sacred art of stealing (2002)

BROOKS, T.
SHANNARA
1 Sword of Shannara (1981)
2 Elfstones of Shannara (1982)
3 Wishsong of Shannara (1984)

BROOKS, T.
MAGIC KINGDOM OF LANDOVER
1 Magic kingdom for sale/sold (1986)
2 The black unicorn (1988)
3 Wizard at large (1988)
4 The tangle box (1994)

BROOKS, T.
THE HERITAGE OF SHANNARA
1 The scions of Shannara (1990)
2 The Druid of Shannara (1991)
3 The Elf-Queen of Shannara (1992)
4 The talismans of Shannara (1993)

BROOKS, T.
JOHN ROSS
1 Running with the demon (1997)
2 A knight of the word (1998)
3 Angel fire east (1999)

BROOKS, T.
THE VOYAGE OF THE JERLE SHANNARA
1 Isle witch (2000)
2 Antrax (2001)
3 Morgawr (2002)
4 Jarka Ruus (2003)

BROSNAN, J.
SKY LORDS TRILOGY
1 The sky lords (1988)
2 War of the sky lords (1989)
3 The fall of the sky lords (1991)

BROWN, D.
MAJOR PAT MCLANAHAN
1 Flight of the old dog (1988)
2 Day of the Cheetah (1989)
3 Night of the hawk (1992)
4 Shadows of steel (1998)

5 Warrior class (2001)
6 Wings of fire (2002)
7 Air battle force (2003)
8 Electric sky (2004)

BROWN, D.
REAR ADMIRAL IAN HARDCASTLE
1 Hammerheads (1988)
2 Storming heaven (1994)

BROWN, FRANCES
ROMANY SERIES
1 The haresfoot legacy (1990)
2 Dancing on the rainbow (1991)
3 The other sister (1992)

BROWN, HOSANNA
FRANK LE ROUX
1 Ispy, you die (1984)
2 Death upon a spear (1986)

BROWN, LIZBIE
ELIZABETH BLAIR
1 Broken star (1994)
2 Turkey tracks (1996)
3 Shoofly (1998)
4 Double wedding ring (1999)
5 Jacob's ladder (2000)
6 Cat's cradle (2001)

BRUCE, L.
CAROLUS DEENE
1 Cold blood (1952)
2 At death's door (1955)
3 Death of cold (1956)
4 Dead for a ducat (1956)
5 Dead men's shoes (1958)
6 A louse for the hangman (1959)
7 Our jubilee is death (1959)
8 Jack on the gallows tree (1960)
9 Furious old women (1960)
10 A bone and a hank of hair (1960)
11 Die all, die merrily (1961)
12 Nothing like blood (1961)
13 Crack of doom (1962)
14 Death in Albert Park (1963)
15 Death at Hallow's End (1963)
16 Death in the Black Sands (1964)
17 Death at Saint Asprey's School; (1967)
18 Death of a commuter (1967)
19 Death on Romney Marsh (1968)
20 Death with blue ribbon (1969)
21 Death on All Hallowe'en (1970)
22 Death by the lake (1971)
23 Death in the middle watch (1974)
24 Death of a bovver boy (1974)

BRUST, S.
VLAD TALTOS
1 Jhereg (1990)
2 Yeudi (1990)
3 Teckla (1990)
4 Taltos (1990)

BUCHAN, J.
1 John MacNab (1925)
2 The return of John MacNab, by A.Greig (1996)

BUCHANAN, E.
BRITT MONTERO
1 Contents under pressure (1994)
2 Miami, it's murder (1995)

BUCKLEY, F.
URSULA BLANCHARD
1 The Robsart mystery (1997)
2 The doublet affair (1998)

BUCKLEY, W. F.
BLACKFORD OAKES
1 Saving the Queen (1976)
2 Stained glass (1978)
3 Who's on first? (1980)
4 The story of Henri Tod (1984)
5 Marco polo if you can (1982)
6 See you later, alligator (1986)
7 High jinx (1987)
8 Mongoose R.I.P. (1988)
9 Tucker's last stand (1991)

BUECHNER, T. F.
LEO BEBB, EVANGELIST
1 Lion country (1971)
2 Open heart (1972)
3 The love feast (1975)
4 Treasure hunt (1978)

BUJOLD, L.M.
MILES VORKOSIGAN
1 Shards of honour (1986)
2 Barrayar (1994)
3 The warrior's apprentice (1988)
4 Komarr
5 Young Miles
6 Miles mystery and mayhem
7 Diplomatic immunity

BULL, P.
1 To sea in a sieve (1956)
2 Bulls in the meadows (1957)
3 I know the face, but... (1959)
4 I say, look here (1965)

5 It isn't all Greek to me (1967)
6 Life is a cucumber (1973)
  NF Autobiography

BULMER, K.
SEA WOLF
1 Steel shark
2 Shark north
3 Shark pack
4 Shark hunt
5 Shark Africa
6 Shark raid
7 Shark America
8 Shark trap

BUNCH, C.
NUMANTIA
1 The seer king
2 The demon king
3 The warrior king

BUNCH, C.
STEN
1 Sten
2 The wolf worlds
3 The court of a thousand suns
4 Fleet of the damned
5 Revenge of the damned
6 Return of the emperor
7 Vortex
8 Empire's end

BUNCH, C.
DRAGONMASTER
1 Storm of wings (2002)
2 Knighthood of the dragon (2003)
3 The last battle (2004)

BURDEN, P.
DET. CHIEF SUPT. BASSETT
1 Screaming bones (1989)
2 Wreath of honesty (1990)
3 Bury him kindly (1991)
4 Father, forgive me (1993)

BURGESS, A.
ENDERBY
1 Inside Mr. Enderby (1964)
2 Enderby outside (1968)
3 The clockwork testament, or Enderby
4 Enderby's dark lady or No end to
  Enderby (1984)

BURGH, A.
DAUGHTERS OF A GRANITE LAND
1 The azure bowl (1989)

2 The golden butterfly (1990)
3 The stone mistress (1991)

BURKE, J. L.
DAVE ROBICHEAUX
1 The neon rain (1989)
2 Heaven's prisoners (1990)
3 Black cherry blues (1991)
4 In the electric mist with the Confederate
  dead (1993)
5 Dixie City jam (1994)
6 Burning angel (1995)
7 Cadillac jukebox (1996)
8 Sunset limited (1998)
9 Purple cane road (2000)
10 Robicheaux (2000)
11 Jolie Blon's bounce (2002)
12 Last car to Elysian Fields (2003)

BURKE, J. L.
BILLYBOB HOLLAND
1 Cimarron rose (1997)
2 Heartwood (1999)
3 Bitterroot (2001)

BURKE, JAN
IRENE KELLY
1 Goodnight Irene (1994)
2 Sweet dreams, Irene (1995)
3 Dear Irene (1996)
4 Remember me, Irene (1997)
5 Hours (1998)
6 Liar (1999)
7 Bones (2000)

BURKHOLZ, H.
1 The sensitives (1988)
2 Strange bedfellows (1989)
3 Brain damage (1992)

BURKHOLZ, H.
MANCUSO AND BORGNEFF
1 The death freak (1983)
2 The sleeping spy (1984)

BURLEY, W. J.
DR. PYM
1 A taste of power (1966)
2 Death in willow pattern (1969)

BURLEY, W. J.
DET. SUPT. WYCLIFFE
1 Three-toed pussy (1969)
2 To kill a cat (1970)
3 Guilt edged (1971)
4 Death in a salubrious place (1972)

5 Death in Stanley Street (1973)
6 Wycliffe and the pea green boat (1975)
7 Wycliffe and the schoolgirls (1976)
8 Wycliffe and the scapegoat (1978)
9 Wycliffe in Paul's Court (1980)
10 Wycliffe's wild goose chase (1982)
11 Wycliffe and the Beales (1983)
12 Wycliffe and the four Jacks (1985)
13 Wycliffe and the quiet virgin (1986)
14 Wycliffe and the Winsor Blue (1987)
15 Wycliffe and the tangled web (1988)
16 Wycliffe and the cycle of death (1990)
17 Wycliffe and the dead flautist (1991)
18 Wycliffe and the last rites (1992)
19 Wycliffe and the dunes mystery (1993)
20 Wycliffe and the house of fear (1995)
21 Wycliffe and the redhead (1997)
22 Wycliffe and the Guild of Nine (2001)

BURNETT, F. H.
1 The secret garden (1911)
2 Misselthwaite, by S.Moody (1995)

BURNS, J.
MAX CHARD
1 Snap (1998)
2 Nark (1999)
3 Spike (2000)

BURNS, P.
1 Stacey's flyer (1986)
2 Kezzy (1988)

BURNS, P.
PACKARDS
1 Packards (1997)
2 Goodbye Piccadilly; Packards at war (1998)

BURNS, R.
GABE WAGER
1 The Alvarez journal
2 The Farnsworth score
3 Speak for the dead
4 Angle of attack
5 The avenging angel
6 Strip search
7 Ground money

BURROUGHS, E. R.
TARZAN SERIES
1 Tarzan of the apes (1914)
2 The return of Tarzan (1915)
3 The beasts of Tarzan (1916)
4 The son of Tarzan (1917)
5 Tarzan and the jewels of Opar (1918)
6 Jungle tales of Tarzan (1919)

7 Tarzan the untamed (1920)
8 Tarzan the terrible (1921)
9 Tarzan and the golden lion (1923)
10 Tarzan and the Antmen (1924)
11 Tarzan, Lord of the jungle (1928)
12 Tarzan and the lost empire (1929)
13 Tarzan at the Earth's core (1930)
14 Tarzan the invincible (1931)
15 Tarzan triumphant (1932)
16 Tarzan and the city of gold (1933)
17 Tarzan and the lion man (1934)
18 Tarzan and the leopard men (1935)
19 Tarzan's quest (1936)
20 Tarzan and the forbidden city (1938)
21 Tarzan the magnificent (1939)
22 Tarzan and the Foreign Legion (1947)
23 Tarzan and the madman (1965)
24 Tarzan and the castaways (1965)
25 Tarzan and the valley of gold (1965)
26 Tarzan lives, by P.J.Farmer (1974)

BURROUGHS, E. R.
MARTIAN SERIES
1 A princess of Mars
2 The gods of Mars
3 The warlord of Mars
4 Thuvia, maid of Mars
5 Chessmen of Mars
6 A fighting man of Mars
7 Master mind of Mars
8 Synthetic men of Mars
9 Swords of Mars
10 Llana of Gathol
11 John Carter of Mars

BURROUGHS, W.
1 Cities of red night (1981)
2 The place of dead woods (1984)
3 The western lands (1988)

BURROWES, J.
GORBALS TRILOGY
1 Jamsie's people (1984)
2 Incomers (1988)
3 Mother Glasgow (1991)

BURTON, B.
NUGENT FAMILY
1 Jude (1986)
2 Jaen (1986)
3 Women of no account (1988)
4 Hard loves, easy riches (1989)

BUSHBY, J.
CAPT. JAMES ROLLO
1 The Spanish General (1982)
2 Mondego Bay (1983)

BUTLER, D.
1 We'll meet again (1982)
2 The end of an era (1983)

BUTLER, G.
INSPECTOR COFFIN SERIES
1 The murdering kind (1958)
2 The interloper (1959)
3 Death lives next door (1960)
4 Make me a murderer (1961)
5 Coffin in Oxford (1962)
6 Coffin on the water (1986)
7 Coffin for baby (1963)
8 Coffin waiting (1964)
9 Coffin in Malta (1964)
10 A nameless Coffin (1966)
11 Coffin following (1968)
12 Coffin's dark number (1969)
13 A Coffin from the past (1970)
14 A Coffin for the canary (1974)
15 Coffin in fashion (1987)
16 Coffin underground (1988)
17 Coffin in the Black Museum (1989)
18 Coffin and the paper man (1990)
19 Coffin on Murder Street (1991)
20 Cracking open a Coffin (1992)
21 A Coffin for Charley (1993)
22 The Coffin tree (1994)
23 A dark coffin (1995)
24 A double coffin (1996)
25 Coffin's game (1997)
26 A grave Coffin (1998)
27 Coffin's ghost (1999)
28 A cold Coffin (2000)
29 Coffin knows the answer (2002)

BUTLER, O.
XENOGENESIS
1 Dawn (1987)
2 Adulthood rites (1988)
3 Imago (1989)

BUTLER, O.
PATTERNMAKER
1 Wild seed (1989)
2 Mind of my mind (1990)

BYATT, A.
FREDERICA
1 The virgin in the garden (1978)
2 Still life (1985)
3 Babel Tower (1996)

BYRD, M.
MIKE HALLER
1 California thriller (1984)

2 Fly away Jill (1984)
3 Finders weepers (1985)

BYRNE, B.
MENDOZA FAMILY TRILOGY
1 The lasting fire (1992)
2 The flames of vengeance (1992)

CALDECOTT, M.
EGYPTIAN SERIES
1 Daughter of Amun (1989)
2 The son of the sun (1986)
3 Daughter of the Ra (1990)

CALLISON, B.
CAPT.EDWARD TRAPP
1 Trapp's war (1973)
2 Trapp's peace (1979)
3 Trapp and World War Three (1988)
4 Crocodile Trapp (1993)

CALLOWAY SISTERS
1 Mariah, by Sandra Canfield (1989)
2 Jo, by Tracy Hughes (1989)
3 Tess, by Katherine Burton (1990)
4 Eden, by Penny Richards (1990)

CAMERON, D. K.
1 The ballad and the plough (1978)
2 Willie Gavin, Crofterman (1980)
3 The cornkister days (1984)
   NF Life in the Scottish Highlands

CAMP, J.
KIDD
1 The fool's run (1990)
2 The empress file (1992)

CAMPBELL, D.
HOPEWELL SAGA
1 Broken promises
2 Silent dreams
3 Stolen passions
4 Tomorrow

CAMPBELL, ROBERT
WHISTLER
1 In La-La land we trust (1987)
2 Alice in La-La land (1988)
3 Sweet La-La land (1990)

CAMPBELL, ROBERT
JIMMY FLANNERY
1 The junkyard dog (1989)
2 The cat's meow (1990)
3 Thinning the turkey herd (1990)

4 The gift horse's mouth (1992)
5 Nibbled to death by ducks (1991)
6 In a pig's eye (1993)

CANDY, E. [A. NEVILLE]
BURNIVEL
1 Which doctor (1953)
2 Bones of contention (1954)

CANNAM, H.
1 The last ballad (1991)
2 A stranger in the land (1992)

CANNELL, D.
ELLIE HASKELL
1 The thin woman (1990)
2 Mum's the word (1991)
3 Femmes fatal (1993)

CANNELL, S. J.
SHANE SCULLY
1 The tin collectors (2001)
2 The Viking funeral (2002)
3 Hollywood tough (2003)
4 Vertical coffin (2004)

CANNING, V.
BIRDCAGE
1 Birdcage (1977)
2 The Satan sampler (1979)
3 Vanishing point (1982)

CANNING, V.
ARTHURIAN TRILOGY
1 The crimson chalice (1976)
2 Circle of the Gods (1977)
3 The immortal wound (1978)

CANNING, V.
MR. FINCHLEY
1 Mr. Finchley discovers his England (1934)
2 Mr. Finchley goes to Paris (1936)
3 Mr. Finchley takes the road (1939)

CANNING, V.
SMILER MILES TRILOGY
1 The runaways (1970)
2 Flight of the grey goose (1973)
3 The painted tent (1974)

CANNING, V.
REX CARVER
1 Whiphand (1965)
2 Doubled in diamonds (1966)

3 Python project (1967)
4 The melting man (1968)

CAO, XUEGIN
THE STORY OF THE STONE
1 Golden days
2 The crab-flower club
3 The warning voice
4 The debt of tears
5 The dreamer wakes

CAPE, T.
DEREK SMAILES
1 The Cambridge theorem (1990)
2 The last defector (1991)

CARD, O. S.
TALES OF ALVIN MAKER
1 Seventh son (1988)
2 Red prophet (1989)
3 Prentice Alvin (1989)
4 Alvin journeyman
5 Heartfire

CARD, O. S.
HOMECOMING
1 The memory of earth (1992)
2 The call of earth (1993)
3 The ships of earth (1994)

CARD, O. S.
ENDER WIGGINS
1 Ender's game (1985)
2 Speaker for the dead (1987)
3 Ender's shadow (1999)
4 Shadow of the hegemon (2000)
5 Shadow puppets (2002)

CAREY, H.
LAVENDER ROAD
1 Lavender Road (1996)
2 Some sunny day (1996)
3 On a wing and a prayer (1997)

CARNEY, D.
1 The wild geese (1977)
2 The square circle (1983)

CARR, C.
DR. LASZLO KREISLER
1 The alienist (1996)
2 The angel of darkness (1998)

CARR, J. L.
HETTY BEAUCHAMP
1 What Hetty did (1988)
2 Harpole and Foxberrow (1992)

CARR, P.
DAUGHTERS OF ENGLAND
1 The miracle at St. Bruno
2 The lion triumphant (1974)
3 The witch from the sea (1975)
4 Saraband for two sisters (1976)
5 Lament for a lost lover (1977)
6 The lovechild (1978)
7 Song of the siren (1980)
8 The drop of the dice (1981)
9 The adulteress (1982)
10 Zipporah (1983)
11 Voices in a haunted room (1984)
12 The return of the gypsy (1985)
13 Midsummer's eve (1986)
14 The pool of St.Branok (1987)
15 The changeling (1989)
16 Black swan (1990)
17 A time for silence (1991)
18 The gossamer cord (1992)
19 We'll meet again (1993)

CARROLL, G.
GHOSTS
1 North star
2 Ghostrider one
3 No place to hide

CARROLL, J.
FRANNIE MCCABE
1 Kissing the beehive (1999)
2 The marriage of sticks (2000)
3 The wooden sea (2001)

CARSON, M.
MARTIN BENSON
1 Sucking sherbet lemons (1988)
2 Stripping penguins bare (1991)
3 Yanking up the yo-yo (1992)

CARTER, A.
BLACKOAKS
1 Master of Blackoaks (1977)
2 Sword of the golden stud (1978)
3 Secrets of Blackoaks (1980)
4 Heritage of Blackoaks (1982)
5 A farewell to Blackoaks (1984)

CARTER, C.
NANETTE HAYES
1 Rhode island red (1997)
2 Drumsticks (2001)

CARTER, NICHOLAS
SHADOW ON THE CROWN
1 Turncoat's drum (1995)
2 Storming party (1996)
3 King's men crow (1997)
4 Harvest of swords (1998)
5 Stand by the colours (1999)

CASLEY, D.
CHIEF INSPECTOR JAMES ODHIAMBO
1 Death underfoot (1993)
2 Death undertow (1994)
3 Death understates (1995)
4 Death under par (1997)

CASSADA, J.
IMMORTAL EYES TRILOGY
1 Immortal eyes
2 Shadows on the hill
3 Court of all kings

CAUDWELL, S.
PROFESSOR HILARY TAMAR
1 Thus was Adonis murdered (1981)
2 The shortest way to Hades (1984)
3 The sirens sang of murder (1989)
4 The sybil in her grave (2002)

CELINE, L-F.
1 Journey to the end of the night (1932)
2 Death on credit (1936)

CHADBOURN, M.
THE AGE OF MISRULE
1 World's end (1999)
2 Darkest hour (2000)
3 Always forever (2001)

CHADWICK, E.
1 The wild hunt (1990)
2 The running vixen (1991)
3 The leopard unleashed (1992)

CHALKER, J. L.
THE WELLWORLD SAGA
1 Midnight at the Well of Souls
2 Exiles at the Well of Souls
3 Quest for the Well of Souls
4 The return of Nathan Brazil
5 Twilight at the Well of Souls
6 Echoes of the Well of Souls
7 Shadows of the Well of Souls

CHALKER, J. L.
DANCING GODS
1 Demons of the Dancing Gods

2 Vengeance of the Dancing Gods
3 The river of the Dancing Gods

CHALKER, J. L.
RINGS OF THE MASTER
1 Lords of the middle dark
2 Pirates of the thunder
3 Warriors of the storm
4 Marks of the martyrs

CHALKER, J. L.
CHANGEWINDS
1 When the changewinds blow
2 Riders of the winds
3 War of the maelstrom

CHALKER, J. L.
GOD INC.
1 The labyrinth of dreams
2 The shadow dancers
3 The maze in the mirrors

CHALKER, J. L.
FOUR LORDS OF THE DIAMOND
1 Lilith
2 Cerberus
3 Charon
4 Medusa

CHALKER, J. L.
SOUL RIDER
1 Spirits of Flux and Anchor
2 Empires of Flux and Anchor
3 Masters of Flux and Anchor
4 The birth of Flux and Anchor
5 Children of Flux and Anchor

CHALLONER, R.
COMMANDER LORD CHARLES
OAKSHOTT
1 Run out the guns (1984)
2 Give fire! (1986)
3 Into battle! (1987)

CHAMBERS, P.
MARK PRESTON
1 This'll kill you (1963)
2 Nobody lives forever (1964)
3 You're better off dead (1966)
4 Always take the big ones (1966)
5 No gold where you go (1966)
6 The bad die young (1967)
7 Don't bother to knock (1968)
8 The blonde wore black (1968)
9 No peace for the wicked (1968)
10 Speak ill of the dead (1968)

11 They call it murder (1969)
12 Somebody has to lose (1975)
13 The deader they fall (1976)
14 Lady, you're killing me (1977)
15 The day of the big dollar (1978)
16 The beautiful golden frame (1979)
17 Nothing personal (1980)
18 The deep blue cradle (1980)
19 A long time dead (1980)
20 The lady who never was (1981)
21 Female - handle with care (1981)
22 Murder is its own reward (1982)
23 The highly explosive case (1982)
24 A miniature murder mystery (1982)
25 Jail bait (1983)
26 Dragons can be dangerous (1983)
27 Bomb scare - Flight 147 (1984)
28 The moving picture writes (1984)
29 The vanishing holes murders (1985)

CHAMBERS, R.
HANK MOODY
1 Moth in a rag shop (1969)
2 The lesser evil (1971)

CHANCE, J. N.
JOHN MARSH
1 The case of the death computer (1967)
2 The case of the fear makers (1968)
3 Thug executive (1969)
4 The three masks of death (1970)

CHANCE, J. N.
JONATHAN BLAKE
1 The affair at Dead End (1966)
2 The double death (1966)
3 The mask of pursuit (1966)
4 The death woman (1967)
5 The hurricane drift (1967)
6 Dead men's shoes (1968)
7 Man trap (1968)
8 Death of the wild bird (1968)
9 Fate of the lying jade (1968)
10 The rogue aunt (1968)
11 The Hallowe'en murders (1968)
12 Involvement in Austria (1969)
13 The Abel coincidence (1969)
14 The killer reaction (1969)
15 The killing experiment (1969)
16 The ice maidens (1969)
17 The mists of treason (1970)
18 The mirror train (1970)
19 A ring of liars (1970)
20 A wreath of bones (1971)
21 The cat watchers (1971)
22 The faces of a bad girl (1971)
23 The man with two heads (1972)
24 Last train to Limbo (1972)

25 The dead tale tellers (1972)
26 A bad dream of death (1973)
27 The farm villains (1973)
28 The grab operation (1973)
29 The starfish affair (1974)
30 Girl in the crime belt (1974)
31 The shadows of the killer (1975)
32 Hill fog (1975)
33 The monstrous regiment (1975)
34 The devil's edge (1975)
35 The murder makers (1976)
36 Return to Death Alley (1976)
37 A fall out of thieves (1976)
38 House of dead ones (1977)
39 The frightened fisherman (1977)
40 Mists of treason (1977)
41 The Ducrow folly (1978)
42 A drop of hot gold (1978)
43 The guilty witnesses (1979)
44 The death watch ladies (1980)
45 Mayhem Madchen (1980)
46 The reluctant agent (1988)

CHANDLER, B.
RIM RUNNERS
1 The rim of space (1981)
2 When the dream dies (1981)
3 Bring back yesterday (1982)
4 Beyond the galactic rim (1982)

CHANDLER, R.
PHILIP MARLOWE
1 The big sleep (1939)
2 Farewell my lovely (1940)
3 The high window (1942)
4 Lady in the lake (1944)
5 Little sister (1949)
6 The simple art of murder (1950)
7 The long goodbye (1953)
8 Playback (1958)
9 Poodle Springs, completed by
   R.B.Parker (1990)
10 Perchance to dream, completed by
   R.B.Parker (1991)

CHANDRARATNA, B.
SAYEED
1 Mirage (1998)
2 An eye for an eye (2001)

CHARLES, K.
DAVID MIDDLETON-BROWN
1 A drink of deadly wine (1991)
2 The snares of death (1992)
3 Appointed to die (1993)
4 A dead man out of mind (1994)
5 Evil angels among them (1995)

CHARLES, P.
INSPECTOR CHRISTY KENNEDY
1 I love the sound of breaking glass (1997)
2 Last boat to Camden (1998)
3 Fountain of sorrow (1998)
4 The ballad of Sean and Wilko (2000)
5 Hissing of the silent lonely room (2001)
6 I've heard the banshee sing (2002)
7 The justice factory (2004)

CHARRETTE, R. N.
MITSUTOMO
1 A prince among men (1994)
2 A king beneath the mountain (1995)
3 A knight among knaves (1995)

CHARTERIS, L.
THE SAINT
1 Meet the tiger (1928)
2 Enter the Saint (1936)
3 The Saint closes the case (1936)
4 Knight Templar (1936)
5 Featuring the Saint (1936)
6 Alias the Saint (1936)
7 The Saint meets his match (1936)
8 The Saint versus Scotland Yard (1936)
9 Getaway (1936)
10 The Saint and Mr. Teal (1936)
11 The brighter buccaneer (1936)
12 The Saint in London (1936)
13 The Saint intervenes (1936)
14 The Saint goes on (1936)
15 The Saint in New York (1936)
16 Saint overboard (1936)
17 The ace of knaves (1937)
18 The Saint bids diamonds (1937)
19 The Saint plays with fire (1938)
20 Follow the Saint (1938)
21 The happy highwayman (1939)
22 The Saint in Miami (1941)
23 The Saint goes west (1942)
24 The Saint steps in (1944)
25 The Saint on guard (1945)
26 The Saint sees it through (1946)
27 Call for the Saint (1948)
28 Saint errant (1948)
29 The Saint in Europe (1954)
30 The Saint in the Spanish Main (1955)
31 Saint around the world (1959)
32 Thanks to the Saint (1961)
33 Senor Saint (1961)
34 Trust the Saint (1962)
35 The Saint in the sun (1963)
36 Vendetta for the Saint (1964)

CHARYN, J.
ISAAC SIDEL
1 Marilyn the wild (1991)

2 The good policeman (1991)
3 Blue eyes
4 The education of Patrick Silver
5 Secret Isaac

CHASE, J. H.
HELGA ROLFE
1 An ace up my sleeve (1971)
2 The joker in the pack (1975)
3 I hold the four aces (1977)

CHAUDHURI, N. C.
1 Autobiography of an unknown Indian (1951)
2 A passage to England (1963)
3 Thy hand, great Anarch (1987)
NF Autobiography

CHEEK, M.
1 Pause between acts (1988)
2 Parlour games (1989)

CHERRYH, C. J.
MORGAINE CHRONICLES
1 Gate of Ivrel (1981)
2 Well of Shuian
3 The fires of Azeroth

CHERRYH, C. J.
MERCHANTER
1 Downbelow station
2 Cyteen
3 Merchanter's luck
4 Rimrunners
5 Heavy time
6 Hellburner
7 Finity's end

CHERRYH, C. J.
CHANUR
1 Pride of Chanur
2 Chanur's venture
3 Chanur's homecoming

CHERRYH, C. J.
RUSALKA
1 Chernevog (1991)
2 Rusalka (1989)
3 Yvgenie (1992)

CHERRYH, C. J.
FOREIGNER
1 Foreigner (1994)
2 Invader (1995)

CHERRYH, C. J.
GALASIEN
1 Fortress in the eye of time
2 Fortress of eagles

CHESNEY, M.
SIX SISTERS
1 Minerva (1983)
2 The taming of Annabelle (1983)
3 Deirdre and desire (1984)
4 Daphne (1984)
5 Diana the huntress (1985)
6 Frederica in fashion (1986)

CHESNEY, M.
A HOUSE FOR THE SEASON
1 The miser of Mayfair (1987)
2 Plain Jane (1987)
3 The wicked godmother (1988)
4 Rakes progress (1988)
5 The adventuress (1989)
6 Rainbird's revenge (1989)

CHESNEY, M.
SCHOOL FOR MANNERS
1 Refining Felicity (1989)
2 Perfecting Fiona (1990)
3 Enlightened Delilah (1990)
4 Finessing Clarissa (1991)
5 Animating Maria (1991)
6 Marrying Harriet (1992)

CHESNEY, M.
TRAVELLING MATCHMAKER
1 Emily goes to Exeter
2 Belinda goes to Bath
3 Penelope goes to Portsmouth
4 Beatrice goes to Brighton
5 Deborah goes to Dover
6 Yvonne goes to York

CHETWYND-HAYES, R.
CLAVERING GRANGE
1 Tales of darkness (1981)
2 Tales of the other side (1983)
3 Ghosts from the mists of time (1985)
4 The King's ghost (1985)
5 Tales from the haunted house (1987)
6 Tales from the hidden world (1988)

CHILD, L.
JACK REACHER
1 Killing floor (1997)
2 Die trying (1998)
3 The visitor (2000)
4 Echo burning (2001)
5 Without fail (2002)

6 Persuader (2003)
7 The enemy (2004)

CHILDERS, E.
1 The riddle of the sands (1903)
2 The shadow in the sands, by Sam
  Llewellyn (1998)

CHISHOLM, M.
MACALLISTER
1 On the Comanche crossing
2 Macallister and the Spanish gold
3 Macallister never surrenders
4 Macallister and the Cheyenne death
5 Macallister:quarry
6 Diehard
7 Wolfbait
8 Firebrand

CHISHOLM, P. F.
SIR ROBERT CAREY
1 A famine of horses (1994)
2 A season of knives (1995)
3 A surfeit of guns (1996)
4 A plague of angels (1998)

CHRISTIE, AGATHA
MISS MARPLE
1 Murder at the vicarage (1930)
2 The body in the library (1942)
3 The thirteen problems (1942)
4 The moving finger (1943)
5 A murder is announced (1950)
6 They do it with mirrors (1952)
7 A pocket full of rye (1953)
8 The 4.50 from Paddington (1957)
9 The mirror crack'd from side to side
  (1962)
10 A Caribbean mystery (1964)
11 At Bertram's Hotel (1965)
12 Nemesis (1971)
13 Sleeping murder (1976)
14 Miss Marple's final cases (1979)

CHRISTIE, AGATHA
HERCULE POIROT
1 The mysterious affair at Styles (1920)
2 The murder on the links (1923)
3 Poirot investigates (1924)
4 The murder of Roger Ackroyd (1926)
5 The big four (1927)
6 The mystery of the blue train (1928)
7 Peril at End House (1932)
8 Lord Edgeware dies (1933)
9 Murder on the Orient Express (1934)
10 The ABC murders (1935)
11 Three act tragedy (1935)

12 Death in the clouds (1935)
13 Murder in Mesopotamia (1936)
14 Cards on the table (1936)
15 Dumb witness (1937)
16 Death on the Nile (1937)
17 Appointment with death (1938)
18 Murder in the mews (1938)
19 Hercule Poirot's Christmas (1939)
20 Sad cypress (1940)
21 One two, buckle my shoe (1940)
22 Evil under the sun (1941)
23 Five little pigs (1943)
24 The hollow (1946)
25 Labours of Hercules (1947)
26 Taken at the flood (1948)
27 Mrs. McGinty's dead (1952)
28 After the funeral (1953)
29 Hickory, dickory, dock (1955)
30 Dead man's folly (1956)
31 Cat among the pigeons (1959)
32 The adventure of the Christmas pudding
   (1959)
33 The clocks (1963)
34 Third girl (1966)
35 Hallowe'en party (1969)
36 Elephants can remember (1972)
37 Poirot's early cases (1974)
38 Curtain:Poirot's last case (1976)

CHRISTIE, AGATHA
SUPT. BATTLE
1 The secret of Chimneys (1925)
2 Murder is easy (1929)
3 Towards zero (1944)
4 The seven dials mystery

CHRISTIE, AGATHA
TOMMY AND TUPPENCE BERESFORD
1 The secret adversary (1922)
2 Partners in crime (1929)
3 N or M (1941)
4 By the pricking of my thumbs (1968)
5 Postern of fate (1973)

CHRONICLES OF ATHAS
1 The brazen gambit, by L.Abbey
2 The darkness before dawn, by R.Hughes
3 The broken blade, by S.Hawke
4 Cinnabar shadows, by L.Abbey

CHUN CHAN YEH
QUIET ARE THE MOUNTAINS
1 The mountain village
2 The open fields (1988)

CIRNI, J.
FRANK FONTANA
1 The kiss off (1988)
2 The come on (1989)

CLANCY, TOM
JACK RYAN
1 Patriot games (1987)
2 The Cardinal of the Kremlin (1988)
3 Debt of honour (1994)
4 Executive orders (1996)
5 The bear and the dragon (2000)
6 Red rabbit (2002)
7 The teeth of the tiger (2003)

CLANCY, TOM
JOHN KELLY
1 The hunt for Red October (1985)
2 Clear and present danger (1989)
3 The sum of all fears (1991)
4 Without remorse (1993)
5 Rainbow six (1998)

CLARE, A.
HAWKENLYE
1 Fortune like the moon (1999)
2 Ashes of the elements (2000)
3 The tavern in the morning (2000)
4 The chatter of the maidens (2001)
5 A dark night hidden (2003)

CLARK, C. H.
REGAN REILLY
1 Decked (1992)
2 Snagged (1993)
3 Iced (1996)
4 Twanged (1998)

CLARK, D.
CHIEF INSPECTOR MASTERS
1 Nobody's perfect (1969)
2 Death after evensong (1969)
3 Deadly pattern (1970)
4 Sweet poison (1970)
5 Sick to death (1971)
6 The miracle makers (1971)
7 Premedicated murder (1975)
8 Dread and water (1976)
9 Table d'hote (1977)
10 The gimmel flask (1977)
11 The Libertines (1978)
12 Heberden's seat (1979)
13 Poacher's bag (1979)
14 Golden rain (1980)
15 Roast eggs (1981)
16 The longest pleasure (1981)
17 Shelf life (1982)

18 Doone walk (1982)
19 Vicious circle (1983)
20 The Monday theory (1983)
21 Bouquet garni (1984)
22 Dead letter (1984)
23 Performance (1985)
24 Jewelled eye (1985)
25 Storm centre (1986)
26 The big grouse (1986)
27 Plain sailing (1987)

CLARKE, A. C.
THE FALL OF NIGHT
1 Against the fall of night (1953)
2 Beyond the fall of night, by G.Benford (1991)

CLARKE, A. C.
RAMA
1 Rendezvous with Rama (1973)
2 Rama II (with Lee Gentry) (1989)
3 The garden of Rama (with Lee Gentry) (1991)
4 Rama revealed (with Lee Gentry) (1993)

CLARKE, A. C.
ODYSSEY
1 2001:a space odyssey (1968)
2 2010: odyssey 2 (1982)
3 2061:odyssey 3 (1988)
4 3001:the final odyssey (1997)

CLARKE, R.
SUMMER WINE CHRONICLES
1 Gala Week (1986)
2 The moonbather (1987)

CLAVELL, J.
ASIAN SAGA
1 Shogun (1975)
2 Tai-pan (1966)
3 King Rat (1962)
4 Noble house (1981)
5 Gai-jin (1993)

CLAYTON, C. G.
THE BLAKENEY PAPERS
1 Daughter of the Revolution (1984)
2 Such mighty rage (1985)
3 Bordeaux red (1986)

CLAYTON, M.
DET. CHIEF INSPECTOR JOHN REYNOLDS
1 Pearls before swine (1995)
2 Dead men's bones (1996)

3 The prodigal's return (1996)
4 The word is death (1997)
5 Death is the inheritance (1999)

CLEARY, J.
SCOBIE MALONE
1 The High Commissioner (1970)
2 Helga's web (1971)
3 Ransom (1972)
4 Dragons at the party (1987)
5 Now and then, Amen (1988)
6 Babylon south (1989)
7 Murder song (1990)
8 Pride's harvest (1991)
9 Bleak spring (1993)
10 Dark summer (1994)
11 Autumn maze (1994)
12 Winter chill (1995)
13 Endpeace (1996)
14 A different turf (1997)
15 Dilemma (1999)
16 The bear pit (2000)
17 Yesterday's shadows (2001)

CLEEVES, A.
GEORGE PALMER-JONES
1 A bird in the hand (1986)
2 Come death and high water (1987)
3 Murder in Paradise (1988)
4 A prey to murder (1989)
5 Another man's poison (1992)
6 Sea fever (1993)
7 The mill on the shore (1994)
8 High island blues (1996)

CLEEVES, A.
INSPECTOR RAMSAY
1 A lesson in dying (1990)
2 Murder in my back yard (1991)
3 A day in the death of Dorothea Cassidy (1992)
4 Killjoy (1993)
5 The healers (1995)
6 The babysnatcher (1997)
7 Where birds don't sing (1999)

CLEMENS, J.
THE BANNED AND BANISHED
1 Witch storm (1999)
2 Wit'ch gate (2001)
3 Wit'ch fire (2002)
4 Witch star (2002)
5 Witch war (2002)

CLEVERLY, B.
DET. INSPECTOR JOE SANDILANDS
1 The last Kashmiri rose (2001)

2 Ragtime in Simla (2002)
3 Damascene blade (2003)

CLEWES, D.
GRANT FAMILY
1 Missing from home (1975)
2 Testing year (1977)

CLIFFORD, R.
1 Just here doctor (1976)
2 Not there, doctor (1978)
3 What next, doctor? (1979)
4 Oh dear, doctor (1980)
5 Look out, doctor (1983)
6 Surely not, doctor (1985)
7 There you are, doctor (1986)
8 On holiday again, doctor? (1987)
9 You're still a doctor, Doctor (1989)

CLYNES, M.
SIR ROGER SHALLOTT
1 The white rose murders (1991)
2 The poisoned chalice (1992)
3 The Grail murders (1993)
4 A brood of vipers (1994)
5 The gallows murders (1995)
6 The relic murders (1996)

COBB, R.
1 Still life (1983)
2 A classical education (1986)
3 Something to hold on to (1988)

COBEN, H.
MYRON BOLITAR
1 One false move (1998)
2 Drop shot (1999)
3 The final detail (1999)
4 Deal breaker (1999)
5 Fade away (2000)
6 Back spin (2000)
7 Darkest fear (2001)

COBURN, L.
KATHERINE HARROD
1 A desperate call (1995)
2 An uncertain death (1996)

COCKEY, T.
HITCHCOCK SEWELL
1 The hearse you came in on (2000)
2 Hearse of a different colour (2001)
3 The hearse case scenario (2003)
4 Murder in the hearse degree (2003)

CODY, L.
ANNA LEE AND BRIERLEY SECURITY
1 Head case (1985)
2 Dupe (1980)
3 Bad company (1982)
4 Stalker (1984)
5 Under contract (1986)
6 Backhand (1991)

CODY, L.
EVA WYLIE
1 Bucket nut (1992)
2 Monkey wrench (1994)
3 Musclebound (1997)

COE, D. B.
LON TOBYN CHRONICLES
1 Children of Amarid
2 The outlanders
3 Eagle and sage (2000)

COFFMAN, V.
LOMBARD FAMILY
1 Pacific cavalcade (1986)
2 The Lombard cavalcade (1986)
3 The Lombard heiress (1986)

COFFMAN, V.
THE ROYLES
1 The Royles (1992)
2 Dangerous loyalties (1993)
3 The princess Royal (1994)
4 Heir to a throne (1995)

COFFMAN, V.
JEWELS
1 Emerald flame (1996)
2 The wine dark opal (1997)
3 Tiger's eye (1998)
4 A splash of rubies (1999)

COFFMAN, V.
MOURA
1 Moura (1959)
2 The beckoning (1965)
3 The Vicar of Moura (1972)
4 The dark beyond Moura (1977)
5 The vampyre of Moura (1997)

COGGIN, J.
DUBLIN TRILOGY
1 McIlhenney (1989)
2 Leaving (1989)
3 Northside (1990)

COHEN, ANTHEA
NURSE CARMICHAEL
1 Angel without mercy (1981)
2 Angel of vengeance (1982)
3 Angel of death (1983)
4 Fallen angel (1984)
5 Guardian angel (1985)
6 Hell's angel (1986)
7 Ministering angel (1987)
8 Destroying angel (1988)
10 Recording angel (1991)
11 Angel in action (1992)
12 Angel in love (1993)
13 Angel in autumn (1995)
14 Dedicated angel (1997)
15 Angel of retribution (1998)
16 Angel and the French widow (2000)
17 Angel and the deadly secret (2003)

COHEN, N. J.
MARLA SHORE
1 Hair raiser (2001)
2 Murder by manicure (2002)
3 Body wave (2003)
4 Highlights to heaven (2004)

COLE, A.
OMARAN SAGA
1 A place among the fallen (1986)
2 Throne of fools (1987)
3 The King of light and shadows (1988)
4 The gods in anger (1988)

COLE, A.
STAR REQUIEM
1 Mother of storms (1989)
2 Thief of dreams (1989)
3 Warlord of heaven (1990)
4 Labyrinth of worlds (1990)

COLE, A.
TIMURA TRILOGY
1 When the gods slept (1997)
2 Wolves of the gods (1998)
3 The gods awaken (1999)

COLE, A. & BUNCH, C.
1 The far kingdoms (1993)
2 The warrior's tale (1994)

COLE, H.
1 Policeman's patch
2 Policeman's lot
3 Policeman's progress
4 Policeman's patrol
5 Policeman's story
6 Policeman's prelude

COLEMAN, L.
BEULAH LAND
1 Beulah land (1973)
2 Look away, Beulah land (1977)
3 The legacy of Beulah land (1980)

COLEMAN, V.
BILBURY
1 Bilbury chronicles (1992)
2 Bilbury Grange (1993)
3 The Bilbury revels (1994)
4 Bilbury country (1994)
5 Bilbury pie (1994)

COLES, P. J. C.
CHAMPION
1 Champion's folly (1984)
2 Champion's chariot (1985)
3 Champion's calamity (1987)

COLLARD, T.
DET. SUPT. JAMES BYRD
1 Murder at the Tower (1991)
2 Murder at Hampton Court Palace (1992)
3 Murder at the Royal Shakespeare (1994)

COLLENETTE, E. J.
BEN GRANT
1 90 feet to the sun (1984)
2 The Gemini plot (1985)
3 The secret of the Kara Sea (1986)
4 The Monday mutiny (1987)
5 A capful of glory (1988)
6 Sea wolf hunter (1989)

COLLEY, B.
CHARLOTTE LA RUE
1 Maid for murder (2002)
2 Death tidies up (2003)

COLLIER, C.
DET. INSPECTOR DOUGLAS MCBRIDE
1 Spring tide (1996)
2 Requiem (1997)
3 Innocent blood (1998)

COLLIER, C.
PONTYPRIDD SAGA
1 Hearts of gold (1991)
2 One blue moon (1993)
3 All that glitters (1995)
4 A silver lining (1996)
5 Such sweet sorrow (1996)
6 Past remembering (1997)
7 Broken rainbows (1999)
8 The spoils of war (2000)

9 Swansea summer (2002)
10 Homecoming (2003)
11 Beggars and choosers (2003)

COLLINS, J.
LUCKY
1 Chances (1982)
2 Lucky (1885)
3 Lady boss (1995)
4 Vendetta:Lucky's revenge (1996)
5 Dangerous kiss (1999)

COLLINS, M. A.
MALLORY
1 The baby-blue ripoff (1984)
2 Cure for death (1985)

COLLINS, M. A.
NATHAN HELLER
1 True detective
2 True crime
3 The million-dollar wound (1989)
4 Neon mirage (1989)

COLLINS, W.
1 Challenge (1990)
2 New world (1991)
3 Death of an angel (1992)

COLLINS, W.
GRANGE & HARWOOD
1 The rationalist (1998)
2 The marriage of souls (1999)

COMPTON, D. G.
ALEC DUNCAN
1 Justice city (1994)
2 Back of town blues (1996)

CONDON, R.
PRIZZI
1 Prizzi's honour (1984)
2 Prizzi's family (1986)
3 Prizzi's glory (1988)
4 Prizzi's money (1994)

CONEY, M.
GRANGE & HARWOOD
1 The celestial steam locomotive (1984)
2 Gods of the greataway (1986)

CONLON, K.
GRANGE & HARWOOD
1 A forgotten season (1980)
2 Consequences (1981)

CONNELLY, M.
HARRY BOSCH
1 The black echo (1992)
2 The black ice (1993)
3 The concrete blond (1994)
4 The last coyote (1995)
5 The poet (1996)
6 Trunk music (1997)
7 Angels flight (1999)
8 A darkness more than light (2000)
9 City of bones (2002)
10 Lost light (2003)

CONNERY, T.
MARKHAM OF THE MARINES
1 A shred of honour (1996)
2 Honour redeemed (1997)
3 Honour be damned (1999)

CONNOR, B.
LYNDSAY CHAMBERLAIN
1 Questionable remains (2001)
2 Skeleton crew (2001)
3 Airtight case (2001)
4 A rumour of bones (2002)
5 Dressed to die (2002)

CONRAD, P.
1 Down home (1988)
2 Where I fell to earth (1990)

CONRAN, S.
1 Lace (1982)
2 Lace II (1985)

CONSTANTINE, K. C.
MARIO BALZIC
1 The Rocksburg railroad murders
2 The man who liked to look at himself (1986)
3 The blank page
4 A fix like this
5 The man who liked to grow tomatoes (1984)
6 Always a body to trade (1985)
7 Upon some midnight's clear (1986)
8 Joey's case (1988)
9 Sunshine enemies (1990)
10 Bottom line blues
11 Cranks and shadows (1995)
12 Good sons (1996)
13 Family values (1997)
14 Blood mud (1999)

CONSTANTINE, S.
WRAETHTHU
1 The enchantments of flesh and spirit (1987)
2 The bewitchments of love and hate (1988)
3 The fulfilments of fate and desire (1989)

CONWAY, P.
INSPECTOR NEWTON
1 Victims of circumstance (1977)
2 30 days to live (1979)
3 Nut case (1980)
4 Needle track (1981)
5 Dead drunk (1982)
6 Cryptic clue (1984)

CONYNGHAM, J.
1 The arrowing of the cane (1988)
2 The desecration of the graves (1992)

COOK, BOB
MICHAEL WYMAN
1 Disorderly elements (1986)
2 Questions of identity (1987)

COOK, G.
THE BLACK COMPANY
1 The Black Company
2 Shadows linger
3 The white rose

COOK, GLORIA
PENGARRON
1 Pengarron land (1992)
2 Pengarron pride (1993)
3 Pengarron's children (1993)
4 Pengarron dynasty (2002)
5 Pengarron rivalry (2004)

COOK, H.
CHRONICLES OF AN AGE OF DARKNESS
1 The wizards and the warriors (1987)
2 The wordsmiths and the warguild (1987)
3 The women and the warlords (1988)
4 The walrus and the warwolf (1988)
5 The wicked and the witless (1989)
6 The wishstone and the wonderworkers (1990)
7 The Wazir and the witch (1990)
8 The werewolf and the wormlord (1991)
9 The worshippers and the way (1992)

COOK, J.
DR. SIMON FORMAN
1 Death of a lady's maid (1997)
2 Murder at the Rose (1998)
3 Blood on the Borders (1999)
4 Kill the witch (1999)
5 School of the night (2000)

COOK, T. H.
1 Sacrificial ground (1988)
2 Flesh and blood (1989)
3 Streets of fire (1990)
4 Night secrets (1992)

COOKE, C.
1 The winged assassin
2 Realm of the gods

COOKSON, C.
TILLY TROTTER
1 Tilly Trotter (1980)
2 Tilly Trotter wed (1981)
3 Tilly Trotter widowed (1982)

COOKSON, C.
HAMILTON
1 Hamilton (1983)
2 Goodbye Hamilton (1984)
3 Harold (1985)

COOKSON, C.
BILL BAILEY
1 Bill Bailey (1986)
2 Bill Bailey's lot (1987)
3 Bill Bailey's daughter (1988)

COOKSON, C.
MALLEN FAMILY
1 The Mallen streak (1973)
2 The Mallen girl (1973)
3 The Mallen litter (1974)

COOKSON, C.
MARY ANN SHAUGHNESSY
1 A grand man (1956)
2 The Lord and Mary Ann (1956)
3 The devil and Mary Ann (1958)
4 Love and Mary Ann (1961)
5 Life and Mary Ann (1962)
6 Marriage and Mary Ann (1964)
7 Mary Ann's angels (1965)
8 Mary Ann and Bill (1967)

COONTS, S.
JAKE GRAFTON
1 Flight of the intruder (1987)

2 Final flight (1989)
3 The minotaur (1990)
4 Under siege (1990)
5 The intruders (1994)
6 Liberty (2003)

COONTS, S.
DEEP BLACK
1 Deep black (2003)
2 Biowar (2004)

COOPER, BRIAN
CHIEF INSPECTOR TENCH AND JOHN LUBBOCK
1 The cross of San Vincente (1991)
2 The singing stones (1993)
3 Covenant with death (1994)
4 Shadows on the sand (1995)
5 The travelling dead (1997)
6 The Blacknock woman (1999)
7 The Norfolk triangle (2000)
8 The murder column (2003)

COOPER, DIANA
1 Animal hotel (1979)
2 Up to scratch (1981)
3 Mere folly (1982)

COOPER, JILLY
RUTSHIRE
1 Riders (1985)
2 Rivals (1988)
3 Polo (1991)
4 The man who made husbands jealous (1993)
5 Appasssionata (1996)
6 Score (1999)

COOPER, L.
DET. CHIEF INSPECTOR CORBY
1 Tea on Sunday (1973)
2 Unusual behaviour (1986)

COOPER, LOUISE
TIME MASTER TRILOGY
1 The initiate (1986)
2 The outcast (1986)
3 The master (1987)

COOPER, LOUISE
INDIGO
1 Nemesis (1993)
2 Inferno
3 Infanta
4 Nocturne
5 Troika

6 Avatar
7 Revenant
8 Aisling

COOPER, LOUISE
CHAOS GATE
1 The deceiver
2 The pretender
3 The avenger

COOPER, LOUISE
STAR SHADOW TRILOGY
1 Star ascendant (1994)
2 Eclipse (1994)
3 Moonset (1995)

COOPER, N.
WILLOW KING
1 Festering lilies (1990)
2 Poison flowers (1991)
3 Bloody roses (1993)
4 Bitter herbs (1993)
5 Rotten apples (1995)
6 Fruiting bodies (1996)
7 Sour grapes (1997)

COOPER, LOUISE
TRISH MAGUIRE
1 Creeping ivy (1998)
2 Fault lines (1999)
3 Prey to all (2000)
4 Out of the dark (2001)
5 A place of safety (2003)
6 Keep me alive (2004)

COOPER, W.
1 Scenes from provincial life (1950)
2 Scenes from married life (1961)
3 Scenes from metropolitan life (1982)
4 Scenes from later life (1983)

COPPER, B.
MIKE FARADAY
1 The dark mirror (1965)
2 Night frost (1966)
3 No flowers for the general (1967)
4 Scratch on the dark (1967)
5 Die now, live later (1967)
6 Don't bleed on me (1968)
7 The marble orchard (1969)
8 Dead file (1970)
9 No letters from the grave (1971)
10 Big chill (1972)
11 Strong-arm (1972)
12 A great year for dying (1973)
13 shockwave (1973)
14 The breaking point (1974)

15 A voice from the dead (1974)
16 Feedback (1974)
17 Ricochet (1974)
18 The high wall (1975)
19 Impact (1975)
20 A good place to die (1976)
21 The lonely place (1976)
22 Crack in the sidewalk (1976)
23 Tight corner (1976)
24 The year of the dragon (1977)
25 Death squad (1977)
26 Murder one (1977)
27 A quiet room in Hell (1978)
28 The big ripoff (1978)
29 The Caligari complex (1979)
30 Flip-side (1980)
31 The long rest (1981)
32 The empty silence (1981)
33 Dark entry (1981)
34 Hang loose (1982)
35 Shoot-out (1982)
36 The far horizon (1982)
37 Trigger-man (1983)
38 Pressure point (1983)
39 The narrow corner (1983)
40 Hard contract (1984)
41 The hook (1984)
42 You only die once (1984)
43 Tuxedo Park (1985)
44 The far side of fear (1985)
45 Snow job (1985)
46 Jet-lag (1986)
47 Blood on the moon (1986)
48 Heavy iron (1987)
49 Turn down an empty glass (1987)
50 Bad scene (1987)
51 House-dick (1988)
52 Print-out (1988)

CORDELL, A.
1 This proud and savage land (1988)
2 Rape of the fair country (1966)
3 Song of the earth (1969)
4 The fire people (1972)
5 This sweet and bitter earth (1977)
6 Land of my fathers (1983)
7 Beloved exile (1993)

CORK, B.
INSPECTOR ANGUS STRAUN
1 Dead ball (1988)
2 Unnatural hazard (1989)
3 Laid dead (1990)
4 Winter rules (1991)
5 Endangered species (1992)

CORLEY, E.
DET. CHIEF INSPECTOR ANDREW
FENWICK
1 Requiem mass (1999)
2 Fatal legacy (2000)

CORNWELL, B.
RICHARD SHARPE
1 Sharpe's tiger (Siege of Seringapatam
  1799) (1998)
2 Sharpe's triumph (1803) (1998)
3 Sharpe's fortress (Siege of Gawilghur
  1803) (1999)
4 Sharpe's prey (1807) (2000)
5 Sharpe's havoc (Oporto 1809) (2003)
6 Sharpe's rifles (Galicia 1809) (1988)
7 Sharpe's eagle (Talavera 1809) (1980)
8 Sharpe's gold (Almeida 1810) (1981)
9 Sharpe's escape (Bussaco 1810) (2004)
10 Sharpe's company (Badajoz 1812) (1982)
11 Sharpe's sword (Salamanca 1812) (1983)
12 Sharpe's enemy (Defence of Portugal
  1812) (1984)
13 Sharpe's honour (Vitoria 1813) (1985)
14 Sharpe's regiment (1813) (1985)
15 Sharpe's siege (1814) (1987)
16 Sharpe's revenge (1814) (1989)
17 Sharpe's Waterloo (1815) (1990)
18 Sharpe's devil(Sharpe and the Emperor
  1820-21) (1992)

CORNWELL, B.
NATHANIEL STARBUCK
1 Rebel (1993)
2 Copperhead (1994)
3 Battle flag (1994)
4 The bloody ground (1996)

CORNWELL, B.
THE WARLORD CHRONICLES
1 The winter king (1995)
2 Enemy of God (1996)
3 Excalibur (1997)

CORNWELL, B.
THE GRAIL
1 Harlequin (2001)
2 Vagabond (2002)
3 Heretic (2003)

CORNWELL, P. D.
DR. KAY SCARPETTA
1 Post mortem (1991)
2 Body of evidence (1991)
3 All that remains (1992)
4 Cruel and unusual (1993)
5 The body farm (1994)

6 From Potter's field (1995)
7 Cause of death (1996)
8 Unnatural exposure (1997)
9 Point of origin (1998)
10 Black notice (1999)
11 The last precinct (2000)
12 Blow fly (2003)

CORNWELL, P. D.
DEPUTY CHIEF VIRGINIA WEST
1 Hornet's nest (1998)
2 Southern Cross (1999)
3 Isle of dogs (2002)

CORY, D.
PROFESSOR DOBIE
1 The strange attractor (1991)
2 The mask of Zeus (1992)
3 The Dobie paradox (1993)

COSGRAVE, P.
COLONEL CHEYNEY
1 Cheyney
2 The three Colonels (1979)
3 Adventure of state (1984)

COUGHLIN, W. J.
1 Shadow of a doubt (1992)
2 Death penalty (1993)

COULTER, C.
SHERBROOKE FAMILY
1 The Sherbrooke bride (1994)
2 The heiress bride (1994)
3 The hellion bride (1994)

COULTER, C.
NIGHT
1 Night shadow
2 Night storm
3 Night fire

COULTER, C.
STAR
1 Wild star
2 Evening star
3 Midnight star
4 Jade star

COUPER, L.
PHILIPPA
1 Philippa's farm (1995)
2 Philippa's folly (1996)

COURTENAY, B.
1 The power of one (1989)
2 Tandia (1991)

COURTER, G.
HANNAH SOKOLOW
1 The midwife (1986)
2 The midwife's advice (1993)

COURTNEY, D.
AUTOBIOGRAPHY
1 Stop the ride, I want to get off (2001)
2 The ride's back on (2002)

COURTNEY, E.
KIT HEMSWORTHY
1 The price of loving (1987)
2 Over the bridge (1988)

COWPER, R.
BIRD OF KINSHIP SAGA
1 Piper at the gates of dawn (1976)
2 The road to Corlay (1978)
3 A dream of Kinship (1981)
4 A tapestry of time (1982)

COX, J.
EMMA GRADY
1 Outcast (1990)
2 Alley urchin (1991)
3 Vagabonds (1992)

CRADOCK, F.
THE LORMES OF CASTLE RISING
1 The Lormes of Castle Rising (1975)
2 Shadows over Castle Rising (1977)
3 War comes to Castle Rising (1977)
4 Wind of change over Castle Rising
  (1978)
5 Uneasy peace at Castle Rising (1979)
6 Thunder over Castle Rising (1980)
7 Gathering clouds at Castle Rising (1981)
8 Fateful years at Castle Rising (1982)
9 The defence of Castle Rising (1984)
10 The loneliness of Castle Rising (1986)

CRAGOE, E.
1 Buttercups and Daisy (1974)
2 Cowslips and clover (1978)
3 Yorkshire relish (1979)
4 Sweet nothings (1980)
5 The untidy gardener (1982)
  NF Country life

CRAIG, D.
DET. INSPECTOR BRADE & SERGEANT
JENKINS
1 Forget it! (1997)
2 The tattooed detective (1998)

CRAIS, R.
ELVIS COLE
1 The monkey's raincoat (1988)
2 Stalking the angel (1990)
3 Lullaby town (1992)
4 Indigo slam (1998)
5 Devil's cantina (1999)
6 LA requiem (1999)
7 Sunset express (2000)
8 Demolition angel (2001)
9 Hostage (2002)
10 The last detective (2002)
11 The forgotten man (2004)

CRANE, T.
1 Tomorrow, Jerusalem (1989)
2 Green and pleasant land (1991)

CRAWLEY, A.
SULEIMAN THE MAGNIFICENT
1 The bride of Suleiman (1981)
2 The shadow of God (1982)
3 The house of war (1984)

CRICHTON, M.
JURASSIC PARK
1 Jurassic Park (1989)
2 The lost world (1995)

CRISP, W.
WESTFALL
1 Spytrap (1984)
2 Vengeance is thine (1986)

CRISPIN, E.
GERVASE FEN
1 The case of the gilded fly (1944)
2 Holy disorders (1945)
3 The moving toyshop (1846)
4 Swan song (1947)
5 Love lies bleeding (1948)
6 Buried for pleasure (1949)
7 Frequent hearses (1950)
8 The long divorce (1951)
9 Beware of the trains (1953)
10 Glimpses of the moon (1977)
11 Fen country (1979)

CROFT-COOKE, R.
THE SENSUAL LIFE
1 The gardens of Camelot (1958)
2 The altar in the loft (1960)
3 The drums of morning (1961)
4 The glittering pastures (1962)
5 The numbers came (1963)
6 The last of Spring (1964)
7 The purple streak (1966)
8 The wild hills (1966)
9 The happy highways (1967)
10 The sound of revelry (1969)
11 The moon in my pocket (1970)
12 The licentious soldiery (1971)
13 The blood red island (1967)
14 The gorgeous east (1965)
15 The dogs of peace (1968)
16 The life for me (1970)
17 The verdict of you all (1970)
18 The tangerine house (1956)
19 The quest for Quixote (1961)
20 The wintry sea (1964)
21 The ghost of June (1969)
22 The caves of Hercules (1974)
23 The long way home (1974)
24 The green green grass (1977)
NF Autobiography

CROMBIE, D.
SUPT. DUNCAN KINCAID
1 A share in death (1994)
2 All shall be well (1995)
3 Leave the grave green (1996)
4 Mourn not your dead (1996)
5 Dreaming of the bones (1997)
6 Kissed a sad goodbye (1999)
7 A finer end (2001)
8 And justice there is none (2002)
9 Now may you weep (2004)

CROSBY, J.
HORATIO CASSIDY
1 An affair of strangers (1975)
2 The company of friends (1977)
3 Party of the year (1980)
4 Men at arms (1984)
5 Take no prisoners (1986)

CROSS, A.
KATE FANSLER
1 In the last analysis (1966)
2 The James Joyce murder (1967)
3 Poetic justice (1970)
4 The Theban mysteries (1972)
5 The question of Max (1976)
6 A death in the faculty (1981)
7 Sweet death, kind death (1984)
8 No word from Winifred (1987)
9 A trap for fools (1990)
10 An imperfect spy (1995)

CROSS, R. A.
THE ETERNAL GUARDIANS
1 The fourth guardian (1994)
2 The lost guardian (1995)
3 The white guardian (1998)

CROSSLEY, B.
ANNA KNIGHT
1 Candyfloss coast (1993)
2 Rollercoaster (1994)

CROWDER, H.
DAVID LLEWELLYN
1 Ambush at Osirak (1990)
2 Missile zone (1991)

CROWLEY, E.
O'HARA FAMILY
1 Dreams of other days (1984)
2 Waves upon the shore (1989)

CRUISE, T. E.
WINGS OF GOLD
1 Wings of gold (1989)
2 Skies of gold (1990)
3 Pilots of gold (1991)

CRUMLEY, J.
MILO MILOGRADOVITCH
1 The wrong case (1975)
2 Dancing bear (1983)
3 Bordersnakes (1997)

CRUMLEY, J.
C.W.SUGHRUE
1 The last good kiss (1991)
2 The Mexican tree duck (1994)
3 One to count cadence (1995)

CULLEN, S.
1 A noose of light
2 The Sultan's turret

CUNNINGHAM, E. V.
MASAO MASUTO
1 The case of the one-penny orange (1978)
2 The case of the Russian diplomat (1979)
3 The case of the poisoned eclairs (1980)
4 The case of the sliding pool (1982)
5 The case of the kidnapped angel (1983)
6 The case of the murdered Mackenzie (1985)

CURRAN, S.
ERICA MASSEN
1 Mine (1994)
2 Communion with death (1995)

CURRIE, E.
PARLIAMENTARY SERIES
1 A Parliamentary affair (1994)
2 A woman's place (1996)

CURRY, G.
SADDLER
1 A dirty way to die
2 Colorado crossing
3 Hot as a pistol
4 Wild wild women

CURZON, C.
DET. SUPT. MIKE YEADINGS
1 I give you five days (1983)
2 Masks and faces (1984)
3 The Trojan hearse (1985)
4 Cat's cradle (1991)
5 First wife, twice removed (1992)
6 Death prone (1992)
7 Nice people (1993)
8 Past mischief (1994)
9 Close quarters (1996)
10 All unwary (1997)
11 Cold hands (1999)
12 Don't leave me (2001)
13 Body of a woman (2002)
14 A meeting of minds (2003)

CUSSLER, C.
DIRK PITT
1 Pacific vortex (1983)
2 Raise the Titanic (1980)
3 Night probe (1981)
4 Deep six (1984)
5 Cyclops (1986)
6 Treasure (1988)
7 Dragon (1990)
8 Sahara (1992)
9 Inca gold (1994)
10 Shock wave (1996)
11 Flood tide (1997)
12 Atlantis found (2000)
13 Valhalla rising (2001)
14 Trojan odyssey (2004)

CUSSLER, C.
KURT AUSTIN AND NUMA
1 Serpent (1999)
2 Blue gold (2000)

CUTLER, J.
DET. SERGEANT KATE POWER
1 Power on her own (1997)
2 Staying power (1999)
3 Power games (2000)
4 Will Power (2001)
5 Hidden Power (2002)
6 Power shift (2003)

CUTLER, J.
SOPHIE RIVERS
1 Dying to fall (1995)
2 Dying to write (1996)
3 Dying on principle (1996)
4 Dying for millions (1997)
5 Dying for power (1998)
6 Dying to score (1999)
7 Dying by degrees (2000)
8 Dying by the book (2001)
9 Dying in discord (2002)
10 Dying to deceive (2003)

DA SILVA, C.
1 Winds of Sinhala (1982)
2 Founts of Sinhala (1984)
3 The fires of Sinhala (1986)
4 The last Sinhala lions (1987)

DACRE, R.
SAM HOSKINS
1 The blood runs hot (1987)
2 Scream blue murder (1988)
3 Money with menaces (1989)

DAHL, R.
1 Boy (1984)
2 Going solo (1986)
   NF Autobiography

DAILEY, J.
CALDERS
1 This Calder range (1983)
2 The Calder sky (1982)
3 Stands a Calder man (1983)
4 Calder born, Calder bred (1984)
5 Green Calder grass (2003)

DAILEY, J.
TEXAS
1 The proud and the free (1994)
2 Legacies (1995)

DAISH, E.
COPPINS BRIDGE
1 The shop on Coppins Bridge (1985)

2 The family on Coppins Bridge (1986)
3 Ebbtide at Coppins Bridge (1988)

DAISH, E.
EMMA
1 Emma's war (1989)
2 Emma's peace (1995)
3 Emma's haven (1995)
4 Emma's family (1996)
5 Emma's Christmas rose (1997)
6 Emma's journey (1999)
7 Emma and the leprechauns (2000)

DALEY, B.
CORAMONDE
1 The doomfarers of Coramonde
2 The starfollowers of Coramonde

DALEY, B.
ALACRITY FITZHUGH AND HOBART FLOYT
1 Requiem for a ruler of worlds
2 Jinx on a terran inheritance
3 Fall of the white ship Avatar

DANIEL, A. B.
INCAS
1 The puma's shadow (2002)
2 The gold of Cuzco (2002)
3 The light of Machu Picchu (2003)

DANIELSON, P.
1 Children of the lion (1985)
2 The shepherd kings (1985)
3 Vengeance of the lion (1985)
4 The lion in Egypt (1985)

DANIKEN, E.VON
GODS
1 Chariots of the gods (1969)
2 Return to the stars (1971)
3 The gold of the gods (1973)
4 In search of ancient gods (1974)
5 Miracles of the gods (1975)
6 Signs of the gods (1980)

DANKS, D.
GEORGINA POWERS
1 The pizza house crash (1990)
2 Better off dead (1991)
3 Frame grabber (1992)
4 Wink a hopeful eye (1993)
5 Phreak (1998)
6 Torso (2000)
7 Baby love (2001)

DARBY, C.
FALCON SERIES
1 Falcon for a witch (1975)
2 Game for a falcon (1976)
3 Falcon's claw (1976)
4 Falcon to the lure (1981)
5 Fortune for a falcon (1976)
6 Season of the falcon (1976)
7 A pride of falcons (1977)
8 The falcon tree (1977)
9 The falcon and the moon (1977)
10 Falcon rising (1978)
11 Falcon sunset (1978)
12 Seed of the falcons (1981)

DARBY, C.
ROWAN SERIES
1 Rowan Garth (1982)
2 Rowan for a Queen (1983)
3 A scent of rowan (1983)
4 A circle of rowan (1983)
5 The Rowan maid (1984)
6 Song of the rowan (1984)

DARBY, C.
SABRE
1 Sabre (1984)
2 Sabre's child (1985)
3 The silken sabre (1985)
4 House of Sabre (1986)
5 A breed of Sabre
6 Morning of a Sabre (1987)
7 Gentle Sabre (1988)

DARBY, L.
EYE OF TIME TRILOGY
1 Crystal and steel (1988)
2 Bloodshed (1988)
3 Phoenixfire

DARKE, J.
THE WITCHES
1 The prisoner
2 The trial
3 The torture
4 No escape
5 The meeting
6 The killing

DARKE, S.
GRAHAM FAMILY
1 Conquer the night
2 Come the morning
3 Seize the dawn
4 Knight triumphant

DARKE, S.
VAMPIRE TRILOGY
1 When darkness falls
2 Beneath a blood red moon
3 Deep midnight

DARRELL, E.
SHERIDAN FAMILY
1 At the going down of the sun (1984)
2 And in the morning (1988)

DART, I. R.
1 Beaches (1985)
2 I'll be there (1992)

DART-THORNTON, C.
THE BITTERBYNDE TRILOGY
1 The ill-made mute (2001)
2 The lady of the sorrows (2002)

DAVEY, A. R.
FORRESTER FAMILY
1 Autumn on Angel Street (1995)
2 Winter in Paradise Square (1996)

DAVEY, D.
VICTOR ARLISS (THE VICAR)
1 The case of the golden coins (1990)
2 The death of a Wimbledon finalist (1990)

DAVEY, D.
KATE ENGLAND
1 Caravanserai for Kate (1986)
2 Keyhole for Kate (1987)
3 Coronet for Kate (1987)

DAVIES, A.
1 A very peculiar practice (1987)
2 The new frontier (1988)

DAVIES, F.
1 Death of a hitman (1982)
2 Snow in Venice (1983)

DAVIES, Freda
DET. INSPECTOR TYRELL
1 A fine and private place (2001)
2 Bound in shadows (2003)

DAVIES, P
1 Mare's milk and wild honey (1987)
2 A corner of Paradise (1992)
   NF Autobiography

DAVIES, R.
CORNISH TRILOGY
1 Rebel angels (1981)
2 What's bred in the bone (1985)
3 The lyre of Orpheus (1988)

DAVIES, R.
SALTERTON TRILOGY
1 Tempest-tost
2 Leaven of malice
3 Mixture of frailties

DAVIES, R.
EISENGRIN TRILOGY
1 The fifth business (1971)
2 The Manticore (1973)
3 World of wonders (1977)

DAVIES, T.
1 One winter of the Holy Spirit (1985)
2 Fire in the bay (1989)
3 The dragon's war NYP
4 Black sunlight (1987)

DAVIS, BART
PETER MACKENZIE
1 Raise the Red Dawn (1991)
2 Destroy the Kentucky (1994)

DAVIS, D. S.
JULIE HAYES
1 A death in the life (1980)
2 Scarlet night (1981)
3 Lullaby of murder (1984)

DAVIS, G.
THE SERGEANT
1 Death train
2 Hell harbour
3 Bloody bush
4 The liberation of Paris
5 Doom river
6 Slaughter city
7 Bullet bridge
8 Bloody Bastogne
9 Hammerhead

DAVIS, J. G.
1 Hold my hand, I'm dying (1980)
2 Seize the reckless wind (1984)

DAVIS, K.
MAVIS MIDDLETON
1 Possessions (1998)
2 Shattered illusions (1999)
3 Until the end (2000)

DAVIS, L
FALCO
1 The silver pigs (1989)
2 Shadows in bronze (1990)
3 Venus in copper (1991)
4 The iron hand of Mars (1992)
5 Poseidon's gold (1993)
6 Last act in Palmyra (1994)
7 Time to depart (1995)
8 A dying light in Corduba (1996)
9 Three hands in the fountain (1997)
10 Two for the lions (1998)
11 One virgin too many (1999)
12 Ode to a banker (2000)
13 A body in the bath house (2001)
14 The Jupiter myth (2002)
15 The accusers (2003)
16 Scandal takes a holiday (2004)

DAVIS, M. T.
1 Rag woman, rich woman (1987)
2 Daughters and mothers (1988)
3 Wounds of war (1989)

DAVIS, M. T.
MONKTON FAMILY
1 A woman of property (1991)
2 A sense of belonging (1993)

DAVIS, M. T.
ALEXANDER FAMILY
1 Hold me forever (1994)
2 Kiss me no more (1995)
3 A kind of immortality (1996)

DAVIS, M. T.
GLASGOW TRILOGY
1 The breadmakers (1971)
2 A baby might be crying (1973)
3 A sort of peace (1974)

DAVIS, M. T.
SCOTTISH TRILOGY
1 The prince and the tobacco lords (1975)
2 The roots of bondage (1976)
3 Scorpion in the fire (1977)

DAWES, F. V.
COLE FAMILY
1 A family album (1982)
2 Inheritance (1984)

DAWSON, J.
JERI HOWARD
1 Kindred crimes (1990)
2 Till the old men die (1992)

3 Don't turn your back on the ocean (1993)
4 Take a number (1994)
5 The missing child (1995)

DAY, M.
CLAUDIA VALENTINE
1 The life and crimes of Harry Valentine (1988)
2 The case of the Chinese boxes (1990)
3 The last tango of Dolores Delgada (1992)
4 The disappearance of Madalena Grimaldi (1995)

DAYUS, K.
1 Her people (1982)
2 Where there's life (1985)
3 All my days (1988)
4 The best of times (1991)
5 The people of Lavender Court (1993)
NF Life in the slums of Birmingham

DE BOISSIERE, R.
1 Crown jewel (1982)
2 Rum and coca-cola (1984)

DE CHAIR, S.
1 The golden carpet (1945)
2 Buried pleasures (1986)

DE HAAN, T.
BRYCHMACHRYE
1 A mirror for princes (1988)
2 The child of good fortune (1989)

DE HAVEN, T
1 Walker of worlds
2 The end of everything man

DE MILLE, A.
1 Dance to the piper (1952)
2 And promenade home (1989)
NF Autobiography

DEAN, S. F. X.
NEIL KELLY
1 By frequent anguish (1982)
2 Such pretty toys (1983)
3 It can't be my grave (1983)
4 Ceremony of innocence (1985)
5 Death and the mad heroine (1986)

DEAVER, J.
RUNE
1 Manhattan is my beat (2000)
2 Death of a blue movie star (2000)
3 Hard news (2001)

DEAVER, J.
JOHN PELLAM
1 Shallow graves (2000)
2 Bloody river blues (2001)
3 Hell's kitchen (2001)

DEAVER, J.
LINCOLN RHYME
1 The coffin dancer (1998)
2 The empty chair (2000)
3 The stone monkey (2002)
4 The vanished man (2003)

DEFOE, D.
ROBINSON CRUSOE
1 Robinson Crusoe
2 The return of Robinson Crusoe, by H.Treece (1958)
3 Foe, by J.M.Coetzee (1988)

DEFORGES, R.
THE BLUE BICYCLE
1 The blue bicycle (1985)
2 101 Avenue Henri-Martin (1986)
3 The devil is still laughing (1987)

DEIGHTON, B.
FELICITY TRAVERS
1 A little learning (1987)
2 Good intentions (1988)

DEIGHTON, L.
BERNARD SAMSON
1 Berlin game (1983)
2 Mexico set (1984)
3 London match (1985)
4 Spy hook (1988)
5 Spy line (1989)
6 Spy sinker (1990)
7 Faith (1994)
8 Hope (1995)
9 Charity (1996)

DEIGHTON, L.
HARRY PALMER
1 The Ipcress file (1962)
2 Horse under water (1963)
3 Funeral in Berlin (1964)
4 Billion dollar brain (1966)
5 An expensive place to die (1969)

DELACORTA
GORODISH AND ALBA
1 Nana (1984)
2 Diva (1984)
3 Luna (1985)

4 Lola (1986)
5 Vida (1986)

DELANY, F.
IRISH SAGA
1 The sins of the mothers (1992)
2 Telling the pictures (1993)
3 A stranger in their midst (1995)
4 Desire and pursuit (1999)
5 The bell walk (2002)

DELANY, S. R.
1 Fall of the towers (1971)
2 Out of the dead city (1966)
3 The towers of Toron

DELANY, S. R.
NEVERYON
1 Tales of Neveryon
2 Neveryone
3 Flight from Neveryon
4 Return to Neveryon

DELMAN, D.
JACOB & HELEN HOROWITZ
1 Sudden death (1973)
2 One man's murder (1975)
3 The nice murderers (1977)
4 Death of a nymph (1986)
5 Dead faces laughing (1987)
6 The liar's league (1989)
7 Last gambit (1990)
8 Bye-bye baby (1992)

DENHAM, B.
DEREK THYRDE
1 The man who lost his shadow (1985)
2 Two Thyrdes (1986)
3 Foxhunt (1988)
4 Black rod (1997)

DENISON, M.
1 Overture and beginners (1973)
2 Double act (1985)
   NF Autobiography

DENKER, H.
HOROWITZ
1 Horowitz and Mrs. Washington (1990)
2 Mrs. Washington and Horowitz too (1994)

DENNING, T.
PRISM PENTAD
1 The verdant passage
2 The crimson legion

3 The amber enchantress
4 The obsidian oracle
5 The cerulean storm

DENNING, T.
THE TWILIGHT GIANTS
1 The ogre's pact
2 The giant among us
3 The Titan of twilight

DENNIS, I.
THE PRINCE OF STARS IN THE
CAVERN OF TIME
1 Baghdad
2 The Prince of Stars

DENTINGER, J.
JOCELYN O'ROURKE
1 First hit of the season (1986)
2 Death mask (1988)
3 Murder on cue (1985)

DENVER, L.
CHEYENNE JONES
1 The gun code of Cheyenne Jones (1969)
2 Cheyenne swings a wide loop (1970)
3 Three slugs for Cheyenne (1971)
4 Cheyene pays in lead (1972)
5 Lone trail for Cheyenne (1973)
6 Cheyenne Jones maverick marshal
  (1977)
7 Cheyenne's six-gun justice
8 Cheyenne's trail to perdition
9 Cheyenne's two-gun shoot-out
10 Cheyenne at Dull Knife Pass (1984)

DERWENT, L.
1 A breath of Border air (1975)
2 Another breath of Border air (1977)
3 A Border bairn (1979)
4 God bless the Borders (1981)
5 Lady of the Manse (1983)
6 A mouse in the Manse (1985)
  NF Life in the Scottish Borders

DEUTSCH, D.
THE EQUALISER
1 The equaliser
2 To even the odds
3 Blood and wine

DEVERAUX, J.
MONTGOMERY FAMILY
1 The velvet promise
2 Highland velvet
3 Velvet angel

4 Velvet song
5 The temptress
6 The princess
7 The raider (1988)

DEVERAUX, J.
JAMES RIVER TRILOGY
1 Counterfeit lady
2 Lost lady
3 River lady

DEVERAUX, J.
CHANDLER TWINS
1 Twin of ice
2 Twin of fire

DEVINE, R.
FLESHTRADERS
1 Master of Black River
2 Black River affair
3 Black River breed

DEWHURST, E.
NEIL CARTER
1 Trio in three flats (1982)
2 There was a little girl (1984)
3 A nice little business (1990)

DEWHURST, E.
HELEN JOHNSON
1 Whoever I am (1981)
2 Playing safe (1985)

DEWHURST, E.
ANNE WESTON
1 Death in Candie Gardens (1996)
2 Alias the enemy (1997)

DEWHURST, E.
PHYLLIDA MOON
1 Now you see her (1995)
2 The verdict on winter (1996)
3 Roundabout (1998)
4 Double act (2000)
5 Closing stages (2001)
6 No love lost (2002)
7 Easeful death (2002)
8 Naked witness (2003)

DEXTER, C.
DET. CHIEF INSPECTOR MORSE
1 Last bus to Woodstock (1975)
2 Last seen wearing (1976)
3 The silent world of Nicholas Quinn
  (1977)
4 Service of all the dead (1979)

5 The dead of Jericho (1981)
6 The riddle of the third mile (1983)
7 The secret of Annexe 3 (1986)
8 The wench is dead (1989)
9 The jewel that was ours (1991)
10 The way through the woods (1992)
11 Morse's greatest mystery and other stories (1993)
12 The daughters of Cain (1994)
13 Death is now my neighbour (1996)
14 The remorseful day (1999)

DEXTER, S.
THE WINTER KING'S WAR
1 The ring of Allaire (1987)
2 The sword of Calandra (1987)
3 The mountains of Channadran (1987)

DIBBA, E.
1 Chaff in the wind (1984)
2 Fafa (1989)

DIBDIN, M.
AURELIO ZEN
1 Ratking (1988)
2 Vendetta (1990)
3 Cabal (1992)
4 Dead lagoon (1993)
5 The dying of the light (1994)
6 Cosi fan tutte (1996)
7 A long finish (1998)
8 Blood rain (1999)
9 Thanksgiving (2000)
10 And then you die (2002)
11 Medusa (2003)

DICKASON, C.
ANDROIDS
1 The dragon riders (1988)
2 The years of the tiger (1989)

DICKENS, C.
EDWIN DROOD
1 The mystery of Edwin Drood (1870)
2 The disappearance of Edwin Drood, by P.Rowland (1991)
3 The D case, by G.Dowling (1995)

DICKINSON, B.
LORD IFFY BOATRACE
1 The adventures of Lord Iffy Boatrace (1990)
2 The missionary position (1992)

DICKINSON, D.
LORD FRANCIS POWERSCOURT
1 Goodnight, sweet prince (2002)
2 Death and the Jubilee (2003)
3 Death of an old master (2004)

DICKINSON, M.
ABBEYFORD TRILOGY
1 Sarah (1981)
2 Adeline (1981)
3 Carrie (1982)

DICKINSON, M.
LINCOLNSHIRE
1 Plough the furrow (1994)
2 Sow the seed (1995)
3 Reap the harvest (1996)

DICKINSON, P.
ALTERNATIVE ROYAL FAMILY
1 King and joker (1976)
2 Skeleton-in-waiting (1989)

DICKSON, G.
SEA PEOPLE
1 Home from the shore
2 The Space swimmers

DICKSON, G.
DORSAI
1 Tactics of mistake
2 Dorsai
3 Soldier, ask not
4 The spirit of Dorsai
5 Lost Dorsai

DICKSON, G.
CHILDE CYCLE
1 The final encyclopaedia
2 Chantry guild
3 Young Bleys

DICKSON, G.
DRAGON SERIES
1 The dragon and the George
2 The dragon knight
3 The dragon at war

DIEHL, W.
MARTIN VAIL
1 Primal fear (1992)
2 Show of evil (1995)
3 Reign in hell (1998)

DILLON, A.
1 Seasons (1990)

2 Another time, another season (1991)
3 Season's end (1991)

DILLON, E.
1 Wild geese (1981)
2 Citizen Burke (1984)

DILLON, E.
IRISH SAGA
1 Across the bitter sea (1974)
2 Blood relation (1978)

DILLON, P.
CHIEF INSPECTOR GEORGE
HAVILLAND
1 Truth (1996)
2 Lies (1997)

DISCH, T. M.
EARTH TRILOGY
1 The ruins of Earth (1973)
2 Bad moon rising (1974)
3 The new improved sun (1976)

DJEBAR, A.
ALGERIAN QUARTET
1 Fantasia (1989)
2 A sister to Scheherezade (1989)

DOBBS, M.
FRANCIS URQUHART
1 House of cards (1989)
2 To play the King (1992)
3 The touch of innocents (1994)

DOBBS, M.
THOMAS GOODFELLOWE
1 Goodfellowe, MP (1997)
2 The Buddha of Brewer Street (1998)
3 Whispers of betrayal (1999)

DOBLIN, A.
NOVEMBER 1918: A GERMAN
REVOLUTION
1 A people betrayed (1986)
2 The troops return (1986)
3 Karl and Rosa (1986)

DOBYNS, S.
CHARLIE BRADSHAW
1 Saratoga swimmer
2 Saratoga headhunter
3 Saratoga longshot (1988)
4 Saratoga snapper (1988)
5 Saratoga bestiary (1989)
6 Saratoga hexameter (1990)

DOHERTY, P. C.
CANTERBURY TALES
1 An ancient evil (1993)
2 A tapestry of murders (1994)
3 A tournament of murders (1996)
4 Ghostly murders (1997)
5 The hangman's hymn (2001)
6 A haunt of murder (2002)

DOHERTY, P. C.
HUGH CORBETT
1 Satan in St.Mary's (1986)
2 Spy in chancery (1988)
3 Crown in darkness (1991)
4 The angel of death (1991)
5 The prince of darkness (1992)
6 Murder wears a cowl (1992)
7 The assassin in the greenwood (1993)
8 The song of a dark angel (1994)
9 Satan's fire (1995)
10 The devil's hunt (1996)
11 The demon archer (1999)
12 The treason of the ghosts (2000)
13 Corpse candle (2001)
14 The magician's death (2004)

DOHERTY, P. C.
BROTHER ATHELSTAN
1 The nightingale gallery (1991)
2 The house of the red slayer (1992)
3 Murder most holy (1992)
4 The anger of God (1993)
5 By murder's bright light (1994)
6 The house of crows (1995)
7 The assassin's riddle (1996)
8 The devil's domain (1998)
9 The field of blood (1999)
10 The house of shadows (2003)

DOHERTY, P. C.
ALEXANDER THE GREAT
1 The house of death (2001)
2 The godless man (2002)

DOMINIC, R. B. [E. LATHEN]
CONGRESSMAN BEN SAFFORD
1 Nurder in high places (1970)
2 Murder out of court (1971)
3 Epitaph for a lobbyist (1974)
4 Murder out of commission (1976)
5 Attending physician (1980)
6 A flaw in the system (1983)

DONACHIE, D.
HARRY LUDLOW
1 The devil's own luck (1792) (1991)
2 A dying trade (1794) (1993)

3 A hanging matter (1795) (1994)
4 An element of chance (1994)
5 The scent of betrayal (1996)
6 A game of bones (1997)

DONACHIE, D.
NELSON
1 On a making tide (2000)
2 Taken at the flood (2001)
3 Breaking the line (2002)

DONALD, A.
ALEX TANNER
1 An uncommon murder (1992)
2 In at the deep end (1993)
3 The glass ceiling (1994)
4 The loop (1996)
5 Destroy unopened (1999)

DONALDSON, S. R.
THE CHRONICLES OF THOMAS
COVENANT, UNBELIEVER
1 Lord Foul Bane (1980)
2 The Illearth war (1980)
3 The power that preserves (1980)
4 The wounded land (1980)
5 The one tree (1982)
6 White gold wielder (1983)

DONALDSON, S. R.
MORDANT'S NEED
1 A mirror for her dreams (1986)
2 A man rides through (1988)

DONALDSON, S. R.
THE GAP
1 The gap into conflict:the real story (1990)
2 The gap into vision:forbidden knowledge (1991)
3 Gap into power:a dark and hungry god arises (1992)
4 The gap into madness; chaos and order (1994)
5 The gap into ruins; this day all gods die (1996)

DONALDSON, S. R.
GINNY FISTOULARI
1 The man who fought alone (2002)
2 The man who tried to get away (2004)

DONALDSON, W.
1 Both the ladies and the gentlemen (1975)
2 The balloons in the black bag (1975)
3 The English way of doing things (1984)

DONLEAVY, J. P.
SCHULTZ
1 Schultz
2 Are you listening, Rabbi Low? (1987)

DONLEAVY, J. P.
DARCY DANCER
1 The destinies of Darcy Dancer, gentleman (1978)
2 Leila (1983)
3 That Darcy, that Dancer, that gentleman (1990)

DOODY, M.
ARISTOTLE
1 Aristotle, detective
2 Aristotle and poetic justice (2002)
3 Aristotle and the secrets of life (2003)
4 Poison in Athens (2004)

DOOLITTLE, J.
TOM BETHANY
1 Body scissors (1991)
2 Strangle hold (1992)
3 Bear hug (1994)

D'ORMESSON, J.
1 The winds of evening (1987)
2 Mad about the girl (1988)

DOUGLAS, A.
JONATHAN CRAYTHORNE
1 Last rights (1986)
2 A very wrong number (1987)
3 The goods (1985)
4 A worm turns (1987)

DOUGLAS, C. N.
SWORD AND CIRCLET
1 Keepers of Edenvant
2 Heir of Rengarth
3 Seven of swords

DOUGLAS, COLIN
1 The Houseman's tale (1975)
2 The greatest breakthrough since lunchtime (1977)
3 Bleeders come first (1979)
4 Wellies from the Queen (1981)
5 A cure from living (1983)
6 For services to medicine (1985)
7 Ethics made easy (1986)
8 Hazards of the profession (1987)

DOUGLAS, GARRY

SERGEANT JACK CROSSMAN
1 The devil's own (Battle of the Alma) (1997)
2 The valley of death (The Battle of Balaclava) (1998)
3 Soldiers in the mist (The Battle of Sebastopol) (1999)
4 The winter soldiers (2002)
No.4 was written under the name of Garry Kilworth

DOUGLAS, KIRK

1 Dance with the devil (1990)
2 The gift (1992)

DOUGLASS, S.

AXIS TRILOGY
1 Battle axe
2 Enchanter
3 Starman

DOUGLASS, S.

THE CRUCIBLE
1 The nameless day
2 The wounded hawk
3 The crippled angel

DOYLE, A. C.

SHERLOCK HOLMES
1 A study in scarlet (1888)
2 The sign of four (1890)
3 Adventures of Sherlock Holmes (1892)
4 The memoirs of Sherlock Holmes (1894)
5 The hound of the Baskervilles (1902)
6 The return of Sherlock Holmes (1905)
7 The valley of fear (1915)
8 His last bow (1917)
9 The casebook of Sherlock Holmes (1927)
10 The seven percent solution, by N.Meyer (1976)
11 The West End horror, by N.Meyer (1976)
12 The giant rat of Sumatra, by R.L.Boyer (1977)
13 Exit Sherlock Holmes, by R.L.Hall (1977)
14 Tangled skein, by D.S.Davies (1978)
15 The last Sherlock Holmes story, by M.Dibdin (1978)
16 Sherlock Holmes versus Dracula, by L.D.Estleman (1978)
17 Prisoner of the devil, by M.Hardwick (1979)
18 Aventures of the stalwart companions, by H.Jeffers (1979)
19 Infernal device, by M.Kurland (1979)
20 Puzzle for Sherlock Holmes, by R.Newman (1979)
21 Case of the philosopher's ring, by R.Collins (1980)
22 Curse of the Nibelungen, by M.D'Agreau (1981)
23 Final adventures of Sherlock Holmes, by P.Haining (1983)
24 The Mycroft memoranda, by R.Walsh (1984)
25 Sherlock Holmes, by M.Hardwick (1984)
26 Ten years beyond Baker Street, by C.van Ash (1985)
27 Sherlock Holmes at the 1902 5th Test, by S.Shaw (1985)
28 The private life of Dr. Watson, byM.Hardwick (1985)
29 Sherlock Holmes meets Annie Oakley, by S.Shaw (1986)
30 The Kentish Manor murders, by J.Symons (1988)
31 Revenge of the hound, by M.Hardwick (1988)
32 My dearest Holmes, by R.Piercy (1988)
33 Sherlock Holmes and the eminent thespian, by V. Andrews (1988)
34 S.Holmes investigates the murder in Euston Square (1990)
35 Sherlock Holmes and the Brighton pavilion mystery (1990)
36 Sherlock Holmes revisited, by C.Brooks (1990)
37 Secret files of Sherlock Holmes, by J.Thomson (1990)
38 Disappearance of Edwin Drood. by P.Rowland (1991)
39 Sherlock Holmes and the Hentzau affair, by D.S.Davies (1991)
40 Secret chronicles of Sherlock Holmes, by J.Thomson (1992)
41 Unopened casebook of Sherlock Holmes, by J.Thomson (1993)
42 The case of Emily V., by K.Oatley (1993)
43 Sherlock Holmes and the Egyptian Hall adventure, by V.Andrews (1993)
44 Sherlock Holmes and the railway maniac, by B.Roberts (1994)
45 The singular case of the duplicate Holmes, by J.Walker (1994)
46 Sherlock Holmes and the earthquake machine, by A.Mitchelson (1994)
47 The angel of the opera, by S.Siciliano (1995)
48 Holmes and Watson, by J.Thomson (1995)
49 Sherlock Holmes and the devil's grail, by B.Roberts (1995)
50 The secret cases of Sherlock Holmes, by D.Thomas (1997)
51 The secret documents of Sherlock Holmes, by J.Thomson (1997)

52 Sherlock Holmes and the man from hell, by B.Roberts (1997)
53 Sherlock Holmes and the royal flush, by B.Roberts (1998)
54 Sherlock Holmes and the harvest of death, by B.Roberts (1999)
55 Sherlock Holmes and the Crosby murder, by B.Roberts (2001)
56 Sherlock Holmes and the running noose, by D. Thomas (2001)
57 Sherlock Holmes and the rule of nine, by B.Roberts (2003)

DOYLE, D. & MACDONALD, J. D.
MAGEWORLDS
1 The price of the stars
2 Starpilot's grave

DOYLE, E.
EVELYN
1 Evelyn (2001)
2 Nothing green (2003)
NF Autobiography

DOYLE, R.
RABBITTE FAMILY
1 The commitments (1987)
2 The snapper (1990)
3 The van (1991)

DRABBLE, M.
1 The radiant way (1988)
2 A natural curiosity (1989)
3 The gates of ivory (1991)

DRAGONLANCE
THE DRAGONLANCE CHRONICLES
1 Dragons of autumn twilight
2 Dragons of winter night
3 Dragons of spring dawning
4 Dragons of summer flame

DRAGONLANCE
THE DRAGONLANCE LEGENDS
1 Time of the twins
2 War of the twins
3 Test of the twins

DRAGONLANCE
THE DRAGONLANCE TALES
1 The magic of Krynn
2 Kenders, Gully dwarfs and Gnomes
3 Love and war

DRAGONLANCE
DRAGONLANCE PRELUDES
1 Darkness and light, by P.B.Thompson
2 Kendermore, by M.Kirchoff 3 Brothers Majere, by K.Stein

DRAGONLANCE
DRAGONLANCE PRELUDES II
1 Riverwind the plainsman, by P.B.Thompson
2 Flint the king, by M.Kirchoff
3 Tanis, the shadow years

DRAGONLANCE
DRAGONLANCE SAGA HEROES
1 The legend of Huma, by R.A.Kraak
2 Stormblade
3 Weasel's luck, by M.Williams

DRAGONLANCE
DRAGONLANCE SAGA HEROES II
1 Kaz the monster, by R.A.Kraak
2 The gates of Thorbarden, by D.Parkinson
3 Galen benighted

DRAGONLANCE
THE DRAGONLANCE TALES II
1 The reign of Istar
2 The cataclysm
3 The war of the lance

DRAGONLANCE
ELVEN NATIONS TRILOGY
1 Firstborn
2 The kinslayer wars
3 The Qualinesti

DRAGONLANCE
MEETINGS SEXTET
1 Kindred spirits
2 Wanderlust
3 Dark heart
4 The oath and the measure
5 Steel and stone
6 The companions

DRAGONLANCE
VILLAINS
1 Before the mask, by M.T.Williams
2 The black wing, by M.Kirchoff
3 Emperor of Ansalon, by D.Niles
4 Hederick the theocrat, by E.D.Stevenson
5 Lord Toede, by J.Grubb
6 The dark queen, by M. & T.Williams

DRAGONLANCE
DEFENDERS OF MAGIC TRILOGY
1 Night of the eye
2 The medusa plague

DRAGONLANCE
DWARVEN NATIONS TRILOGY
1 The covenant of the forge, by D.Parkinson
2 Hammer and axe, by D.Parkinson
3 The soulforge, by M.Wei

DRAGONLANCE
THE FIFTH AGE
1 The dawning of a new age, by J.Rabe
2 The day of the tempest, by J.Rabe
3 The eve of the maelstrom, by J.Rabe
4 Relics and omens, by M.Weis & T.Hickman

DRAGONLANCE
CHAOS WAR
1 The second generation, by M.Weis
2 The doom brigade, by M.Weis
3 Murder in Tarsis, by J.M.Robetrs
4 The dragons of Krynn, by M.Weis
5 The dragons at war, by M.Weis

DRAGONLANCE
THE LOST HISTORIES
1 The Kagonesti, by D.Niles
2 The Irda, by L.P.Baker
3 The Dargonesti, by P.B.Thompson
4 The land of the Minotaurs, by R.A.Knaak
5 The gully dwarves, by D.Parkinson
6 The dragons, by D.Niles
7 Dezra's quest, by C.Pierson
8 The thieves' guild, by J.Crook

DRAGONLANCE
THE LOST LEGENDS
1 Vinus Solanus, by R.J.King
2 Fistandantilus reborn, by D.Niles

DRAGONLANCE
DRAGONLANCE WARRIORS
1 The seventh sentinel
2 Swordsheath scroll
3 Marquesta Kar Thorn
4 Knights of the crown, by R.Green
5 Knights of the sword, by R.Green
6 Theros Ironfeld, by D.Perrin
7 Knights of the rose, by R.Green
8 Lord Soth, by E. van Elkom

DRAKE, D.
LORD OF THE ISLES
1 Lord of the isles (1997)
2 Servant of the dragon (1999)
3 Mistress of the catacombs (2002)

DRAPER, A.
CRISPIN PATON, R. N.
1 Grey seal (1982)
2 The restless waves (1983)
3 The raging deep (1985)
4 Storm over Singapore (1986)
5 The great avenging day (1988)

DREHER, S.
STONER MCTAVISH
1 Stoner McTavish (1987)
2 Something shady (1988)
3 Grey magic (1990)
4 Captive time (1991)
5 Other world (1993)

DRESDEN, T.
DET. SUPT. JACK ABBILENE
1 Talking to a stranger (1994)
2 Missing (1995)

DRUMMOND, E.
KNIGHTSHILL
1 That sweet savage land (1992)
2 A distant hero (1994)
3 Act of valour (1996)

DRURY, A.
UNIVERSITY SERIES
1 Toward what bright glory? (1990)
2 Into what far harbour? (1993)

DRURY, A.
SOVIET CONQUEST
1 The hill of summer (1983)
2 The roads of earth (1985)

DRURY, A.
EGYPTIAN DYNASTY
1 A god against gods (1976)
2 Return to Thebes (1977)

DRURY, A.
AMERICAN POLITICS
1 Advise and consent (1962)
2 A shade of difference (1964)
3 Capable of honour (1966)
4 Preserve and protect (1968)
5 Come Nineveh, come Tyre (1974)

6 Promise of joy (1975)
7 Anna Hastings (1978)

DRYSDALE, A.
1 Faint heart never kissed a pig (1982)
2 Sows ears and silk purses (1984)
3 Pearls before swine (1985)
   NF Farming life

DRYSDALE, MARGARET
ROBERT DUDLEY, EARL OF LEICESTER
1 Quest for a crown (1982)
2 Heir for the Earl (1983)

DU BARRY, M.
THE LOVES OF ANGELA CARLYLE
1 Into passion
2 Across captive seas
3 Towards love

DU MAURIER, D.
1 Rebecca (1938)
2 Mrs. De Winter, by Susan Hill (1993)

DUANE, D.
TALE OF THE FIVE
1 The door into fire
2 The door into shadow
3 The door into sunset

DUBUS, E. N.
1 Where love rules (1986)
2 To love and to dream (1987)

DUFFY, MARGARET
PATRICK GILLARD & INGRID
LANGLEY
1 A murder of crows (1987)
2 Death of a raven (1988)
3 Brass eagle (1988)
4 Who killed Cock Robin? (1990)
5 Rook-shoot (1991)
6 Gallows bird (1993)
7 Prospect of death (1995)
8 Music in the blood (1997)
9 A fine target (1998)
10 A hanging matter (2002)
11 Dead trouble (2004)

DUFFY, MAUREEN
METROPOLITAN TRILOGY
1 Wounds (1969)
2 Capital (1975)
3 Londoners (1983)

DUFFY, S.
SAZ MARTIN
1 Calendar girl
2 Wavewalker
3 Beneath the blonde
4 Fresh flesh

DUNANT, S.
HANNAH WOLFE
1 Birth marks (1991)
2 Fatlands (1993)
3 Under my skin (1995)

DUNCAN, A.
COUNTRY DOCTOR
1 To be a country doctor (1980)
2 God and the doctor (1981)
3 Diary of a country doctor (1982)
4 The doctor's affairs all told (1983)

DUNCAN, A.
THE VET
1 It's a vet's life (1962)
2 The vet has nine lives (1962)
3 Vets in the belfry (1963)
4 A vet exposed (1977)
5 Vets in congress (1978)
6 Vets in the manger (1979)
7 Vet among the pigeons (1979)
8 Vet in a state (1980)
9 Vet on vacation (1980)

DUNCAN, D.
A MAN OF HIS WORD
1 Magic casement
2 Faery lands forlorn
3 Perilous seas
4 Emperor and clown

DUNCAN, D.
A HANDFUL OF MEN
1 The cutting edge
2 Upland outlaws

DUNCAN, D.
THE GREAT GAME
1 Past imperative
2 Present tense
3 Future indefinite

DUNN, C.
DAISY DALRYMPLE
1 Styx and stones (2000)
2 To Davey Jones below (2001)
3 Murder on the Flying Scotsman (2002)
4 Damsel in distress (2002)

5 The case of the murdered muckraker (2002)
6 Mistletoe and murder (2003)
7 Die laughing (2004)

DUNN, M.
1 Lady Addle at home (1986)
2 Lady Addle remembers (1985)
3 The memoirs of Mipsie (1986)

DUNN, N.
1 Poor cow (1988)
2 My silver shoes (1996)

DUNNE, C.
JOE HUSSEY
1 Retrieval (1984)
2 Ratcatcher (1985)
3 Hooligan (1987)

DUNNETT, D.
THE HOUSE OF NICCOLO
1 Niccolo rising (1986)
2 The spring of the ram (1987)
3 Race of scorpions (1989)
4 Scales of gold (1991)
5 The unicorn hunt (1993)
6 To lie with lions (1995)
7 Caprice and Rondo (1997)
8 Gemini (1999)

DUNNETT, D.
JOHNSON JOHNSON
1 Tropical issue (1983)
2 Rum affair (1968)
3 Ibiza surprise (1970)
4 Operation Nassau (1971)
5 Roman nights (1973)
6 Split code (1977)
7 Moroccan traffic (1991)

DUNNETT, D.
FRANCIS CRAWFORD OF LYMOND
1 The game of kings (1965)
2 Queen's play (1966)
3 The disorderly knights (1968)
4 Pawn in frankincense (1969)
5 The ringed castle (1971)
6 Checkmate (1975)

DURACK, M.
1 Kings in grass castles (1959)
2 Sons in the saddles (1983)

DURBRIDGE, F.
TIM FRAZER
1 The world of Tim Frazer (1961)
2 Tim Frazer again (1964)
3 Tim Frazer gets the message (1979)

DURBRIDGE, F.
PAUL TEMPLE
1 Send for Paul Temple
2 Paul Temple and the front page men
3 Paul Temple intervenes
4 News of Paul Temple
5 Send for Paul Temple again (1948)
6 Paul Temple and the Kelby affair (1970)
7 Paul Temple and the Harkdale robbery (1970)
8 The Geneva mystery (1972)
9 The Curzon case (1972)
10 Paul Temple and the Margo mystery (1986)
11 Paul Temple and the Madison case (1988)

DURGIN, D.
THE PLANTAGENETS
1 Touched by magic
2 Wolf justice

DURRANT, D.
1 With my little eye (1975)
2 Trunch (1978)
3 Addle (1980)

DURRELL, G.
1 My family and other animals (1956)
2 Birds, beasts and relatives (1969)
3 The garden of the gods (1978)
   NF Autobiography

DURRELL, L.
AVIGNON QUINTET
1 Monsieur (1974)
2 Livia or Buried alive (1978)
3 Constance (1982)
4 Sebastien (1983)
5 Quinx (1985)

DURRELL, L.
ALEXANDRIA QUARTET
1 Justine (1957)
2 Balthasar (1958)
3 Mountolive (1958)
4 Clea (1960)

DURRELL, L.
ANTROBUS
1 Esprit de corps (1957)
2 Stiff upper lip (1958)
3 Sauve qui peut (1966)
4 Antrobus complete (1985)

DURRELL, L.
ISLANDS
1 Prospero's cell (1945)
2 Reflections on a marine Venus (1953)
3 Bitter lemons of Cyprus (1957)

DURRELL, L.
REVOLT OF APHRODITE
1 Tunc (1967)
2 Nunquam (1970)

DUVAL, C.
FAIRFAX AND VALLANCE
1 A moment of madness (1997)
2 A tangled web (1997)

DYMOKE, J.
FRENCH REVOLUTION SERIES
1 The white cockade (1979)
2 The Queen
3 The march to Corunna (1985)
4 Two flags for France (1986)

DYMOKE, J.
HOLLANDER FAMILY
1 Hollander's House (1990)
2 Cry of the peacock (1992)
3 Winter's daughter (1994)

DYMOKE, J.
HENRY I
1 The ring of Earls (1970)
2 Henry of the high rock (1971)
3 The lion's legacy (1972)

DYMOKE, J.
THE PLANTAGENETS
1 A pride of Kings (1978)
2 The royal griffin (1978)
3 The lion of Mortimer (1979)
4 The Lord of Greenwich (1980)
5 The sun in splendour (1980)

EAMES, M.
1 The secret room (1975)
2 Fair wilderness (1976)

EARLY, R. E.
1 The apprentice (1977)

2 Master Weaver (1980)
3 Weavers and war (1984)

EBDON, J.
1 Ebdon's Odyssey (1979)
2 Ebdon's Iliad (1983)
3 Ebdon's England (1985)
NF Travel

EBERSOHN, W.
YUDEL GORDON
1 A lonely place to die (1979)
2 Divide the night (1980)
3 Closed circle (1990)

EBERT, A.
TIERNAN FAMILY
1 Traditions (1982)
2 The long way home (1985)

ECCLES, M.
INSPECTOR GIL MAYO
1 Cast a cold eye (1999)
2 Death of a good woman (1989)
3 Requiem for a dove (1990)
4 More deaths than one (1991)
5 Late of this parish (1992)
6 The company she kept (1993)
7 An accidental shroud (1994)
8 A death of distinction (1995)
9 A species of revenge (1996)
10 Killing me softly (1998)
11 The Superintendent's daughter (1999)
12 A sunset touch (2000)
13 Untimely graves (2001)

ECKHARDT, K.
SS DIVISION VATERLAND
1 Heroes without honour (1980)
2 Stalingrad heroes (1981)
3 Heroes of Cassino (1982)
4 Achtung Normandy (1982)

EDDINGS, D.
THE BELGARIAD
1 Belgarath the sorcerer (1995)
2 Polgara the sorceress (1997)
3 Pawn of prophecy (1982)
4 Queen of sorcery (1982)
5 Magician's gambit (1983)
6 Castle of wizardry (1984)
7 Enchanter's endgame (1985)

EDDINGS, D.
THE MALLOREON
1 Guardians of the West (1987)

2 King of the Murgos (1988)
3 Demon Lord of Karanda (1988)
4 Sorceress of Darshiva (1989)
5 Seeress of Kell (1991)

EDDINGS, D.
ELENIUM
1 The diamond throne (1989)
2 The ruby knight (1990)
3 The sapphire rose (1991)

EDDINGS, D.
TAMULI
1 Domes of fire (1992)
2 The shining ones (1993)
3 The hidden city (1994)

EDDY, P.
GRACE FLINT
1 Flint (2001)
2 Mandrake (2002)

EDGAR, J.
MARGARET NORMANBY
1 Margaret Normanby (1983)
2 A dark and alien rose (1991)

EDGAR, J.
PEERESSES
1 Duchess (1976)
2 Countess (1978)

EDMONDS, J.
LINUS RINTOUL
1 Dog's body (1988)
2 Dead spit (1989)
3 Judge and be damned (1990)
4 Let sleeping dogs lie (1992)
5 Death has a cold nose (1993)

EDWARDS, G.
DRAGONS
1 Dragonscharm
2 Dragonstorm
3 Dragonflame

EDWARDS, G.
STONE TRILOGY
1 Stone and sky
2 Stone and sea

EDWARDS, J. C.
JACOB FLETCHER
1 Fletcher's fortune (1992)
2 Fletcher's glorious 1st of June (1993)

EDWARDS, M.
HARRY DEVLIN
1 All the lonely people (1991)
2 Suspicious minds (1992)
3 I remember you (1993)
4 Yesterday's papers (1994)
5 Eve of destruction (1996)
6 The devil in disguise (1998)
7 First cut is the deepest (1999)

EDWARDS, R.
RICHARD III
1 Fortune's wheel (1978)
2 Some touch of pity (1976)

EDWARDS, R. D.
ROBERT AMISS
1 Corridors of death (1981)
2 The St.Valentine's Day murders (1984)
3 The School of English murder (1990)
4 Clubbed to death (1992)
5 Matricide at St.Martha's (1994)
6 Ten lords a-leaping (1995)
7 Murder in a cathedral (1996)
8 Publish and be murdered (1998)
9 The Anglo-Irish murders (2001)
10 Carnage on the committee (2004)

EGAN, L.
GLENDALE POLICE DEPT.
1 A case for appeal (1962)
2 Scenes of crime (1976)
3 A dream apart (1978)
4 Random death (1982)
5 Crime for Christmas (1984)
6 Chain of violence (1985)

EGAN, L.
VIC VARALLO
1 The borrowed alibi (1962)
2 Run to evil (1963)
3 Detective's due (1965)
4 The nameless ones (1967)
5 The wine of violence (1970)
6 Malicious mischief (1972)
7 The hunters and the hunted (1980)
8 A choice of crimes (1981)

EGAN, L.
JESSE FALKENSTEIN
1 Against the evidence (1963)
2 My name is death (1965)
3 Some avenger, rise! (1967)
4 A serious investigation (1969)
5 In the death of a man (1970)
6 Paper chase (1973)
7 The blind search (1977)

8 Look back on death (1979)
9 Motive in shadow (1980)
10 The miser (1982)
11 Little boy lost (1984)
12 The wine of life (1986)

EGLETON, C.
CHARLES WINTER
1 The Winter touch (1981)
2 The Russian enigma (1983)

EGLETON, C.
PETER ASHTON
1 Hostile intent (1993)
2 A killing in Moscow (1994)
3 Death throes (1994)
4 Warning shot (1996)
5 Blood money (1997)
6 Dead reckoning (1999)
7 One man running (2001)
8 Cry havoc (2002)

EICKHOFF, R. L.
CUCHULAIN
1 The raid (1999)
2 The feast (1999)
3 The destruction of the inn (2001)

ELDER, M.
PHILIP STEVENSON
1 Mindslip (1976)
2 Mindquest (1977)

ELDER, M.
THE BARCLAYS
1 Nowhere on earth (1972)
2 The perfumed planet (1973)
3 Down to earth (1975)
4 The seeds of frenzy (1976)

ELGIN, E.
SUTTON FAMILY
1 I'll bring you buttercups (1994)
2 Daisychain summer (1995)
3 Where bluebells chime (1996)
4 Windflower wedding (1997)

ELGIN, S. H.
NATIVE TONGUE
1 Native tongue
2 The Judas rose

ELIS, I. F.
WALES
1 Shadow of the sickle (1999)
2 Return to Lleifior (1999)

ELKINS, A.
GIDEON OLIVER
1 Murder in the Queen's Armes (1990)
2 Icy clutches (1991)
3 Make no bones (1992)

ELLIOTT, K.
CROWN OF STARS
1 King's dragon (1997)
2 Prince of dogs (1998)
3 The burning stone (1999)
4 Child of flame (2000)
5 The gathering storm (2003)

ELLIS, A. T.
1 The clothes in the wardrobe (1987)
2 The skeleton in the cupboard (1988)
3 The fly in the ointment (1989)

ELLIS, H. F.
1 A.J.Wentworth, BA (1980)
2 The swansong of A.J.Wentworth (1982)

ELLIS, K.
DET. SERGEANT WES PETERSON
1 The merchant's house (1998)
2 The Armada boy (1999)
3 An unhallowed grave (1999)
4 The funeral boat (2000)
5 The bone garden (2001)
6 A painted doom (2002)
7 The skeleton room (2003)
8 The plague maiden (2004)

ELLIS, R.
JOHNNY ACE
1 Ears of the city (1997)
2 Mean streets (1998)
3 Framed (1999)
4 The singing dead (2000)
5 Grave mistake (2001)
6 Single shot (2002)

EMECHETA, B.
1 Second class citizen (1974)
2 In the ditch (1979)

EMERSON, R.
THE TALE OF NEDAO
1 To the haunted mountains
2 In the caves of exile
3 On the seas of destiny

EMERSON, S.
1 Second sight (1980)
2 The listeners (1983)

EMPIRES TRILOGY

1 Horselords, by David Cook
2 Dragonwell, by Troy Denning
3 Crusade, by James Lowden

ENEFER, D.

SAM BAWTRY

1 Pierhead 627 (1968)
2 13 steps to Lime Street (1969)
3 Riverside 90 (1970)
4 Girl in a million (1972)
5 A long way to Pitt Street (1972)
6 Girl on the M6 (1973)
7 Lakeside zero (1973)
8 The jade green judy (1974)
9 Last train to Rock Ferry (1975)
10 The sixth raid (1979)
11 The deadly streak (1982)
12 The last leap (1983)

ENGEL, H.

BENNY COOPERMAN

1 The ransom game (1982)
2 Murder on location (1983)
3 The suicide murders (1984)
4 Murder sees the light (1985)
5 A city called July (1987)
6 A victim must be found (1988)

ERDRICH, L.

1 Love medicine (1984)
2 The beet queen (1987)
3 Tracks (1988)

ESTES, R.

GREYHAWK ADVENTURES

1 Master Wolf
2 The price of power
3 The demon hand

ESTES, R.

THE HUNTER

1 The hunter
2 The hunter on Arena
3 The hunter victorious

ESTLEMAN, L. D.

AMOS WALKER

1 Motor City blues (1981)
2 Angel eyes (1982)
3 The midnight man (1983)
4 The glass highway (1984)
5 Sugartown (1986)
6 Every brilliant eye (1986)
7 Lady yesterday (1987)
8 Downriver (1988)
9 General murders (1989)

10 Silent thunder (1989)
11 Sweet women lie (1990)
12 Never Street (1997)
13 The hours of the virgin (1999)
14 The witchfinder (1999)
15 The smile on the face of the tiger (2001)
16 Sinister heights (2002)

ETCHELLS, O.

JERICHO

1 The jericho rose (1993)
2 The Jericho trumpet (1996)

ETTINGER, E.

1 Kindergarten (1988)
2 Quicksand (1989)

EVANOVICH, J.

STEPHANIE PLUM

1 One for the money (1995)
2 Two for the dough (1996)
3 Three to get deadly (1997)
4 Four to score (1998)
5 High five (1999)
6 Hot six (2000)
7 Seven up (2001)
8 Hard eight (2002)
9 To the nines (2003)
10 Ten big ones (2004)
(Visions of sugar plums, 2002, is a volume of short stories)

EVANOVICH, J.

MAX HOLT

1 Full house (2002)
2 Full tilt (2003)
3 Full speed (2003)
4 Full blast (2003)

EVANS, A.

COMMANDER SMITH

1 Thunder at dawn (1979)
2 Ship of force (1979)
3 Dauntless (1980)
4 Seek out and destroy (1982)

EVANS, GERALDINE

INSPECTOR RAFFERTY

1 Dead before morning (1993)
2 Down among the dead men (1994)
3 Death time (1995)
4 The hanging tree (1996)
5 Absolute poison (2002)
6 Dying for you (2004)

EVANS, J.
HABBAKUK PARTON
1 The Portobello virgin (1986)
2 The Mexico novice (1987)
3 The Alamo design (1989)

EVANS, LIZ
GRACE SMITH
1 Who killed Marilyn Monroe (1997)
2 JFK is missing (1999)
3 Don't mess with Mrs. Inbetween (2000)
4 Barking (2001)
5 Sick as a parrot (2004)

EVANS, MARGARET
HANNAH HYWEL
1 Song of the hills (1995)
2 Inheritors (1997)

EVANS, Q. T.
MERLIN'S LEGACY
1 Daughter of fire
2 Daughter of the mist
3 Daughter of Camelot

EVANS, R. P.
1 The Christmas box (1995)
2 The timepiece (1996)

EVANS, S.
WINDMILL HILL
1 Centres of ritual (1978)
2 Occupational debris (1979)
3 Temporary hearths (1982)
4 Houses on the site (1984)
5 Seasonal tribal feasts (1987)

EVANS, T.
LONGARM
1 Longarm
2 Longarm on the border
3 Longarm and the avenging angels
4 Longarm and the Wendigo
5 Longarm in the Indian Nation
6 Longarm and the logger
7 longarm and the high graders
8 Longarm and the nesters
9 Longarm and the hatchetmen
10 Longarm and the Molly Maguires
11 Longarm and the Texas Rangers
12 Longarm in Lincoln County

EXLEY, F.
1 A fan's notes
2 Last notes from home (1990)

EYRE, E.
SIGISMONDO
1 Death of a Duchess (1991)
2 Curtains for the Cardinal (1992)
3 Poison for the Prince (1993)
4 Bravo for the bride (1994)
5 Axe for an abbot (1995)
6 Dirge for a doge (1996)

FAIRSTEIN, L.
ALEXANDRA COOPER
1 Final jeopardy (1996)
2 Likely to die (1997)
3 The dead house (2000)
4 The bone vault (2002)

FALCONER, E.
1 The golden years (1995)
2 The love of women (1996)
3 The counter-tenor's daughter (1997)
4 Wings of the morning (1998)
5 A barefoot wedding (1999)
6 Frost at midnight (2000)

FANTE, J.
ARTURO BANDINI
1 Wait until Spring, Bandini (1938)
2 Ask the dust (1939)
3 Dreams from Bunker Hill (1982)

FANTONI, M.
MIKE DIME
1 Mike Dime (1981)
2 Stickman (1982)

FARAH, N.
VARIATIONS ON THE THEME OF
AFRICAN DICTATORSHIP
1 Sweet and sour milk (1979)
2 Sardines (1981)
3 Close Sesame (1983)

FARLAND, D.
THE RUNELORDS
1 The sum of all men (1997)
2 Brotherhood of the wolf (1999)
3 Wizard born (2001)

FARMER, P. J.
DOC CALIBAN
1 Lord of the trees (1981)
2 Keepers of secrets (1985)

FARMER, P. J.
WORLD OF THE TIERS
1 Makers of Universes

2 Private cosmos
3 The gates of Creation
4 Behind the walls of Terra
5 The lavalite world

FARMER, P. J.
AN EXORCISM
1 Blown
2 The image of the beast

FARMER, P. J.
DAYWORLD
1 Dayworld (1987)
2 Dayworld rebel (1988)
3 Dayworld break-up (1992)

FARMER, P. J.
RIVERWORLD SAGA
1 To your scattered bodies go
2 The fabulous riverboat
3 The dark design (1987)
4 The magic labyrinth
5 Gods of Riverworld (1987)

FARRINGTON, R.
HENRY MORANE
1 The killing of Richard the Third (1972)
2 Tudor agent (1974)
3 The traitors of Bosworth (1978)

FAST, H.
LAVETTE FAMILY
1 The immigrants (1977)
2 Second generation (1979)
3 The establishment (1980)
4 The legacy (1981)
5 The immigrant's daughter (1983)
6 An independent woman (1998)

FAULCON, R.
NIGHTHUNTER
1 The stalking
2 The talisman
3 The ghost dance
4 The shrine
5 The labyrinth
6 The hexing

FAULKS, S.
FRENCH TRILOGY
1 The girl at the Lion d'Or (1990)
2 Birdsong (1997)
3 Charlotte Gray (1998)

FAVIER, P.
THE FRENCH LEGACY
1 A masquerade too far (1997)
2 A price too high (1998)
3 A temptation too great (1999)

FAWCETT, Q.
MADAME VERNET
1 Napoleon must die
2 Death wears a crown

FAWCETT, Q.
MYCROFT HOLMES
1 Embassy rout (1998)
2 The Flying Scotsman (2000)
3 The Scottish ploy (2001)

FEINTUCH, D.
THE SEAFORT SAGA
1 Midshipman's hope (1996)
2 Challenger's hope (1996)
3 Prisoner's hope (1997)
4 Fisherman's hope (1997)
5 Voices of hope (1997)
6 Prince of the blood (1991)

FEIST, R. E.
RIFTWAR
1 Magician (1983)
2 Silverthorn (1985)
3 A darkness at Sethanon (1986)
4 Prince of the blood (1989)

FEIST, R. E.
SERPENTWAR SAGA
1 Shadow of a dark queen (1994)
2 Rise of a merchant prince (1995)
3 Rage of a demon king (1997)
4 Shards of a broken crown (1999)

FEIST, R. E.
THE RIFTWAR LEGACY
1 Krondor; the betrayal (1998)
2 Krondor; the assassins (1999)
3 Krondor:tear of the Gods (2000)

FEIST, R. E.
LEGENDS OF THE RIFTWAR
1 Honoured enemy (2001)
2 Murder in Lamut (2002)
3 Jimmy the hand (2003)

FEIST, R. E. & WURTS, J.
EMPIRE
1 Daughter of the Empire (1989)

2 Servant of the Empire (1990)
3 Mistress of the Empire (1992)

FENNELLY, T.
MATTY SINCLAIR
1 The glory hole murders (1986)
2 The closet hanging (1987)

FENSON, J.
ROSCOE SUMMERFIELD
1 Roscoe, Emily and all the little bastards (1998)
2 More little bastards (1999)

FENTON, S.
1 All the beasts in the field (1984)
2 Creature comforts (1985)

FERGUSON, F.
DET. SERGEANT JANE PERRY
1 Missing person (1993)
2 No fixed abode (1994)
3 Identity unknown (1995)
4 With intent to kill (1996)

FERMOR, P. L.
1 Between the woods and the water (1986)
2 A time of gifts (1977)
   NF Travel

FERRARS, E.
FELIX FREER
1 I met murder (1985)
2 Last will and testament (1979)
3 Frog in the throat (1980)
4 Thinner than water (1981)
5 Death of a minor character (1983)
6 Woman slaughter (1989)
7 Sleep of the unjust (1990)
8 Beware of the dog (1992)

FERRARS, E.
ANDREW BASNETT
1 Something wicked (1983)
2 Root of all evil (1984)
3 The crime and the crystal (1985)
4 The other devil's name (1986)
5 A murder too many (1988)
6 Smoke without fire (1990)
7 A hobby of murder (1994)
8 A choice of evils (1995)

FERRIS, C.
1 The darkness is light enough (1986)

2 Out of the darkness (1988)
3 The badgers of Ashcroft woods (1990)
   NF Animal protection

FERRIS, P.
BUCKLEY FAMILY
1 Children of dust (1988)
2 The divining heart (1995)

FFORDE, J.
THURSDAY NEXT
1 The Eyre affair (2001)
2 Lost in a good book (2002)
3 The well of lost plots (2003)

FIELDING, G.
JOHN BLAYDON
1 Brotherly love (1947)
2 In the time of the greenbloom (1956)
3 Pretty doll houses (1979)
4 The women of Guinea Lane (1986)

FIELDING, H.
BRIDGET JONES
1 Bridget Jones' diary (1998)
2 Bridget Jones, the edge of reason (1999)

FIELDING, K.
RAVENSDALE
1 Untrodden ways (1996)
2 A secret place (1997)
3 Ravensdale spring (1999)

FINLAY, D. G.
BAYLESS FAMILY
1 Watchman (1984)
2 The grey regard (1985)
3 Deadly relations (1986)
4 Graven image (1987)

FINN, R. L.
1 Time remembered (1963)
2 Spring in Aldgate (1968)
   NF Autobiography

FINN, T.
1 Knapworth at war (1982)
2 Knapworth fights on (1989)

FINNEY, P.
SIMON AMES AND DAVID BECKET
1 Firedrake's eye (1992)
2 Unicorn's blood (1998)

FINNEY, P.
LUGH THE HARPER
1 Shadow of gulls (1977)
2 The crow goddess (1978)

FISHER, D. E.
1 The man you sleep with (1982)
2 Variation on a theme (1982)

FITZGERALD, JULIA
1 Desert queen (1986)
2 Taboo (1985)

FITZGIBBON, T.
1 With love (1982)
2 Love lies at a loss (1982)

FITZROY, R.
MALLAMSHIRE SERIES
1 The Manor of Braye (1979)
2 The widow's might (1980)
3 The American Duchess (1980)
4 Ill fares the land (1987)
5 Barnaby's Charity (1988)
6 The Rockport rubies (1989)

FLANDERS, P.
1 Doctor, doctor (1986)
2 Mercenary doctor (1987)

FLEISCHER, L.
1 Saturday night fever (1980)
2 Staying alive (1983)

FLEMING, A.
DET. CHIEF INSPECTOR JOHN CHARTER
1 There goes Charlie (1990)
2 Sophie is gone (1994)
3 Death and deconstruction (1995)
4 This means mischief (1996)

FLEMING, I
JAMES BOND
1 Casino Royale (1953)
2 Live and let die (1954)
3 Moonraker (1955)
4 Diamonds are forever (1956)
5 From Russia with love (1957)
6 Dr. No (1958)
7 Goldfinger (1959)
8 For your eyes only (1960)
9 Thunderball (1961)
10 The spy who loved me (1961)
11 On her Majesty's Secret Service (1963)
12 You only live twice (1964)
13 The man with the golden gun (1965)
14 Octopussy and The living daylights (1966)
15 Dr. Sun, by R.Markham, i.e.K.Amis (1975)
16 Licence renewed, by J. Gardner (1981)
17 For special services, by J.Gardner (1982)
18 Role of honour, by J. Gardner (1984)
19 Icebreaker, by J.Gardner (1983)
20 Nobody lives forever, by J.Gardner (1986)
21 No deals, Mr. Bond, by J.Gardner (1987)
22 Scorpius, by J.Gardner (1988)
23 Brokenclaw, by J.Gardner (1990)
24 Win lose or die, by J.Gardner (1990)
25 The man from Barbarossa, by J.Gardner (1991)
26 Death is forever, by J.Gardner (1992)
27 Never send flowers, by J.Gardner (1993)
28 Seafire, by J.Gardner (1994)
29 COLD, by J.Gardner (1996)
30 Zero minus ten, by R.Benson (1997)
31 Tomorrow never dies, by R.Benson (1997)
32 The facts of death, by R.Benson (1998)
33 High time to kill, by R.Benson (1999)
34 Double shot, by R.Benson (2000)
35 Never dream of dying, by R.Benson (2001)
36 The man with the red tattoo, by R.Benson (2002)
37 Die another day, by R.Benson (2002)

FLETCHER, A.
OUTBACK SAGA
1 Outback (1978)
2 Outback station (1991)
3 Walkabout (1992)
4 Wallaby track (1994)

FLETCHER, B.
1 The wood burners (1992)
2 The iron mouth (1994)

FLETCHER, D.
RAINBOW
1 Rainbow in hell (1983)
2 Rainbows end in tears (1984)

FLETCHER, D.
ROBERT LUMAN
1 The accident of Robert Luman (1988)
2 A wagon-load of monkeys (1988)

FLINT, K. C.
THE SIDHE LEGENDS
1 The hound of Culain

2 Riders of the Sidhe
3 Champions of the Sidhe
4 Master of the Sidhe
5 The challenge of the Clans
6 Storm shield
7 The dark druid

FLUKE, J.
HANNAH SWENSON
1 Chocolate chip cookie murder (2000)
2 Strawberry shortcake murder (2001)
3 Blueberry muffin murder (2002)

FLYNN, K.
MERSEYSIDE
1 A Liverpool lass (1993)
2 The Mersey girls (1994)

FLYNN, R.
EDDATHORPE MYSTERIES
1 Seascape with body (1995)
2 A public body (1996)
3 A fine body of men (1997)
4 Busy body (1998)
5 The body beautiful (1998)
6 Over my dead body (2000)

FLYNN, V.
MITCH RAPP
1 Transfer of power (1999)
2 The third option (2001)
3 Separararation of power (2002)
4 Executive power (2003)

FOLEY, H.
THE FOREST
1 A child in the forest (1974)
2 No pipe dreams for Father (1978)
3 Back to the forest (1981)
4 In and out of the forest (1984)
   NF Life in the Forest of Dean

FOLLETT, J.
EARTHSEARCH
1 Earthsearch (1981)
2 Deathship (1982)

FORBES, BRYAN
HILLSDEN TRILOGY
1 The endless game (1986)
2 A song at twilight (1989)
3 Quicksand (1996)

FORBES, C.
TWEED & NEWMAN
1 Cover story (1985)

2 The Janus man (1987)
3 Deadlock (1987)
4 The Greek key (1988)
5 Terminal (1984)
6 Shockwave (1989)
7 Whirlpool (1990)
8 Cross of fire (1991)
9 By stealth (1992)
10 The power (1993)
11 Fury (1995)
12 Precipice (1996)
13 The cauldron (1997)
14 The sisterhood (1998)
15 This united state (1999)
16 Sinister tide (2000)
17 Rhinoceros (2001)
18 The vorpal blade (2002)
19 The cell (2002)
20 No mercy (2003)

FORBES, G.
CLAIRE FLEETWOOD
1 A handful of summers (1987)
2 Too soon to panic (1997)

FORBES, L.
1 Bombay ice (1999)
2 Fish, blood and bone (2000)

FORD, R.
FARADAWN
1 Quest for Faradawn (1982)
2 Melvaig's vision (1984)
3 Children of Ashgaroth (1986)

FORDE, N.
MARK URGENT
1 Urgent enquiry (1973)
2 Urgent action (1974)
3 Urgent delivery (1975)
4 Urgent trip (1977)
5 Urgent wedding (1979)
6 Urgent honeymoon (1981)

FORESTER, C. S.
HORNBLOWER
1 Mr. Midshipman Hornblower (1950)
2 Lieutenant Hornblower (1952)
3 Hornblower and the Atropos (1956)
4 Hornblower and the Hotspur (1962)
5 The happy return (1937)
6 Ship of the line (1937)
7 Flying colours (1938)
8 The Commodore (1945)
9 Lord Hornblower (1946)
10 Hornblower in the West Indies (1958)
11 Hornblower and the crisis (1967)

FORREST, A.
CAPTAIN JUSTICE
1 Captain Justice (1981)
2 The Pandora secret (1982)
3 A balance of dangers (1984)

FORREST, K. V.
KATE DELAFIELD
1 Amateur city
2 At the Nightwood Bar
3 Beverly Malibu (1989)
4 Murder by tradition (1991)

FORREST, R.
LYON WENTWORTH
1 Death through the looking glass (1978)
2 The wizard of death (1979)
3 A child's garden of death (1979)
4 Death in the willows (1980)
5 Death at Yew Corner (1981)

FORRESTER, H.
1 Twopence to cross the Mersey (1974)
2 Minerva's step-child (1979)
3 By the waters of Liverpool (1981)
4 Lime Street at two (1985)

FORSYTHE, M.
DET. CHIEF INSPECTOR MILLSON &
DET. SGT. SCOBIE
1 Without a trace (1991)
2 A cousin removed (1992)
3 The book lady (1993)
4 A fatal reunion (1995)
5 Death of a secretary (1996)
6 Only living witness (2000)
7 Last known address (2001)

FORTSCHER, W.
THE LOST REGIMENT
1 Rally cry
2 Union forever
3 Terrible swift sword

FORWARD, R.
THE OWL
1 The owl
2 Scarlet serenade

FOSS, J.
DR. JEFFREY FLINT
1 Shadow in the corn (1993)
2 Byron's shadow (1994)
3 Shadesmoor (1995)
4 Lady in the lake (1996)

FOSSUM, K.
KONRAD SEJER
1 He who fears the wolf (2003)
2 When the devil holds the candle (2004)

FOSTER, A. D.
SPELLSINGER
1 Spellsinger (1986)
2 The hour of the gate (1986)
3 The day of the dissonance
4 The moment of the magician
5 The paths of the Perambulator (1986)
6 The time of the transference (1988)
7 Son of Spellsinger (1993)
8 Chorus skating (1995)

FOSTER, A. D.
FLINX AND PIP
1 The Tar Aiym Krang (1972)
2 Nor crystal tears (1983)
3 Flix in flux (1989)
4 The end of the matter (1991)
5 For love of mother-not (1992)
6 Mid-Flinx (1996)

FOSTER, A. D.
ICERIGGER TRILOGY
1 Ice rigger (1978)
2 Mission to Moulokin (1979)
3 The deluge drivers (1990)

FOSTER, A. D.
THE DAMNED
1 A call to arms
2 The great escape
3 The spoils of war

FOSTER, A. D.
ALIEN
1 Alien (1986)
2 Aliens (1990)
3 Alien 3 (1992)
4 Earth hive, by S.Perry (1994)
5 Nightmare asylum, by S.Perry (1994)
6 The female war, by S.Perry (1994)
7 Genocide, by S.Perry (1994)
8 Predator prey, by S. & S.Perry (1995)
9 Hunter's planet, by D.Bischoff (1996)
10 Alien resurrection, by A.C.Crispin (1997)

FOUNTAINE, M.
1 Love among the butterflies (1980)
2 Butterflies and late loves (1986)
   NF Autobiography

FOX, A.
1 Slightly foxed (1986)
2 Completely foxed (1989)
NF Autobiography

FOXELL, N.
EMMA HAMILTON
1 Loving Emma (1986)
2 Emma expects (1987)

FRAME, J.
1 To the Is-land (1983)
2 An angel at my table (1984)
3 The envoy from Mirror City (1985)
NF Autobiography

FRANCIS, D.
KIT FIELDING
1 Break-in (1985)
2 Bolt (1986)

FRANCIS, D.
SID HALLEY
1 Odds against (1965)
2 Whip hand (1980)
3 Come to grief (1995)

FRASER, ANTHEA
CHIEF INSPECTOR NEIL WEBB
1 A shroud for Delilah (1984)
2 A necessary end (1985)
3 Pretty maids all in a row (1986)
4 Death speaks softly (1987)
5 The nine bright shiners (1987)
6 Six proud walkers (1988)
7 The April rainers (1989)
8 Symbols at your door (1990)
9 The lily-white boys (1991)
10 Three, three, the rivals (1992)
11 The gospel makers (1994)
12 The seven stars (1995)
13 One is one and all alone (1996)
14 The ten commandments (1997)
15 Eleven that went up to heaven (1999)
16 The twelve apostles (1999)

FRASER, ANTONIA
JEMIMA SHORE
1 Quiet as a nun (1977)
2 The wild island (1978)
3 A splash of red (1981)
4 Cool repentance (1982)
5 Oxford blood (1985)
6 Jemima Shore's first case and other stories (1986)
7 Your Royal Hostage (1987)
8 The Cavalier case (1990)

9 Jemima Shore at the sunny grave (1991)
10 Political death (1994)

FRASER, C. M.
1 Blue above the chimneys (1980)
2 Roses round the door (1986)
3 Green are my mountains (1990)
NF Autobiography

FRASER, C. M.
RHANNA
1 Rhanna (1978)
2 Rhanna at war (1979)
3 Children of Rhanna (1984)
4 Return to Rhanna (1984)
5 A song of Rhanna (1985)
6 Storm over Rhanna (1988)
7 Stranger on Rhanna (1992)
9 A Rhanna mystery (1996)

FRASER, C. M.
THE GRANTS OF ROTHIEDRUM
1 King's Croft (1986)
2 King's Acre (1987)
3 King's exile (1989)
4 King's Close (1991)
5 King's farewell (1993)

FRASER, C. M.
NOBLE
1 Noble beginnings (1994)
2 Noble deeds (1995)
3 Noble seed (1997)

FRASER, C. M.
KINVARA
1 Kinvara wives (1999)
2 Kinvara summer (2000)
3 Kinvara affairs (2001)

FRASER, CARO
CAPER COURT
1 The pupil (1993)
2 Judicial whispers (1995)
3 An immoral code (1997)
4 A hallowed place (1999)
5 A calculating heart (2004)

FRASER, D.
TREASON IN ARMS
1 A kiss for the enemy (1985)
2 The killing times (1986)
3 The dragon's teeth (1987)
4 The seizure (1987)
5 A candle for Judas (1989)

FRASER, D.
THE HARDROW CHRONICLES
1 Adam Hardrow (1991)
2 Codename Mercury (1992)
3 Adam in the breach (1993)
4 The pain of winning (1994)

FRASER, G. M.
1 The general danced at dawn (1973)
2 McAuslan in the rough (1974)
3 The Sheikh and the dustbin (1988)

FRASER, G. M.
FLASHMAN
1 Flashman in the great game (1836-8) (1975)
2 Flashman (1839-42) (1969)
3 Royal Flash (1842-3) (1970)
4 Flashman's lady (1842-5) (1977)
5 Flash for freedom (1848-9) (1971)
6 Flashman at the charge (1854-5) (1972)
7 Flashman and the dragon (1860) (1985)
8 Flashman and the Redskins (1849 & 1875/6) (1982)
9 Flashman and the mountain of light (1990)
10 Flashman and the angel of the lord (1994)
11 Flashman and the tiger (1999)

FRASER, S.
TILDY CRAWFORD
1 Tildy (1985)
2 Poorhouse woman (1986)
3 Nursing woman (1987)
4 Pointing woman (1988)
5 Radical woman (1989)
6 Gang woman (1989)
7 Widow woman (1991)
8 Invincible woman (1991)

FRASER, S.
GRAINNE MCDERMOTT
1 The bitter dawning (1989)
2 The harsh noontide (1990)
3 The healing might fall (1992)

FRASER, S.
SUFFRAGETTES
1 The summer of the fancy man (1993)
2 The sisterhood (1994)
3 The dreamers (1995)

FRASER, S.
SPECS
1 Specs war
2 Beau Specs

FRASER, S.
LIDDY
1 The surgeon's apprentice (1999)
2 The workhouse doctor (2001)

FREE, C.
POLLITT FAMILY
1 Vinegar Hill
2 Bay of shadows
3 Brannan (1981)

FREELING, N.
HENRI CASTANG
1 Dressing of diamond (1974)
2 What are the bugles blowing for (1975)
3 Lake Isle (1976)
4 Night lords (1978)
5 Castang's city (1980)
6 Wolfnight (1982)
7 Back of the north wind (1983)
8 No part in your death (1984)
9 Cold iron (1986)
10 Lady Macbeth (1988)
11 Not as far as Velma (1989)
12 Those in peril (1990)
13 The pretty how town (1992)
14 You who know (1993)
15 The sea coast of Bohemia (1994)
16 A dwarf kingdom (1996)

FREELING, N.
ARLETTE VAN DER VALK
1 The widow (1979)
2 One damn thing after another (1981)
3 Sand castle (1989)

FREELING, N.
VAN DER VALK
1 Love in Amsterdam (1962)
2 Because of the cats (1963)
3 Guns before butter (1963)
4 Double-barrel (1964)
5 Criminal conversations (1965)
6 The king of the rainy country (1966)
7 The Dresden green (1966)
8 Strike out where not applicable (1967)
9 Tsing-boum (1969)
10 Over the high side (1971)
11 A long silence (1972)

FREEMANTLE, B.
CHARLIE MUFFIN
1 Charlie Muffin (1977)
2 Clap hands, here comes Charlie (1978)
3 The inscrutable Charlie Muffin (1979)
4 Charlie Muffin's Uncle Sam (1980)
5 Madrigal for Charlie Muffin (1981)

6 Charlie Muffin and Russian Rose (1985)
7 Charlie Muffin San (1987)
8 The run around (1988)
9 Comrade Charlie (1989)
10 Charlie's apprentice (1993)
11 Charlie's chance (1996)
12 Dead men living (2001)
13 Kings of many castles (2002)

FREEMANTLE, B.
DIMITRI DANILOV
1 The button man (1993)
2 No time for heroes (1994)

FRENCH, N.
KIT QUINN
1 The memory game (1997)
2 Safe house (1998)
3 Killing me softly (1999)
4 The red room (2001)

FRERE, R.
1 Maxwell's ghost (1976)
2 Beyond the Highland line (1984)

FREWEN, F.
FENBY FAMILY
1 The sunlight on the garden (1997)
2 A woman's judgement (1999)

FREYDONT, S.
LINDY HAGGERTY
1 Backstage murder (1999)
2 High seas murder (2000)
3 A merry little murder (2004)

FRIEDMAN, K.
KINKY FRIEDMAN
1 The Kinky Friedman crime club (1992)
2 More Kinky Friedman (1994)
3 Elvis, Jesus and Coca-cola (1994)
4 Armadillos and old lace (1995)
5 God bless John Wayne (1996)
6 Blast from the past (1998)
7 Frequent flyer (1998)
8 The mile high club (2000)
9 Steppin' on a rainbow (2001)
10 Meanwhile, back at the ranch (2002)

FRIEDMAN, M.
GEORGINA LEE MAXWELL
1 Deadly reflections (1989)
2 Temporary ghost (1990)

FRIEDMAN, R.
1 A loving mistress (1983)
2 A second wife (1985)

FRIEDMAN, R.
SHELTON FAMILY
1 Proofs of affection (1982)
2 Rose of Jericho (1984)
3 To live in peace (1988)

FRIESNER, E.
1 Here be demons
2 Demon blues
3 Hooray for Hellywood

FRITCHLEY, A.
LETTY CAMPBELL
1 Chicken run (1997)
2 Chicken feed (1998)
3 Chicken out (1999)
4 Chicken shack (2001)

FULLER, K.
RIVERVIEW
1 Bitter legacy (1988)
2 The lion's share (1988)
3 Pride of place (1989)

FULLER, R.
1 Souvenirs (1981)
2 Vamp until ready (1982)
3 Home and dry (1984)
NF Autobiography

FULLERTON, A.
NICK EVERARD
1 Sixty minutes for St.George (1975)
2 The blooding of the guns (1976)
3 Patrol to the Golden Horn (1978)
4 Storm force to Narvik (1979)
5 Last lift from Crete (1980)
6 All the drowning seas (1981)
7 A share of honour (1982)
8 The torch bearers (1983)
9 The gate-crashers (1984)

FULLERTON, A.
SBS
1 Special deliverance (1986)
2 Special dynamic (1987)
3 Special deception (1988)

FULLERTON, A.
BOB COWAN
1 Bloody sunset (1991)
2 Look to the wolves (1992)

FULLERTON, A.
ROSIE EWING
1 Into the fire (1995)
2 Return to the field (1997)
3 In at the kill (1999)
4 Single to Paris (2001)

FUREY, M.
ARTEFACTS OF POWER
1 Aurian (1994)
2 Harp of winds (1994)
3 The sword of flame (1995)
4 Dhiamarra (1997)

FUREY, M.
SHADOWLEAGUE
1 The heart of Myrial (1999)
2 Spirit of the stone (2001)
3 The eye of eternity (2002)

FURST, A.
JEAN CASSON
1 The world at night (1997)
2 Red gold (1999)

FURST, R.
ROGER LEVIN
1 The Paris drop (1982)
2 The Caribbean account (1983)

FUSSEY, J.
1 Milk my ewes and weep (1974)
2 Cows in the corn (1978)
3 Calf love (1984)
4 Cats in the coffee (1986)
   NF Autobiography

FYFIELD, F.
HELEN WEST
1 A question of guilt (1988)
2 Trial by fire (1990)
3 Deep sleep (1991)
4 Shadow play (1993)
5 A clear conscience (1994)
6 Without consent (1996)

FYFIELD, F.
SARAH FORTUNE
1 Shadows on the mirror (1989)
2 Perfectly pure and good (1994)
3 Staring at the light (1999)

GAAN, M.
OPIUM WAR TRILOGY
1 Red barbarian (1984)

2 White poppy (1986)
3 Blue mountain (1987)

GABALDON, D.
SARAH FORTUNE
1 Cross stitch (1991)
2 Dragonfly in amber (1993)
3 Voyager (1995)
4 Drums of autumn (1997)

GADNEY, R.
ALAN ROSSLYN
1 Just when we are safest (1995)
2 The Achilles heel (1996)
3 Mother, son and Holy Ghost (1998)
4 Strange police (2000)
5 The scholar of extortion (2003)

GAGE, N.
1 Eleni (1983)
2 A place for us (1990)
   NF Autobiography

GAGNON, M.
DEIRDRE O'HARA
1 The inner ring (1985)
2 A dark night offshore (1986)
3 Doubtful motives (1987)

GALLACHER, T.
BILL THOMPSON
1 Apprentice (1983)
2 Journeyman (1984)
3 Survivor (1985)

GALLAGHER, J.
THE ARCHERS
1 To the victors the spoils (1987)
2 Return to Ambridge (1987)
3 Borchester echoes (1987)

GALLISON, K.
1 Unbalanced accounts (1986)
2 The death tape (1987)

GANDOLFI, S.
TRENT
1 Golden girl (1992)
2 Golden triangle (1993)
3 Golden web (1993)
4 Golden vengeance (1994)
5 White sands (1996)

GANN, E. K.
1 The triumph (1986)
2 The antagonists (1971)

GANO, J.
FLORIA TOSCA GRAND OPERA
COMPANY
1 Death at the opera (1996)
2 Arias of blood (1997)

GANO, J.
INSPECTOR PROBY
1 Inspector Proby's Christmas (1994)
2 Inspector Proby in court (1995)
3 Inspector Proby's weekend (1996)

GARDNER, C. S.
1 A difficulty with dwarves
2 A disagreement with death
3 An excess of enchantments
4 A malady of magicks
5 A multitude of monsters
6 A night in the Netherhells

GARDNER, C. S.
ARABIAN NIGHTS TRILOGY
1 The other Sinbad
2 A bad day for Ali Baba
3 Scheherezade's night out

GARDNER, C. S.
CINEVERSE CYCLE
1 Bride of the slime monster
2 Slaves of the volcano god
3 Revenge of the fluffy bunnies

GARDNER, C. S.
DRAGON CIRCLE
1 Raven walking (1994)
2 Dragon waking (1995)

GARDNER, J.
DIPSPRING SERIES
1 Gunman
2 Dilemma at Dipspring (1976)
3 The underhand mail (1976)
4 The oldtimers (1979)
5 Confession at Dipspring (1982)
6 The jayhawk legacy (1983)

GARDNER, JOHN
1 The secret generations (1987)
2 The secret houses (1988)
3 The secret families (1989)

GARDNER, JOHN
BOYSIE OAKES
1 The liquidator (1964)
2 The understrike (1965)
3 Amber nine (1967)

4 Madrigal (1967)
5 Founder member (1969)
6 Traitor's exit (1970)
7 The airline pilots (1970)
8 The champagne communist (1971)
9 A killer for a song (1974)

GARDNER, JOHN
HERBIE KRUGER
1 The Nostradamus traitor (1978)
2 The garden of weapons (1980)
3 The quiet dogs (1982)
4 Maestro (1993)
5 Confessor (1995)

GARDNER, JOHN
MORIARTY
1 The return of Moriarty (1974)
2 The revenge of Moriarty (1975)

GARDNER, JOHN
DEREK TORRY
1 A complete state of death (1969)
2 The corner men (1974)

GARLOCK, D.
WABASH RIVER TRILOGY
1 Dream river (1990)
2 Lonesome river (1990)
3 River of tomorrow (1991)

GARNER, W.
JOHN MORPURGO
1 Think big, think dirty (1983)
2 Rats alley (1984)

GARNETT, W.
1 Farmer Gribbins and Farmer Green
2 Wrangledale Chase (1989)

GARWOOD, J.
CLAYBORNE FAMILY
1 For the roses
2 One pink rose
3 One white rose
4 One red rose
5 Come the spring

GASH, J.
LOVEJOY
1 The Judas pair (1978)
2 Gold from Gemini (1979)
3 The Grail tree (1979)
4 The spend game (1980)
5 The Vatican rip (1981)
6 The firefly gadroon (1982)

7 The sleepers of Erin (1983)
8 The gondola scam (1984)
9 Pearlhanger (1985)
10 The Tartan ringers (1986)
11 Moonspender (1986)
12 Jade woman (1988)
13 The very last gambado (1989)
14 The great California game (1990)
15 The lies of fair ladies (1991)
16 Paid and loving eyes (1993)
17 The sin within her smile (1993)
18 The grace in older women (1995)
19 The possessions of a lady (1996)
20 The rich and the profane (1997)
21 A rag, a bone and a hank of hair (1999)
22 Every last cent (2001)
23 The ten word game (2003)

GASH, J.
DR. CLARE BURTONALL
1 Different women dancing (1997)
2 Prey dancing (1998)
3 Die dancing (2000)
4 Bone dancing (2002)

GASTON, B.
LT. JASON WINTER
1 Winter and the 'Wild Cat' (1980)
2 Winter and the 'White Witch' (1981)
3 Winter and the 'Wild Rover' (1982)
4 Winter and the widowmakers (1984)
5 Winter and the "Wanderer" (1986)

GAVIN, C.
1 A light woman (1986)
2 The glory road (1987)

GAVIN, C.
RESISTANCE TRILOGY
1 Traitor's gate (1977)
2 None dare call it treason (1979)
3 How sleep the brave (1980)

GAVIN, C.
NAPOLEONIC TRILOGY
1 A dawn of splendour (1989)
2 The French fortune (1991)
3 One candle burning (1996)

GAVIN, C.
WORLD WAR I
1 The devil in the harbour (1968)
2 The house of war (1970)
3 Give me the daggers (1972)
4 The snow mountain (1973)

GAY, A.
1 Dancing on the volcano (1993)
2 To bathe in lightning (1995)

GEAR, K. O.
ANAZAZIA MYSTERIES
1 The visitant (1999)
2 The summoning God (2000)
3 Bone walker (2002)

GEAR, W. M. & K. O.
PREHISTORIC AMERICA
1 People of the wolf
2 People of the fire
3 People of the earth
4 People of the river
5 People of the sea
6 People of the owl (2003)

GEDDES, P.
VENNIKER
1 The high game (1968)
2 A November wind (1970)
3 The Ottawa allegation (1973)
4 A state of corruption (1985)

GEDGE, P.
LORD OF THE THE TWO LANDS
1 Lord of the two lands (2001)
2 The oasis (2001)
3 The Horus road (2002)

GEE, M.
1 Plumb (1979)
2 Meg (1981)
3 Sole survivor (1983)

GELLIS, R.
ROSELYNDE CHRONICLES
1 Roselynde (1978)
2 Alinor (1979)
3 Joanna (1979)
4 Gilliane (1980)
5 Rhiannon (1984)
6 Sybelle (1984)

GEMMELL, D.
1 Lion of Macedon (1991)
2 Dark Prince (1991)

GEMMELL, D.
THE DRENAI SAGA
1 Legend (1984)
2 The King beyond the gate (1985)
3 Waylander (1986)
4 Quest for lost heroes (1990)

5 In the realm of the wolf (Waylander II) (1992)
7 The first chronicles of Druss the Legend (1996)
8 Winter warriors (1997)
9 Hero in the shadows (Waylander III) (2000)
10 The swords of night and day (2004)

GEMMELL, D.
SIPSTRASSI TALES
1 Wolf in shadow (1987)
2 Ghost king (1988)
3 Last sword of power (1988)
4 The last guardian (1989)
5 Knights of dark renown (1990)
6 Morningstar (1992)
7 Bloodstone (1994)

GEMMELL, D.
HAWK QUEEN
1 Ironhand's daughter (1995)
2 The hawk eternal (1995)

GEMMELL, D.
THE RIGANTES
1 Sword in the storm (1998)
2 Midnight falcon (1999)
3 Ravenheart (2001)
4 Stormrider (2002)

GEMS, P.
MRS. FRAMPTON
1 Mrs. Frampton (1988)
2 Bon voyage, Mrs. Frampton (1990)

GENTLE, M.
1 Golden witchbreed (1983)
2 Ancient light (1987)

GENTLE, M.
WHITE CROW
1 Rats and gargoyles (1990)
2 The architecture of desire (1991)
3 Left to his own devices (1994)

GEORGE, E.
DET. CHIEF INSPECTOR LYNLEY
1 A great deliverance (1989)
2 Payment in blood (1989)
3 A suitable vengeance (1991)
4 Well-schooled in murder (1990)
5 For the sake of Elena (1991)
6 Missing Joseph (1993)
7 Playing for the ashes (1994)
8 In the presence of the enemy (1996)

9 Deception on his mind (1997)
10 In pursuit of the proper sinner (1999)
11 A traitor to memory (2001)
12 A place of hiding (2003)

GEORGESON, V.
SHADOW OF THE ELEPHANT
1 Seeds of love (1986)
2 Whispering roots (1987)
3 The haunted tree (1989)
4 The garden (1992)

GERBER, M.
BARRY TROTTER
1 Barry Trotter and the shameless parody (2002)
2 Barry Trotter and the unnecessary sequel (2003)

GERROLD, D.
WAR AGAINST THE CHTORR
1 A matter for men
2 A day for damnation

GERSON, J.
INSPECTOR LOHMANN
1 Deaths head Berlin (1987)
2 Death squad London (1989)

GETHIN, D.
WYATT
1 Wyatt (1982)
2 Wyatt and the Moresby legacy (1983)
3 Wyatt's orphan (1985)

GETHIN, D.
HALLORAN
1 Jack Lane's Browning (1985)
2 Dane's testament (1986)

GIBB, NEIL
ALEX BRIERLEY
1 Blood red sky (1999)
2 Bleached white (2000)

GIBBONS, S.
COLD COMFORT FARM
1 Cold Comfort Farm (1932)
2 Christmas at Cold Comfort Farm (1940)
3 Conference at Cold Comfort Farm (1949)

GIBSON, M.
1 One man's medicine (1983)
2 Doctor in the west (1984)
   NF Reminiscences of a doctor

GIBSON, W.
CYBERSPACE
1 Neuromancer (1984)
2 Count Zero (1986)
3 Mona Lisa overdrive (1988)

GIFFORD, B.
1 Wild at heart (1990)
2 59 and raining (1992)

GILBERT, M.
CALDER AND BEHRENS
1 Game without rules (1965)
2 Mr. Calder and Mr. Behrens (1982)

GILBERT, M.
CHIEF INSPECTOR HAZELRIGG
1 Close quarters (1947)
2 They never looked inside (1948)
3 The doors open (1949)
4 Smallbone deceased 11950
5 Death has deep roots (1951)
6 Fear to tread (1953)

GILBERT, M.
PETRELLA
1 Young Petrella (1988)
2 Petrella at Q (1977)
3 Roller-coaster (1993)

GILCHRIST, E.
NORA JANE
1 Light can be both wave and particle (1993)
2 The age of miracles (1995)
3 Nora Jane and company (1997)

GILCHRIST, R.
SLAVES WITHOUT MASTERS
1 A girl called Friday Night (1983)
2 The house at 3 o'clock (1982)
3 The wrong side of town (1985)

GILCHRIST, R.
DRAGONARD
1 Dragonard (1975)
2 Master of Dragonard Hill (1976)
3 Dragonard blood (1977)
4 Dragonard rising (1978)
5 The siege of Dragonard Hill (1979)
6 Guns of Dragonard (1980)

GILL, A.
EGYPTIAN MYSTERIES
1 City of the horizon (1991)

2 City of dreams (1993)
3 City of the dead (1995)

GILL, B.
CHIEF INSPECTOR MCGARR
1 McGarr and the Sienese conspiracy (1978)
2 McGarr and the politician's wife (1979)
3 McGarr on the Cliffs of Moher (1980)
4 McGarr at the Dublin Horse Show (1981)
5 McGarr and the Prime Minister of Belgrave Square
6 McGarr and the method of Descartes (1985)
7 McGarr and the legacy of a woman scorned (1987)
8 The death of a Joyce scholar (1989)
9 The death of love (1992)
10 Death on a cold wild river (1993)
11 The death of an ardent bibliophile (1995)
12 The death of an Irish seawolf (1996)
13 Death of a busker king (1997)
14 Death in Dublin (2003)

GILL, B. M.
DET. CHIEF INSPECTOR MAYBRIDGE
1 Seminar for murder (1985)
2 The fifth Rapunzel (1991)

GILLULY, S.
1 Greenbriar Queen (1989)
2 The crystal keep (1989)
3 Ritmyin's daughter (1989)

GILLULY, S.
PAINTER
1 The boy from the Burren (1991)
2 The giant of Inishkerry (1992)
3 The emperor of Earth-Above (1993)

GILMAN, D.
MRS. POLLIFAX
1 The unexpected Mrs. Pollifax (1966)
2 The amazing Mrs. Pollifax (1970)
3 The elusive Mrs. Pollifax (1973)
4 A palm for Mrs. Pollifax (1974)
5 Mrs. Pollifax on the China Station (1985)
6 Mrs. Pollifax and the Hong KongBuddha (1986)
7 Mrs. Pollifax and the golden triangle (1989)

GLANFIELD, J.
1 Hotel Quadriga (1987)
2 Viktoria (1989)

GLASSER, R.
1 Growing up in the Gorbals (1986)
2 Gorbals boy at Oxford (1988)
3 Gorbals voices, siren songs (1990)
NF Autobiography

GLAZEBROOK, P.
1 Captain Vinegar's commission (1988)
2 The gate at the end of the world (1989)

GLOVER, J.
FLYNN FAMILY
1 The stallion man (1982)
2 Sisters and brothers (1984)
3 To everything a season (1986)
4 Birds in a gilded cage (1987)

GODDARD, R.
HARRY BARNETT
1 Into the blue (1992)
2 Out of the sun (1996)

GODDEN, R.
1 A time to dance, a time to weep (1987)
2 A house with four rooms (1989)

GODFREY, E.
JANE TREGAR
1 Murder behind locked doors (1989)
2 Georgia disappeared (1992)

GOLDING, W.
EDMUND TALBOT
1 Rites of passage (1980)
2 Close quarters (1987)
3 Fire down below (1989)

GOLDMAN, W.
1 Marathon man (1974)
2 Brothers (1986)

GOLDREICH, G.
LEAH
1 Leah's journey (1983)
2 Leah's children (1985)

GOLDSBOROUGH, R.
NERO WOLFE
1 Murder in E minor (1986)
2 Death on deadline (1989)
3 The bloodied ivy (1989)
4 The last coincidence (1991)

GOLLIN, J.
1 The Verona Passamezzo (1987)
2 Eliza's galiardo (1988)

GOODEN, P.
NICK REVILL
1 Sleep of death (2000)
2 Death of Kings (2001)
3 The pale companion (2002)
4 Alms for oblivion (2003)
5 The mask of night (2004)

GOODKIND, T.
THE SWORD OF TRUTH
1 Wizard's first rule (1994)
2 Stone of tears (1995)
3 Blood of the fold (1996)
4 Temple of the winds (1997)
5 Soul of the fire (1999)
6 Faith of the fallen (2000)
7 The pillars of creation (2001)

GOODMAN, P.
EMPIRE CITY
1 The state of nature (1946)
2 The dead of spring (1950)
3 The holy terror (1959)
4 Grand piano (1942)

GOODWIN, S.
1 Winter spring (1978)
2 Winter sisters (1980)

GORDON, GILES
1 About a marriage (1972)
2 Scenes from married life (1976)

GORDON, K.
PEACOCKS
1 Emerald peacock (1978)
2 Peacock in flight (1979)
3 In the shadow of the peacock (1980)
4 The peacock ring (1981)
5 Peacock in jeopardy (1982)
6 The peacock fan (1996)
7 The peacock garden (2000)

GORDON, N.
ROB COLE
1 The physician (1990)
2 Shaman (1992)
3 Choices (1996)

GORDON, R.
DOCTOR SIMON SPARROW
1 Doctor in the house (1952)

2 Doctor at sea (1954)
3 Doctor at large (1955)
4 Doctor in love (1957)
5 Doctor and son (1958)
6 Doctor in clover (1960)
7 Doctor on toast (1961)
8 Doctor in the swim (1962)
9 The summer of Sir Lancelot (1963)
10 Love and Sir Lancelot (1965)
11 Doctor on the boil (1970)
12 Doctor on the brain (1972)
13 Doctor in the nude (1973)
14 Doctor on the job (1976)
15 Doctor in the nest (1979)
16 Doctor on the ball (1985)
17 Doctor in the soup (1986)

GORDON, S.
THE WATCHERS
1 The watchers
2 The hidden world
3 The mask

GOSLING, P.
LT. JACK STRYKER
1 Monkey puzzle (1988)
2 Backlash (1989)
3 Ricochet (2002)

GOSLING, P.
LUKE ABBOT
1 The Wychford murders (1986)
2 Death penalties (1991)

GOSLING, P.
BLACKWATER BAY MYSTERIES
1 The body in Blackwater Bay (1992)
2 A few dying words (1993)
3 The dead of winter (1995)
4 Death and shadows (1999)
5 Underneath every stone (2000)

GOTLIEB, P.
1 Flesh and gold (1999)
2 Violent stars (1999)

GOUGH, L.
WILLOWS & PARKER
1 The goldfish bowl (1987)
2 Death on a No.8 hook (1988)
3 Hot shots (1989)
4 Serious crimes (1990)
5 Accidental deaths (1991)
6 Killers (1993)
7 Heartbreaker (1996)
8 Memory lane (1997)

GOULD, J.
LOVEMAKERS TRILOGY
1 The Texas years (1989)
2 The lovemakers (1985)
3 Second love (1998)

GOWER, I.
1 The copper cloud (1976)
2 Return to Tip Row (1977)
Published in one volume in 1987 as 'The loves of Catrin'

GOWER, I.
SWEYNESEYE
1 Copper kingdom (1983)
2 Proud Mary (1984)
3 Spinners Wharf (1985)
4 Morgan's woman (1986)
5 Fiddler's ferry (1987)
6 Black gold (1988)

GOWER, I.
CORDWAINERS
1 The shoemaker's daughter (1991)
2 The oyster catchers (1992)
3 Honey's Farm (1993)
4 Arian (1994)
5 Sea mistress (1995)
6 The wild seed (1996)

GOWER, I.
POTTERS
1 Firebird (1997)
2 Dream catcher (1998)
3 Sweet Rosie (1999)
4 Kingdom's dream (2001)
5 Paradise Park (2002)

GRAFTON, S.
KINSEY MILLHONE
1 A is for alibi (1985)
2 B is for burglar (1986)
3 C is for corpse (1987)
4 D is for deadbeat (1987)
5 E is for evidence (1988)
6 F is for fugitive (1989)
7 G is for gumshoe (1990)
8 H is for homicide (1991)
9 I is for innocent (1992)
10 J is for judgment (1993)
11 K is for killer (1994)
12 L is for lawless (1996)
13 M is for malice (1996)
14 N is for noose (1998)
15 O is for outlaw (1999)
16 P is for peril (2001)
17 Q is for quarry (2003)

GRAHAM, C.
CHIEF INSPECTOR TOM BARNABY
1 The killings at Badger's Drift (1987)
2 Death of a hollow man (1989)
3 Death in disguise (1992)
4 Written in blood (1994)
5 Faithful unto death (1996)
6 A place of safety (1999)
7 A ghost in the machine (2004)

GRAHAM, WINSTON
POLDARK
1 Ross Poldark (1783-87) (1945)
2 Demelza (1788-90) (1946)
3 Jeremy Poldark (1790-91) (1950)
4 Warleggan (1792-93) (1953)
5 The black moon (1794-95) (1973)
6 The four swans (1795-97) (1976)
7 The angry tide (1798-99) (1977)
8 The stranger from the sea (1810-11) (1981)
9 The miller's dance (1812-13) (1982)
10 The loving cup (1813-15) (1984)
11 Twisted sword (1990)
12 Bella Poldark (2002)

GRAHAME, K.
THE WILLOWS
1 The wind in the willows (1908)
2 A fresh wind in the willows, by D.Scott (1983)
3 The willows at Christmas, by W.Horwood (1999)
4 The willows in winter, by W.Horwood (1993)
5 Toad triumphant, by W.Horwood (1995)
6 The willows and beyond, by W.Horwood (1996)

GRANGER, ANN
FRAN VARADY
1 Asking for trouble (1997)
2 Keeping bad company (1997)
3 Running scared (1998)
4 Risking it all (2001)
5 Watching out (2003)

GRANGER, ANN
MEREDITH MITCHELL AND SUPT. ALAN MARKBY
1 Say it with murder (1990)
2 A season for murder (1991)
3 Cold in the earth (1992)
4 Murder among us (1992)
5 Where old bones lie (1993)
6 A fine place for death (1994)
7 Flowers for his funeral (1994)
8 Candle for a corpse (1995)
9 A touch of mortality (1996)
10 A word after dying (1996)
11 Call the dead again (1998)
12 Beneath these stones (1999)
13 Shades of murder (2000)
14 A restless evil (2002)
15 That way murder lies (2004)

GRANGER, B.
THE NOVEMBER MAN
1 The November man (1980)
2 Schism (1982)
3 The shattered eye (1984)
4 The British Cross (1985)
5 The Zurich numbers (1985)
6 Hemingway's notebook (1986)
7 There are no spies (1992)
8 The infant of Prague (1988)
9 Henry McGee is not dead (1989)
10 League of terror (1991)
11 The man who heard too much (1993)

GRANGER, P.
PARADISE GARDENS
1 Not all tarts are apple (2002)
2 The widow ginger (2003)
3 Trouble in Paradise (2004)

GRANT, JAMES
MACE
1 Mace (1984)
2 Mace's luck (1985)

GRANT, JOAN
1 The owl on the teapot (1991)
2 The cuckoo on the kettle (1993)
   NF Country life

GRANT, JOHN
1 Albion (1991)
2 The world (1992)

GRANT, JONATHAN
SEALANDINGS
1 Shores of Sealandings (1991)
2 Storms at Sealandings (1992)
3 Mehala;lady of Sealandings (1993)

GRANT-ADAMSON, L.
RAIN MORGAN
1 Patterns in the dust (1984)
2 Faces of death (1985)
3 Guilty knowledge (1987)
4 Wild justice (1987)
5 Curse the darkness (1990)

GRANT-ADAMSON, L.
JIM RUSH
1 A life of adventure (1993)
2 Dangerous games (1994)

GRASS, G.
THE DANZING TRILOGY
1 The tin drum (1959)
2 Cat and mouse (1966)
3 Dog years (1965)

GRAVE, S.
MIAMI VICE
1 China white
2 Hellhole
3 Probing by fire
4 The razor's edge

GRAY, CAROLINE
1 A woman of her time (1994)
2 A child of fortune (1995)

GRAY, CAROLINE
JOANNA ORTON
1 The promised land (1997)
2 The phoenix (1998)
3 The torrent (1999)

GRAY, CAROLINE
HELIER L EREE
1 Spawn of the devil (1993)
2 Sword of the devil (1994)
3 Death of the devil (1994)

GRAY, J.
GUARDIAN CYCLE
1 Ice mage (1999)
2 The dark moon (2000)
3 The Jasper forest (2001)
4 The red glacier (2002)
5 Alyssa's ring (2002)

GRAY, S.
1 Unnatural pursuit (1985)
2 How's that for telling 'em, fat lady?
(1988)
NF Autobiography

GRAYSON, RICHARD
INSPECTOR GAUTIER
1 The murders at the Impasse Louvain
(1979)
2 The Monterant affair (1980)
3 The death of Abbe Didier (1981)
4 The Montmartre murders (1982)
5 Crime without passion (1983)

6 Death en voyage (1986)
7 Death on the cards (1988)
8 Death off stage (1991)
9 Death au gratin (1994)
10 And death the prize (1996)
11 Death in the skies (1998)
12 For blood and wine are red (2000)
13 Let slip the dogs of war (2002)

GREATOREX, W.
AIRLINE
1 Take-off (1981)
2 Ruskin's Berlin (1982)

GREAVES, J.
STEVE WALKER
1 The boss (1980)
2 The second half (1981)

GREELEY, A. M.
FATHER "BLACKIE" RYAN
1 Happy are the meek (1986)
2 Happy are the clean of heart (1987)
3 Happy are those who thirst for justice
(1988)
4 Happy are the merciful (1993)
5 Happy are the peacemakers (1994)
6 Happy are the poor in spirit (1995)
7 Happy are those who mourn (1996)
8 Happy are the oppressed (1996)
9 Blackie at sea (1998)
10 The Bishop and the three kings (1999)
11 The Bishop and the missing L train
(2000)
12 The Bishop and the beggar girl of
St.Germain (2001)
13 The Bishop in the West Wing (2002)
14 The Bishop goes to the university (2004)

GREELEY, A. M.
TIME BETWEEN THE STARS
1 Virgin and martyr (1985)
2 Angels of September (1986)
3 Patience of a saint (1988)
4 Rite of spring (1988)
5 Love song (1990)
6 St.Valentine's night (1990)

GREELEY, A. M.
THE PASSOVER TRILOGY
1 Thy brother's wife (1982)
2 Ascent into hell (1983)
3 Lord of the dance (1988)

GREELEY, A. M.
NUALA ANN MCGRAIL
1 Irish gold (1996)

2 Irish lace (1997)
3 Irish whiskey (1998)
4 Irish mist (1999)
5 Irish eyes (2000)
6 Irish love (2001)
7 Irish stew (2002)

GREELEY, A. M.
O MALLEY FAMILY
1 A midwinter's tale (1999)
2 Younger than springtime (2000)
3 A Christmas wedding (2001)
4 September song (2002)

GREEN, CHLOE
DALLAS OCONNOR
1 Going out in style (2000)
2 Designed to die (2001)

GREEN, CHRISTINE
KATE KINSELLA
1 Deadly errand (1991)
2 Deadly admirer (1992)
3 Deadly practice (1994)
4 Deadly partners (1996)
5 Deadly bond (2001)
6 Deadly echo (2002)
7 Deadly choice (2004)

GREEN, E.
1 Adam's empire (1990)
2 Kalinda (1991)

GREEN, H.
TRIPLE S AGENTS
1 A woman called Omega (1984)
2 The Fidelio affair (1985)

GREEN, M.
1 The boy who shot down an airship (1988)
2 Nobody lost in small earthquake (1990)
   NF Autobiography

GREEN, S.
1 The warrior within
2 The warrior enchained

GREEN, S. R.
HAWK AND FISHER
1 No haven for the guilty
2 Devil take the hindmost
3 The God killer
4 Vengeance for a lonely man
5 Guard against dishonour
6 Two kings in haven

7 House of lost souls
8 Fear and loathing in haven

GREEN, S. R.
OWEN DEATHSTALKER
1 Deathstalker prelude
2 Blue moon rising
3 Blood and honour
4 Deathstalker honour
5 Deathstalker legacy (2002)
6 Deathstalker return (2004)

GREEN, S. R.
TWILIGHT OF EMPIRE
1 Mistworld
2 Ghostworld
3 Hellworld

GREENE, B.
1 Summer of the German soldier (1974)
2 Morning is a long time coming (1978)

GREENLAND, C.
TABITHA FLUTE TRILOGY
1 Take back plenty (1994)
2 Seasons of plenty (1995)

GREENLEAF, S.
JOHN TANNER, P. I.
1 Grave error (1981)
2 Death bed (1982)
3 State's evidence (1984)
4 Fatal obsession (1985)
5 Beyond blame (1987)
6 Flesh wounds (1997)
7 Past tense (1997)

GREENWOOD, D. M.
DEACONESS THEODORA
BRAITHWAITE
1 Clerical errors (1990)
2 Unholy ghosts (1991)
3 Idol bones (1993)
4 Holy terrors (1994)
5 Every deadly sin (1995)
6 Mortal spoils (1996)
7 Heavenly vices (1997)
8 A grave disturbance (1998)
9 Foolish ways (1999)

GREENWOOD, J.
DET. INSPECTOR MOSLEY
1 Murder, Mr. Mosley (1983)
2 Mosley by moonlight (1984)
3 Mosley went to mow (1985)
4 Mists over Mosley (1986)

5 The mind of Mr. Mosley (1987)
6 What, me, Mr. Mosley? (1987)

GREGORIAN, J. B.
THE TREDANA TRILOGY
1 The broken citadel
2 Castle-down
3 The great wheel

GREGORY, P
1 Wideacre (1987)
2 The favoured child (1989)
3 Meridon (1990)

GREGORY, P
TRADESCANT FAMILY
1 Earthly joys (1998)
2 Virgin earth (1999)

GREGORY, P
DET. INSPECTOR PERCY PEACH
1 Missing, presumed dead (1997)
2 An unsuitable murder (2000)
3 An accidental murder (2001)
4 An academic death (2001)
5 The Lancashire leopard (2001)
6 A little learning (2002)
7 Murder at the Lodge (2003)
8 The wages of sin (2004)

GREGORY, S.
MATTHEW BARTHOLOMEW
1 A plague on both your houses (1995)
2 An unholy alliance (1996)
3 A bone of contention (1997)
4 A deadly brew (1998)
5 A wicked deed (1999)
6 A masterly murder (2000)
7 An order for death (2001)
8 A summer of discontent (2002)
9 A killer in winter (2003)
10 The hand of justice (2004)

GREGSON, J. M.
SUPT. JOHN LAMBERT
1 Murder on the 19th (1989)
2 For sale, with corpse (1990)
3 Bring forth your dead (1991)
4 Dead on course (1991)
5 The fox in the forest (1992)
6 Stranglehold (1993)
7 Watermarked (1994)
8 Accident by design (1996)
9 Body politic (1997)
10 Girl gone missing (1998)
11 Malice aforethought (1999)
12 A turbulent priest (1999)

13 Death on the eleventh hole (2002)
14 Fly in the ointment (2003)

GREY, ROMER ZANE
LARAMIE NELSON
1 Last stand at Indigo Flats (1970)
2 The other side of the river (1970)

GREY, ROMER ZANE
BUCK DUANE
1 Rider of the distant trails (1969)
2 High valley river (1970)
3 King of the range (1970)
4 Rustlers of the cattle range (1970)
5 Three deaths for Buck Duane (1971)
6 Track the man down (1971)

GRIBBIN, J. & CHOWN, M.
1 Double planet (1988)
2 Reunion (1991)

GRIBBLE, L. R.
ANTHONY SLADE
1 Gillespie suicide murder (1929)
2 The Grand Modena murder (1930)
3 The stolen Home Secretary (1932)
4 Is this revenge? (1931)
5 The secret of Tangles (1933)
6 The riddle of the ravens (1934)
7 Riley of the Special Branch (1936)
8 The case of the Malverne diamonds (1936)
9 The casebook of Anthony Slade (1937)
10 Tragedy in E flat (1938)
11 The Arsenal Stadium mystery (1939)
12 Atomic murder (1947)
13 Hangman's moon (1949)
14 They kidnapped Stanley Matthews (1950)
15 The frightened chameleon (1951)
16 Murder out of season (1952)
17 Death pays the piper (1956)
18 Superintendent Slade investigates (1957)
19 Stand in for murder (1957)
20 Don't argue with death (1958)
21 Wantons die hard (1961)
22 Heads you die (1964)
23 The violent dark (1965)
24 Strip tease macabre (1967)
25 A diplomat dies (1969)
26 Alias the victim (1971)
27 Programmed for death (1973)
28 Midsummer slay ride (1976)
29 You can't die tomorrow (1978)
30 Dead end in Mayfair (1981)
31 The dead don't scream (1984)
32 Violent midnight (1986)

GRIFFIN, W. E. B.
BROTHERHOOD OF WAR
1 The Lieutenants (1988)
2 The Captains (1988)
3 The Majors (1989)
4 The Colonels (1989)
5 The Berets (1989)
6 The Generals (1990)
7 The new breed (1990)
8 Aviators (1990)

GRIFFIN, W. E. B.
BADGE OF HONOUR
1 Men in blue (1982)
2 Special operations (1984)
3 The victim (1986)
4 The witness (1997)
5 The assassin (1998)
6 The murderers (1998)
7 The investigators (2000)

GRIFFIN, W. E. B.
CORPS
1 Semper fi (1992)
2 Call to arms (1993)
3 Counterattack (1993)
4 Battleground (1994)
5 Line of fire (1994)
6 Close combat (1995)
7 Behind the lines (1996)
8 In danger's path (1998)
9 Under fire (2002)
10 Retreat, hell! (2003)

GRIFFIN, W. E. B.
WORLD WAR II
1 Honor bound (1992)
2 Blood and honor (1997)
3 In the line of duty (1999)
4 Secret honor (2000)
5 Give me liberty (2000)
6 Into enemy hands (2001)
7 Special ops (2001)

GRIFFITHS, E.
RUDOLF & KARSTEN NILSEN
1 Murder on Page 3 (1985)
2 The water widow (1986)

GRIMES, M.
CHIEF INSPECTOR RICHARD JURY
1 The man with a load of mischief (1981)
2 The old fox deceiv'd (1982)
3 The anodyne necklace (1984)
4 The Dirty Duck (1986)
5 I am the only Running Footman (1987)
6 Jerusalem Inn (1987)

7 The Five Bells and Bladebone (1988)
8 The Deer Leap (1988)
9 Help the poor struggler (1989)
10 The Old Silent (1990)
11 The Old Contempibles (1991)
12 The horse you came in on (1993)
13 Rainbow's end (1995)
14 The case has altered (1997)
15 The stargazy (1999)
16 The Lamorna wink (1999)
17 The blue last (2001)
18 The grave Maurice (2004)

GRIMES, M.
MID WEST
1 Hotel Paradise (1996)
2 Cold Flat Junction (2001)

GRIMWOOD, J.
ASHRAF BEY
1 Pashazade (2001)
2 Effendi (2002)
3 Felaheen (2003)

GROOM, W.
FORREST GUMP
1 Forrest Gump (1994)
2 Gump & Co. (1995)

GROSS, J.
1 The lives of Rachel (1985)
2 The books of Rachel (1980)

GROSSMITH, G.
1 Diary of a nobody (1892)
2 Mrs. Pooter's diary, by K.Waterhouse (1983)
3 Collected letters of a nobody, by K. Waterhouse (1986)

GUARESCHI, G.
DON CAMILLO
1 The little world of Don Camillo (1953)
2 Don Camillo and the prodigal son (1955)
3 Don Camillo's dilemma (1957)
4 Don Camillo and the devil (1959)
5 Comrade Don Camillo (1960)
6 Don Camillo meets Hell's Angels (1970)

GUILD, N.
1 The Assyrian (1988)
2 The blood star (1989)

GUILLOU, J.
THE CRUSADES TRILOGY
1 The road to Jerusalem (2001)
2 The Knight Templar (2002)

GULLAND, S.
NAPOLEON AND JOSEPHINE
1 The many lives and secret sorrows of
   Josephine B. (1998)
2 Tales of passion, tales of woe (1999)
3 The last great dance on earth (2000)

GULVIN, J.
ADEN VANNER
1 Sleep no more (1996)
2 Sorted (1996)
3 Close quarters (1997)
4 Storm crow (1998)
5 Nom de guerre (1999)

GUTTRIDGE, P.
NICK MADRID
1 No laughing matter (1997)
2 A ghost of a chance (1998)
3 Two to tango (1998)
4 The once and future con (1999)
5 Foiled again (2001)

GUY, R.
1 The friends (1974)
2 Edith Jackson (1979)
3 Ruby (1981)

GYGAX, G.
DANGEROUS JOURNEYS
1 The Anubis murders
2 The Samarkand solution
3 Death in Delhi

HADDAD, C. A.
BECKY BELSKI
1 Caught in the shadows (1993)
2 Root canal (1994)

HAGAN, P.
COLTRANE FAMILY
1 Love and war (1990)
2 Raging hearts (1990)

HAGBERG, D.
KIRK MCGARREY
1 High flight (1995)
2 Joshua's hammer (2000)

HAGGARD, W.
COL.CHARLES RUSSELL
1 The high wire (1963)
2 The antagonists (1964)
3 The powder barrel (1965)
4 The hard sell (1965)
5 The power house (1966)
6 The conspirators (1967)
7 A cool day for killing (1968)
8 The hardliners (1970)
9 The bitter harvest (1971)
10 The old masters (1973)
11 The poison people (1977)
12 Scorpion's tail (1976)
13 The median line (1978)
14 The money men (1981)
15 Visa to limbo (1978)
16 The mischief maker (1982)
17 The heirloom (1983)
18 The need to know (1984)
19 The meritocrats (1985)
20 The doubtful disciples (1969)
21 Slow burner (1958)
22 Venetian blind (1959)
23 The arena (1961)
24 The unquiet sleep (1962)
25 The vendettists (1990)

HAGGARD, W.
PAUL MARTINY
1 The protectors (1972)
2 The kinsmen (1974)

HALDEMAN, J.
WORLDS TRILOGY
1 Worlds
2 Worlds apart
3 Worlds enough and time

HALEY, A.
1 Roots (1977)
2 Queen (1993)
   NF Family history

HALEY, R.
JOHN GOSS
1 Thoroughfare of stones (1995)
2 When beggars die (1996)
3 Written in water (1999)
4 Fear of violence (2000)

HALL, A. [E. TREVOR]
QUILLER
1 The Berlin memorandum (1965)
2 The striker portfolio (1969)
3 The Warsaw document (1971)
4 The Tango briefing (1973)

5 The Mandarin cipher (1975)
6 The Kobra manifesto (1976)
7 The Sinkiang executive (1978)
8 The scorpion signal (1980)
9 The Pekin target (1981)
10 Northlight (1985)
11 Quiller's run (1988)
12 The ninth directive (1966)
13 Quiller KGB (1989)
14 Quiller Baracuda (1991)
15 Quiller bamboo (1992)
16 Quiller solitaire (1992)
17 Quiller meridian (1993)
18 Quiller Salamander (1994)
19 Quiller Balalaika (1996)

HALL, D.
MARTIN KEMP
1 Kemp: the road to Crecy (1996)
2 Kemp: passage at arms (1997)

HALL, J.
THORN
1 Mean high tide (1994)
2 Gone wild (1995)
3 Buzz cut (1996)
4 Blackwater Sound (2002)

HALL, PATRICIA
D.C.I.MICHAEL THACKERAY & LAURA
ACKROYD
1 The poison pool (1991)
2 The coldness of killers (1992)
3 Death by election (1993)
4 Dying fall (1994)
5 In the bleak midwinter (1995)
6 Perils of the night (1997)
7 The Italian girl (1998)
8 Dead on arrival (1999)
9 Skeleton at the feast (2001)
10 Deep freeze (2002)
11 Death in dark waters (2002)
12 Dead reckoning (2003)
13 The masks of darkness (2004)

HALL, R. L.
BENJAMIN FRANKLIN
1 Benjamin Franklin takes the case (1988)
2 Benjamin Franklin and a case of
  Christmas murder (1991)

HAMBLY, B.
SUN WOLF
1 The ladies of Mandrigyu (1984)
2 The witches of Wenshar (1987)
3 Dark hand of magic (1990)

HAMBLY, B.
JOHN AVERSIN
1 Dragonsbane
2 Dragonshadow

HAMBLY, B.
DARWATH TRILOGY
1 The time of the dark
2 The walls of air
3 The armies of daylight

HAMBLY, B.
MAGIC
1 The rainbow abyss (1991)
2 Time like infinity (1991)
3 Magicians of the night (1992)

HAMBLY, B.
JAMES ASHER
1 Immortal blood (1998)
2 Travelling with the devil (2000)

HAMER, M.
CHRIS LUDLOW
1 Sudden death (1991)
2 A deadly lie (1992)
3 Death trap (1993)
4 Shadows on the green (1994)
5 Dead on time (1996)

HAMILTON, H.
GARDA PAT COYNE
1 Headbanger (1997)
2 Sad bastard (1998)

HAMILTON, L. K.
ANNA BLAKE, VAMPIRE HUNTER
1 Guilty pleasures (1993)
2 The laughing corpse (1993)
3 Circus of the damned (1994)
4 The lunatic cafe (1994)
5 Bloody bones (1996)
6 The killing dance (1996)
7 Burnt offerings (1998)
8 Blue moon (1999)
9 Obsidian butterfly (2001)
10 A kiss of shadows (2002)
11 Narcissus in chains (2002)
12 Cerulean sins (2003)

HAMILTON, M.
MONTY
1 Monty:the making of a general, 1887-
  1942 (1981)

2 Monty:master of the battlefield, 1942-44 (1983)
3 Monty the Field Marshal, 1944-46 (1986)
NF Biography

HAMILTON, PETER F.
THE NIGHT S DAWN TRILOGY
1 The reality dysfunction (1997)
2 The neutronium alchemist (1998)
3 The naked god (1999)

HAMILTON, S.
ALEX MCKNIGHT
1 A cold day in Paradise (2000)
2 Winter of the wolf moon (2001)
3 The hunting wind (2001)
4 North of nowhere (2002)
5 Blood is the sky (2003)

HAMMOND, G.
KEITH CALDER
1 Dead game (1979)
2 The reward game (1980)
3 The revenge game (1981)
4 Fair game (1982)
5 The game (1982)
6 Sauce for the pigeon (1984)
7 Cousin once removed (1984)
8 Pursuit of arms (1985)
9 Silver city scandal (1986)
10 The executor (1986)
11 The worried widow (1987)
12 Adverse report (1987)
13 Stray shot (1988)
14 A brace of skeet (1989)
15 Let us prey (1990)
16 Home to roost (1990)
17 Snatch crop (1991)
18 Thin air (1993)
19 Hook or crook (1994)
20 Carriage of justice (1995)
21 Sink or swim (1996)
22 Follow that gun (1997)

HAMMOND, G.
JOHN CUNNINGHAM
1 Dog in the dark (1989)
2 Doghouse (1989)
3 Whose dog are you? (1990)
4 Give a dog a bad name (1992)
5 The curse of the cockers (1993)
6 Sting in the tale (1994)
7 Mad dogs and Scotsmen (1995)
8 Bloodlines (1996)
9 A shocking affair (1999)
10 Dogsbody (1999)
11 Dead weight (2000)

HANCOCK, N.
CIRCLE OF LIGHT
1 Greyfax Grimwald
2 Faragon Fairingay
3 Calix stay
4 Squaring the circle

HANCOCK, N.
THE WILDERNESS OF FOUR
1 Across the far mountain
2 The plains of sea
3 On the boundaries of darkness
4 The road to the Middle Islands

HANFF, H.
CHARING CROSS ROAD
1 84, Charing Cross Road (1973)
2 The Duchess of Bloomsbury Street (1974)
3 Q's legacy (1985)

HANRAHAN, B.
1 The scent of eucalyptus (1973)
2 Kewpie doll (1984)

HANSEN, J.
DAVE BRANDSTETTER
1 Fadeout (1972)
2 Death claims (1973)
3 The troublemaker (1975)
4 The man everybody was afraid of (1978)
5 Skinflick (1980)
6 Gravedigger (1982)
7 A smile in a lifetime (1983)
8 Nightwork (1984)
9 Early graves (2002)
10 Obedience (2003)

HANSON, R.
ADAM MCCLEET
1 Mortal remains (1996)
2 Extreme odds (1999)

HANSON, V. J.
AMOS HATCHER
1 Amos lives! (1990)
2 Shroud for Amos (1990)
3 Legend of Amos (1991)
4 A deal for Amos (1997)

HARBINSON, W. A.
PROJEKT SAUCER
1 Inception
2 Phoenix
3 Genesis
4 Millennium
5 Resurrection

HARDCASTLE, M.
1 Countryman's lot (1998)
2 Luck of a countryman (1998)
3 This country business (1999)
   NF Country life

HARDING, D.
SBS
1 Operation judgment (1994)
2 Operation Stormwind (1996)

HARDING, I.
ASSAULT TROOP
1 Blood beach (1983)
2 Death in the forest (1983)
3 Clash on the Rhine (1984)
4 End run (1984)

HARDWICK, MICHAEL
RACKSTRAW
1 Regency rake (1979)
2 Regency revenge (1980)
3 Regency revels (1982)

HARDWICK, MOLLIE
JULIET BRAVO
1 New arrivals (1981)
2 Calling Juliet Bravo (1981)

HARDWICK, MOLLIE
DORAN FAIRWEATHER CHELMARSH
1 Malice domestic (1986)
2 Parson's pleasure (1987)
3 Uneaseful death (1988)
4 The bandersnatch (1989)
5 Perish in July (1989)
6 The dreaming Damozel (1990)

HARDY, ADAM
STRIKE FORCE FALKLANDS
1 Operation Exocet (1983)
2 Raiders dawn (1984)
3 Red alert
4 Recce patrol
5 Covert op
6 Ware mines!

HARLAN, T.
THE OATH OF EMPIRE
1 The shadow of Arafat (1999)
2 The gate of fire (2000)
3 The storm of heaven (2001)

HARMAN, A.
RHYNGYLL
1 The sorcerer's appendix

2 The frogs of war
3 The tome tunnel
4 101 damnations
5 Fahrenheit 666
6 The scrying game
7 The deity dozen

HARRELL, A.
SAM SHANK
1 The twin bridges murder (1982)
2 Trailersnatch (1983)
3 Rivermist (1983)
4 Kickback (1984)
5 A touch of jade (1985)

HARRER, H.
1 Seven years in Tibet (1952)
2 Tibet is my country (1960)
3 Return to Tibet (1984)
   NF Mountaineering

HARRIS, D. T.
THE MAGES OF GARILLON
1 The burning stone
2 The gauntlet of malice

HARRIS, E.
LARGE LEE
1 Largely luck (1984)
2 Largely trouble (1986)

HARRIS, MARION
1 Soldiers' wives (1987)
2 Officers' ladies (1987)

HARRIS, MARION
HEART OF THE DRAGON
1 Nesta (1988)
2 Amelda (1990)

HARRIS, R. E.
PURCELL SISTERS
1 The silent shore (1986)
2 The beckoning hills (1987)

HARRIS, T.
HANNIBAL LECTER
1 Red dragon (1981)
2 The silence of the lambs (1988)
3 Hannibal (1999)

HARRIS, W.
1 Carnival (1985)
2 Infinite rehearsal
3 Four banks of the river of space (1990)

HARRIS, W.
GUIANA QUARTET
1 The palace of the peacock (1960)
2 The far journey of Oudin (1961)
3 The whole armour (1962)
4 The secret ladder (1962)

HARRISON, C.
1 Arctic rose (1985)
2 Wild flower (1986)

HARRISON, CAREY
TO LISKEARD
1 Richard's feet (1990)
2 Cley (1991)
3 Egon (1993)

HARRISON, H.
TO THE STARS
1 Wheelworld
2 Epic to the stars
3 Starworld (1988)
4 Homeworld

HARRISON, H.
STAINLESS STEEL RAT
1 The stainless steel rat is born (1985)
2 The stainless steel rat (1961)
3 The stainless steel rat's revenge (1971)
4 The stainless steel rat saves the world (1973)
5 The stainless steel rat wants you (1975)
6 The stainless steel rat for President (1983)
7 The Stainless Steel Rat gets drafted (1987)
8 Stainless steel visions (1993)
9 The stainless steel rat sings the blues (1994)
10 The stainless steel rat goes to hell (1997)
11 The stainless steel rat joins the circus (1999)

HARRISON, H.
WEST OF EDEN
1 West of Eden (1986)
2 Winter in Eden (1987)
3 Return to Eden (1988)

HARRISON, H.
BILL THE GALACTIC HERO
1 Bill .... on the planet of robot slaves (1989)
2 Bill ..... on the planet of bottled brains (1990)
3 Bill.... on the planet of tasteless pleasure (1991)
4 Bill.... on the planet of zombie vampires (1992)
5 Bill.... on the planet of hippies from hell (1992)
6 Bill....the final incoherent adventure (1993)

HARRISON, H.
STARS AND STRIPES TRILOGY
1 Stars and Stripes forever (1999)
2 Stars and Stripes in peril (2000)
3 Stars and Stripes triumphant (2001)

HARRISON, H.
THE HAMMER AND THE CROSS
1 The hammer and the cross (1994)
2 One king's way (1995)
3 King and Emperor (1996)

HARRISON, M. J.
1 In Viriconium (1981)
2 Viriconium nights (1985)

HARRISON, RAY.
SGT. BRAGG & P.C.MORTON
1 French ordinary murder (1983)
2 Death of an Honourable member (1984)
3 Death watch (1985)
4 Death of a dancing lady (1985)
5 Counterfeit of murder (1987)
6 A season for death (1987)
7 Tincture of death (1989)
8 Sphere of death (1990)
9 Patently murder (1991)
10 Akin to murder (1992)
11 Murder in Petticoat Square (1993)
12 Hallmark of murder (1995)
13 Murder by design (1996)
14 Facets of murder (1997)
15 Draught of death (1999)

HARRISON, S.
1 Hot breath (1988)
2 Cold feet (1989)
3 Foreign parts (1992)

HARROD-EAGLES, C.
MORLAND DYNASTY
1 The foundling (1980)
2 Dark rose (1981)
3 The princeling (1981)
4 The oak apple (1982)
5 The black pearl (1982)
6 The long shadow (1983)
7 The Chevalier (1984)
8 The maiden (1985)
9 The flood-tide (1986)

10 The tangled thread (1987)
11 The Emperor (1988)
12 The victory (1989)
13 The Regency (1990)
14 Campaigners (1991)
15 The reckoning (1993)
16 The devil's horse (1993)
17 The poison tree (1994)
18 The abyss (1995)
19 The hidden shore (1996)
20 The winter journey (1997)
21 The outcast (1998)
22 The mirage (1999)
23 The cause (2000)
24 The homecoming (2001)
25 The question (2002)
26 The dream kingdom (2003)
27 The Restless Sea (2004)

HARRISON, H.
KIROV SAGA
1 Anna (1990)
2 Fleur (1991)
3 Emily (1992)

28 The White Road
29 The Burning Roses (NOV06)

HARRISON, H.
DET. INSPECTOR BILL SLIDER
1 Orchestrated death (1991)
2 Death watch (1992)
3 Necrochip (1993)
4 Dead end (1994)
5 Blood lines (1996)
6 Killing time (1997)
7 Blood sinister (1999)
8 Gone tomorrow (2001)
9 Dear departed (2004)

HARRY, L.
CORNER HOUSE
1 The Corner House girls (2000)
2 Kiss the girls goodbye (2001)
3 PS. I love you (2002)

HARRISON, H.
PORTSMOUTH SEQUENCE
1 Goodbye sweetheart (1995)
2 The girls they left behind (1995)
3 Keep smiling through (1996)
4 Moonlight and lovesongs (1997)
5 Love and laughter (1998)
6 A girl called Thursday (2002)
7 Tuppence to spend (2003)
8 Under the apple tree (2004)

HART, E.
JANE LAWLESS
1 Robber's wine (1998)
2 Wicked games (1999)

HART, J.
CARL PEDERSON
1 Some die young (1990)
2 A decent killer (1991)

HART, R.
DET. SUPT. ROPER
1 Seascape with dead figures (1987)
2 A pretty place for a murder (1987)
3 A fox in the night (1988)
4 Remains to be seen (1989)
5 Robbed blind (1990)
6 Breach of promise (1990)
7 Blood kin (1991)
8 Final appointment (1993)
9 A deadly schedule (1993)

HARTLAND, M.
DAVID NAIRN
1 Down among the dead men (1983)
2 The third betrayal (1986)

HARTMAN, D.
DIRTY HARRY
1 Duel for cannons
2 Death on the docks
3 The long death
4 The Mexico kill

HARTOG, J.DE
1 The Commodore (1987)
2 The Captain (1987)
3 The Centurion
4 The outer buoy (1995)

HARTON, R.
1 Under the hammer (1992)
2 An auctioneer's lot (1992)
   NF Memoirs of an auctioneer

HARVESTER, S.
BLUNDEN
1 A breastplate for Aaron
2 Sheep may safely graze
3 Obols for Charon

HARVEY, A.
1 Burning houses
2 The web (1987)

HARVEY, J. B.
HART THE REGULATOR
1 Cherokee outlet
2 Blood trail
3 Tago
4 The silver lie

5 Blood on the border
6 Ride the wide country
7 Arkansas breakout
8 John Wesley Hardin
9 California bloodlines
10 The skinning place

HARVEY, JOHN
DET. INSPECTOR CHARLIE RESNICK
1 Lonely hearts (1989)
2 Rough treatment (1990)
3 Cutting edge (1991)
4 Off minor (1992)
5 Wasted years (1993)
6 Cold light (1994)
7 Living proof (1995)
8 Easy meat (1996)
9 Still water (1997)
10 Last rites (1999)
11 Now's the time (short stories) (2000)

HARVEY, M.
1 The dark horseman (1978)
2 The proud hunter (1980)
3 Foxgate (1982)

HASEK, J.
1 The good soldier Schweik
2 Adventures of good comrade Schweik,
  by H.Putz (1969)
3 The red commissar (1981)

HATTERSLEY, R.
1 The maker's mark (1990)
2 In that quiet earth (1991)
3 Skylark's song (1993)

HAWKE, S.
TIME WARS
1 The Ivanhoe gambit
2 The time-keeper conspiracy
3 The Pimpernel plot
4 The Zenda vendetta
5 The Nautilus sanction
6 The Khyber connection
7 The argonaut affair
8 The dracula caper

HAWKE, S.
TRIBE OF ONE
1 The outcast
2 The seeker
3 The nomad

HAWKE, S.
WIZARD SERIES
1 The Wizard of 4th Street
2 The Wizard of Whitechapel
3 The Wizard of Sunset Strip
4 The Wizard of the Rue Morgue
5 The Samurai wizard
6 The wizard of Santa Fe
7 The Wizard of Lovecraft's cafe
8 The Wizard of Camelot
9 The last wizard

HAWKE, S.
SYMINGTON SMYTHE
1 A mystery of errors (2001)
2 The slaying of the shrew (2002)
3 The merchant of vengeance (2003)
4 Much ado about murder (2004)

HAWKEY, R.
PRESIDENTIAL TRILOGY
1 Wild card (1974)
2 Side effect (1979)
3 End stage (1983)

HAWTHORNE, N.
1 The scarlet letter (1850)
2 Pearl, by C.Bigsby (1995)

HAY, HEATHER
THE MONTFORD SAGA
1 Heritage (1990)
2 Honour (1990)
3 Heroes (1991)

HAYDON, E.
RHAPSODY
1 Rhapsody, child of blood (2000)
2 Prophecy, child of earth (2001)
3 Destiny (2002)

HAYMAN, C.
WARFLEET CHRONICLES
1 Missing
2 Greed, crime, sudden death

HAYMAN, C.
LADIES OF LETTERS
1 Ladies of letters (2000)
2 More ladies of letters (2001)
3 Ladies of letters.com (2002)
4 Ladies of letters log on (2002)

HAYMON, S. T.
1 Opposite the Cross keys (1989)
2 The quivering tree (1990)
NF Autobiography

HAYMON, S. T.
DET. INSPECTOR BEN JURNET
1 Death of a pregnant virgin (1980)
2 Ritual murder (1982)
3 Stately homicide (1985)
4 Death of a god (1987)
5 A very particular murder (1989)
6 Death of a warrior queen (1991)
7 Beautiful death (1993)
8 Death of a hero (1996)

HAYNES, C.
PROFESSOR HARRY BISHOP
1 Bishop's gambit, declined (1990)
2 Perpetual check
3 Sacrifice play (1990)

HAYTER, S.
ROBIN HUDSON MYSTERIES
1 What's a girl gotta do? (1997)
2 Nice girls finish last (1998)
3 The last manly man (1999)
4 The Chelsea girl murders (2000)
5 Naked brunch (2002)

HAYTHORNE, J.
OLIVER MANDRAKE
1 The Streslan dimension (1981)
2 Mandrake in Granada (1984)
3 Mandrake in the monastery (1985)

HAYTON, S.
DARK AGE TRILOGY
1 Hidden daughters (1992)
2 The governors (1992)
3 The last flight (1993)

HAYWOOD, G. A.
AARON GUNNER
1 Fear of the dark (1988)
2 Not long for this world (1991)

HAZEL, P.
FINNBRANCH SAGA
1 Yearwood
2 Undersea
3 Winterking

HEADLEY, V.
CRACK
1 Yardie (1992)

2 Excess (1993)
3 Yush! (1994)

HEALD, T.
SIMON BOGNOR
1 Unbecoming habits (1973)
2 Blue blood will out (1974)
3 Deadline (1975)
4 Let sleeping dogs lie (1976)
5 Just desserts (1977)
6 Murder at Moose Jaw (1981)
7 Masterstroke (1982)
8 Red herrings (1985)
9 Brought to book (1988)
10 Business unusual (1989)
11 Death and the visiting fellow (2004)

HEALY, J.
J.F.CUDDY
1 Blunt darts (1986)
2 The tethered goat (1986)
3 So like sleep (1987)
4 Swan dive (1988)
5 Yesterday's news (1989)
6 Right to die (1991)

HEARN, L.
TALES OF THE OTORI
1 Across the nightingale floor (2002)
2 Grass for his pillow (2003)
3 Brilliance for the moon (2004)

HEATH, R.
1 From the heat of the day (1978)
2 One generation (1980)
3 Genetha (1981)

HEAVEN, C
1 House of Kuragin (1972)
2 The Astrov inheritance (1973)
3 Heir to Kuragin (1978)

HEAVEN, C
AYLSHAM FAMILY
1 Lord of Ravensley (1980)
2 The Ravensley touch (1982)
3 The raging fire (1987)
4 The fire still burns (1989)

HEBDEN, M.
INSPECTOR PEL
1 Death set to music (1978)
2 Pel and the faceless corpse (1979)
3 Pel under pressure (1980)
4 Pel is puzzled (1981)
5 Pel and the staghound (1982)

6 Pel and the bombers (1983)
7 Pel and the predators (1984)
8 Pel and the pirates (1984)
9 Pel and the prowler (1985)
10 Pel and the Paris mob (1986)
11 Pel among the pueblos (1987)
12 Pel and the touch of pitch (1987)
13 Pel and the picture of innocence (1988)
14 Pel and the party spirit (1989)
15 Pel and the missing persons (1990)
16 Pel and the promised land (1991)
17 Pel and the sepulchre job (1992)
18 Pel picks up the pieces (1993)
19 Pel and the perfect partner (1994)
20 Pel the patriarch (1996)
21 Pel and the precious parcel (1997)
22 Pel is provoked (1999)
23 Pel and the death of the detective (2000)
24 Pel and the butcher's blade (2001)
25 Pel and the nickname game (2002)

HEINLEIN, R.
FUTURE HISTORY
1 Universe
2 Common sense
3 Methusaleh's children (1941)
4 The man who sold the moon (1950)
5 The green hills of Earth (1951)
6 Revolt in 2100 (1953)
7 Time enough for love (1973)
8 Number of the beast (1979)
9 The cat who walks through walls (1985)
10 To sail beyond the sunset

HELEY, V.
ELLIE QUICKE
1 Murder at the altar (2000)
2 Murder by suicide (1992)
3 Murder of innocence (2003)
4 Murder by accident (2004)

HELLER, J.
1 Catch 22 (1961)
2 Closing time (1994)

HELLER, K.
GEORGE MAN
1 Man's illegal life (1984)
2 Man's storm (1985)
3 Man's loving family (1986)

HELM, E.
VIETNAM GROUND ZERO
1 Strike
2 The raid
3 Incident at Plei Soi

4 Tet
5 Red dust

HENDERSON, L.
SAMANTHA JONES
1 Dead white female (1995)
2 Too many blondes (1996)
3 The black rubber dress (1997)
4 Freeze my margarita (1998)
5 The strawberry tattoo (1999)
6 Chained (2000)
7 Pretty boy (2001)

HENNESSEY, M.
CAVALRY TRILOGY
1 Soldier of the Queen (1980)
2 Regimental lance (1981)
3 The iron stallions (1982)

HENNESSEY, M.
KELLY MAGUIRE
1 The lion at sea (1977)
2 The dangerous years (1978)
3 Back to battle (1979)

HENNESSEY, M.
RFC TRILOGY
1 The bright blue sky (1982)
2 The challenging heights (1983)
3 Once more the hawks (1984)

HERBERT, B.
DUNE PRELUDE
1 House Atreides (1999)
2 House Harkonnen (2000)
3 House Corrino (2001)

HERBERT, F.
DUNE
1 Dune (1967)
2 Dune Messiah (1971)
3 Children of Dune (1976)
4 God Emperor of Dune (1981)
5 Heretics of Dune (1984)
6 Chapterhouse Dune (1985)

HERBERT, F.
JORJ AND MCKIE
1 Whipping star (1979)
2 The Dosadi experiment (1978)

HERBERT, J.
1 The rats (1977)
2 Lair (1979)
3 Domain (1984)

HERBERT, K.
DARK AGES
1 Queen of the lightning (1984)
2 Ghost in the sunlight (1986)
3 Bride of the spear (1988)

HERBERT, M. H.
DARK HORSE
1 Valorian
2 Dark horse
3 Lightning's daughter
4 City of the sorcerers

HERMAN, R.
MATT PONTOWSKI
1 Warbirds (1989)
2 Force of eagles (1990)
3 Dark wing (1994)
4 Iron gate (1995)

HERON, J.
JASON TRASK
1 Trask the avenger (1982)
2 Trask and the fighting Irishman (1983)

HERRIOT, J.
VET
1 If only they could talk (1964)
2 It shouldn't happen to a vet (1971)
3 Let sleeping vets lie (1973)
4 Vet in harness (1974)
5 Vets might fly (1976)
6 Vet in a spin (1977)
7 The Lord God made them all (1981)
8 Every living thing (1992)

HERVEY, E.
MISS UNWIN
1 The governess (1984)
2 The man of gold (1985)
3 Into the valley of death (1986)

HESS, J.
CLARE MALLOY
1 Murder at Mimosa Inn (2000)
2 Roll over and play dead (2002)
3 Death by the light of the moon (2003)

HEWITT, E.
THE CARTWRIGHT SAGA
1 Where waters meet (1997)
2 The harbinger of doom (1997)
3 The miller's daughter (1998)

HEY, S.
FRANK BRENNAN
1 Filling spaces (1995)
2 Sudden unprovided death (1996)
3 Scare story (1999)

HIGGINS, G. V.
JERRY KENNEDY
1 Kennedy for the defense (1980)
2 Penance for Jerry Kennedy (1985)
3 Defending Billy Ryan (1993)
4 Sandra Nicholls found dead (1996)

HIGGINS, J.
SEAN DEVLIN
1 The eagle has landed (1975)
2 Touch the devil (1983)
3 Confessional (1985)
4 The eagle has flown (1991)

HIGGINS, J.
SEAN DILLON
1 Eye of the storm (1992)
2 Thunder point (1993)
3 On dangerous ground (1994)
4 Angel of death (1995)
5 Drink with the devil (1996)
6 The President's daughter (1997)
7 The White House connection (1999)
8 Day of reckoning (2000)
9 Edge of danger (2001)
10 Midnight runner (2002)
11 In a darker place (2003)

HIGHSMITH, D.
JERRY KENNEDY
1 Leonora (1992)
2 Lukan (1993)

HIGHSMITH, DOMINI
1 Frankie (1990)
2 Mammy's boy (1991)

HIGHSMITH, DOMINI
SIMEON DE BEVERLEY
1 Keeper at the shrine (1994)
2 Guardian at the gate (1995)
3 Master of the keys (1996)

HIGHTOWER, L. S.
SONORA BLAIR
1 Flashpoint (1995)
2 Eyeshot (1996)
3 No good deed (1998)
4 The debt collector (1999)
5 Borderline (2001)

HILL, D.
APOTHEOSIS TRILOGY
1 The lightless dome (1993)
2 The leafless forest (1994)

HILL, PAMELA
1 Fenfallow (1987)
2 The Sutburys (1988)

HILL, PORTER
CAPT.ADAM HORNE
1 The Bombay Marines (1985)
2 The war chest (1986)
3 China flyer (1987)

HILL, R.
DALZIEL AND PASCOE
1 A clubbable woman (1971)
2 Fell of dark (1971)
3 An advancement of learning (1971)
4 A fairly dangerous thing (1972)
5 Ruling passion (1974)
6 An April shroud (1976)
7 A pinch of snuff (1978)
8 Pascoe's ghost and other stories (1979)
9 A killing kindness (1980)
10 Deadheads (1983)
11 Exit lines (1984)
12 Child's play (1986)
13 Under world (1988)
14 Bones and silence (1990)
15 One small step (1990)
16 Recalled to life (1992)
17 Pictures of perfection (1994)
18 The wood beyond (1996)
19 On Beulah Height (1998)
20 Arms and the woman (2000)
21 Dialogues of the dead (2001)
22 Death's jest-book (2002)
23 Good morning, midnight (2004)

HILL, R.
JOE SIXSMITH
1 Blood sympathy (1993)
2 Born guilty (1994)
3 Killing the lawyers (1997)
4 Singing the sadness (1999)

HILLERMAN, T.
JIM CHEE
1 People of darkness (1982)
2 The dark wind (1983)
3 The ghostway (1985)
4 Skinwalkers (1988)

HILLERMAN, T.
LIEUT. JOE LEAPHORN
1 The blessing way (1970)
2 The fly on the wall (1971)
3 Dance hall of the dead (1973)
4 Listening women (1979)
5 Skinwalkers (1988)

HILLERMAN, T.
LEAPHORN AND CHEE
1 A thief of time (1989)
2 Talking God (1990)
3 Coyote waits (1991)
4 Sacred clowns (1994)
5 The fallen man (1997)
6 The first eagle (1999)
7 Hunting badger (2000)

HILLIARD, N.
1 Maori girl (1960)
2 Power of joy (1965)
3 Maori woman (1974)
4 Glory and the dream (1975)

HILTON, J. B.
SGT. BRUNT
1 The quiet stranger (1985)
2 Gamekeeper's gallows (1973)
3 Rescue from the Rose (1975)
4 Dead nettle (1977)
5 Mr. Fred (1983)
6 Slickensides (1987)

HILTON, J. B.
SUPT. SIMON KENWORTHY
1 Death of an Alderman (1968)
2 Death in midwinter (1969)
3 Hangman's tide (1972)
4 No birds sang (1975)
5 Some run crooked (1977)
6 The anathema stone (1979)
7 Playground of death (1980)
8 Surrender value (1981)
9 The green frontier (1982)
10 The sunset law (1982)
11 The asking price (1983)
12 Corridors of guilt (1984)
13 The Hobbema prospect (1984)
14 Passion in the Peak (1985)
15 Moondrop to murder (1986)
16 The innocents at home (1986)
17 Displaced person (1987)

HIMES, C.
GRAVE DIGGER JONES AND COFFIN
ED JOHNSON
1 Cotton comes to Harlem (1965)

2 The heat's on (1966)
3 Run man run (1967)
4 Blind man with a pistol (1968)
5 All shot up (1969)
6 The real cool killers (1970)

HINES, J.
CIVIL WAR TRILOGY
1 The Cornish girl (1994)
2 The Puritan's wife (1996)
3 The lost daughter (1999)

HINXMAN, M.
DET. INSPECTOR RALPH BRAND
1 One way cemetery (1977)
2 Death of a good woman (1981)
3 The telephone never tells (1983)
4 The sound of murder (1986)

HOAG, T.
SAM KOVAC
1 Ashes to ashes (1999)
2 Dust to dust (2000)

HOBB, R.
FARSEER TRILOGY
1 The assassin's apprentice (1995)
2 Royal assassin (1996)
3 Assassin's quest (1997)

HOBB, R.
THE LIVESHIP TRADERS
1 Ship of magic (1998)
3 Ship of destiny (2000)

HOBB, R.
THE TAWNY MAN
1 Fool's errand (2002)
2 The golden fool (2002)
3 Fool's fate (2003)

HOCKE, M.
1 The ancient solitary reign (1989)
2 The lost domain (1993)

HOCKEN, E.
1 Emma and I (1977)
2 Emma VIP (1980)
3 Emma and Co. (1983)
4 After Emma (1988)
 NF life with a guide dog

HOCKING, M.
FAIRLEYS
1 Good daughters (1984)

2 Indifferent heroes (1985)
3 Welcome strangers (1986)

HODGE, J. A.
PURCHIS FAMILY
1 Judas flowering (1979)
2 Wide is the water (1981)
3 Savannah Purchase (1971)
4 Runaway bride (1977)

HODGE, J. A.
LISTENBURG
1 Last act (1979)
2 First night (1989)
3 Leading lady (1990)

HODGSON, H.
STILLION STONE
1 Six feet under (2000)
2 Exhumed innocent (2002)

HOFF, B. J.
EMERALD BALLAD
1 Song of the silent harp (1991)
2 Heart of the lonely exile (1992)
3 Land of a thousand dreams (1993)
4 Sons of an ancient glory (1993)

HOGAN, J. P.
GIANTS
1 Inherit the stars
2 The gentle giants of Ganymede
3 Giants' star

HOGGART, R.
1 A local habitation (1918-40) (1988)
2 A sort of clowning (1940-59) (1990)
3 An imagined life (1992)
 NF Autobiography

HOLBROOK, D.
PAUL GRIMMER
1 Flesh wounds (1966)
2 A play of passion (1978)
3 Nothing larger than life (1987)
4 A little Athens (1990)
5 The gold in Father's heart (1992)

HOLDEN, U.
1 Tin toys (1986)
2 The unicorn sisters (1988)

HOLDSTOCK, R.
MYTHAGO
1 Mythago Wood (1985)
2 Lavondyss (1988)

3 The bore forest (1991)
4 The hollowing (1993)
5 Merlin's wood (1994)

HOLLAND, I.
ST.ANSELM'S
1 Death at St.Anselm's (1985)
2 Bump in the night (1989)
3 Thief (1989)
4 A fatal Advent (1991)
5 The long search (1991)

HOLLICK, H.
1 Pendragon's banner (1994)
2 The kingmaking (1994)
3 Shadow of the king (1997)

HOLME, T.
INSPECTOR ACHILLE PERONI
1 The Neapolitan streak (1980)
2 A funeral of gondolas (1981)
3 The devil and the dolce vita (1982)
4 The Assisi murders (1985)
5 At the lake of sudden death (1987)

HOLMS, J.
FIZZ AND BUCHANAN
1 Payment deferred (1996)
2 Foreign body (1997)
3 Bad vibes (1998)
4 Thin ice (1999)
5 Mr. Big (2000)
6 Bitter end (2001)
7 Hot potato (2003)

HOLROYD, M.
GEORGE BERNARD SHAW
1 The search for love (1988)
2 The pursuit of power (1988)
3 The lure of fantasy (1991)
4 The last laugh (1992)
   NF Biography

HOLT, H.
SHEILA MALLORY
1 Gone away (1990)
2 The cruellest month (1991)
3 The shortest journey (1992)
4 Uncertain death (1993)
5 Murder on campus (1994)
6 Superfluous death (1995)
7 Death of a Dean (1996)
8 The only good lawyer (1997)
9 Dead and buried (1998)
10 The fatal legacy (1999)
11 Lilies that fester (2000)
12 Delay of execution (2001)

13 Leonora (2002)
14 Death in practice (2003)
15 The silent killer (2004)

HOLT, T.
THE WALLED ORCHARD
1 Goatsong (1989)
2 The walled orchard (1990)

HOLT, T.
HEAVEN, INC.
1 Grailblazers (1993)
2 Faust among equals (1994)
3 Odds and gods (1995)

HOLT, T.
PAUL CARPENTER
1 The portable door (2003)
2 In your dreams (2004)

HOLZER, H.
AMITYVILLE
1 Murder in Amityville (1980)
2 The Amityville curse (1981)
3 The secret of Amityville (1985)

HOOD, E.
1 A stranger in the town (1985)
2 Silver bells, white linen (1988)

HORANSKY, R.
NIKKI TRAKOS
1 Dead ahead (1992)
2 Dead centre (1993)

HORNIG, D.
LOREN SWIFT
1 Hardball (1986)
2 The dark side (1987)

HORST, K.
1 Sink the Ark Royal (1981)
2 Caribbean pirate (1982)

HORWOOD, W.
DUNCTON CHRONICLES
1 Duncton Wood (1980)
2 Duncton quest (1988)
3 Duncton found (1989)
4 Duncton tales (1991)
5 Duncton rising (1992)
6 Duncton stone (1993)

HORWOOD, W.
WOLVES OF TIME
1 Journeys to the heartland (1995)
2 Seekers at the Wulfrock (1997)

HOUGH, R.
BULLER
1 Buller's guns (1981)
2 Buller's dreadnought (1982)
3 Buller's victory (1984)

HOUSEHOLD, G.
1 Rogue male (1939)
2 Rogue justice (1982)

HOUSEHOLD, G.
ROGER TAINE
1 Rough shoot (1951)
2 Time to kill (1952)

HOUSEMAN, J.
1 Run-through (1973)
2 Front and centre (1979)
3 Final dress (1983)
   NF Autobiography

HOWARD, A.
CHAPMAN FAMILY
1 The mallow years (1990)
2 Shining threads (1991)
3 Strand of dreams (1997)

HOWARD, A.
OSBORNE FAMILY
1 Ambitions (1986)
2 All the dear faces (1992)
3 There is no parting (1993)

HOWARD, E. J.
CAZALET CHRONICLES
1 Light years (1990)
2 Marking time (1991)
3 Confusion (1993)
4 Casting off (1995)

HOWARD, L.
FYTTON OF GAWSWORTH
1 Elizabeth Fytton of Gawsworth Hall (1985)
2 The master of Littlecote Manor (1986)
3 The squire of Holdenby (1986)
4 Isabel the girl (1989)
5 Isabel the woman (1990)

HOWARD, R. E.
CONAN
1 Conan
2 Conan the usurper, by L.Sprague de Camp
3 Conan the wanderer, by L.Sprague de Camp
4 Conan the conqueror
5 Conan the adventurer
6 Conan the avenger
7 Conan of the Isles, by L.Sprague de Camp
8 Conan the warrior
9 Conan the buccaneer, by L.Sprague de Camp
10 Conan of Cimmeria, by L.Sprague de Camp
11 Conan the freebooter
12 Conan of Aquilonia, by L.Sprague de camp
13 Conan the swordsman, byL.Sprague de Camp
14 Conan the liberator, by A.J.Offut
15 Conan the mercenary, by A.J.Offut
16 The sword of Skelos, by A.J.Offut
17 The road of kings, by K.E.Wagner
18 Conan and the spider god, by L.Sprague de Camp
19 Conan the rebel, by P.Anderson
20 Conan the invincible, by R.Jordan
21 Conan the defender, by R.Jordan
22 Conan the unconquered, by R.Jordan
23 Conan the triumphant, by R.Jordan
24 Conan the barbarian, by R.Jordan
25 Conan the magnificent, by R.Jordan
26 Conan the victorious, by R.Jordan
27 Conan the valorous, by J.M.Roberts
28 Conan the champion, by J.M.Roberts
29 Conan the fearless, by S.Perry

HOWARD, RICHARD
NAPOLEONIC WARS
1 Bonaparte's sons (1997)
2 Bonaparte's invaders (1998)
3 Bonaparte's conqueror (1999)
4 Bonaparte's warriors (2000)
5 Bonaparte's avengers (2001)
6 Bonaparte's horsemen (2002)

HOWATCH, SUSAN
CHURCH OF ENGLAND SERIES
1 Glittering images (1987)
2 Glamorous powers (1988)
3 Ultimate prizes (1989)
4 Scandalous risks (1990)
5 Mystical paths (1992)
6 Absolute truths (1994)

HOWELL, L.
KATE WILKINSON
1 After the break (1995)
2 The director's cut (1996)
3 A job to die for (1997)

HOWELLS, B.
MAY AND OTLEY
1 Wuthering depths (1990)
2 Silver riding (1991)
3 Dandelion days (1991)

HOYT, R.
JOHN DENSON
1 Decoy
2 30 for a Harry (1982)
3 Fish story (1987)

HUBBARD, L. R.
MISSION EARTH
1 The invaders plan (1986)
2 Black genesis (1986)
3 The enemy within (1987)
4 An alien affair (1987)
5 Fortune of fear (1987)
6 Death quest (1987)
7 Voyage of vengeance (1988)
8 Disaster (1988)
9 Villainy victorious (1988)
10 The doomed planet (1988)

HUDSON, J. F.
JUDEA
1 Rabshakah (1993)
2 Zoheleth (1994)

HUGHART, B.
1 Bridge of birds (1989)
2 The story of the stone (1989)
3 Eight skilled gentlemen (1991)

HUGHES, G.
GEORGE WILLIS
1 Split on red (1980)
2 Cover zero (1981)
3 The French deal (1982)

HUGHES, GLYN
1 The hawthorn goddess (1986)
2 The rape of the rose (1987)

HUGHES, R. D.
PELMAN THE POWERSHAPER
1 The prophet of Lamath
2 The wizard in waiting

HUGHESDON, B.
1 Roses have thorns (1993)
2 Silver fountains (1994)

HUGO, V.
LES MISERABLES
1 Les Miserables (1862)
2 Cosette, by L.Kalpakian (1996)

HULME, A.
1 The flying man (1988)
2 Whisper in the wind (1989)

HUMMER, G. B.
WHITMORE FAMILY
2 West of the sun (1994)
3 Red branch (1993)

HUMPHREYS, E.
1 Flesh and blood (1974)
2 The best of friends (1978)
3 Salt of the earth (1985)
4 An absolute hero (1986)
5 Open secrets (1988)
6 Bonds of attachment (1991)

HUNT, R.
DET. CHIEF INSPECTOR SYDNEY WALSH
1 Death in ruins (1991)
2 Death sounds grand (1991)
3 Death of a merry widow (1992)
4 Deadlocked (1994)
5 Murder benign (1995)
6 A cure for killers (1995)
7 The man trap (1997)
8 A ring of vultures (1998)
9 Dead men's shoes (1999)

HUNTER, A.
SUPT. GEORGE GENTLY
1 Gently does it (1955)
2 Gently by the shore (1956)
3 Gently down the stream (1957)
4 Landed Gently (1958)
5 Gently through the mill (1958)
6 Gently in the sun (1959)
7 Gently with the painters (1960)
8 Gently to the summit (1960)
9 Gently go man (1961)
10 Gently where the roads go (1962)
11 Gently floating (1963)
12 Gently Sahib (1964)
13 Gently with the ladies (1965)
14 Gently northwest (1966)
15 Gently continental (1968)
16 Gently coloured (1969)

17 Gently with the innocents (1970)
18 Gently at a gallop (1971)
19 Vivienne:Gently where she lay (1972)
20 Gently French (1973)
21 Gently in trees (1974)
22 Gently with love (1975)
23 Gently where the birds are (1976)
24 Gently instrumental (1977)
25 Gently to a sleep (1978)
26 The Honfleur decision (1980)
27 Gabrielle's way (1981)
28 Fields of heather (1981)
29 Gently between the tides (1982)
30 Amorous Leander (1983)
31 The unhung man (1983)
32 Once a prostitute... (1984)
33 The Chelsea ghost (1985)
34 Goodnight, sweet prince (1986)
35 Strangling man (1987)
36 Traitor's end (1988)
37 Gently with the millions (1989)
38 Gently scandalous (1990)
39 Gently to a kill (1991)
40 Gently tragic (1992)
41 Gently in the glens (1993)
42 Bomber's moon (1994)
43 Jackpot (1995)
44 The love of gods (1997)
45 Over here (1998)
46 Gently mistaken (1999)

HUNTER, C.
1 Fiercely the tempest (1984)
2 Island of stone (1982)

HUNTER, J. D.
BRUNO STACHEL
1 The blue Max (1965)
2 Blood order (1980)
3 The tin cravat (1981)

HUNTER, R.
SIMON QUARRY
1 The fourth angel (1986)
2 Quarry's contract (1987)

HUNTER, S.
BOB LEE SWAGGER
1 Point of impact (1997)
2 Time to hunt (1998)
3 Black light (1995)

HURLEY, G.
JOE FARADAY
1 The take (2001)
2 Angels passing (2002)

HUTSON, S.
1 Slugs (1984)
2 Breeding ground (1985)

HUTSON, S.
SGT. ROLF KESSLER
1 No survivors (1985)
2 Sledgehammer (1981)
3 Kessler's raid (1982)
4 Convoy of steel (1982)
5 Slaughterhouse (1983)
6 Men of blood (1984)
7 Taken by force (1987)

HUXLEY, E.
1 The flame trees of Thika (1959)
2 The mottled lizard (1962)
3 Love among the daughters (1968)
4 Out in the midday sun (1985)
   NF Life in Kenya

IBARGUENGOITIA, J.
1 Two dead girls (1983)
2 Two crimes (1984)

IGGULDEN, C.
EMPEROR
1 The gates of Rome (2003)
2 The death of King (2004)

INCHBALD, P.
INSPECTOR FRANCO CORTI
1 Tondo for Short (1981)
2 The sweet short grass (1982)
3 Short break in Venice (1983)
4 Or the bambino dies (1985)

INFANTE, A.
MICKEY DOUGLAS
1 Death on a hot summer night (1989)
2 Death among the dunes (1990)
3 Deathwater (1991)
4 Death in green (1992)
5 Death launch (1993)

INNES, B.
1 The Red Baron lives (1982)
2 The red Red Baron (1983)

INNES, H.
IAIN WARD AND PETER KETTIL
1 Isvik (1991)
2 Target Antarctica (1993)

INNES, M.
SIR JOHN APPLEBY
1 Death at the President's lodging (1936)
2 Hamlet, revenge! (1937)
3 Lament for a maker (1938)
4 Stop press (1939)
5 There came both mist and snow (1940)
6 The secret vanguard (1940)
7 Appleby on Ararat (1941)
8 The daffodil affair (1942)
9 The weight of the evidence (1944)
10 Appleby's end (1945)
11 From London far (1946)
12 What happened at Hazelwood (1947)
13 A night of errors (1948)
14 Operation Pax (1951)
15 A private view (1952)
16 Appleby talking (1954)
17 Appleby talks again (1956)
18 Appleby plays chicken (1956)
19 The long farewell (1958)
20 Hare sitting up (1959)
21 Silence observed (1961)
22 A connoisseur's case (1962)
23 Money from Holme (1964)
24 The bloody wood (1966)
25 A change of heir (1966)
26 Appleby at Allington (1968)
27 A family affair (1969)
28 Death at the chase (1970)
29 An awkward lie (1971)
30 The open house (1972)
31 Appleby's answer (1973)
32 Appleby's other story (1974)
33 The Appleby file (1975)
34 The gay phoenix (1976)
35 The Ampersand papers (1978)
36 Sheiks and adders (1982)
37 Appleby and Honeybath (1983)
38 Carson's conspiracy (1984)
39 Appleby and the Ospreys (1986)

INNES, M.
HONEYBATH
1 The mysterious commission (1974)
2 Honeybath's haven (1977)
3 Lord Mullion's secret (1981)
4 Appleby and Honeybath (1983)

IRISH, L.
COLONIAL TRILOGY
1 And the wild birds sing (1984)
2 The place of the swan (1986)
3 The house of O'Shea (1990)

IRVINE, I.
THE VIEW FROM THE MIRROR
1 A shadow on the glass

2 The tower on the rift
3 Dark is the moon
4 The way between the worlds

IRVINE, I.
THE WELL OF ECHOES
1 Geomancer (2002)
2 Tetrarch (2003)

IRVINE, L.
1 Runaway (1986)
2 Castaway (1983)
   NF Autobiography

ISHERWOOD, C.
SALLY BOWLES
1 Goodbye to Berlin
2 After the cabaret, by H.Bailey (1998)

ISON, G.
DET. CHIEF SUPT. JOHN GAFFNEY
1 Cold light of dawn (1988)
2 Confirm or deny (1989)
3 A damned serious business (1990)

ISON, G.
DET. CHIEF SUPT. TOMMY FOX
1 The Home Secretary will see you now (1989)
2 Lead me to the slaughter (1990)
3 Tomfoolery (1992)
4 The taming of Tango Harris (1993)
5 Underneath the arches (1994)
6 Rough diamonds (1995)
7 Blue murder (1996)

JACK, D.
THE JOURNALS OF BARTHOLOMEW DANDY
1 Three cheers for me (1973)
2 That's me in the middle (1974)
3 It's me again
4 Me Dandy, you Cissie
5 Me too (1984)
6 Hitler versus me (1997)

JACKSON, A.
1 Tales from a country practice (1986)
2 More tales from a country practice (1987)

JACKSON, B
AIR DETECTIVE
1 Crooked flight (1985)
2 Spy's flight (1986)
3 Terror flight (1988)

JACKSON, J. A.
DET. SGT. FANG MULHEISEN
1 Hit on the house (2000)
2 Dead folks (2001)
3 La Donna Detroit (2002)

JACKSON, R.
HURRICANE SQUADRON
1 Yeoman goes to war (1978)
2 Squadron scramble (1978)
3 Target Tobruk (1979)
4 Malta victory (1980)
5 Mosquito squadron (1981)
6 Operation diver (1981)
7 Tempest squadron (1981)
8 The last battle (1982)
9 Operation Firedog (1982)
10 Korean combat (1983)
11 Venom squadron (1983)
12 Hunter squadron (1984)

JACKSON, R.
SAS
1 Desert Commando (1986)
2 Partisan! (1987)
3 Attack at night (1988)
4 Wind of death (1990)
5 The last secret (1991)

JACKSON, R.
THE SECRET SQUADRON
1 The intruders (1997)
2 Desert combat (1998)
3 The rising sun (1999)

JACOBS, A.
GIBSON AND HALLAM FAMILIES
1 Salem Street (1994)
2 High Street (1994)
3 Ridge Hill (1995)
4 Hallam Square (1996)
5 Spinner's Lake (1997)

JACOBY, K.
ELITA
1 Exile's return (1998)
2 Voice of the demon (1999)
3 Black eagle rising (2000)
4 The rebel's cage (2001)
5 Trial of fire (2002)

JACQ, C.
STONE OF LIGHT
1 The wise woman (1999)
2 Nefer the silent (2000)
3 Paneb the ardent (2000)
4 The place of truth (2001)

JACQ, C.
RAMSES
1 The son of the light (1997)
2 The temple of a million years (1998)
3 The battle of Kadesh (1998)
4 The lady of Abu Simbel (1998)
5 Under the Western acacia (1999)

JACQ, C.
QUEEN OF FREEDOM
1 The Empire of darkness (2002)
2 The war of the crowns (2003)
3 The flaming sword (2003)

JACQ, C.
PAZAIR
1 Beneath the pyramid (2004)
2 Shadow of the Sphinx (2004)

JAFFE, R.
1 Class reunion
2 After the reunion (1985)

JAGGER, B.
BARFORTH FAMILY
1 The clouded hills (1980)
2 Flint and roses (1981)
3 The sleeping sword (1982)

JAKEMAN, J.
LORD AMBROSE
1 Let there be blood (1997)
2 The Egyptian coffin (1997)
3 Fool's gold (1999)

JAKES, J.
1 North and South (1983)
2 Love and war (1985)
3 Heaven and hell (1987)

JAKES, J.
BRAK THE BARBARIAN
1 Brak the barbarian
2 The sorcerers
3 The mark of the demons

JAKES, J.
KENT FAMILY CHRONICLES
1 The bastard
2 The rebels
3 The seekers
4 The warriors
5 The titans (1990)
6 The furies (1990)
7 Lawless (1990)
8 Americans (1990)

JAMES, B.
DET. CHIEF SUPT. COLIN HARPUR
1 You'd better believe it (1985)
2 The Lolita man (1986)
3 Halo parade (1987)
4 Protection (1988)
5 Come clean (1989)
6 Take (1990)
7 Club (1991)
8 Astride a grave (1991)
9 Gospel (1992)
10 Roses, roses (1993)
11 In good hands (1994)
12 The detective is dead (1995)
13 Top banana (1996)
14 Panicking Ralph (1997)
15 Lovely mover (1998)
16 Eton crop (1999)
17 Kill me (2000)
18 Pay days (2001)
19 Naked at the window (2002)
20 The girl with the long back (2003)

JAMES, B.
BRITISH INTELLIGENCE
1 Split (2002)
2 A man's enemies (2003)

JAMES, D.
CONSTANTIN VADIM
1 Monstrum (1998)
2 The fortune teller (1999)

JAMES, E.
1 Life class (1990)
2 Life lines (1991)

JAMES, E.
HULME WELFORD
1 A breath of fresh air (1996)
2 Time for a change (1997)
3 Lovers and friends (1999)

JAMES, HENRY
1 The turn of the screw (1924)
2 Miles and Flora, by H.Bailey (1997)

JAMES, L. D.
RED KINGS OF WYNNAMYR
1 Sorcerer's stone
2 Kingslayer
3 Book of stones

JAMES, M.
LAWRENCE FAMILY
1 A touch of earth (1988)

2 Fortune's favourite child (1989)
3 The treasures of existence (1989)

JAMES, MARGARET
1 A green bay tree (1994)
2 The ash grove (1995)

JAMES, P. D.
CORDELIA GRAY
1 An unsuitable job for a woman (1972)
2 The skull beneath the skin (1982)

JAMES, P. D.
SUPT. ADAM DALGLEISH
1 Cover her face (1962)
2 A mind to murder (1963)
3 Unnatural causes (1963)
4 Shroud for a nightingale (1971)
5 The black tower (1975)
6 Death of an expert witness (1977)
7 A taste for death (1985)
8 Devices and desires (1989)
9 Original sin (1994)
10 A certain justice (1997)
11 Death in holy orders (2000)
12 The murder room (2003)

JAMES, PETER
MAX FLYNN
1 Dead letter drop (1981)
2 Atom bomb angel (1982)

JAMES, W.
SUNFALL TRILOGY
1 The earth is the Lord's (1991)
2 The other side of heaven (1992)
3 Before the sun falls (1993)

JAMESON, D.
1 Touched by angels (1989)
2 Last of the hot metal men (1990)
NF Autobiography

JANCE, J. A.
DET. J. P. BEAUMONT
1 Until proven guilty
2 Injustice for all
3 Trial by fury
4 Taking the fifth
5 Improbable cause
6 A more perfect union
7 Dismissed with prejudice (1989)
8 Birds of prey
9 Payment in kind (2003)

JANCE, J. A.
JOANNE BRADY
1 Shoot don't shoot
2 Tombstone courage
3 Devil's claw (2001)
4 Paradise lost (2002)
5 Partner in crime (2002)

JANES, J. R.
JEAN-LOUIS ST.CYR AND HERMANN KOHLER
1 Mayhem (1991)
2 Carousel (1992)
3 Kaleidoscope (1993)
4 Salamander (1994)
5 Mannequin (1994)
6 Dollmaker (1995)
7 Stonekiller (1995)
8 Sandman (1996)
9 Gypsy (1997)
10 Madrigal (1998)
11 Beekeeper (2001)
12 Flykiller (2002)

JANES, P, N,
GALAXY GAME
1 Galaxy game (1993)
2 Fission impossible (1993)
3 I, Arnold (1995)

JARDINE, Q.
OZ BLACKSTONE
1 Blackstone's pursuits (1995)
2 A coffin for two (1997)
3 Wearing purple (1999)
4 Screen savers (2000)
5 On honeymoon with death (2001)
6 Poisoned cherries (2002)
7 Unnatural justice (2003)

JARDINE, Q.
ASST.CHIEF CONSTABLE BOB SKINNER
1 Skinner's rules (1993)
2 Skinner's festival (1994)
3 Skinner's trail (1994)
4 Skinner's round (1995)
5 Skinner's ordeal (1996)
6 Skinner's mission (1997)
7 Skinner's ghosts (1998)
8 Murmuring the judges (1999)
9 Gallery whispers (1999)
10 Thursday legends (2000)
11 Autographs in the rain (2001)
12 Head shot (2002)
13 Fallen gods (2003)

JARMAN, R. H.
RICHARD III
1 We speak no treason (1970)
2 The King's grey mare (1972)
3 The courts of illusion (1983)

JECKS, M.
SIR BALDWIN FURNSHILL
1 The last Templar (1995)
2 The merchant's partner (1995)
3 Moorland hanging (1996)
4 The Crediton killings (1997)
5 The abbot's gibbet (1998)
6 The leper's return (1999)
7 Squire Throwleigh's heir (1999)
8 Bellsdonna at Belstone (1999)
9 The boy bishop's glovemaker (2000)
9 The traitor of St.Giles (2000)
10 The tournament of blood (2001)
11 The sticklepath stranger (2001)
12 The devil's acolyte (2002)
13 The mad monk of Gidleigh (2002)
14 The templar's penance (2003)
15 The outlaws of Ennor (2004)
16 The tolls of death (2004)

JEFFREY, E.
CHISWELL FAMILY
1 Stranger's Hall (1988)
2 Gin and gingerbread (1989)

JEFFRIES, M.
THE HEIRS TO GNARLSMYRE
1 Glitterspike Hall
2 Hall of whispers

JEFFRIES, M.
LOREMASTERS OF ELUNDIUM
1 The road to Underfall (1987)
2 Palace of kings (1988)
3 Shadowlight (1989)

JEFFRIES, R.
INSPECTOR ALVAREZ
1 Mistakenly in Mallorca (1973)
2 Two-faced death (1975)
3 Troubled deaths (1977)
4 Murder begets murder (1979)
5 Just desserts (1980)
6 Unseemly end (1981)
7 Deadly petard (1983)
8 Three and one make five (1984)
9 Layers of deceit (1985)
10 Almost murder (1986)
11 Relatively dangerous (1987)
12 Death trick (1988)
13 Dead clever (1989)

14 Too clever by half (1990)
15 Murder's long memory (1991)
16 A fatal fleece (1992)
17 Murder confounded (1993)
18 Death takes time (1994)
19 An Arcadian death (1995)
20 An artistic way to go (1996)
21 A maze of murders (1997)
22 An enigmatic disappearance (1998)
23 The ambiguity of murder (1999)
24 An awful death (2000)
25 Definitely deceased (2001)
26 Seeing is deceiving (2002)
27 An intriguing murder (2002)
28 An air of murder (2003)

JEN, G.
1 Typical American
2 Mona in the promised land

JETER, K. W.
1 Dr. Adder
2 The glass hammer
3 Death arms (1987)

JOHNSON, B.
COLLEEN FITZGERALD
1 The beach affair (1997)
2 Bad moon rising (1998)

JOHNSON, O.
THE LIGHTBRINGER TRILOGY
1 The forging of the shadows (1996)
2 The nations of the night (1999)

JOHNSON, P. H.
1 The good listener (1975)
2 The good husband (1978)

JOHNSTON, B.
1 It's been a lot of fun (1976)
2 It's a funny game (1976)
3 It's been a piece of cake (1989)
   NF Cricketing reminiscences

JOHNSTON, P.
QUINT DALRYMPLE
1 The body politic (1997)
2 The bone yard (1998)
3 Water of death (1999)
4 The blood tree (2000)
5 The house of dust (2001)

JOHNSTONE, W. M.
HALLOWEEN HORROR
1 The devil's kiss

2 The devil's heart
3 The devil's touch
4 The devil's cat
5 Cat's cradle
6 Cat's eye

JOLLEY, E.
1 My father's moon (1989)
2 Cabin fever (1991)

JON, M.
STEVEN KALE
1 The Wallington case (1981)
2 Chuck reducks (1996)

JONES, D. W.
DALEMARK
1 Cart and Cwidder
2 Drowned Annet
3 Spellcoats
4 Crown of Dalemark

JONES, ELWYN
CHIEF INSPECTOR BARLOW
1 Barlow (1972)
2 Barlow in charge (1973)
3 Barlow comes to judgment (1974)
4 The Barlow casebook (1975)
5 Barlow exposed (1976)
6 Barlow down under (1978)

JONES, G.
1 Lord of misrule (1983)
2 Noble savage (1985)

JONES, GWYNETH
ALEUTIAN SEQUENCE
1 White queen (1991)
2 North wind (1994)
3 Phoenix Cafe (1997)

JONES, GWYNETH
AX
1 Bold as love (2001)
2 Castles made of sand (2002)
3 Midnight lamp (2003)

JONES, H. W.
EMMA SHAW
1 Death and the trumpets of Tuscany
   (1988)
2 Shot on location (1990)

JONES, I. H.
1 Sister (1987)
2 Senior sister (1988)

JONES, J. V.
THE BOOK OF WORDS
1 The baker's boy (1995)
2 A man betrayed (1996)
3 Master and fool (1997)

JONES, J. V.
SWORD OF SHADOWS
1 A cavern of black ice (1999)
2 A fortress of grey ice (2001)
3 A sword from red ice (2003)

JONES, JENNY
FLIGHT OVER FIRE
1 Fly by night (1990)
2 The edge of vengeance (1991)
3 Lies and flames (1992)

JONES, R. W.
INSPECTOR EVANS & SGT. BEDDOES
1 Saving Grace (1986)
2 Cop out (1987)
3 The green reapers (1988)

JONES, T.
1 A steady trade (1982)
2 Heart of oak (1984)
3 The incredible voyage (1977)
4 Ice (1979)
5 Saga of a wayward sailor (1980)
6 Adrift (1981)
7 A star to steer her by (1985)
8 The improbable voyage (1986)
   NF Autobiogrpahy of a sailor

JONES, TANYA
OPHELIA O.
1 Ophelia O. and the mortgage bandits (1995)
2 Ophelia O. and the ante-natal mysteries (1995)
3 Trotter's bottom (1997)

JONG, E.
ISADORA WING
1 Fear of flying (1975)
2 How to save your own life (1977)
3 Parachutes and kisses (1985)

JORDAN, J.
THE VAUGHANS
1 A good weekend for murder (1987)
2 Murder under the mistletoe (1988)

JORDAN, R.
THE WHEEL OF TIME
1 Eye of the world (1990)
2 The great hunt (1991)
3 The dragon reborn (1992)
4 The shadow rising (1992)
5 The fires of heaven (1993)
6 Lord of chaos (1994)
7 A crown of swords (1996)
8 The path of daggers (1998)
9 Winter's heart (2000)
10 Crossroads of twilight (2002)

JOSEPH, A.
SISTER AGNES
1 Sacred hearts (1994)
2 The hour of our death (1995)
3 The quick and the dead (1996)
4 A dark and sinful death (1997)
5 The dying light (1999)
6 The night watch (2000)

JOSEPH, M.
DAISY PENNY
1 A better world than this (1987)
2 A world apart (1988)

JOSS, M.
SARA SELKIRK
1 Funeral music (1998)
2 Fearful symmetry (1999)
3 Fruitful bodies (2001)

JOYCE, C.
GREG ALLARD
1 Errant witness (1981)
2 Errant target (1982)
3 Errant ssleuth (1983)

JOYCE, C.
INSPECTOR PAT STOCKTON
1 Run a golden mile (1978)
2 Sentence suspended (1979)
3 A hitch in time (1980)
4 Death of a left-handed woman (1980)
5 Calculated risk (1981)
6 A bullet for Betty (1981)
7 From the grave to the cradle (1982)
8 Murder is a pendulum (1983)

JUDD, B.
FORREST EVERS
1 Formula one (1989)
2 Indy (1990)
3 Monza (1991)
4 Phoenix (1992)
5 Silverstone (1993)

KAHN, J.
NEW WORLD TRILOGY
1 World enough and time
2 Time

KAKONIS, T.
WAVERLEY
1 Michigan role (1991)
2 Double down (1992)

KALLEN, L.
C.B.GREENFIELD
1 Introducing C.B. Greenfield (1979)
2 C.B.Greenfield and the tanglewood
  murder (1980)
3 C.B.Greenfield:lady in the house (1982)
4 C.B.Greenfield:the piano bird (1984)
5 A little madness (1986)

KALMAN, Y.
YARDLEY FAMILY
1 Greenstone land (1982)
2 Juliette
3 Riversong (1985)

KALMAN, Y.
MORGAN AND RENNIE FAMILIES
1 Mists of heaven (1988)
2 After the rainbow (1989)

KALOGRIDIS, J.
DRACUL TRILOGY
1 Covenant with the vampire (1994)
2 Children of the vampire (1995)
3 Lord of the vampires (1996)

KAMADA, A.
1 A love so bold (1980)
2 Richer than a crown (1981)

KAMINSKY, S. M.
INSPECTOR PORFIRY ROSTNIKOV
1 Rostnikov's corpse (1981)
2 Black Knight in Red Square (1988)
3 Cold red sunrise (1990)
4 The man who walked like a bear (1991)
5 Fall of a cosmonaut (2000)
6 Murder on the Trans-Siberian Express
  (2002)

KAMINSKY, S. M.
TOBY PETERS
1 The Howard Hughes affair (1980)
2 Bullet for a star (1981)
3 Murder on the Yellow Brick Road (1981)
4 High midnight (1982)

5 Buried Caesars (1990)
6 The devil met a lady (1993)
7 Tomorrow is another day (1996)
8 Dancing in the dark (1997)
9 A few minutes past midnight (2002)
10 To catch a spy (2003)

KAPP, C.
CAGEWORLD
1 Search for the sun
2 The lost world of Cronos
3 The tyrant of Hades
4 Star search

KAPP, Y.
ELEANOR MARX
1 Family life (1972)
2 The crowded years (1976)

KARON, J.
MITFORD
1 At home in Mitford (1995)
2 A light in the window (1996)
3 These high, green hills (1996)

KARTUN, D.
ALFRED BAUM
1 Beaver to fox (1983)
2 Flittermouse (1984)
3 Megiddo (1987)
4 Safe house (1989)

KAUFMAN, P.
1 Shield of three lions (1986)
2 Banners of gold (1987)

KAVA, A.
MAGGIE O'DELL
1 A perfect evil (2001)
2 Split second (2002)

KAVANAGH, D.
DUFFY
1 Duffy (1980)
2 Fiddle City (1981)
3 Putting the boot in (1985)
4 Going to the dogs (1987)

KAVANAGH, P. J.
1 Perfect stranger (1966)
2 Finding connections (1990)

KAY, G. G.
THE FIONAVAR TAPESTRY
1 The summer tree (1985)

2 The wandering fire (1986)
3 The darkest road (1987)

KAY, G. G.
THE SARANTINE MOSAIC
1 Sailing to Sarantium (1998)
2 Lord of Emperors (2000)

KAZAN, E.
1 America, America (1969)
2 The Anatolian (1983)

KEARNEY, P.
THE MONARCHIES OF GOD
1 Hawkwood's voyage (1995)
2 The heretic kings (1996)
3 The iron wars (1999)
4 The second empire (2000)
5 Ships from the west (2001)

KEAST, F.
DARRYL KRUSTOV
1 Sunburst
2 Cloudburst (1986)

KEATING, H. R. F.
INSPECTOR GHOTE
1 The perfect murder (1964)
2 Inspector Ghote's good crusade (1966)
3 Inspector Ghote caught in meshes (1967)
4 Inspector Ghote hunts the peacock (1968)
5 Inspector Ghote plays a joker (1969)
6 Inspector Ghote breaks an egg (1970)
7 Inspector Ghote goes by train (1971)
8 Inspector Ghote trusts the heart (1972)
9 Bats fly up for Inspector Ghote (1974)
10 Filmi, filmi Inspector Ghote (1976)
11 Inspector Ghote draws a line (1979)
12 Go West, Inspector Ghote (1981)
13 The Sherriff of Bombay (1984)
14 Under a monsoon cloud (1986)
15 The body in the billiard room (1987)
16 Dead on time (1988)
17 The iciest sin (1990)
19 Cheating death (1992)
20 Doing wrong (1994)
21 Asking questions (1996)
22 Bribery, corruption also (1999)
23 Breaking and entering (2000)

KEATING, H. R. F.
DET. CHIEF INSPECTOR PHIL BENHOLME
1 The rich detective (1994)
2 The good detective (1995)

3 The bad detective (1996)
4 The soft detective (1997)

KEATING, H. R. F.
DET. CHIEF INSPECTOR HARRIET MARTINEAU
1 The hard detective (2000)
2 A detective in love (2001)
3 A detective under fire (2002)
4 The dreaming detective (2003)

KEILLOR, G.
LAKE WOBEGONE
1 Lake Woebegone days (1986)
2 Leaving home (1988)
3 Wobegon boy (1998)
4 Wobegon summer (2000)

KEITH, W. H.
INVADERS OF CHARON
1 The genesis web
2 Nomads of the sky
3 Warlords of Jupiter

KELLERMAN, F.
SGT. PETE DECKER
1 Ritual bath (1987)
2 Sacred and profane (1989)
3 The quality of mercy (1989)
4 Day of atonement (1991)
5 False prophet (1992)
6 Grievous sin (1993)
7 Sanctuary (1994)
8 Justice (1995)
9 Prayers for the dead (1996)
10 Serpent's tooth (1997)
11 Jupiter's bones (1999)
12 Stalker (2000)
13 The forgotten (2001)
14 Stone kiss (2002)
15 Street dreams (2003)

KELLERMAN, J.
ALEX DELAWARE
1 Shrunken heads (1985)
2 Blood test (1985)
3 The butcher's theatre (1988)
4 Silent partner (1989)
5 Time bomb (1990)
6 Private eyes (1991)
7 Devil's waltz (1992)
8 Bad love (1993)
9 Self defence (1994)
10 The web (1995)
11 The clinic (1996)
12 Survival of the fittest (1997)
13 Monster (1998)

14 Doctor Death (2000)
15 Flesh and blood (2001)

KELLEY, L. P.
LUKE SUTTON
1 Outlaw (1981)
2 Gunfighter (1982)
3 Indian fighter (1983)
4 Avenger (1984)
5 Outrider (1986)
6 Bounty hunter (1991)
7 Hired gun (1991)
8 Lawman (1992)
9 Mustanger (1992)

KELLOGG, M.B. & ROSSOW, W. B.
LEAR'S DAUGHTERS
1 The wave and the flame (1987)
2 Reign of fire (1988)

KELLS, S.
LAZENDER FAMILY
1 A crowning mercy (1983)
2 The fallen angels (1984)

KELLY, N.
GILLIAN ADAMS
1 In the shadow of King's (1990)
2 My sister's keeper (1992)
3 Bad chemistry (1993)
4 Old wounds (1998)

KELLY, SHEELAGH
FEENEY FAMILY
1 A long way from heaven (1985)
2 For my brother's sins (1986)
3 Erin's child (1987)
4 Dickie (1989)

KELLY, SHEELAGH
KILMASTER FAMILY
1 A sense of duty (1999)
2 Family of the Empire (2001)

KELLY, SHEELAGH
PRINCE FAMILY
1 Shoddy prince (1995)
2 A complicated woman (1997)

KELLY, SUSAN
DET. INSPECTOR NICK TREVELYAN
1 Hope against hope (1989)
2 Time of hope (1990)
3 Hope will answer (1992)
4 Kid's stuff (1995)
5 Death is sweet (1996)

KELLY, SUSAN
DET. SUPT. GREGORY SUMMERS
1 The lone traveller (2000)
2 Killing the fatted calf (2001)
3 Little girl lost (2002)

KELLY, T.
JORDAN SAGE
1 The cut (1999)
2 The shuffle (2000)

KELNER, T. P. L.
LAURA FLEMING
1 Death of a damn Yankee (1999)
2 Mad as the Dickens (2001)

KEMP, S.
DR. TINA MAY
1 No escape (1985)
2 The lure of sweet death (1986)
3 What dread hand? (1987)

KENNEALY, P.
THE KELTIAD
1 The copper crown
2 The throne of Scone
3 The hawk's grey feather
4 The oak above the kings
5 The hedge of mist

KENNEDY, A.
BRADSHAW TRILOGY
1 No place to cry (1986)
2 The fires of summer (1987)
3 All dreams denied (1988)

KENNEDY, A.
KINCAID TRILOGY
1 Passion never knows (1990)
2 Dancing in the shadows (1991)
3 Love, come no more (1992)

KENNEDY, W.
ALBANY CYCLE
1 Legs (1975)
2 Billy Phelan's greatest game (1978)
3 Ironweed (1983)
4 Quinn's book (1988)
5 Very old bones (1992)
6 The flaming corsage (1998)

KENT, A.
RICHARD BOLITHO
1 Richard Bolitho - Midshipman (1772)
  (1970)

2 Midshipman Bolitho and the "Avenger"(1773) (1971)
3 Stand into danger (1774) (1980)
4 In gallant company (1777) (1977)
5 Sloop of war (1778) (1972)
6 To glory we steer (1782) (1967)
7 Command a King's ship (1789) (1973)
8 Passage to mutiny (1789) (1976)
9 Form line of battle (1793) (1969)
10 With all despatch (1792) (1988)
11 Enemy in sight (1794) (1970)
12 The flag captain (1795) (1971)
13 Signal - close action (1798) (1974)
14 Inshore squadron (1800) (1978)
15 A tradition of victory (1801) (1981)
16 Success to the brave (1802) (1983)
17 Colours aloft (1803) (1986)
18 Honour this day (1804-5) (1987)
19 The only victor (1806) (1990)
20 Beyond the reef (1808) (1992)
21 The darkening sea (1809-10) (1993)
21 Sword of honour (1814) (1998)
22 For my country's freedom (1811) (1995)
23 Cross of St.George (1813) (1996)
25 Second to none (1815) (1999)
26 Relentless pursuit (1818) (2001)
27 Man of war (2003)

KENWORTHY, C.
MATTHEW AND SON
1 In the dark of the moon (1981)
2 Ride a dark tide (1982)
3 A storm in the dark (1983)
4 Against a dark shore (1985)

KENYON, M.
HARRY PECKOVER
1 The rapist (1979)
2 Zigzag (1981)
3 The God squad bod (1982)
4 A free range wife (1983)
5 A healthy way to die (1986)
6 Peckover holds the baby (1988)
7 Kill the butler (1991)
8 Peckover joins the choir (1992)
9 Peckover and the bog man (1994)

KERR, K.
DEVERRY
1 Daggerspell (1987)
2 Darkspell (1988)
3 Dawnspell;the bristling wood (1989)
4 Dragonspell;the Southern sea (1990)

KERR, K.
DEVERRY-WESTLANDS CYCLE
1 A time of exile (1991)

2 A time of omens (1992)
3 A time of war;days of blood and fire (1993)
4 A time of justice; days of air and darkness (1994)

KERR, K.
THE DRAGON MAGE
1 The black raven (1999)
2 The fire dragon (2000)

KERR, P.
SPY SERIES
1 The pale criminal (1990)
2 A German requiem (1991)
3 A philosophical investigation (1992)

KERRIGAN, J.
SBS
1 Fireball (1983)
2 Bluebeard (1984)
3 Watchdog (1984)

KERRIGAN, J.
THE O SULLIVANS OF THE SAS
1 Kill Rommel (1995)
2 Surprise attack (1996)
3 Revenge! (1996)

KERSHAW, V.
MITCH MITCHELL
1 Murder is too expensive (1993)
2 Funny money (1994)
3 Late knights (1995)
4 Juicy Lucy (1996)
5 Head wounds (2000)

KESSLER, L.
COSSACKS
1 Black Cossacks
2 Sabres of the Reich
3 The mountain of skulla
4 Breakthrough

KESSLER, L.
STORM TROOP
1 Storm troop (1983)
2 Blood mountain (1982)
3 Valley of the assassins (1984)
4 Red assault (1983)
5 Himmler's gold (1983)
6 Fire over Kabul (1983)
7 Wave of terror (1983)
8 Fire over Africa (1984)

KESSLER, L.
OTTO STAHL
1 Otto's phoney war (1981)
2 Otto's blitzkrieg (1982)
3 Otto and the Reds (1982)
4 Otto and the Yanks (1983)
5 Otto and the SS (1984)
6 Otto and the Himmler loveletters (1984)

KESSLER, L.
SEA WOLVES
1 Sink the Scharnhorst (1982)
2 Death to the Deutschland (1982)

KESSLER, L.
ROMMEL
1 Ghost division (1981)
2 Massacre

KESSLER, L.
STUKA SQUADRON
1 The black knights (1983)
2 The hawks of death (1983)
3 The tank busters (1984)
4 Blood mission (1984)

KESSLER, L.
WOTAN/PANZER DIVISION
1 SS Panzer Battalion (1975)
2 Death's head (1978)
3 Claws of steel (1978)
4 Guns at Cassino (1978)
5 The march on Warsaw (1988)
6 Hammer of the Gods (1979)
7 Forced march (1979)
8 Blood and ice (1977)
9 Sand panthers (1977)
10 Counter attack (1979)
11 Hell fire (1978)
12 Panzer hunt (1979)
13 Slaughter ground (1980)
14 Flash point (1980)
15 Cauldron of blood (1981)
16 Schirmer's head hunters (1981)
17 Whores of war (1982)
18 Schirmer's death legions (1983)
19 Slaughter at Salerno (1985)
20 Death ride
21 The Hess assault (1987)
22 March or die

KESSLER, L.
REBEL
1 Cannon fodder (1986)
2 The die-hards (1987)
3 Death match (1987)
4 Breakout (1988)

KESSLER, L.
SUBMARINE
1 The wolf pack (1985)
2 Operation deathwatch (1985)
3 Convoy to catastrophe (1986)
4 Fire in the west (1986)
5 Flight to the Reich (1987)

KESSLER, L.
SS WOTAN
1 Assault on Baghdad (1992)
2 Flight from Moscow (1992)
3 Fire over Serbia (1993)
4 Operation longjump (1993)
5 SS attacks! (1994)
6 Flight from Berlin (1995)
7 Breakout from Stalingrad (1995)
8 The Wotan mission (1996)
9 March of death (1996)
10 Operation fury (1997)
11 Death from Arctic skies (1997)
12 Death's eagles (1998)
13 Stalag assault (2000)
14 Battle for Hitler's Eagles Nest (2000)
15 The screaming eagles (2001)
16 Operation Glenn Miller (2001)
17 Hitler Youth attacks! (2004)

KHANNA, B.
1 Nation of fools (1984)
2 Sweet chilies (1991)

KIENZLE, W. X.
FATHER KOESLER
1 The rosary murders (1978)
2 Death wears a red hat (1980)
3 Mind over murder (1981)
4 Assault with intent (1984)
5 Shadow of death (1984)
6 Kill and tell (1985)
7 Sudden death (1986)
8 Deathbed (1989)
9 Deadline for a critic (1991)
10 Masquerade (1992)
11 Eminence (1992)
12 Chameleon (1993)
13 Body count (1994)
14 Dead wrong (1994)
15 Bishop as pawn (1995)
16 Marked for murder (1996)
17 Call no man father (1996)
18 Requiem for Moses (1997)
19 The man who loved God (1999)

KIJEWSKI, K.
KAT COLORADO
1 Kat walk

2 Katapult
3 Kat's cradle (1994)
4 Copy Kat (1994)
5 Alley Kat blues (1995)
6 Honky tonk Kat (1996)
7 Kat scratch fever (1997)

KILWORTH, G.
ANGEL
1 Angel (1993)
2 Archangel (1994)

KILWORTH, G.
THE NAVIGATOR KINGS
1 The roof of voyaging (1996)
2 The princely flower (1997)
3 Land-of-mists (1998)

KING, B.
NORDIC TRILOGY
1 Starkadder (1985)
2 Vargr moon (1986)

KING, B.
MASTERFUL INVENTION
1 The destroying angel
2 The time-fighters
3 Skyfire

KING, G.
CATS
1 The wild road (1998)
2 The golden cat (1999)

KING, J.
THE BEAUTIFUL GAME
1 The football factory (1996)
2 The headhunters (1997)
3 England away (1998)

KING, L. R.
KATE MARTINELLI
1 A grave talent (1995)
2 To play the fool (1996)
3 With child (1997)
4 Night work (2000)

KING, L. R.
MARY RUSSELL
1 The beekeeper's apprentice (1994)
2 A monstrous regiment of women (1997)
3 The moor (1998)
4 A letter of Mary (1999)
5 O Jerusalem (2000)
6 Justice Hall (2002)
7 The game (2004)

KING, P.
THE GOURMET DETECTIVE
1 The gourmet detective (1998)
2 Spiced to death (1999)

KING, S.
THE DARK TOWER
1 The gunslinger (1988)
2 The drawing of the three (1989)
3 The wastelands (1992)
4 Wizard and glass (1997)
5 Wolves of the Calla (2003)

KINGSTON, B.
EASTER EMPIRE
1 Tuppeny times (1988)
2 Fourpenny flier (1989)
3 Sixpenny stalls (1990)

KINGSTON, G.
1 A wing and a prayer
2 Main force
3 The boys of Coastal

KINSELLA, S.
REBECCA BLOOMFIELD
1 The secret dreamworld of a shopaholic (2000)
2 Shopaholic abroad (2001)
3 Shopaholic ties the knot (2002)
4 Shopaholic & sister (2004)

KIPLING, R.
1 Kim (1904)
2 The Imperial agent, by T.N.Murari (1987)
3 The last victory, by T.N.Murari (1988)

KIRKUP, J.
CHILDHOOD
1 The only child (1957)
2 Sorrows, passions and alarms (1959)
3 I, of all people (1988)

KIRKWOOD, G.
FAIRLYDEN
1 Fairlyden (1990)
2 Mistress of Fairlyden (1991)
3 The family at Fairlyden (1992)
4 Fairlyden at war (1993)

KIRST, H. H.
MUNICH TRILOGY
1 A time for scandal (1972)
2 A time for truth (1974)
3 A time for payment (1976)

KIRST, H. H.
ZERO EIGHT-FIFTEEN
1 The strange mutiny of Gunner Asch (1955)
2 Gunner Asch goes to war (1956)
3 The return of Gunner Asch (1958)
4 What became of Gunner Asch (1964)

KIRSTEN, A.
RALPH WHITGIFT
1 Young Lucifer (1984)
2 Satan's child (1985)

KLEIN, D.
ED BUCK AND GERRY KEEGAN
1 Fourth down (1999)
2 Kilos in the keys (2001)

KLEIN, N.
1 Sunshine (1983)
2 The sunshine years (1984)

KLINE, P.
ANNA MCCOLL
1 Dying to help (1993)
2 Feeling bad (1994)
3 A crushing blow (1995)
4 Turning nasty (1995)
5 Ending in tears (1996)
6 Living in dread (1998)

KNAAK, R.
DRAGONREALM
1 Firedrake
2 Ice dragon

KNIEF, C.
JOHN CAINE
1 Diamond head (1998)
2 Sand dollars (1999)
3 Emerald flash (1999)

KNIGHT, A.
INSPECTOR JEREMY FARO
1 Enter second murderer (1988)
2 Blood line (1989)
3 Deadly beloved (1989)
4 Killing cousins (1990)
5 A quiet death (1991)
6 To kill a queen (1992)
7 The evil that men do (1993)
8 The missing Duchess (1994)
9 The bull slayers (1995)
10 Murder by appointment (1996)
11 The Coffin Lane murders (1998)
12 The final enemy (2002)

KNIGHT, A.
ROSE MCQUINN
1 The Inspector's daughter (2000)
2 Dangerous pursuits (2002)
3 An Orkney murder (2003)

KNIGHT, B.
CROWNER JOHN
1 The sanctuary seeker (1997)
2 The poisoned chalice (1998)
3 Crowner's quest (1999)
4 The awful secret (2000)
5 The tinner's corpse (2001)
6 The grim reaper (2002)
7 Fear in the forest (2003)

KNOWLES, A.
1 Single in the field (1984)
2 An ark on the flood (1985)

KNOWLES, A.
MATTHEW RATTON
1 Matthew Ratton (1979)
2 The raven tree (1981)

KNOX, B.
WEBB CARRICK, FISHERY PROTECTION
1 The scavengers (1964)
2 Devilweed (1965)
3 Blacklight (1966)
4 The Klondyker (1968)
5 Blueback (1969)
6 Seafire (1970)
7 Stormtide (1972)
8 Whitewater (1974)
9 Hellspout (1976)
10 Witchrock (1977)
11 Bombship (1979)
12 Bloodtide (1982)
13 Wavecrest (1985)
14 Dead man's mooring (1987)
15 The drowning nets (1991)

KNOX, B.
THANE AND MOSS
1 Dead line for a dream (1957)
2 Death department (1958)
3 Leave it to the hangman (1959)
4 Little drops of blood (1960)
5 Sanctuary isle (1961)
6 The man in the bottle (1962)
7 Taste of proof (1965)
8 Deep fall (1966)
9 Justice on the rocks (1967)
10 The tallyman (1969)
11 Children of the mist (1970)

12 To kill a witch (1971)
13 Draw batons (1973)
14 Rally to kill (1975)
15 Pilot error (1976)
16 Live bait (1978)
17 A killing in antiques (1981)
18 The hanging tree (1983)
19 The crossfire killings (1986)
20 The interface man (1989)
21 The counterfeit killers (1996)
22 Blood proof (1997)
23 Death bytes (1998)
24 The Lazarus widow (1999)
25 The deep fall (2001)

KNOX-MAWER, J.
1 The sultans came to tea (1961)
2 A gift of islands (1984)

KOESTLER, A.
1 Arrow in the blue (1969)
2 The invisible writing (1954)
3 Stranger in the square (1984)

KONRAD, K.
RUSSIAN SERIES
1 First blood (1981)
2 March on Moscow (1981)
3 Front swine (1982)

KOONTZ, D.
CHRISTOPHER SNOW
1 Fear nothing (1997)
2 Seize the night (1998)

KOSTOV, K. N.
PUNISHMENT BATTALION
1 Baptism of blood
2 The Gulag rats
3 Blood on the Baltic
4 The Steppe wolves

KRAFT, E.
1 Little follies
2 Sweet mysteries
3 Wishful thinking
4 Where do you stop

KRANTZ, J.
SCRUPLES
1 Scruples (1978)
2 Scruples two (1993)

KURTZ, K.
THE LEGENDS OF CAMBER OF CULDI
1 Camber of Culdi (1986)

2 Saint Camber
3 Camber the heretic

KURTZ, K.
DERYNI CHRONICLES
1 Deryni rising
2 Deryni checkmate
3 High Deryni
4 Deryni archives

KURTZ, K.
THE HISTORIES OF KING KELSON
1 The Bishop's heir
2 The King's justice (1986)
3 The quest for Saint Camber (1987)

KURTZ, K. & HARRIS, D.
ADEPT
1 The adept (1992)
2 The lodge of the lynx (1993)
3 The Templar treasure (1994)
4 Dagger magic (1995)
5 Death of an adept (1997)

LA PLANTE, R.
TEGNE
1 Warlord of Zendow
2 The killing blow

LACEY, P.
"MAUDIE"MORGAN
1 The limit (1988)
2 The bagman (1989)

LACEY, S.
LEAH HUNTER
1 File under:deceased (1992)
2 File under:missing (1993)
3 File under:arson (1994)
4 File under:jeopardy (1995)

LACKEY, M.
BARDIC VOICES
1 The lark and the wren (1993)
2 The robin and the kestrel (1994)

LACKEY, M.
MAGE STORMS
1 Storm warning (1994)
2 Storm rising (1995)
3 Storm breaking (1996)

LACKEY, M.
MAGE WARS
1 The black gryphon (1994)

2 The white gryphon (1995)
3 The silver gryphon (1996)

LACKEY, M.
THE LAST HERALD-MAGE
1 Magic's pawn
2 Magic's promise
3 Magic's price

LACKEY, M.
SERRATED EDGE
1 Born to run
2 Wheels of fire
3 When the bough breaks

LACKEY, M.
HERALDS OF VALDEMAR
1 Owlsight (1999)
2 Owl knight (2000)
3 Brightly burning (2001)

LADD, J.
ABILENE
1 The peacemaker (1989)
2 The sharpshooter
3 The prizefighter (1993)
4 The night riders (1989)
5 The half-breed (1990)

LAKE, D.
JOHN RAWLINGS
1 Death in the dark walk (1994)
2 Death at the Beggar's Opera (1995)
3 Death at the Devil's Tavern (1996)
4 Death on the Romney Marsh (1998)
5 Death in the Peerless Pool (1999)
6 Death at Apothecaries' Hall (2000)
7 Death in the west wind (2001)
8 Death at St.James Palace (2002)
9 Death in the valley of shadows (2003)

LAMONT, M.
1 Nine moons wasted (1977)
2 Horns of the moon (1979)

L'AMOUR, L.
SACKETT
1 Sackett's land (1964)
2 To the far blue mountains (1975)
3 The warrior's path (1975)
4 Jubal Sackett (1986)
5 Ride the river
6 The daybreakers
7 Sackett
8 Lando
9 Mojave crossing

10 The Sackett brand
11 The lonely men
12 Treasure mountain
13 Mustang men
14 Galloway
15 The sky-liners
16 The man from Broken Hills
17 Ride the dark trail
18 Lonely on the mountain

L'AMOUR, L.
THE CHANTRY FAMILY
1 Fair blows the wind (1985)
2 Over on the dry side (1988)

LAMPITT, D.
SUTTON PLACE
1 Sutton Place (1983)
2 The silver swan (1984)
3 Fortune
4 Zachary (1990)

LANE, K.
1 Diary of a medical nobody (1982)
2 West country doctor (1984)
   NF Memoirs of a doctor

LANGLEY, L.
1 Changes of address (1987)
2 Persistent rumours (1992)
3 A house in Pondicherry (1995)

LANGSFORD, A. E.
NAVAL SERIES
1 HMS Marathon (1989)
2 HMS Crusader (1990)
3 HMS Inflexible (1991)

LANGTON, J.
HOMER KELLY
1 Emily Dickinson is dead (1989)
2 The Memorial Hall murder (1990)
3 The Dante game (1991)

LANSDALE, J. R.
HAP COLLINS AND LEONARD PINE
1 Mucho mojo (1995)
2 The two-bear mambo (1996)
3 Bad chili (1997)
4 Rumble tumble (1998)
5 Captains outrageous (2002)

LANSDOWNE, J. A.
LORD NIGHTINGALE
1 Lord Nightingale's debut
2 Lord Nightingale's love song

3 Lord Nightingale's triumph
4 Lord Nightingale's Christmas

LAPIERRE, J.
MEG HALLORAN
1 Unquiet grave (1988)
2 Children's games (1990)
3 The cruel mother (1991)

LASGARN, H.
1 A vet for all seasons (1986)
2 Vet in a storm (1987)
3 Vet in the village (1988)

LASHNER, W.
VICTOR CARL
1 Hostile witness (1996)
2 Veritas (1997)

LATHEN, E.
JOHN PUTNAM THATCHER
1 Banking on death (1962)
2 A place for murder (1963)
3 Accounting for murder (1965)
4 Murder makes the wheels go round (1966)
5 Death shall overcome (1967)
6 Murder against the grain (1967)
7 A stitch in time (1968)
8 When in Greece (1969)
9 Come to dust (1970)
10 Murder to go (1970)
11 Pick up sticks (1971)
12 Ashes to ashes (1971)
13 The longer the thread (1972)
14 Murder without icing (1973)
15 Sweet and low (1974)
16 By hook and by crook (1975)
17 Double, double, oil and trouble (1979)
18 Going for gold (1981)
19 Green grow the dollars (1982)
20 Something in the air (1988)
21 East is east (1991)
22 Right on the money (1993)

LAU, M.
LAST CLANSMAN
1 Talisker (2002)
2 Dark Thane (2002)

LAUBEN, P.
HOMER CLAY
1 A nice sound alibi (1981)
2 A surfeit of alibis (1982)
3 A sort of tragedy (1985)

LAUCK, J.
CHILDHOOD
1 Blackbird (2000)
2 Still waters (2001)
NF Autobiography

LAUMER, K.
RETIEF
1 Envoy to new worlds (1963)
2 Retief and the Warlords
3 Retief's war (1965)
4 Retief's ransome (1971)
5 Retief of the CDT (1971)

LAUMER, K.
LAFAYETTE O'LEARY
1 The tune bender (1975)
2 The world bender (1973)
3 The shape changer (1977)

LAUMER, K.
MR. CURLON
1 Worlds of the Imperium (1968)
2 The other side of time (1969)
3 Assignment in nowhere (1971)

LAURENCE, J.
DARINA LISLE
1 A deepe coffyne (1989)
2 A tasty way to die (1990)
3 Hotel morgue (1991)
4 Recipe for death (1992)
5 Death and the epicure (1993)
6 Death at the table (1994)
7 Death a la Provencale (1995)
8 Diet for death (1996)
9 Appetite for death (1999)
10 The mermaid's feast (2000)

LAURENCE, J.
CANALETTO
1 Canaletto and the case of Westminster bridge (1997)
2 Canaletto and the case of the privy garden (1999)
3 Canaletto and the case of Bonnie Prince Charlie (2002)

LAWHEAD, S.
EMPYRION
1 Search for Fierra
2 The siege of Dome

LAURENCE, J.
DRAGON KING SAGA
1 In the hall of the Dragon King

2 The warlords of Nin
3 The sword and the flame

LAURENCE, J.
THE PENDRAGON CYCLE
1 Taliesin
2 Merlin
3 Arthur
4 Pendragon (1994)
5 Grail (1997)

LAURENCE, J.
SONG OF ALBION
1 The paradise war (1991)
2 The silver hand (1992)
3 The endless knot (1993)

LAURENCE, J.
THE CELTIC CRUSADES
1 The iron lance (1999)
2 The black rood (2000)
3 The mystic rose (2001)

LAWRENCE, D. H.
LADY CHATTERLEY
1 Lady Chatterley's lover (1929)
2 Lady Chatterley's confession, by
   E.Feinstein (1995)

LAWRENCE, M. C.
DR. ELIZABETH CHASE
1 Murder in Scorpio (1995)
2 The cold heart of Capricorn (1996)
3 Aquarius descending (1999)

LAWRENCE, MARGARET
HANNAH TREVOR
1 Hearts and bones (1996)
2 Blood red roses (1998)

LAWTON, J.
FREDERICK TROY
1 Riptide (2001)
2 Blackout (1995)
3 Old flames (1996)
4 A little white death (1998)

LAYBERRY, L. G. J.
OAKLEIGH FARM
1 Hayseed (1980)
2 Gleanings (1981)
3 To be a farmer's girl (1982)
4 A pocket full of rye (1984)
5 Tangled harvest (1984)
6 The last mophrey (1987)

7 As long as the fields are green (1987)
8 A new earth (1988)

LEACH, B.
VANESSA CARTER
1 I'm a vegetarian (1992)
2 Summer without Mum (1993)
3 Vanessa (1994)

LEAHY, S.
1 Family ties (1983)
2 Family truths (1985)

LEAHY, S.
CHRISTINE BENNETT
1 The Good Friday murder (1993)
2 The atonement murder (1994)
3 The St.Patrick's Day murder (1996)

LEAN, F.
DAVE CUNANE
1 Red for Rachel (1994)
2 Nine lives (1995)
3 The reluctant investigator (1997)
4 Kingdom gone (1999)
5 Boiling point (2000)
6 Above suspicion (2001)
7 Raised in silence (2002)

LEASOR, J.
CHINA SERIES
1 Follow the drum (1972)
2 Mandarin gold (1973)
3 The Chinese widow (1975)
4 Jade gate (1976)

LEASOR, J.
DR. JASON LOVE
1 Passport to oblivion (1965)
2 Passport to peril (1966)
3 The Yang meridian (1967)
4 Passport in suspense (1967)
5 Passport for a pilgrim (1968)
6 A week for Love (1969)
7 Love-all (1971)
8 Love and the land beyond (1979)
9 Frozen assets (1989)
10 Love down under (1992)

LEATHER, E.
RUPERT CONWAY
1 The Vienna elephant (1977)
2 The Mozart score (1979)
3 The Duveen collection (1980)

LECKIE, R.
ROME
1 Hannibal (1996)
2 Scipio (1998)
3 Carthage (2000)

LEDWITH, F.
1 The best of all possible worlds (1987)
2 Ships that go bump in the night (1974)
3 Ships afloat in the city (1977)
   NF Autobiography

LEE, C.
INSPECTOR LEONARD
1 The Bath detective (1995)
2 The killing of Sally Keemer (1997)
3 The killing of Cinderella (1999)

LEE, J.
1 The unicorn quest (1987)
2 The unicorn dilemma (1989)

LEE, L.
1 Cider with Rosie (1959)
2 As I walked out one midsummer
   morning (1969)
3 A moment of war (1991)
4 I can't stay longer (1976)
   NF Autobiography

LEE, M.
HEARTS OF FIRE
1 Seduction and sacrifice (1994)
2 Desire and deception (1994)
3 Passion and the past (1994)
4 Fantasies and the future (1994)
5 Scandals and secrets (1994)
6 Marriage and miracles (1994)

LEE, MAUREEN
PEARL STREET
1 Lights out in Liverpool (1995)
2 Put out the fires (1996)
3 Through the storm (1997)

LEE, S.
OWEN LIGHTBRINGER
1 The quest for the sword of infinity
2 The land where the serpents rule
3 The path through the circle of time

LEE, T.
THE SECRET BOOKS OF PARADYS
1 The book of the damned (1988)
2 The book of the beast (1988)

LEE, T.
BIRTHGRAVE
1 Birthgrave
2 The storm cloud
3 Shadow fire
4 Quest for the white witch

LEE, T.
BLOOD OPERA
1 Dark dance (1992)
2 Personal darkness (1993)
3 Darkness, I (1994)

LEES-MILNE, J.
1 Ancestral voices (1975)
2 Prophesying peace (1977)
3 Caves of ice (1983)
4 Midway on the waves (1985)
   NF Autobiography

LEGAT, M.
1 The silk maker (1985)
2 The cast iron man (1987)

LEIBER, F.
SWORDS
1 Swords and deviltry
2 Swords against death
3 Swords in the mist
4 Swords against wizardry
5 Swords of Lankhmar
6 Swords and ice magic
7 The knight and knave of swords

LEIGH, H.
THE VINTAGE YEARS
1 The grapes of Paradise
2 Wild vines
3 Kingdoms of the vine

LEIGH, R.
SAM CARROLL
1 The cheap dream (1982)
2 The girl with the bright head (1982)

LEITCH, D.
1 God stand up for bastards (1973)
2 Family secrets (1984)
   NF Autobiography

LEITH, A.
TALES FROM SARSON MAGNA
1 Molly's flashings (1991)
2 Hector's hobbies (1994)

LEITH, V.
EVERIEN
1 The company of glass (1999)
2 The riddled night (2000)

LEJEUNE, A.
1 Professor in peril (1987)
2 Key without a door (1988)

LEMARCHAND, E.
DET. SUPT. TOM POLLARD
1 Death of an old girl (1967)
2 The Affacombe affair (1968)
3 Alibi for a corpse (1969)
4 Death on doomsday (1970)
5 Cyanide with compliments (1972)
6 Let or hindrance (1973)
7 Buried in the past (1974)
8 A step in the dark (1976)
9 Unhappy returns (1977)
10 Suddenly, while gardening (1978)
11 Change for the worse (1980)
12 Nothing to do with the case (1981)
13 Troubled waters (1982)
14 The wheel turns (1983)
15 Light through glass (1984)
16 Who goes home? (1986)
17 The Glade Manor murder (1988)

LEON, D.
COMMISSARIO GUIDO BRUNETTI
1 Death in La Fenice (1992)
2 Death in a strange country (1993)
3 The anonymous Venetian (1994)
4 A Venetian reckoning (1995)
5 Acqua alta (1996)
6 The death of faith (1997)
7 A noble radiance (1998)
8 Fatal remedies (1999)
9 Friends in high places (2000)
10 A sea of troubles (2001)
11 Wilful behaviour (2002)
12 Uniform justice (2003)
13 Doctored evidence (2004)

LEONARD, E.
CHILI PALMER
1 Get Shorty (1992)
2 Be cool (1999)

LEROUX, G.
PHANTOM
1 The Phantom of the Opera (1918)
2 The Phantom of Manhattan, by F.
  Forsyth (1999)

LESLIE, A.
1 The gilt and the gingerbread (1981)
2 A story half told (1983)

LESLIE, C.
HOUSE OF GODWIN
1 A farrago of foxes (1975)
2 Feud royal (1977)

LESLIE, R.
VICTORY TRILOGY
1 Dawn readiness (1984)
2 The raging skies (1985)
3 The hunters (1986)

LESLIE, R.
HERACLES TRILOGY
1 Trouble in the wind (1984)
2 The fateful dawn (1984)
3 Under a shrieking sky (1984)

LESSING, D.
CANOPUS IN ARGOS
1 Shikasta (1979)
2 The marriages between Zones 3, 4 & 5
  (1980)
3 The Sirian experiments (1981)
4 The making of the representative for
  Planet 8 (1983)
5 Documents relating to the sentimental
  agents in the Volyen Empire (1983)

LESSING, D.
CHILDREN OF VIOLENCE
1 Martha Quest (1952)
2 A proper marriage (1956)
3 A ripple from the storm (1958)
4 Landlocked (1965)
5 The four-gated city (1966)

LESSING, D.
BEN
1 The fifth child (1985)
2 Ben in the world (2000)

LEVI, P.
BEN JONSON
1 Grave witness (1985)
2 Knit one, drop one (1987)

LEVIN, I.
1 Rosemary's baby (1967)
2 Son of Rosemary (1998)

LEVINE, L.
JAINE AUSTEN
1 This pen for hire (2002)
2 Last writes (2003)

LEWIN, M. Z.
ALBERT SAMSON & DET. LT. POWDER
1 Ask the right question (1972)
2 The enemies within (1973)
3 The way we die now (1974)
4 The silent salesman (1976)
5 Missing woman (1982)
6 Out of time (1984)
7 Night cover (1976)
8 Hard line (1983)
9 Late payments (1986)
10 Child proof (1988)
11 Called by a Panther (1991)
12 Called by a partner (1992)

LEWIS, C.
HOWARD HAYES
1 The golden grin
2 Acid test
3 Hot rain

LEWIS, H.
MARY OF ENGLAND
1 Rose of England (1977)
2 Heart of a rose (1978)

LEWIS, H.
MARY TUDOR
1 I am Mary Tudor (1971)
2 Mary the Queen (1973)
3 Bloody Mary (1974)

LEWIS, R.
INSPECTOR CROW
1 A lover too many (1967)
2 Wolf by the ears (1970)
3 Error of judgment (1971)
4 A secret singing (1972)
5 Blood money (1973)
6 A part of virtue (1976)
7 A question of degree (1976)
8 Nothing but foxes (1977)
9 A relative distance (1981)

LEWIS, R.
ERIC WARD
1 A certain blindness (1980)
2 Dwell in danger (1982)
3 A limited vision (1983)
4 Once dying, twice dead (1984)
5 A blurred reality (1985)
6 Premium on death (1986)

7 The salamander chill (1988)
8 A necessary dealing (1989)
9 A kind of transaction (1991)
10 A form of death (2001)
11 The nightwalker (2002)
12 Dead man running (2003)

LEWIS, R.
ARNOLD LANDON
1 A gathering of ghosts (1983)
2 Most cunning workmen (1984)
3 A trout in the milk (1986)
4 Men of subtle craft (1987)
5 The devil is dead (1989)
6 A wisp of smoke (1991)
7 A secret dying (1992)
8 Bloodeagle (1993)
9 Cross bearer (1994)
10 A short-lived ghost (1995)
11 Angel of death (1996)
12 Suddenly as a shadow (1997)
13 The shape-shifter (1998)
14 The ghost dancers (1999)
15 An assumption of death (2000)
16 Dead secret (2001)
17 The ways of death (2002)

LEWIS, R. H.
MATTHEW COLL
1 A cracking of spines (1980)
2 The manuscript murders (1981)
3 A pension for death (1983)
4 Where agents fear to tread (1984)
5 Death in Verona (1989)

LEY, A. C.
JUSTIN & ANTHEA RUTHERFORD
1 A fatal assignation (1987)
2 Masquerade of vengeance (1989)

LIDDELL, R.
1 Kind relations (1939)
2 Stepsons (1969)
3 The last enchantments (1991)

LIDE, M.
ANN OF CAMBRAY
1 Ann of Cambray
2 Gifts of the Queen
3 Hawks of Sedgemont

LIDE, M.
CORNISH SERIES
1 The homecoming (1998)
2 Polmena Cove (1999)

LIGHTFOOT, F. M.
MANCHESTER SERIES
1 Manchester pride (1999)
2 Polly's war (2000)

LIMB, S.
DULCIE DOMUM
1 Dulcie Domum's manual of bad
   housekeeping (1991)
2 More bad housekeeping (1992)
3 Dulcie dishes the dirt (1994)
4 Dulcie goes native (1998)

LIN-CHANDLER, I.
HOLLY-JEAN HO
1 The healing of Holly-Jean (1995)
2 Grievous angel (1996)
3 The hour of the tigress (1998)

LINDHOLM, M.
1 The reindeer people (1987)
2 Wolf's brother (1989)

LINDSAY, F.
DET. INSPECTOR JIM MELDRUM
1 A kind of dying (1998)
2 Idle hands (1999)
3 Death knock (2000)

LINDSAY, JOAN
1 Picnic at Hanging Rock (1968)
2 The secret of Hanging Rock (1987)

LINDSEY, D. L.
1 Cold mind (1984)
2 Heat from another sun (1985)
3 Spiral (1987)

LINDSEY, R.
1 The falcon and the snowman (1980)
2 The flight of the falcon (1985)
   NF Travels in the Arctic

LING, P.
JUDGE FAMILY
1 High water (1991)
2 Flood water (1992)
3 Storm water (1993)

LING, P.
MINSTER FAMILY
1 Crown House (1989)
2 Crown papers (1990)
3 Crown wars (1996)

LINSCOTT, G.
BIRDY AND NIMUE HAWTHORN
1 A healthy body (1984)
2 Murder makes tracks (1985)
3 A whiff of sulphur (1987)

LINSCOTT, G.
NELL BRAY
1 Sister beneath the sheet (1991)
2 Hanging on the wire (1992)
3 Stage fright (1993)
4 Widow's peak (1994)
5 Crown witness (1995)
6 Dead man's music (1996)
7 Dance on blood (1998)
8 Dead man riding (2002)
9 Blood on the wood (2003)

LINZEE, D.
INQUIRIES INC.
1 Discretion (1981)
2 Belgravia (1982)

LIPPMAN, L.
TESS MONAGHAN
1 Baltimore blues (1997)
2 Butcher's Hill (1998)
3 In big trouble (1999)
4 The sugar house (2000)
5 Charm City (2001)
6 In a strange city (2001)
7 The last place (2003)

LISLE, H.
THE SECRET TEXTS
1 Diplomacy of wolves (1999)
2 Vengeance of dragons (2000)
3 Courage of falcons (2001)

LITCHFIELD, M.
DET. SUPT. FERGUS MCQUEEN
1 See how they run (1984)
2 Murder circus (1985)

LIVINGS, H.
RAVENSGILL
1 Pennine tales (1983)
2 Flying eggs and things (1986)

LIVINGSTON, J.
JOE BINNEY
1 A piece of the silence (1983)
2 Die again, Macready (1984)
3 The nightmare file (1987)

LIVINGSTON, N.
MR. PRINGLE
1 The trouble at Aquitaine (1985)
2 Fatality at Bath and Wells (1986)
3 Incident at Parga (1987)
4 Death in a distant land (1988)
5 Death in close-up (1989)
6 Mayhem in Parva (1990)
7 Unwillingly to Las Vegas (1991)
8 A quiet murder (1992)

LIVINGSTON, N.
MCKIE FAMILY
1 The far side of the hill (1987)
2 The land of our dreams (1989)

LLEWELLYN, R.
THE VALLEY
1 How green was my valley (1939)
2 Up, into the singing mountain (1963)
3 Down where the moon is small (1966)
4 Green, green my valley now (1975)

LLEWELLYN, R.
EDMUND TROTHE
1 The end of the rug (1969)
2 But we didn't get the fox (1970)
3 White horse to Banbury Cross (1972)
4 The night is a child (1974)

LLEWELLYN, S.
CHARLIE AGUTTER
1 Dead reckoning (1987)
2 Blood orange (1988)

LLEWELLYN, S.
GURNEY
1 Gurney's revenge (1977)
2 Gurney's reward (1978)
3 Gurney's release (1979)

LLOYD, A. R.
THE KINE SAGA
1 Marshworld (Kine) (1982)
2 Witchwood (1989)
3 Dragonpond (1990)

LLYWELYN, M.
THE ODYSSEY OF THE IRISH
1 Lion of Ireland (1980)
2 The horse goddess (1983)
3 Bard (1985)

LOCHTE, D.
SERENDIPITY DALHQUIST
1 Sleeping dog (1987)
2 Laughing dog (1988)

LOCK, J.
INSPECTOR ERNEST BEST
1 Dead letters (2003)
2 Dead fall (2004)

LODGE, D.
1 Changing places (1975)
2 Small world (1984)

LOFTS, N.
1 Gad's Hall (1977)
2 The haunted house (1978)

LOFTS, N.
A HOUSE IN SUFFOLK
1 The town house (1959)
2 The house at Old Vine (1961)
3 The house at sunset (1963)

LOFTS, N.
SUFFOLK TRILOGY
1 Knight's Acre (1974)
2 The homecoming (1975)
3 The lonely furrow (1976)

LOMER, M.
1 Robert of Normandy (1991)
2 Fortune's knave (1992)

LONES, L. S.
1 Daughters of Eve (1991)
2 A woman's reach (1993)

LONGSTREET, S.
FIORE FAMILY
1 All or nothing (1984)
2 Our father's house (1986)

LONGSTREET, S.
PEDLOCK FAMILY
1 The Pedlocks (1967)
2 Pedlock and sons (1969)
3 Pedlock saint, Pedlock sinner (1970)
4 The Pedlock inheritance (1971)
5 The strange case of Sarah Pedlock (1977)

LORRIMER, C.
ROCHFORD FAMILY
1 The Chatelaine (1981)

2 The wilderling (1982)
3 Fool's curtain (1994)

LORRIMER, C.
SISTERS
1 Mavreen (1977)
2 Tamarisk (1978)
3 Chantal (1980)

LOUVISH, S.
AVRAM BLOK
1 The therapy of Avram Blok (1985)
2 City of Blok (1988)
3 The last trump of Avram Blok (1990)

LOVELL, M.
APPLETON PORTER
1 The spy game (1981)
2 The spy with his head in the clouds (1982)

LOVESEY, P.
DETECTIVE MEMOIRS OF KING EDWARD VII
1 Bertie and the tin man (1987)
2 Bertie and the seven bodies (1990)
3 Bertie and the crime of passion (1993)

LOVESEY, P.
SERGEANT CRIBB AND CONSTABLE THACKERAY
1 Wobble to death (1969)
2 The detective wore silk drawers (1971)
3 Abracadaver (1972)
4 Mad hatter's holiday (1973)
5 Invitation to a dynamite party (1974)
6 A case of spirits (1975)
7 Swing, swing together (1976)
8 Waxwork (1978)

LOVESEY, P.
PETER DIAMOND
1 The last detective (1991)
2 Diamond solitaire (1992)
3 The summons (1993)
4 Bloodhounds (1996)
5 Upon a dark night (1997)
6 The vault (1999)
7 Diamond dust (2002)

LOW, O.
ARVO LAURILA
1 To his just deserts (1986)
2 Murky shallows (1987)

LUDLUM, R.
BOURNE
1 The Bourne identity (1980)
2 The Bourne supremacy (1986)
3 The Bourne ultimatum (1990)

LUDLUM, R.
MATARESE
1 The Matarese circle (1979)
2 The Matarese countdown (1997)

LUDLUM, R.
THE HAWK
1 The road to Gandolfo (1976)
2 The road to Omaha (1992)

LUMLEY, B.
NECROSCOPE
1 Necroscope
2 Wamphyri
3 The source
4 Deadspeak
5 Deadspawn
6 The lost years, vol. 1. (1995)
7 The lost years, vol. 2. (1996)

LUMLEY, B.
TALES OF THE PRIMAL LAND
1 The house of Cthulu
2 Tarra Khash throssak
3 Sorcery in Shad

LUMLEY, B.
E BRANCH
1 E Branch invaders
2 Necroscope defilers
3 Necroscope invaders

LUNN, J.
KILLIGREW
1 Killigrew RN (2000)
2 Killigrew and the golden dragon (2001)
3 Killigrew and the incorrigibles (2002)
4 Killigrew and the North West Passage (2003)
5 Killigrew's run (2004)

LUSBY, J.
INSPECTOR CARL MCCADDEN
1 Making the cut (1995)
2 Flashback (1996)
3 A waste of shame (2000)
4 Serial (2002)

LUSTBADER, E.
CHINA MAROC
1 Jian (1985)
2 Shan (1987)

LUSTBADER, E.
SUNSET WARRIOR
1 The sunset warrior (1979)
2 Shallows of night (1980)
3 Dai-San (1980)
4 Beneath an opal moon (1981)
5 Dragons on a sea of night (1997)

LUSTBADER, E.
NICHOLAS LINNEAR
1 The Ninja (1980)
2 The Miko (1984)
3 White Ninja (1990)
4 The Kaisho (1993)
5 Floating city (1994)
6 Second skin (1995)

LUSTBADER, E.
THE PEARL SAGA
1 The ring of five dragons (2001)
2 The veil of one thousand tears (2002)
3 The cage of nine banestones (2003)

LUTZ, G.
NAZI PARATROOPER
1 Storm Belgium
2 Crete must fall
3 Cassino corpse factory

LUTZ, J.
FRED CARVER
1 Tropical heat (1986)
2 Scorcher (1988)
3 Kiss (1989)
4 Flame (1990)
5 Blood fire (1991)

LYALL, F.
SUPT. MASON
1 A death in time (1987)
2 Death and the remembrancer (1988)
3 The croaking of the raven (1990)
4 Death in the winter garden (1993)

LYALL, G.
HARRY MAXIM
1 The secret servant (1980)
2 The conduct of Major Maxim (1982)
3 The crocus list (1985)
4 Uncle Target (1988)

LYALL, G.
CAPTAIN MATTHEW RANKLIN
1 Spy's honour (1995)
2 Flight from honour (1996)
3 All honourable men (1997)
4 Honourable intentions (1999)

LYNN, E. A.
CHRONICLES OF TORNOR
1 Watchtower
2 The dancers of Arun
3 The Northern girl

LYONS, A.
JACOB ASCH
1 The dead are discreet (1977)
2 All God's children (1977)
3 The killing floor (1977)
4 Dead ringer (1983)
5 Castles burning (1983)
6 Hard trade (1984)
7 Three with a bullet (1987)
8 Other people's money (1990)
9 Fast fade (1990)
10 False pretences (1997)

LYONS, G.
1 Slievelea (1985)
2 The green years (1987)

MACAVOY, R. A.
DAMIANO TRILOGY
1 Damiano
2 Damiano's lute
3 Raphael

MACAVOY, R. A.
NAZURHET OF SORDALING
1 Lens of the heart (1992)
2 King of the dead (1992)
3 Winter of the wolf (1993)

MACCOLLUM, M,
1 Antares passage (1989)
2 Antares dawn (1989)

MACDONALD, F. J.
1 Crowdie and cream (1982)
2 Crotal and white (1983)
   NF Autobiography of a Scots minister

MACDONALD, MALCOLM
STEVENSON FAMILY
1 The world from rough stones (1975)
2 The rich are with you always (1977)

3 Sons of fortune (1978)
4 Abigail (1979)

MACDONALD, MARIANNE
DIDO HOARE
1 Death's autograph (1996)
2 Ghost walk (1997)
3 Smoke screen (1999)
4 Road kill (2000)
5 Blood lies (2001)
6 Die once (2002)

MACDONALD, PETER
BEN HART
1 The hope of glory (1980)
2 Wide horizons (1980)
3 One way street (1981)
4 Exit (1983)
5 Dead end (1986)

MACENROE, R. S.
FAR STARS AND FUTURE TIMES
1 The shattered stars
2 Flight of honour
3 Skinner

MACINNES, H.
ROBERT RENWICK
1 The hidden target (1981)
2 The cloak of darkness (1982)

MACINTYRE, L.
CHRONICLES OF INVERNEVIS
1 Cruel in the shadow (1979)
2 The blind bend (1981)

MACKAY, AMANDA
1 Death is academic (1976)
2 Death on the river (1983)

MACKENZIE, DONALD
RAVEN
1 Raven in flight (1976)
2 Raven and the ratcatcher (1976)
3 Raven and the Kamikaze (1977)
4 Deep, dark and dead (1977)
5 Raven settles a score (1978)
6 Raven feathers his nest (1979)
7 Raven and the paper-hangers (1980)
8 Raven's revenge (1982)
9 Raven's longest night (1984)
10 Raven's shadow (1985)
11 Nobody here by that name (1986)
12 A savage state of grace (1988)
13 By any illegal means (1990)
14 Loose cannon (1991)

15 The eyes of the goat (1992)
16 The sixth deadly sin (1993)

MACLAINE, SHIRLEY
1 Don't fall off the mountain (1972)
2 You can get there from here (1975)
3 Out on a limb (1983)
4 Dancing in the light (1985)
5 It's all in the playing (1987)
6 Going within (1989)
   NF Autobiography and philisophy

MACLEAN, A.
NAVARONE
1 The guns of Navarone (1957)
2 Force ten from Navarone (1968)
3 Storm force from Navarone, by
   S.Llewellyn (1996)
4 Thunderbolt from Navarone, by
   S.Llewellyn (1998)

MACLEOD, C.
PETER SHANDY
1 Rest you merry (1980)
2 The luck runs out (1981)
3 Wrack anf rune (1982)
4 Something the cat dragged in (1984)
5 The corpse in Oozak's pond (1986)
6 Vane pursuit (1989)
7 An owl too many (1991)
8 Something in the water (1994)
9 Exit the milkman (1997)

MACLEOD, C.
SARAH KELLING
1 The family vault (1980)
2 The withdrawing room (1981)
3 The palace guard (1982)
4 The Bilbao looking glass (1983)
5 The convivial codfish (1984)
6 The plain old man (1985)
7 The recycled citizen (1987)
9 The Gladstone bag (1989)
10 The resurrection man (1992)
11 The odd job (1995)
12 The balloon man (2000)

MACLEOD, K.
ENGINES OF LIGHT
1 Cosmonaut keep (2000)
2 Dark light (2001)
3 Engine city (2002)

MACLEOD, R.
JONATHAN GAUNT
1 A witch dance in Bavaria (1975)
2 A pay-off in Switzerland (1977)

3 Incident in Iceland (1979)
4 A problem in Prague (1981)
5 A property in Cyprus (1970)
6 A killing in Malta (1972)
7 A burial in Portugal (1973)
8 A legacy from Tenerife (1984)
9 The money mountain (1987)
10 Spanish maze game (1990)

MACLEOD, R.
ANDREW LAIRD
1 All other perils (1974)
2 Dragonship (1976)
3 Salvage job (1978)
4 Cargo risk (1980)
5 Mayday from Malaga (1983)
6 A cut in diamonds (1985)
7 Witchline (1988)

MACVICAR, A.
1 Silver in my sporran (1980)
2 Salt in my porridge (1972)
3 Heather in my ears (1974)
4 Rocks in my scotch (1976)
5 Bees in my bonnet (1982)
6 Golf in my gallowses (1983)
7 Gremlins in my garden (1985)
8 Capers in the Kirk (1987)
   NF Autobiography

MAHFOUZ, N.
CAIRO TRILOGY
1 Palace walk (1990)
2 Palace of desire (1991)
3 Sugar Street (1992)

MAIMAN, J.
ROBIN MILLER
1 I left my heart
2 Crazy for love
3 Under my skin (1994)

MAITLAND, B.
DET. SGT. KATHY KOLLA AND DET.
CHIEF INSP. DAVID BROCK
1 The Marx sisters (1994)
2 The malcontents (1995)
3 All my enemies (1996)
4 The Chalonheads (1999)
5 Silvermeadow (2000)
6 Babel (2002)

MALCOLM, A.
DAUGHTERS OF CAMERON
1 The taming (1982)
2 Ride out the storm (1982)

MALCOLM, J.
TIM SIMPSON
1 A back room in Somers Town (1983)
2 The Godwin sideboard (1984)
3 The Gwen John sculpture (1985)
4 Whistler in the dark (1986)
5 Gothic pursuit (1987)
6 Mortal ruin (1987)
7 The wrong impression (1989)
8 Sheep, goats and soap (1991)
9 A deceptive appearance (1992)
10 The burning ground (1993)
11 Hung over (1994)
12 Into the vortex (1996)
13 Simpson's Homer (2001)
14 Circles and squares (2003)

MALING, A.
BROCK POTTER
1 Schroeder's game (1977)
2 Lucky devil (1978)
3 The Rheingold route (1979)
4 The Koberg link (1980)
5 A taste of treason (1983)

MALLINSON, A.
MATTHEW HERVEY
1 A close run thing (1999)
2 The Nizam's daughters (2000)
3 A regimental affair (2001)
4 A call to arms (2002)
5 The sabre's edge (2003)
6 Rumours of war (2004)

MALLOY, L.
MARTIN MOON
1 JoJo and the private eye (1980)
2 The happiest ghost in town (1981)
3 Beware the yellow Packard (1982)
4 So help me Hannah (1982)
5 The bullet proof toga (1984)

MALMONT, V. S.
TORI MIRACLE
1 Death pays the rose rent (1995)
2 Death, lies and apple pies (1998)

MALONE, M.
CUDDY MANGUM
1 Uncivil seasons (1983)
2 Handling sin (1986)
3 Time's witness (1989)

MALPASS, E.
PENTECOST FAMILY
1 Morning's at seven (1966)
2 At the height of the moon (1967)

3 Fortinbras has escaped (1970)
4 Oh my darling daughter (1974)

MALPASS, E.
WILL SHAKESPEARE
1 Sweet Will (1972)
2 The Cleopatra boy (1974)
3 House of women (1975)

MANFREDI, V. M.
ALEXANDER THE GREAT
1 Alexander, child of a dream (2001)
2 Alexander; the sands of Ammon (2001)
3 Alexander; the ends of the earth (2001)

MANKELL, H.
INSPECTOR KURT WALLANDER
1 Faceless killers (2000)
2 Sidetracked (2000)
3 The fifth woman (2001)
4 The dogs of Riga (2001)
5 Firewall (2004)

MANN, J.
TAMARA HOYLAND
1 Funeral sites (1981)
2 No man's island (1983)
3 Grave goods (1984)
4 A kind of healthy grave (1986)
5 Death beyond the Nile (1988)
6 Faith, hope and homicide (1991)

MANN, P.
THE STORY OF THE GARDENER
1 Master of Paxwax (1986)
2 The fall of the families (1987)

MANN, P.
LAND FIT FOR HEROES
1 Escape to the wild wood (1993)
2 Stand alone Stan (1994)
3 The dragon wakes (1995)
4 The burning forest (1996)

MANNERS, A.
THE ISLAND
1 Echoing yesterday
2 Karran Kinrade (1986)
3 The red bird (1987)

MANNING, O.
BALKAN TRILOGY
1 The great fortune (1960)
2 The spoilt city (1962)
3 Friends and heroes (1964)

MANNING, O.
LEVANT TRILOGY
1 The danger tree (1977)
2 The battle lost and won (1978)
3 The sum of things (1980)

MANTEL, H.
1 Every day is Mother's Day (1985)
2 Vacant possession (1986)

MANTELL, L.
STEVEN ARROW
1 Murder in fancy dress (1978)
2 A murder or three (1980)
3 Murder and chips (1981)
4 Murder to burn (1983)
5 Murder in vain (1984)

MAPSON, J.
CHLOE
1 Hank and Chloe
2 Loving Chloe (1998)

MARACOTTA, L.
LUCY FREERS
1 Turn around, your'e dead (1996)
2 The dead celeb (1997)
3 Playing dead (1999)

MARCH, H.
ROBERT FAIRFAX
1 The complaint of the dove (1998)
2 The devil's highway (1999)
3 A distinction of blood (2000)
4 Death be my theme (2000)
5 A necessary evil (2001)

MARCHMONT, G.
CORDOVAN CHRONICLES
1 Wild grapes (1996)
2 A roving eye (1997)

MARCO, J.
TYRANTS AND KINGS
1 The jackal of Nar (1999)
2 The grand design (2000)
3 The saints of the sword (2001)

MARCUS, D.
1 A land not theirs (1986)
2 A land in flames (1987)

MARCUS, J.
THE MARSH
1 A few days in Endel (1979)

2 Marsh blood (1980)
3 The sinister side (1996)

MARILLIER, J.
THE SEVENWATERS TRILOGY
1 Daughter of the forest (2000)
2 Son of the shadows (2001)
3 Child of the prophecy (2002)

MARILLIER, J.
VIKINGS
1 Wolfskin (2003)
2 Foxmask (2004)

MARLEY, S.
CHINESE TRILOGY
1 Spirit mirror
2 Dark mask
3 Shadow sisters (1993)

MARLOW, J.
WHITWORTH FAMILY
1 Kessie (1985)
2 Sarah (1988)
3 Anne (1989)

MARON, M.
LT. SIGRID HAROLD
1 One coffee with (1988)
2 Death of a butterfly (1988)
3 Death in blue folders (1989)

MARON, M.
JUDGE DEBORAH KNOTT
1 Bootlegger's daughter (1993)
2 Shooting at loons (1994)
3 Southern discomfort (1995)
4 Up jumps the devil (2002)
5 Slow dollar (2003)

MARQUIS, M.
DET. INSPECTOR HARRY TIMBERLAKE
1 Vengeance (1992)
2 Elimination (1993)
3 Written in blood (1995)
4 Death of a good woman (1998)

MARSH, J.
HOUSE OF ELIOT
1 The House of Eliot (1993)
2 A house at war, by E O'Leary (1994)

MARSH, N.
RODERICK ALLEYN
1 A man lay dead (1934)
2 Enter a murderer (1935)

3 The Nursing Home murder (1936)
4 Death in ecstasy (1937)
5 Vintage murder (1937)
6 Artists in crime (1938)
7 Death in a white tie (1938)
8 Overture to death (1939)
9 Death at the bar (1940)
10 Death and the dancing footman (1942)
11 Died in the wool (1945)
12 Surfeit of lampreys (1941)
13 Colour scheme (1943)
14 Final curtain (1947)
15 Swing brother swing (1948)
16 Opening night (1951)
17 Spinsters in jeopardy (1953)
18 Scales of justice (1954)
19 Off with his head (1957)
20 Singing in the shrouds (1959)
21 False scent (1960)
22 Hand in glove (1962)
23 Dead water (1964)
24 Death at the Dolphin (1967)
25 A clutch of constables (1968)
26 When in Rome (1970)
27 Tied up in tinsel (1972)
28 Black as he's painted (1974)
29 Last ditch (1977)
30 Grave mistake (1978)
31 Photo finish (1980)
32 Light thickens (1982)

MARSHALL, S.
A NORFOLK VILLAGE
1 A nest of magpies (1993)
2 Sharp through the hawthorn (1994)
3 Ring the bell backwards (1998)

MARSHALL, W. L.
YELLOWTHREAD STREET
1 Yellowthread Street (1975)
2 The hatchet man (1976)
3 Gelignite (1976)
4 Thin air (1977)
5 Skulduggery (1979)
6 Sci Fi (1981)
7 Perfect end (1981)
8 War machines (1982)
9 The faraway man (1984)
10 Roadshow (1985)
11 Head first (1986)
12 Frogmouth (1987)

MARSHALL, W. L.
MANILA BAY MYSTERIES
1 Manila Bay (1896)
2 Whisper (1988)

MARSTON, E.
NICHOLAS BRACEWELL
1 The Queen's Head (1988)
2 The merry devils (1989)
3 The Trip to Jerusalem (1990)
4 The nine giants (1991)
5 The mad courtesan (1992)

MARSTON, E.
DOMESDAY BOOKS
1 The wolves of Savernake (1994)
2 The ravens of Blackwater (1995)
3 The dragons of Archenfield (1995)
4 The lions of the north (1996)
5 The serpents of Harbledown (1996)
6 The stallions of Woodstock (1997)
7 The hawks of Delamere (1998)
8 The foxes of Warwick (1999)
9 The wild cats of Exeter (1999)
10 The owls of Gloucester (2000)
11 The elephants of Norwich (2001)

MARSTON, E.
CHRISTOPHER REDMAYNE
1 The King's evil (1999)
2 The amorous nightingale (2000)
3 The repentant rake (2001)
4 The Frost Fair (2003)

MARTELL, D.
PASCUAL
1 Lying, crying, dying (1998)
2 The republic of night (1999)

MARTIN, G. R. R.
A SONG OF ICE AND FIRE
1 A game of thrones (1996)
2 A clash of kings (1999)
3 A storm of swords (2000)
4 A feast for crows (2003)

MARTIN, L.
DEB RALSTON
1 Too sane a murder (1987)
2 A conspiracy of strangers (1988)
3 Murder at the Blue Owl (1989)

MARTIN, R.
1 Gallows wedding (1978)
2 The unicorn summer (1984)

MARVIN, J. W.
CROW
1 The red hills
2 Worse than death
3 Tears of blood

4 The black trail
5 Bodyguard
6 The sisters
7 One-eyed death
8 A good day

MASSIE, A.
1 The last peacock (1981)
2 These enchanted woods (1993)

MASSIE, A.
THE EMPERORS
1 Caesar (1993)
2 Augustus (1986)
3 Tiberius (1990)

MASTERS, A.
MINDER
1 Minder (1984)
2 Minder - back again (1985)
3 Minder - yet again (1986)

MASTERS, A.
MARIUS LARCHE
1 Murder is a long time coming (1991)
2 Confessional (1993)
3 Death's door (1994)

MASTERS, A.
INSIDER
1 The good and faithful servant (1999)
2 Murder is a pretty business (2000)
3 Lifers (2001)
4 Asylum (2003)

MASTERS, P.
DET. INSPECTOR JOANNA PIERCY
1 Winding up the serpent (1995)
2 Catch the fallen sparrow (1996)
3 A wreath for my sister (1997)
4 And none shall sleep (1997)
5 Stone dead (1999)
6 Scaring crows (2000)
7 Embroidering shrouds (2001)
8 Endangering innocents (2003)

MASTERTON, G.
MANITOU
1 The Manitou (1976)
2 Revenge of the Manitou (1984)

MASTERTON, G.
JIM ROOK
1 Rook (1996)
2 Tooth and claw (1997)
3 The terror (1998)

4 Snowman (1999)
5 The swimmer (2001)

MATHER, BERKELEY
STAFFORD FAMILY
1 The pagoda tree (1979)
2 The midnight gun (1981)
3 Hour of the dog (1982)

MATHER, L.
JO HUGHES
1 Blood of an Aries (1993)
2 Beware Taurus (1994)
3 Gemini doublecross (1995)

MATTHEW, C.
SIMON CRISP
1 Diary of a somebody (1978)
2 Loosely engaged (1980)
3 The crisp report (1981)
4 Family matters (1986)

MATTHEWS, B.
WEBSTER FAMILY
1 The open door (2002)
2 Wings of the morning (2003)
3 Time of peace (2004)

MATTHEWS, L.
HORATIO PARKER
1 Unseen witness (1993)
2 A conviction of guilt (1995)
3 A picture of innocence (1996)

MATTHEWS, P.
CASEY FARRELL
1 Scent of fear (1992)
2 Vision of death (1993)
3 Taste of evil (1993)
4 Touch of terror (1995)

MATTHIESON, P.
WATSON TRILOGY
1 Killing Mr. Watson (1995)
2 Lost man's river (1998)

MAUPIN, A.
1 Tales of the city (1978)
2 More of the city (1980)
3 Further tales of the city (1982)
4 Babycakes (1986)
5 Significant others (1988)
6 Sure of you (1990)

MAY, J.
THE EXILES
1 The many coloured land
2 The golden torc
3 The non-born king
4 The adversary

MAY, J.
GALACTIC MILIEU
1 Jack the bodiless (1992)
2 Diamond mask (1994)
3 Magnificat (1996)

MAY, J.
TRILLIUM
1 Black trillium (1991)
2 Blood trillium (1992)
3 Sky trillium (1997)

MAY, J.
THE RAMPART WORLD
1 Perseus spur (1998)
2 Orion arm (1999)
3 Sagittarius whorl (2001)

MAYNARD, K.
LIEUT. LAMB
1 Lieutenant Lamb (1984)
2 First Lieutenant (1985)
3 Lamb in command (1986)
4 Lamb's mixed fortunes (1987)

MAYO, J. K.
HARRY SEDDALL
1 The hunting season (1985)
2 Wolf's head (1987)
3 Cry havoc (1990)
4 A shred of honour (1993)
5 The masterless men (1995)
6 The interloper (1997)

MAYOR, A.
LT. JOE GUNTHER
1 Open season (1990)
2 Borderlines (1991)
3 Scent of evil (1993)
4 The skeleton's knee (1994)
5 Fruits of the poisonous tree (1995)

MCAULEY, P. J.
CONFLUENCE
1 Child of the river (1997)
2 Ancients of days (1998)
3 Shrine of stars (1999)

MCBAIN, E.
MATTHEW HOPE
1 Goldilocks (1978)
2 Rumpelstiltskin (1981)
3 Beauty and the beast (1982)
4 Jack and the beanstalk (1984)
5 Snow white and rose red (1985)
6 Cinderella (1986)
7 Puss in Boots (1987)
8 The house that Jack built (1988)
9 Three blind mice (1991)
10 Mary, Mary (1992)
11 There was a little girl (1994)
12 Glady the cross-eyed bear (1996)
13 The last best Hope (1998)

MCBAIN, E.
THE 87TH PRECINCT
1 Cop hater (1956)
2 The mugger (1956)
3 The pusher (1956)
4 The con man (1957)
5 Killer's choice (1958)
6 Killer's payoff (1958)
7 Lady killer (1958)
8 Killer's wedge (1959)
9 'Til death (1959)
10 King's ransom (1959)
11 Give the boys a great big hand (1960)
12 The heckler (1961)
13 See them die (1961)
14 Lady lady I did it (1961)
15 The empty hours (1962)
16 Like love (1962)
17 Ten plus one (1963)
18 Axe (1964)
19 He who hesitates (1964)
20 Doll (1965)
21 Eighty million eyes (1966)
22 Fuzz (1968)
23 Shotgun (1969)
24 Jigsaw (1970)
25 Hail, hail, the gang's all here (1971)
26 Sadie when she died (1972)
27 Let's hear it for the deaf man (1972)
28 Hail to the chief (1973)
29 Bread (1974)
30 Blood relatives (1975)
31 So long as you both shall live (1976)
32 Long time no see (1977)
33 Calypso (1979)
34 Ghosts (1980)
35 Heat (1981)
36 Ice (1983)
37 Lightning (1984)
38 Eight black horses (1985)
39 Poison (1987)
40 Tricks (1987)

41 McBain's ladies:women of the 87th
Precinct (1988)
42 Lullaby (1989)
43 McBain's ladies, too (1990)
44 Vespers (1990)
45 Widows (1991)
46 Kiss (1992)
47 Mischief (1993)
48 Romance (1995)
49 Nocturne (1997)
50 The big bad city (1999)
51 The last dance (2000)
52 Money, money, money (2001)
53 Fat Ollie's book (2002)
54 The frumious bandersnatch (2003)

MCCAFFERTY, J.
DR. MACKENZIE GREEN
1 Star gazer (1994)
2 Artist unknown (1995)
3 Finales and overtures (1996)

MCCAFFREY, A.
PERN AND THE RED PLANET
1 Dragonflight (1971)
2 Dragonquest (1973)
3 Dragonsong (1974)
4 Dragonsinger (1977)
5 The white dragon (1979)
6 Dragondrums (1979)
7 Moreta, Dragonlady of Pern (1983)
8 Dragonsdawn (1988)
9 The renegades of Pern (1990)
10 All the weyrs of Pern (1991)
11 First fall (1993)
12 The dolphins of Pern (1994)
13 Red star rising (1996)
14 The MasterHarper of Pern (1997)
15 The skies of Pern (2001)
16 Dragon's kin (2003)

MCCAFFREY, A.
ACORNA SERIES
1 Acorna the unicorn girl (1997)
2 Acorna's quest (1998)
3 Acorna's people (2001)
4 Acorna's world (2001)
5 Acorna's search (2003)
6 Acorna's rebels (2003)

MCCAFFREY, A.
CATENI SEQUENCE
1 Freedom's landing (1995)
2 Freedom's choice (1997)
3 Freedom's challenge (1998)
4 Freedom's ransom (2002)

MCCAFFREY, A.
CRYSTAL
1 Crystalsinger (1982)
2 Killashandra (1986)
3 Crystal line (1992)

MCCAFFREY, A.
DINOSAUR PLANET SAGA
1 Dinosaur planet (1977)
2 Survivors (1997)

MCCAFFREY, A.
THE SHIP
1 The ship who sang (with M.Lackey) (1993)
2 The ship who searched (with M.Lackey) (1994)
3 Partnership (with M.Ball) (1994)
4 The city who fought (with J.Nye) (1995)
5 The ship who won (with J.Nye) (1995)
6 The ship errant (with J.Nye) (1997)

MCCAFFREY, A.
THE TOWER AND THE HIVE
1 The rowan (1990)
2 Damia (1992)
3 Damia's children (1993)
4 Lyon's pride (1994)
5 The tower and the hive (1999)

MCCAFFREY, A. & MOON, E.
PLANET PIRATES
1 Sassinak (1991)
2 The death of sleep (1991)
3 Generation warriors (1992)

MCCAFFREY, A. & NYE, J.
DOONA
1 Crisis on Doona (1992)
2 Treaty planet (1994)

MCCAFFREY, A. & SCARBOROUGH, E.
POWER
1 Powers that be (1993)
2 Power lines (1994)
3 Power play (1995)

MCCALL SMITH, A.
MORITZ-MARIA VON IGELFELD
1 At the villa of reduced circumstances (2003)
2 The finer points of sausage dogs (2003)
3 Portuguese irregular verbs (2003)

MCCALL SMITH, A.
PRECIOUS RAMOTSWE
1 The No.1 Ladies' Detective Agency (1999)
2 Tears of the giraffe (2000)
3 The morality of beautiful girls (2001)
4 The Kalahari typing school for men (2001)
5 The full cupboard of life (2003)

MCCARRY, C.
PAUL CHRISTOPHER
1 The Miernik dossier (1974)
2 Tears of autumn (1975)
3 Secret lovers (1977)
4 The better angels (1979)
5 The last supper (1983)
6 Second sight (1991)

MCCARTHY, C.
BORDER TRILOGY
1 All the pretty horses (1993)
2 The crossing (1994)
3 Cities of the plain (1998)

MCCARTHY, N.
LOVE ON THE INTERNET
1 Chat
2 Connect
3 Crash

MCCAUGHREN, T.
1 Run with the wind (1983)
2 Run to earth (1984)

MCCLELLAN, J.
TRU NORTH
1 KC bomber (1997)
2 Penn Valley phoenix (1998)
3 River Quay (1998)

MCCLURE, J.
LIEUT.KRAMER AND SGT. ZONDI
1 The steam pig (1970)
2 The caterpillar cop (1972)
3 Four and twenty virgins (1973)
4 The gooseberry fool (1974)
5 Snake (1976)
6 Killers (1976)
7 The Sunday hangman (1977)
8 The blood of an Englishman (1990)
9 The artful egg (1984)
10 The song dog (1992)

MCCORMAC, R.
FRANK SANSOM
1 Playing dead (1996)
2 Shattered (1999)
3 Malpractice (2001)

MCCOURT, F.
A LIMERICK CHILDHOOD
1 Angela's ashes (1998)
2 'Tis (2000)

MCCRUMB, S.
ELIZABETH MCPHERSON
1 The Windsor knot (1990)
2 Paying the piper (1991)
3 Sick of shadows (1992)
4 Highland laddie gone (1993)
5 Lovely in her bones (1993)
6 Missing Susan (1994)
7 McPherson's lament (1992)
8 If I'd killed him when I met him (1995)

MCCULLOUGH, C.
MASTERS OF ROME
1 First man in Rome (1990)
2 The grass crown (1991)
3 Fortune's favourites (1993)
4 Caesar's women (1996)
5 Caesar (1997)

MCCUTCHAN, P.
LIEUT. HALFHYDE
1 Beware, beware the Bight of Benin (1974)
2 Halfhyde's island (1975)
3 The guns of arrest (1976)
4 Halfhyde to the narrows (1977)
5 Halfhyde for the Queen (1978)
6 Halfhyde ordered south (1979)
7 Halfhyde and the Flag Captain (1980)
8 Halfhyde on the Yangtze (1981)
9 Halfhyde on Zanatu (1982)
10 Halfhyde outward bound (1983)
11 The Halfhyde line (1984)
12 Halfhyde and the chain gang (1985)
13 Halfhyde goes to war (1986)
14 Halfhyde on the Amazon (1987)
15 Halfhyde and the Admiral (1990)
16 Halfhyde and the Fleet Review (1991)

MCCUTCHAN, P.
CAMERON
1 Cameron, Ordinary Seaman (1979)
2 Cameron comes through (1980)
3 Cameron of the 'Castle Bay'
4 Lieut.Cameron RNVR (1981)
5 Cameron's convoy (1982)
6 Cameron in the gap (1982)
7 Orders for Cameron (1983)
8 Cameron in command (1983)
9 Cameron and the Kaiserhof (1984)
10 Cameron's raid (1985)
11 Cameron's chase (1986)
12 Cameron's trooplift (1987)
13 Cameron's commitment (1988)
14 Cameron's crossing (1993)

MCCUTCHAN, P.
SIMON SHARD
1 Call for Simon Shard (1973)
2 A very big bang (1975)
3 Blood runs East (1976)
4 The Eros affair (1977)
5 Blackmail north (1979)
6 Shard calls the tune (1980)
7 The hoof (1983)
8 Shard at bay (1985)
9 The executioners (1986)
10 Overnight express (1988)
11 The Logan file (1991)
12 The Abbot of Stockbridge (1992)

MCCUTCHAN, P.
JOHN MASON KEMP
1 The convoy Commodore (1986)
2 Convoy north (1987)
3 Convoy south (1988)
4 Convoy east (1989)
5 Convoy of fear (1990)
6 Convoy homeward (1992)

MCCUTCHAN, P.
TOM CHATTO
1 Tom Chatto, apprentice (1994)
2 Tom Chatto, second mate (1995)
3 Tom Chatto, RNR (1996)

MCCUTCHAN, P.
COMMANDER SHAW
1 Gibraltar Road (1960)
2 Redcap (1961)
3 Bluebolt one (1961)
4 The man from Moscow (1962)
5 Warmaster (1963)
6 The Moscow coach (1964)
7 Deadline (1965)
8 Skyprobe (1966)
9 The screaming red balloons (1968)
10 The bright red businessmen (1969)
11 The all-purpose bodies (1969)
12 Hartinger's mouse (1970)
13 This Drakotny.... (1971)
14 Sunstrike (1979)
15 Corpse (1980)
16 Werewolf (1982)

17 Rollerball (1984)
18 Greenfly (1987)
19 The boy who liked monsters (1989)
20 The spatchcock plan (1990)
21 Polecat Brennan (1994)
22 Burn-out (1995)

MCDERMID, V.
LINDSAY GORDON
1 Report for murder (1987)
2 Common murder (1989)
3 Final edition (1991)
4 Union Jack (1993)
5 Booked for murder (1997)
6 Hostage to murder (2003)

MCDERMID, V.
KATE BRANNIGAN
1 Dead beat (1992)
2 Kick back (1993)
3 Crack down (1994)
4 Clean break (1995)
5 Blue genes (1996)
6 Star struck (1998)

MCDERMID, V.
TONY HILL
1 The mermaids singing (1995)
2 The wire in the blood (1997)
3 The last temptation (2002)
4 The torment of others (2004)

MCDONALD, GREGORY
INSPECTOR FLYNN
1 Flynn (1976)
2 Snatched (1980)
3 The buck passes Flynn (1982)
4 Flynn's Inn (1985)

MCDONALD, GREGORY
FLETCH
1 Fletch, too (1987)
2 Fletch won (1985)
3 Fletch and the Widow Bradley (1981)
4 Fletch (1975)
5 Confess, Fletch (1977)
6 Fletch's fortune (1979)
7 Fletch's Moxie (1983)
8 Fletch and the man who (1984)
9 Fletch forever (1978)
10 Carioca Fletch (1984)
11 Son of Fletch (1994)
12 Fletch reflected (1995)

MCDONALD, I.
KILLIGREW
1 Chaga (1996)
2 Kirinya (1998)

MCDONALD, J. D.
TRAVIS MCGEE
1 The deep blue goodbye (1965)
2 Nightmare in pink (1966)
3 A purple place for dying (1966)
4 The quick red fox (1967)
5 A deadly shade of gold (1967)
6 Bright orange for the shroud (1967)
7 Darker than amber (1968)
8 One fearful yellow eye (1968)
9 Pale grey for guilt (1969)
10 The girl in the pale brown wrapper (1969)
11 Dress her in indigo (1971)
12 Flash of green (1972)
13 The long lavender look (1972)
14 A tan and sandy silence (1973)
15 McGee (1974)
16 The scarlet ruse (1975)
17 The turquoise lament (1975)
18 The dreadful lemon sky (1976)
19 Dead low tide (1976)
20 Murder for the bride (1977)
21 You live once (1978)
22 The empty copper sea (1979)
23 The green ripper (1980)
24 Free fall in crimson (1982)
25 Cinnamon skin (1982)
26 The lonely silver rain (1985)

MCDOWELL, C.
CONSTANCE CASTELFRANCO
1 A woman of style (1992)
2 A woman of spirit (1993)

MCELDOWNEY, E.
SUPT. CECIL MEGARRY
1 A kind of homecoming (1994)
2 A stone of the heart (1995)
3 The sad case of Harpo Higgins (1996)
4 Murder at Piper's Gut (1997)

MCGARRITY, M.
KEVIN KERNEY
1 Tularosa (1997)
2 Mexican hat (1998)
3 Hermit's peak (1999)
4 Serpent gate (1999)
5 The Judas judge (2001)
6 The big gamble (2003)

MCGOWN, J.
INSPECTOR LLOYD AND SERGEANT HILL
1 A perfect match (1983)
2 Redemption (1988)
3 Death of a dancer (1989)
4 The murders of Mrs. Austin and Mrs. Beale (1991)
5 The other woman (1992)
6 Murder......now and then (1993)
7 A shred of evidence (1995)
8 Verdict unsafe (1997)
9 Picture of innocence (1998)
10 Plots and errors (1999)
11 Scene of crime (2001)
12 Births, deaths and marriages (2002)
13 Unlucky for some (2004)

MCILVANNEY, W.
LAIDLAW
1 Laidlaw (1980)
2 The papers of Tony Veitch (1983)
3 Strange loyalties (1991)

MCINERNY, R.
FATHER DOWLING
1 Her death of cold (1977)
2 The seventh station (1978)
3 Bishop as pawn (1979)
4 Lying there (1980)
5 Second Vespers (1981)
6 Thicker than water (1982)
7 Getting a way with murder (1987)
8 Sleight of body (1989)
9 The Judas priest (1991)
10 The basket case (1992)
11 Getting away with murder (1992)
12 Desert sinner (1994)

MCKENNA, J. E.
TALES OF EINARINN
1 The thief's gamble
2 The swordsman's craft
3 The gambler's fortune
4 The warrior's bond
5 The assassin's edge

MCKENZIE, N.
GUINEVERE AND ARTHUR
1 The child queen (1994)
2 The high queen (1995)

MCKEOWN, J.
1 Back crack boy
2 Liam at large

MCKEVETT, G. A.
SAVANNAH REID
1 Sugar and spite (2000)
2 Sour grapes (2001)
3 Peaches and screams (2002)
4 Death by chocolate (2003)
5 Cereal killer (2004)

MCKILLIP, P. A.
CHRONICLES OF MORGAN, PRINCE OF HED
1 Riddlemaster of Hed
2 Heir of sea and fire
3 Harpist in the wind

MCKILLIP, P. A.
CYGNET
1 The sorceress and the cygnet
2 The cygnet and the firebird

MCKINLAY, M.
JOHN LEITH
1 Double entry (1991)
2 Legacy (1992)
3 The caring game (1993)

MCKINNEY, J.
ROBOTECH
1 Genesis
2 Battlecry
3 Homecoming
4 Battlehymn
5 Force of arms
6 Doomsday
7 Southern cross
8 Metal fire
9 The final nightmare
10 Invid invasion
11 Metamorphosis
12 Symphony of light

MCKINNEY, J.
SENTINELS
1 The devil's hand
2 Dark powers
3 Death dance
4 World killers
5 Rubicon

MCKINNEY, J.
THE BLACK HOLE TRAVEL AGENCY
1 Event horizon
2 Artifact of the system
3 Free radicals
4 Hostile takeover

MCLEAVE, H.
BRODIE AND SHANE
1 A borderline case (1979)
2 Double exposure (1980)
3 The Icarus threat (1984)
4 Under the icefall (1987)

MCLEAVE, H.
GREG MACLEAN
1 Second time around (1984)
2 Death masque (1985)

MCMULLEN, J.
1 My small country living (1984)
2 The wind in the ashtree (1988)
3 A small country living goes ever on
(1990)
   NF Country life

MCMURTRY, L.
AURORA GREENWAY
1 Terms of endearment (1977)
2 The evening star (1992)

MCMURTRY, L.
GUS MACRAE AND WOODROW CALL
1 Comanche moon (1997)
2 Dead man's walk (1995)
3 Lonesome dove (1986)
4 Streets of Laredo (1993)
   Listed in chronological order

MCMURTRY, L.
HARMONY PALMER
1 The desert rose (1983)
2 The late child (1996)

MCMURTRY, L.
TEXAS
1 The last picture show (1966)
2 Texasville (1987)
3 Duane's depressed (1999)

MCMURTRY, LARRY
1 All my friends are going to be strangers
2 Some can whistle (1990)

MCNAB, C.
CAROL ASHTON
1 The Shipley report (1990)
2 Death down under (1991)
3 Cop out (2003)

MCNALLY, C.
GHOST HOUSE
1 The ghost house (1979)
2 The ghost house revenge (1987)

MCNAMARA, J. D.
1 The first directive
2 Fatal command (1988)

MCNEILL, B.
ALEX FRASER
1 Busker (1998)
2 To answer the peacock (1999)

MCNEILL, E.
1 A bridge in time (1994)
2 Wild heritage (1995)

MEEK, M. R. D.
LENNOX KEMP
1 Hang the consequences (1983)
2 The sitting ducks (1984)
3 The split second (1985)
4 In remembrance of Rose (1986)
5 A worm of doubt (1987)
6 A mouthful of sand (1988)
7 A loose connection (1989)
8 This blessed plot (1990)
9 Touch and go (1992)
10 Postscript to murder (1996)
11 If you go down to the woods (2001)
12 The vanishing point (2002)

MEHTA, V.
CONTINENTS OF EXILE
1 Daddiji (1977)
2 Mammaji (1979)
3 Vedi (1983)
4 The ledge between the streams (1984)
5 Sound shadows of the New World
(1986)
6 The stolen light (1989)
7 Up at Oxford (1993)
   NF Autobiography

MEIER, L.
LUCY STONE
1 Back to school murder (1997)
2 Trick or treat murder (1997)
3 Tippy toe murder (1998)
4 Turkey Day murder (1998)
5 Mistletoe murder (1999)
6 Christmas cookie murder (2000)
7 Wedding day murder (2001)

MELLY, G.
1 Scouse mouse (1984)
2 Rum, bum and concertina (1977)
3 Owning up (1965)
   NF Autobiography

MELVILLE, A.
LORIMER SAGA
1 The Lorimer line (1977)
2 Lorimer legacy (1979)
3 Lorimers at war (1980)
4 Lorimers in love (1981)
5 The last of the Lorimers (1983)
6 Lorimer loyalties (1984)

MELVILLE, A.
THE HOUSE OF HARDIE
1 The House of Hardie (1987)
2 Grace Hardie (1988)
3 The Hardie inheritance (1990)

MELVILLE, JAMES
SUPT. OTANI
1 The wages of Zen (1978)
2 The chrysanthemum chain (1980)
3 A sort of Samurai (1981)
4 The ninth netsuke (1982)
5 Sayonara.sweet Amaryllis (1983)
6 Death of a Diamyo (1984)
7 The death ceremony (1985)
8 Go gently Gaijin (1986)
9 Kimono for a corpse (1987)
10 The reluctant ronin (1988)
11 A Haiku for Hanae (1989)
12 Bogus Buddha (1990)
13 The body wore brocade (1992)

MELVILLE, JAMES
BEN LAZENBY
1 Diplomatic baggage (1995)
2 The reluctant spy (1994)

MELVILLE, JENNIE
CHARMIAN DANIELS
1 Come home and be killed (1962)
2 Burning is a substitute for loving (1963)
3 Murderers' houses (1964)
4 There lies your love (1965)
5 Nell alone (1966)
6 A different kind of summer (1967)
7 A new kind of killer, an old kind of death (1970)
8 Murder wears a pretty face (1981)
9 Windsor red (1987)
10 A cure for dying (1989)
11 Witching murder (1990)
12 Footsteps in the blood (1990)

13 Dead set (1992)
14 Whoever has the heart (1993)
15 Baby drop (1994)
16 The morbid kitchen (1995)
17 The woman who was not there (1996)
18 Revengeful death (1997)
19 Stone dead (1999)
20 Dead again (2000)
21 Loving murder (2001)

MELVILLE-ROSS, A.
HARDING
1 Shadow (1984)
2 Trigger (1983)
3 Talon (1983)
4 Command (1985)

MEREDITH, R. C.
TIMELINE TRILOGY
1 At the narrow passage
2 No brother, no friend
3 Vestiges of time

MERRICK, G.
PETER AND CHARLIE TRILOGY
1 The Lord won't mind
2 One for the Gods
3 Forth into the light

MEYNELL, L. W.
HOOKY HEFFERMAN
1 Death by arrangement (1972)
2 The fatal flaw (1973)
3 The thirteen trumpeters (1973)
4 The fairly innocent little man (1974)
5 Don't stop for Hooky Hefferman (1975)
6 Hooky and the crock of gold (1975)
7 The lost half-hour (1976)
8 Hooky gets the wooden spoon (1977)
9 Hooky and the villainous chauffeur (1979)
10 Hooky and the prancing horse (1980)
11 Hooky goes to blazes (1981)
12 The open door (1984)
13 The affair at Barwold (1985)
14 Hooky catches a tartar (1986)
15 Hooky on loan (1987)
16 Hooky hooked (1988)

MICHAEL, J.
DECEPTION
1 Deceptions (1994)
2 A tangled web (1995)

MICHAEL, S.
CHARLES HOLROYD
1 The cut throat (1991)
2 The long lie (1992)

MICHAELS, B.
GREYHAVEN MANOR
1 Black rainbow (1982)
2 Someone in the house (1981)

MICHAELS, F.
TEXAS
1 Texas rich (1988)
2 Texas heat (1989)
3 Texas fury (1991)
4 Texas sunrise (1993)

MICHAELS, F.
THE CAPTIVE
1 Captive passions (1992)
2 Captive embraces (1993)
3 Captive splendours (1994)
4 Captive innocence (1995)
5 Captive secrets (1996)

MICHAELS, F.
SINS
1 Sins of the flesh (1992)
2 Sins of omission (1993)

MICHAELS, F.
THORNTON AND COLEMAN
FAMILIES
1 Vegas rich (1996)
2 Vegas heat (1997)
3 Vegas sunrise (1997)
4 Kentucky rich (2001)
5 Kentucky heat (2002)
6 Kentucky sunrise (2003)

MICHELET, C.
PROVENCAL SERIES
1 Firelight and woodsmoke (1993)
2 Applewood (1994)
3 Scent of herbs (1994)

MIDDLETON, H.
MORDRED CYCLE
1 The King's evil (1995)
2 The Queen's captive (1996)
3 The knight's vengeance (1997)

MILES, K.
ALAN SAXON
1 Bullet hole (1986)
2 Double eagle (1987)

3 Green murder (1990)
4 Flagstick (1991)

MILES, R.
EDEN
1 Bitter legacy (1985)
2 Return to Eden (1986)

MILES, R.
GUENEVERE SERIES
1 Queen of the summer country (1999)
2 The knight of the sacred lake (2000)
3 The child of the Holy Grail (2000)

MILES, R.
ISOLDE
1 Isolde (2002)
2 The maiden of white hands (2004)

MILLER, HUGH
DISTRICT NURSE
1 The District Nurse (1986)
2 Snow on the wind (1987)

MILLER, HUGH
EASTENDERS
1 Home fires burning (1986)
2 Swings and roundabouts (1986)
3 Good intentions (1986)
4 The flower of Albert Square (1986)
5 Blind spots (1986)
6 Hopes and horizons (1987)
7 The baffled heart (1987)
8 Growing wild (1987)
9 A place in life (1988)
10 A single man (1988)
11 Taking chances (1988)
12 Elbow room (1988)

MILLER, HUGH
DET. INSPECTOR MIKE FLETCHER
1 Echo of justice (1990)
2 Skin deep (1991)

MILLER, HUGH
UNACO
1 Prime target (1997)
2 Borrowed time (1997)

MILLER, J.
CALLAGHAN BROTHERS
1 Gone to Texas (1984)
2 War clouds (1984)
3 Comanche trail (1988)
4 Riding shotgun (1988)

MILLER, W.
LEIBOWITZ
1 A canticle for Leibowitz
2 Saint Leibowitz and the wild horse
woman

MILLHISER, M.
CHARLIE GREENE
1 Murder at Moot Point (1992)
2 Death of the office witch (1993)

MILLIGAN, S.
MY WAR
1 Adolf Hitler; my part in his downfall
(1971)
2 Rommel? Gunner who? (1973)
3 Monty; his part in my victory (1976)
4 Mussolini; his part in my downfall
(1978)
5 Where have all the bullets gone (1985)
6 Goodbye, soldier (1986)
NF Wartime experiences

MILNE, C.
THE REAL CHRISTOPHER ROBIN
1 The enchanted places (1979)
2 The path through the trees (1980)
3 The hollow hill (1982)
NF Autobiography

MILNE, J.
JIMMY JENNER
1 Dead birds (1986)
2 Shadow play (1987)
3 Daddy's girl (1988)

MILSTED, D.
1 The chronicles of Craigfieth (1988)
2 Market forces (1989)

MINA, D.
MAUREEN O'DONNELL
1 Garnethill (1999)
2 Exile (2000)
3 Resolution (2002)

MINTON, M.
1 Yesterday's road (1986)
2 The marriage bowl (1987)
3 The weeping doves (1987)

MITCHELL, G.
DAME BEATRICE BRADLEY
1 Speedy death (1929)
2 Mystery of a butcher
3 The longer bodies

4 The Saltmarsh murders
5 Death at the opera
6 The devil at Saxon Wall
7 Dead men's morris (1936)
8 Come away death (1937)
9 St.Peter's finger (1938)
10 Printer's error (1939)
11 Brazen tongue (1940)
12 Hangman's curfew (1940)
13 When last I died (1941)
14 The greenstone griffins (1983)
15 Laurels are poison (1942)
16 The worsted viper (1942)
17 Sunset over Soho (1943)
18 My father sleeps (1944)
19 The rising of the moon (1945)
20 Here comes a chopper (1946)
21 Death and the maiden (1947)
22 The dancing druids (1948)
23 Tom Brown's body (1949)
24 Groaning spinney (1950)
25 The devil's elbow (1951)
26 The echoing strangers (1952)
27 Merlin's furlong (1953)
28 Faintley speaking (1954)
29 Watson's choice (1955)
30 Twelve horses and the hangman's noose
(1956)
31 The twentythird man (1957)
32 Spotted hemlock (1958)
33 The man who grew tomatoes (1959)
34 Say it with flowers (1960)
35 The nodding canaries (1961)
36 My bones will keep (1962)
37 Adders on the heath (1963)
38 Death of a delft blue (1964)
39 Pageant of murder (1965)
40 The croaking raven (1966)
41 Skeleton island (1966)
42 Three quick and five dead (1968)
43 Dance to your daddy (1969)
44 Gory dew (1970)
45 Lament for Leto (1971)
46 A hearse on Mayday (1972)
47 The murder of busy Lizzie (1973)
48 A javelin for Jonah (1973)
49 Winking at the brim (1974)
50 Convent on Styx (1975)
51 Late, late in the evening (1976)
52 Fault in the structure (1977)
53 Noonday and night (1977)
54 Wraiths and changelings (1978)
55 Mingled with venom (1978)
56 Nest of vipers (1979)
57 The mudflats of the dead (1979)
58 Uncoffined clay (1980)
59 The whispering knights (1980)
60 The death-cap dancers (1981)
61 Here lies Gloria Mundy (1982)

62 Death of a burrowing mole (1982)
63 Cold, lone and still (1983)
64 The hangman's noose (1983)
65 No winding sheet (1984)
66 The Crozier pharaohs (1984)

MITCHELL, J.
RON HOGGET
1 Sometimes you could die (1985)
2 Dead Ernest (1986)

MITCHELL, J.
JOE CAVE
1 Dead Ernest (1986)
2 KGB kill (1987)
3 Dying day (1988)

MITCHELL, JAMES
1 A woman to be loved (1990)
2 An impossible woman (1992)

MITCHELL, JOHN
1 Class struggle
2 Chalked off
3 Absolutely chalked off
4 Chalk's away! (1993)

MODESSIT, L. E.
THE FOREVER HERO
1 Down from a distant earth
2 The silent warrior
3 The endless twlight

MODESSIT, L. E.
THE SPELLSONG CYCLE
1 The soprano sorceress (1998)
2 The Spellsong war (1999)
3 The darksong rising (2001)
4 Shadowsinger (2002)

MODESSIT, L. E.
RECLUCE
1 The magic of Recluce
2 The towers of the sunset
3 The magic engineer
4 The order war
5 The death of chaos
6 Fall of angels
7 The chaos balance
8 The white order
9 Colours of chaos
10 Magi'i of Cyador
11 Scion of Cyador

MODESSIT, L. E.
COREAN CHRONICLES
1 Legacies (2003)
2 Darknesses (2004)

MOFFAT, G.
MISS PINK
1 Lady with a cool eye (1973)
2 Deviant death (1974)
3 The corpse road (1975)
4 Miss Pink at the edge of the world (1975)
5 Hard option (1976)
6 Over the sea to death (1976)
7 A short time to live (1977)
8 Persons unknown (1978)
9 Die like a dog (1982)
10 Last chance country (1983)
11 Grizzly trail (1984)
12 Snare (1987)
13 The stone hawk (1989)
14 Rage (1990)
15 Raptor zone (1990)
16 Veronica's sisters (1992)
17 The lost girls (1998)
18 Private sins (1999)
19 Retribution (2002)

MOFFAT, G.
JACK PHARAOH
1 Pit bull (1991)
2 The outside edge (1992)

MOLLOY, M.
THE GAZETTE MYSTERIES
1 Sweet sixteen (1992)
2 Cat's paw (1993)
3 Home before dark (1994)
4 Dogsbody (1996)

MONACO, R.
PARSIVAL
1 Parsifal (1977)
2 The Grail war (1979)
3 The final quest (1980)
4 Blood and dreams (1985)

MONK, C.
1 A field of bright laughter (1990)
2 Flame of courage (1992)

MOODY, S.
PENNY WANAWAKE
1 Penny black (1983)
2 Penny dreadful (1984)
3 Penny post (1985)
4 Penny royal (1986)
5 Penny wise (1988)

6 Penny pinching (1989)
7 Penny saving (1991)

MOODY, S.
CASSIE SWANN
1 Takeout double (1993)
2 Grand slam (1994)
3 King of hearts (1995)
4 Doubled in spades (1996)
5 Sacrifice bid (1997)
6 Dummy hand (1998)

MOON, E.
THE LEGACY OF GIRD
1 Surrender none
2 Liar's oath

MOON, E.
THE DEAD OF PAKESNARRION
1 Sheepfarmer's daughter
2 Divided allegiance
3 Oath of gold
4 The deed of Paksenarrion (2003)

MOON, E.
SERRANO LEGACY
1 Hunting party
2 Sporting chance
3 Winning colours
4 Against the odds

MOORCOCK, M.
CORUM
1 The knight of the swords
2 The queen of the swords
3 The king of the swords
4 The bull and the spear
5 The oak and the ram
6 The sword and the stallion

MOORCOCK, M.
DANCERS AT THE END OF TIME
1 Alien heat (1974)
2 The hollow lands (1975)
3 The end of all songs (1976)
4 Legends from the end of time (1976)
5 The transformation of Miss Mavis Ming (1977)

MOORCOCK, M.
ELRIC
1 Elric of Melnibone (1972)
2 Sailor on the seas of fate (1976)
3 The weird of the white wolf
4 The vanishing tower
5 The bane of the black sword

6 Stormbringer
7 Elric at the end of time; short stories
8 The fortress of the pearl (1989)
9 The revenge of the rose (1991)
10 The dreamthief's daughter (1999)

MOORCOCK, M.
HAWKMOON
1 The jewel in the skull (1973)
2 The mad god
3 The sword of dawn (1973)
4 The runestaff (1974)
5 Count Brass
6 The champion of Garathorn
7 The quest for Tanelorn

MOORCOCK, M.
JERRY CORNELIUS
1 The final programme (1969)
2 A cure for cancer (1970)
3 The English assassin (1972)
5 The condition of Muzak (1976)
6 The entropy tango (1981)

MOORCOCK, M.
OSWALD BASTABLE
1 War lord of the air (1973)
2 The land leviathan (1974)
3 The steel Tsar (1981)

MOORCOCK, M.
JOHN DAKER, ETERNAL CHAMPION OF EREKOSE
1 The eternal champion
2 Phoenix in Obsidian
3 The dragon in the sword (1987)

MOORCOCK, M.
VON BEK FAMILY
1 The war hound and the world's pain (1982)
2 The city in the autumn stars (1986)
3 Fabulous harbours (1995)
4 Blood (1995)
5 The war against the angels (1996)

MOORCOCK, M.
PYAT
1 Byzantium endures (1981)
2 Laughter at Carthage (1986)
3 Jerusalem commands (1992)

MOORCOCK, M.
MICHAEL KANE
1 The city of the beast

2 The lord of the spiders
3 Masters of the pit

MOORE, G.
1 Am I too loud? (1962)
2 Farewell recital (1978)
3 Furthermoore (1983)
  NF Autobiography

MOORE, M.
DET. INSPECTOR RICHARD BAXTER
1 Forests of the night (1988)
2 Dangerous conceits (1989)
3 Murder in good measure (1990)
4 Fringe ending (1991)

MORAY, H.
HENRI, LADY RHONDA
1 Four winds (1983)
2 Before the dawn (1984)

MORGAN, C.
LILY WALTERS
1 Lily of the valleys (1989)
2 Lily among thorns (1990)
3 Comfort me with apples (1991)

MORGAN, D.
RALPH DE GIRET
1 The second son (1980)
2 The Kingmaker's knight (1981)
3 Sons and roses (1981)

MORGAN, R.
CODY WALLACE
1 Tall dead wives (1990)
2 Low mean men (1992)

MORGAN, F.
COUNTESS ASHBY DE LA ZOUCHE
1 Unnatural fire (2000)
2 The rival Queens (2001)
3 Fortune's slave (2003)

MORICE, A.
TESSA CRICHTON
1 Death in the grand manor (1970)
2 Murder in married life (1970)
3 Death of a gay dog (1971)
4 Murder on French leave (1972)
5 Death and the dutiful daughter (1973)
6 Death of a heavenly twin (1974)
7 Killing with kindness (1974)
8 Nursery tea and poison (1975)
9 Death of a wedding guest (1976)
10 Murder in mimicry (1977)

11 Scared to death (1977)
12 Murder by proxy (1978)
13 Murder in outline (1978)
14 Death in the round (1980)
15 The men in her death (1981)
16 Hollow vengeance (1982)
17 Sleep of death (1982)
18 Murder post-dated (1983)
19 Getting away with murder (1984)
20 Dead on cue (1985)
21 Publish and be killed (1986)
22 Treble exposure (1987)
23 Design for dying (1988)
24 Fatal charm (1988)
25 Planning for murder (1990)

MORRELL, D.
ISRAEL SAUL GRISMAN
1 The Brotherhood of the Rose (1985)
2 The Fraternity of the Stone (1986)
3 The League of Night and Fog (1987)

MORRELL, D.
RAMBO
1 First blood (1975)
2 First blood II
3 Rambo III

MORRIS, G. H.
THE BRIGHTSIDE TRILOGY
1 Doves and silk handkerchiefs (1986)
2 Grandmother, grandmother, come and see (1989)
3 The Brightside dinosaur (1991)

MORRIS, J.
THE KERRION SAGA
1 Dream dancer
2 Cruiser dreams

MORSON, I.
WILLIAM FALCONER
1 Falconer's crusade (1994)
2 Falconer's judgment (1995)
3 Falconer and the face of God (1996)
4 A psalm for Falconer (1997)
5 Falconer and the great beast (1998)

MORTIMER, J.
RUMPOLE
1 Rumpole of the Bailey (1978)
2 The trials of Rumpole (1979)
3 Rumpole's return (1980)
4 Regina v Rumpole (1981)
5 Rumpole and the golden thread (1983)
6 Rumpole's last case (1987)
7 Rumpole and the age of miracles (1988)

8 Rumpole a la carte (1990)
   9 Rumpole on trial (1992)
  10 The best of Rumpole (1993)
  11 Rumpole and the angel of death (1995)
  12 Rumpole rests his case (2001)
  13 Rumpole and the Primrose Path (2002)

MORTIMER, J.
THE RAPSTONE CHRONICLES
1 Paradise postponed (1987)
2 Titmuss regained (1990)
3 The sound of trumpets (1999)

MORWOOD, P.
ALDRIC TALVARIN
1 The horse lord (1984)
2 The demon lord (1985)
3 The dragon lord (1987)
4 The warlord's domain (1989)

MORWOOD, P.
CLAN WARS
1 Greylady (1993)
2 Widowmaker (1994)

MORWOOD, P.
PRINCE IVAN
1 Prince Ivan (1990)
2 Firebird (1992)
3 The golden horde (1993)

MOSCO, M.
1 The waiting game (1987)
2 After the dream (1988)

MOSCO, M.
ALISON PLANTAINE
1 Between two worlds (1983)
2 A sense of place (1984)
3 The price of fame (1985)

MOSCO, M.
MANCHESTER SERIES
1 Almonds and raisins (1979)
2 Scattered seed (1980)
3 Children's children (1981)
4 Out of the ashes (1989)
5 New beginnings (1991)

MOSLEY, N.
1 Catastrophe practice (1979)
2 Imago bird (1980)
3 Serpent (1981)
4 Judith (1986)
5 Hopeful monsters (1990)

MOSLEY, W.
SOCRATES FORTLOW
1 Always outnumbered, always
   outgunned (1997)
2 Walkin' the dog (2000)

MOSCO, M.
EASY RAWLINS
1 Devil in a blue dress (1992)
2 A red death (1993)
3 Black Betty (1994)
4 Gone fishin' (1997)
5 Bad boy Brawly Brown (2002)
6 The man in my basement (2004)

MOTION, A.
FRANCIS MAYNE
1 The pale companion (1989)
2 Famous for the creatures (1991)

MOYES, P.
CHIEF INSPECTOR HENRY TIBBETT
1 Dead men don't ski (1960)
2 The sunken sailor (1961)
3 Death on the agenda (1962)
4 Murder a la mode (1963)
5 Falling star (1964)
6 Johnny underground (1965)
7 Murder fantastical (1967)
8 Death and the Dutch uncle (1968)
9 Who saw him die? (1970)
10 Season of snow and sins (1971)
11 The black widower (1975)
12 To kill a coconut (1976)
13 Who is Simon Warwick? (1978)
14 Angel death (1980)
15 A six-letter word for death (1983)
16 Night ferry to death (1985)
17 Black girl, white girl (1990)
18 Twice in a blue moon (1993)

MULLER, M.
SHARON MCCONE
1 Edwin of the iron shoes (1981)
2 Ask the cards a question (1983)
3 The Cheshire Cat's eye (1984)
4 Games to keep the dark away (1985)
5 Trophies and dead things (1990)
6 Where echoes live (1991)
7 There's something in a Sunday (1992)
8 The shape of dread (1992)
9 Pennies on a dead woman's eyes (1993)
10 Wolf in the shadows (1994)
11 Till the butchers cut him down (1995)
12 Both ends of the night (1997)
13 While other people sleep (1998)
14 A walk through the fire (1999)

MURARI, T. N.
KIM
1 The Imperial agent (1987)
2 The last victory (1988)

MURDOCH, M. S.
THE MARTIAN WARS
1 Rebellion (2456)
2 Hammer of Mars
3 Armageddon off Vesta

MURPHY, E.
1 The land is bright (1989)
2 To give and to take (1990)
3 There is a season (1991)

MURPHY, H.
REUBEN FROST
1 Murder for lunch (1986)
2 Murder takes a partner (1987)
3 Murders and acquisitions (1988)
4 Murder keeps a secret (1989)
5 Murder times two (1990)
6 Murder saves face (1991)
7 A very Venetian murder (1994)

MURPHY, M.
SHIVAS IRONS
1 Golf in the kingdom (1983)
2 The kingdom of Shivas Irons (1998)

MURPHY-GIBB, D.
CORMAC
1 The seers (1992)
2 The king making (1993)

MURRAY, S.
DET. INSPECTOR ALEC STAINTON
1 A cool killing (1988)
2 The noose of time (1989)
3 Salty waters (1989)
4 Fetch out no shroud (1990)
5 Fatal opinions (1991)
6 Offences against the person (1993)
7 Death and transfiguration (1994)

MYERS, A.
AUGUSTE DIDIER
1 Murder in Pug's Parlour (1986)
2 Murder in the limelight (1987)
3 Murder at Plum's (1989)
4 Murder at the masque (1991)
5 Murder makes an entree (1992)
6 Murder under the kissing bough (1992)
7 Murder in the smoke house (1994)
8 Murder at the music hall (1995)

9 Murder in the motor stable (1996)
10 Murder with majesty (1999)
11 Murder in the Queen's boudoir (2000)

MYERS, P.
MARK HOLLAND
1 Deadly variations (1985)
2 Deadly cadenza (1986)
3 Deadly aria (1987)
4 Deadly sonata (1987)
5 Deadly score (1988)
6 Deadly crescendo (1989)

NABB, M.
MARSHAL GUARNACCIA
1 Death of an Englishman (1981)
2 Death of a Dutchman (1982)
3 Death in Springtime (1983)
4 Death in Autumn (1984)
5 The Marshal and the murderer (1987)
6 The Marshal and the madwoman (1988)
7 The Marshal's own case (1990)
8 The Marshal makes his report (1991)
9 The Marshal at the Villa Torrini (1993)
10 The monster of Florence (1996)
11 Some bitter taste (2003)
12 Property of blood (2004)

NADEL, B.
INSPECTOR CETIN IKMEN
1 Belshazzar's daughter (1999)
2 Arabesk (2001)
3 Petrified (2004)

NADELSON, R.
ARTIE COHEN
1 Red mercury blues (1995)
2 Hot poppies (1997)
3 Bloody London (1999)
4 Sex dolls (2001)
5 Disturbed earth (2004)

NARAYAN, R. K.
MALGUDI
1 Waiting for the Mahatma (1955)
2 The financial expert (1952)
3 Mr. Sampath (1949)
4 The English teacher (1949)
5 The dark room (1938)
6 Swami and friends (1935)
7 The guide (1958)
8 The man-eater of Malgudi (1961)
9 The sweet vendor (1967)
10 A horse and two goats (1970)
11 Malgudi days (1982)
12 The tiger of Malgudi (1983)
13 Under the banyan tree (1985)

14 The talkative man (1986)
15 The world of Nagaraj (1990)

NASH, P.
GRASS
1 Grass (1982)
2 Grass's fancy (1982)
2 Grass
3 Coup de Grass (1983)
4 Grass in idleness (1983)
5 Wayward seeds of Grass (1983)
6 Grass and supergrass (1984)
7 Grass makes hay (1985)
8 Sheep grass (1986)

NATHANSON, E. M.
1 The dirty dozen (1966)
2 A dirty distant war (1988)

NAUGHTON, B.
1 On the pig's back (1987)
2 Saintly Billy (1988)
   NF Autobiography

NAYLOR, G.
RED DWARF
1 Red Dwarf (1989)
2 Better than life (1990)
3 Last human (1995)
4 Backwards (1996)

NEATE, P.
MUSUNGU JIM
1 Musungu Jim and the Great Chief
   Tuloko (2000)
2 Twelve bar blues (2002)

NEEDLE, J.
SECOND OFFICER WILLIAM BERTLEY
1 A fine boy for killing (1996)
2 The wicked trade (1998)

NEEL, J.
DET. CHIEF INSPECTOR JOHN
MCLEISH
1 Death's bright angel (1988)
2 Death on site (1989)
3 Death of a partner (1991)
4 Death among the dons (1993)
5 A timely death (1996)
6 O gentle death (2001)

NEUMAN, F.
CAPT. REDDER, PSYCHIATRIST
1 The seclusion room (1982)
2 Manoeuvres (1984)

NEWCOMB, R.
CHRONICLES OF BLOOD AND STONE
1 The fifth sorceress (2002)
2 The gates of dawn (2003)

NEWLAND, C.
GREENSIDE ESTATE
1 The scholar
2 Society within

NEWMAN, A.
1 A bouquet of barbed wire (1969)
2 Another bouquet... (1984)

NEWMAN, A.
FELIX CRAMER
1 A sense of guilt (1985)
2 A gift of poison (1991)

NEWMAN, G. F.
JACK BENTHAM
1 Set a thief (1985)
2 The testing ground (1987)

NEWMAN, G. F.
LAW AND ORDER
1 A prisoner's tale (1981)
2 A detective's tale (1981)
3 A villain's tale (1981)

NEWMAN, K.
DRACULA
1 Anno Dracula (1992)
2 The bloody Red Baron (1996)

NEWMAN, S.
ARTHURIAN SERIES
1 Guinevere (1985)
2 The chessboard queen (1985)
3 Guinevere evermore (1986)

NEWTON, W.
JOEY BINNS
1 Someone has to take the fall (1979)
2 The smell of money (1980)
3 The set-up (1981)
4 The Rio contract (1982)

NICHOLLS, D.
BOOTHBY-GRAFFOE FAMILY
1 The dangerous flood (1994)
2 In her own right (1995)

NICHOLLS, D.
LEANDER HAWKSWORTH
1 With magic in her eyes (1990)
2 Heirs to adventure (1991)

NICHOLLS, S.
ORCS
1 Bodyguard of lightning
2 Legion of thunder
3 Warriors of the tempest

NICHOLS, A.
THE WHITEBLADE SAGA
1 The Paladin (1998)
2 The songster (2000)
3 The curer (2001)

NICOLE, C.
CHINA TRILOGY
1 The crimson pagoda (1984)
2 The scarlet princess (1985)
3 Red dawn (1985)

NICOLE, C.
ANDERSON LINE
1 The seas of fortune (1984)
2 The rivals (1985)

NICOLE, C.
BLACK MAJESTY
1 Seeds of rebellion (1984)
2 Wild harvest (1985)

NICOLE, C.
JAPANESE TRILOGY
1 The sun rises (1985)
2 The sun and the dragon (1986)
3 The sun on fire (1987)

NICOLE, C.
MCGANN FAMILY
1 Old Glory (1986)
2 The sea and the sand (1986)
3 Iron ships, iron men (1987)
4 Wind of destiny (1987)
5 Raging sea, searing sky (1988)
6 The passion and the glory (1988)

NICOLE, C.
KENYAN TRILOGY
1 The high country (1988)
2 The happy valley (1989)

NICOLE, C.
ROYAL WESTERN DRAGOON GUARDS
1 The Regiment (1988)

2 The Command (1989)
3 The triumph (1989)

NICOLE, C.
SINGAPORE
1 Pearl of the Orient (1988)
2 Dragon's blood (1989)
3 Dark sun (1990)

NICOLE, C.
RICHARD BRYANT
1 Sword of fortune (1990)
2 Sword of Empire (1991)

NICOLE, C.
DAWSON FAMILY
1 Days of wine and roses (1991)
2 The Titans (1992)

NICOLE, C.
HAGGARD
1 Haggard (1980)
2 Haggard's inheritance (1981)
3 The young Haggards (1982)

NICOLE, C.
RUSSIAN QUARTET
1 The seeds of power (1994)
2 The masters (1995)
3 The red tide (1995)
4 The red gods (1996)

NICOLE, C.
ARMS OF WAR
1 The trade (1997)
2 Shadows in the sun (1998)
3 Guns in the desert (1998)

NILES, D.
THE MOONSHAE TRILOGY
1 Darkwalker on Moonshae
2 Black wizards
3 Darkwell

NILES, D.
THE DRUIDHOLME TRILOGY
1 Prophet of Moonshae
2 The coral kingdom
3 The druid queen

NILES, D.
THE MAZTICA TRILOGY
1 Ironhelm
2 Viperhand
3 Feathered dragon

NICOLE, C
(BERKELEY TOWNSEND)
1) TO ALL ETERNITY
2) THE QUEST
3) BE NOT AFRAID

NIVEN, L.
1 The integral trees (1984)
2 The smoke ring (1987)

NIVEN, L.
RINGWORLD
1 Ringworld (1971)
2 Ringworld engineers (1980)
3 The Ringworld throne (1996)

NIVEN, L. & BARNES, S.
DREAM PARK
1 The Barsoom project (1990)
2 The voodoo game (1991)

NIVEN, L. & POURNELLE, J.
1 The mote in God's eye (1980)
2 The moat around Murcheson's eye (1993)

NIVEN, L. AND OTHERS
HEOROT
1 The legacy of Heorot (1987)
2 The dragons of Heorot (1995)

NOBBS, D.
1 A bit of a do (1989)
2 Fair dos (1990)

NOBBS, D.
HENRY PRATT
1 Second from last in the sack race (1983)
2 Pratt of the Argus (1988)
3 The cucumber man (1994)

NOBBS, D.
REGINALD PERRIN
1 The death of Reginald Perrin (1975)
2 The return of Reginald Perrin (1997)
3 The better world of Reginald Perrin (1978)
4 The legacy of Reginald Perrin (1995)

NOLAN, F.
A CALL TO ARMS
1 A promise of glory (1983)
2 Blind duty (1984)

NOLAN, F.
THE GARRETT DOSSIER
1 Sweet sister death (1989)
2 Alert state black (1990)
3 Designated assassin (1990)
4 Rat run (1991)

NORDHOFF, C. & HALL, J. C.
THE BOUNTY
1 Mutiny on the 'Bounty' (1932)
2 Men against the sea (1934)
3 Pitcairn's Island (1934)
4 Mister Christian, by W. Kinsolving (1996)

NORMAN, B.
BOBBY LENNOX
1 The birddog tape (1992)
2 The Mickey Mouse affair (1995)
3 Death on Sunset (1998)

NORMAN, D.
HENRY II
1 The morning gift (1985)
2 Fitzempress
3 King of the last days (1981)

NORMAN, D.
MAKEPEACE BURKE
1 A catch of consequence (2001)
2 Taking liberties (2003)

NORMAN, G.
MORGAN HUNT
1 Sweetwater Ranch (1995)
2 Blue streak (1996)
3 Deep pursuit (1994)
4 Blue light (1995)

NORTON, A.
JANUS
1 Judgment on Janus
2 Victory on Janus

NORTON, A.
ROSS MURDOCK
1 The tune traders (1979)
2 Galactic derelict (1979)
3 The defiant agents (1979)
4 Key out of tune (1979)

NORTON, A.
WITCHWORLD
1 Witch world
2 Web of Witch World
3 Three against Witch World
4 Warlock of Witch World
5 Sorceress of Witch World
6 Year of the unicorn
7 Spell of Witch World
8 Trey of swords
9 Ware hawk

NORTON, A. & LACKEY, M.
HALFBLOOD CHRONICLES
1 The elvenbane (1993)
2 Elvenblood (1995)

OAKES, P.
1 From middle England (1980)
2 Dwellers all in time and space (1981)
3 At the Jazz Band Ball (1983)
NF Autobiography

O'BRIAN, P.
JACK AUBREY
1 Master and Commander (1969)
2 Post Captain (1972)
3 HMS Surprise (1973)
4 The Mauritius command (1977)
5 Desolation Island (1978)
6 Fortune of war (1979)
7 The surgeon's mate (1980)
8 The Ionian mission (1982)
9 Treason's harbour (1983)
10 The far side of the world (1985)
11 The reverse of the medal (1986)
12 The letter of Marque (1988)
13 The thirteen gun salute (1989)
14 Nutmeg of consolation (1990)
15 Clarissa Oakes (1992)
16 The wine-dark sea (1993)
17 The Commodore (1994)
18 The yellow admiral (1997)
19 The hundred days (1998)
20 Blue at the mizzen (1999)

O'BRIEN, EDNA
GIRLS
1 The country girls (1962)
2 The lonely girl (1963)
3 Girls in their married bliss (1964)

O'BRIEN, EDNA
IRISH TRILOGY
1 The house of splendid isolation (1994)
2 Down by the river (1996)
3 Wild Decembers (1999)

O'BRIEN, MAUREEN
DET. INSPECTOR JOHN BRIGHT
1 Close-up on death (1989)
2 Deadly reflection (1993)
3 Dead innocent (1999)
4 Just revenge (2001)
5 Unauthorised departure (2002)

O'BRIEN, MEG
JESSICA JAMES
1 The Daphne decisions (1993)

2 Salmon in the soup (1993)
3 Hare today, gone tomorrow (1993)
4 Eagles die too (1993)

O'CONNELL, C.
KATHY MALLORY
1 Mallory's oracle (1993)
2 The man who lied to women (1995)
3 Killing critics (1996)
4 Flight of the stone angel (1997)
5 Crime school (2002)
6 The jury must die (2003)

O'DONNELL, L.
MICI ANHALT
1 Leisure dying
2 Falling star (1981)
3 Wicked designs (1983)

O'DONNELL, L.
NORAH MULCAHANEY
1 The phone calls (1972)
2 Don't wear your wedding ring (1973)
3 Dial 577 R.A.P.E. (1975)
4 Aftershock (1977)
5 No business being a cop (1980)
6 The children's zoo (1982)
7 A private crime (1991)

O'DONNELL, PETER
MODESTY BLAISE
1 Modesty Blaise (1965)
2 Modesty Blaise and Sabre Tooth (1966)
3 I, Lucifer (1967)
4 A taste for death (1969)
5 The impossible virgin (1971)
6 The silver mistress (1973)
7 Last day in Limbo (1976)
8 The dragon's claw (1978)
9 The Xanadu talisman (1981)
10 The night of Morningstar (1982)
11 Dead man's handle (1985)
12 Cobra trap (1996)

OKRI, BEN
AZARO
1 The famished road (1991)
2 Songs of enchantment (1993)
3 Infinite riches (1998)

OLBRICH, F.
INSPECTOR DESOUZA
1 Desouza pays the price (1978)
2 Sweet and deadly (1979)
3 Desouza in stardust (1980)

OLDFIELD, J.
PARADISE COURT
1 Paradise Court (1995)
2 After hours (1995)
3 All fall down (1996)

OLDFIELD, P.
FOXEARTH TRILOGY
1 Green harvest (1983)
2 Summer song (1984)
3 Golden tally (1985)

OLDFIELD, P.
THE HERON SAGA
1 The rich earth (retitled Betrothed) (1982)
2 This ravished land (retitled The gilded land) (1982)
3 After the storm (retitled Lowering skies) (1982)
4 White water (retitled The bright dawning) (1983)

OLDHAM, A.
STONED
1 Stoned (2000)
2 2 stoned (2002)
  NF Life in the rock business

OLDHAM, N.
DET. CONSTABLE DANIELLE FURNESS
1 One dead witness (1998)
2 The last big job (1999)
3 Backlash (2001)

OLINTO, A.
1 The water house (1985)
2 The King of Ketu (1987)

OLIVER, A.
1 The Pew Group (1980)
2 Property of a lady (1983)
3 The Ehlberg collection (1985)
4 Cover-up (1987)

O'NEILL, D.
BRIAN SAGA
1 Crucible (1986)
2 Of Gods and men (1987)
3 Sons of death (1988)

O''NEILL, F.
GIOVANNI STEARS
1 Agents of sympathy (1986)
2 Roman circus (1990)

O'NEILL, J.
1 Leaving home (1997)
2 Turn of the tide (1998)

ONSTOTT, K.
FALCONHURST
1 Mandingo (1960)
2 Drum (1963)
3 Master of Falconhurst (1964)
4 Falconhurst fancy (1966)
5 The mustee (1968)
6 Heir to Falconhurst (1968)
7 Flight to Falconhurst (1970)
8 Mistress of Falconhurst (1973)
9 Taproots of Falconhurst (1979)
10 Scandal of Falconhurst (1980)
11 Rogue of Falconhurst (1983)
12 Miz Lucretia of Falconhurst (1985)
13 Falconhurst fugitive (1988)

ORAM, N.
THE WARP
1 The storms howling through Tiflis
2 Lemmings on the edge
3 The balustrade paradox

ORDE, A. J.
JASON LYNX
1 A little neighbourhood murder (1989)
2 Death and the dogwalker (1990)
3 Death for old time's sake (1992)
4 Dead on Sunday (1993)
5 A long time dead (1994)

ORDE, L.
TIGER'S HEART
1 The tiger's heart (1987)
2 The tiger's claw (1988)

ORDE, L.
DANIEL KERR
1 The lion's way (1985)
2 The lion's progress (1987)

ORMEROD, R.
RICHARD AND AMELIA PATTON
1 Stone cold dead (1995)
2 The night she died (1997)

ORMEROD, R.
PHILIPPA LOWE
1 Hung in the balance (1990)
2 Bury him darkly (1991)
3 A shot at nothing (1993)
4 And hope to die (1995)
5 Landscape with corpse (1996)

OSBORNE, H.
1 White poppy (1977)
2 The joker (1978)

OSBOURNE, I.
1 Mango season (1985)
2 Prodigal (1987)

O'SHAUGHNESSY, P.
NINA REILLY
1 Presumption of death (2003)
2 Unlucky in law (2004)

OUDOT, S.
FRIENDSHIP
1 Real women (1996)
2 All that I am (1998)

OWEN, A.
1 Gentlemen of the West (1984)
2 Like birds in the wilderness (1987)

OWENS, V.
POINT BLANK
1 At Point Blank (1991)
2 Congregation (1992)
3 A multitude of sins (1994)

PADFIELD, P.
GUY GREVILLA
1 The lion's claw (1978)
2 The unquiet gods (1980)
3 Gold chains of Empire (1982)

PADGETT, A.
BO BRADLEY
1 Child of silence (1994)
2 Strawgirl (1995)
3 Turtle baby (1995)
4 Moonbird boy (1997)

PAGE, E.
DET. CHIEF INSPECTOR KELSEY
1 Every second Thursday (1981)
2 Last walk home (1982)
3 Cold light of day (1983)
4 Scent of death (1985)
5 Final moments (1986)
6 A violent end (1988)
8 Deadlock (1991)
9 In the event of my death (1994)
10 Murder comes calling (1995)
11 Hard evidence (1996)
12 Intent to kill (1998)
13 Say it with murder (2000)

PAIGE, F.
MCGRATH FAMILY
1 The Sholtie burn (1986)
2 Maeve's daughter (1987)
3 The distaff side (1988)
4 Men who march away (1989)
5 Sholtie flyer (1990)

PAIGE, F.
MACKINTOSH FAMILY
1 Glasgow girls (1994)
2 The painted ladies (1994)
3 The butterfly girl (1995)
4 Kindred spirits (1997)

PALLISER, M.
MATTHEW LOFTUS
1 Devil of a fix (2000)
2 To the bitter end (2001)

PALMER, F.
DET. INSPECTOR JACKO JACKSON
1 Testimony (1992)
2 Unfit to plead (1992)
3 Bent grasses (1993)
4 Blood brother (1993)
5 Nightwatch (1994)
6 China hand (1994)
7 Double exposure (1995)
8 Dead man's handle (1995)

PALMER, F.
PHIL "SWEENEY" TODD
1 Dark forest (1996)
2 Red gutter (1996)
3 Hot Toddy (1997)
4 Murder live (1997)
5 Black gold (1998)
6 Final score (1998)
7 Hoodwinked (1999)
8 Witching hour (1999)
9 Todd's law (2000)

PARETSKY, S.
V.I. WARSHAWSKI
1 Indemnity only (1982)
2 Deadlock (1984)
3 Killing orders (1986)
4 Bitter medicine (1987)
5 Toxic shock (1988)
6 Burn marks (1990)
7 Guardian angel (1992)
8 Tunnel vision (1994)
9 V.I. for short (1995)
10 Hard time (1999)
11 Total recall (2001)
12 Blacklist (2003)

ARK, R.
1 Missus (1985)
2 The harp in the south (1948)
3 Poor man's orange (1949)

ARKER, F. M.
1 Coldiron
2 Shadow of the wolf

ARKER, I.
SOPHIE FITT
2 Something funny (1995)
3 A temporary affair (1994)

ARKER, J.
1 The village cricket match (1978)
2 Test time at Tillingfold (1979)
3 Tillingfold's tour (1986)

ARKER, K. J.
FENCER TRILOGY
1 Colours in the street
2 The belly of the bow
3 The proof house

ARKER, K. J.
SCAVENGER TRILOGY
1 Shadow (2001)
2 Pattern (2002)
3 Memory (2003)

ARKER, R. B.
SPENSER
1 The Godwolf manuscript (1973)
2 God save the child (1975)
3 Mortal stakes (1976)
4 Promised land (1977)
5 The Judas goat (1982)
6 Looking for Rachel Wallace (1982)
7 A savage place (1982)
8 Ceremony (1983)
9 A Catskill eagle (1986)
10 Valediction (1986)
11 Taming a seahorse (1987)
12 Early autumn (1987)
13 Pale kings and princes (1988)
14 Crimson joy (1989)
15 Playmates (1990)
16 The widening gyre (1991)
17 Double deuce (1992)
18 Paper doll (1993)
19 Walking shadow (1995)
20 Thin air (1995)
21 Chance (1996)
22 Small vices (1998)
23 Hush money (2000)
24 Hugger mugger (2000)

25 Perish twice (2000)
26 Potshot (2001)
27 Widow's walk (2002)
28 Back story (2003)
29 Bad business (2004)

PARKER, R. B.
JESSE STONE
1 Night passage (1998)
2 Trouble in Paradise (1999)
3 Death in Paradise (2001)
4 Stone cold (2004)

PARKES, R.
DET. INSPECTOR TAFF ROBERTS
1 Riot (1987)
2 An abuse of justice (1988)
3 Gamelord (1990)

PARKINSON, C. N.
RICHARD DELANCEY
1 The Guernseyman (1982)
2 Devil to pay (1973)
3 Fireship (1974)
4 Touch and go (1977)
5 Dead reckoning (1978)
6 So near, so far (1981)

PARKINSON, D.
PATRICK DALTON
1 The fox and the Fury (1989)
2 The fox and the Fortune (1992)
3 The fox and the flag (1999)

PARKS, T.
1 Cara Massimina (1993)
2 Mimi's ghost (1995)

PARLAND, O.
RIKI
1 The year of the bull (1991)
2 The enchanted way (1991)

PARRISH, F.
DAN MALLETT
1 Fire in the barley (1977)
2 Sting of the honeybee (1978)
3 Snare in the dark (1982)
4 Bait on the hook (1983)
5 Face at the window (1984)
6 Fly in the cobweb (1986)
7 Caught in the birdlime (1987)
8 Voices from the dark (1993)

PARSONS, T.
HARRY SILVER
1 Man and boy (2000)
2 Man and wife (2002)

PARTRIDGE, F.
1 A pacifist's war (1978)
2 Everything to lose (1985)

PASSMORE, R.
1 Blenheim boy (1981)
2 Moving tent (1982)

PATON, A.
1 Towards the mountain (1980)
2 Journey continued (1988)

PATTERSON, J.
ALEX CROSS
1 Along came a spider (1994)
2 Kiss the girls (1995)
3 Jack and Jill (1997)
4 Cat and mouse (1997)
5 Violets are blue (2001)
6 Four blind mice (2002)

PATTERSON, J. & GROSS, A.
WOMENS MURDER CLUB
1 1st to die (2002)
2 2nd chance (2002)

PAUL, B.
MARION LARCH
1 You have the right to remain silent
   (1992)
2 The apostrophe thief (1994)
3 Fare play (1995)
4 Full frontal murder (1998)

PAUL, W.
DET. CHIEF INSPECTOR DAVID FYFE
1 Dance of death (1991)
2 Sleeping dogs (1994)
3 Sleeping pretty (1995)
4 Sleeping partner (1996)
5 Stranger things (1997)

PAWEL, R.
SPANISH CIVIL WAR
1 Death of a nationalist (2003)
2 Law of return (2004)

PAWSON, S.
DET. INSPECTOR CHARLIE PRIEST
1 The Picasso scam (1994)
2 The mushroom man (1995)

3 The Judas sheep (1996)
4 Last reminder (1997)
5 Deadly friends (1998)
6 Some by fire (1999)
7 Chill factor (2001)
8 Laughing boy (2002)
9 Limestone cowboy (2003)

PAXSON, D. L.
WESTRIA
1 Lady of light, lady of darkness
2 Silverhair the warrior
3 The earthstone
4 The sea star
5 The wind crystal
6 The jewel of fire

PAYNE, L.
MARK SAVAGE
1 Take the money and run (1982)
2 Malice in camera (1983)
3 Vienna blood (1985)
4 Dead for a ducat (1985)
5 Late knight (1987)

PEACE, D.
RED RIDING QUARTET
1 Nineteen seventyfour
2 Nineteen seventyseven
3 Nineteen eighty
4 Nineteen eighty three (2002)

PEARCE, M.
THE MAMUR ZAPT
1 The Mamur Zapt and the return of the
   carpet (1988)
2 The Mamur Zapt and the night of the
   dog (1989)
3 The Mamur Zapt and the donkey-vous
   (1990)
4 The Mamur Zapt and the men behind
   (1991)
5 The Mamur Zapt and the girl in the Nile
   (1992)
6 The Mamur Zapt and the spoils of Egypt
   (1992)
7 The Mamur Zapt and the camel of
   destruction (1993)
8 The snake-catcher's daughter (1994)
9 The Mingrelian conspiracy (1995)
10 The fig tree murder (1997)
11 The last cut (1998)
12 Death of an Effendi (1999)
13 A cold touch of ice (2000)
14 The face in the cemetery (2001)

PEARCE, M.
DMITRI KAMERON
1 Dmitri and the milk drinkers (1997)
2 Dmitri and the one-legged lady (1998)

PEARS, I.
JONATHAN ARGYLL
1 The Raphael affair (1990)
2 The Titian committee (1991)
3 The Bernini bust (1992)
4 The last judgment (1993)
5 Giotto's hand (1994)
6 Death and restoration (1996)
7 The immaculate deception (2000)

PEARSON, R.
LOU BOLDT
1 The first victim (2002)
2 The pied piper (2003)
3 The body of David Hayes (2004)

PEGRAM, L.
1 Blood and fire (1978)
2 A day among many (1955)
3 A long way from home (1986)

PELECANOS, G. P.
NICK STEFANOS
1 Down by the river where the dead men
  go (1996)
2 A firing offense (1997)
3 Nick's trip (2000)

PELLA, J. & PHILLIPS, M.
JOURNALS OF CORRIE BELLE
HOLLISTER
1 My father's world
2 Daughters of grace
3 On the trail of the truth
4 A place in the sun
5 Sea to shining sea
6 Into the long dark night
7 Land of the brave and free

PELLA, J. & PHILLIPS, M.
THE RUSSIANS
1 The crown and the crucible (1991)
2 A house divided (1992)
3 Travail and triumph (1992)

PELLA, J. & PHILLIPS, M.
THE STONEWYCKE TRILOGY
1 The heather hills of Stonewycke
2 Shadows over Stonewycke
3 Treasure of Stonewycke

PELLOW, J.
A VILLAGE PARSON
1 Pastor's green (1980)
2 Parson's progress (1981)
3 Parson's princess (1983)

PELZER, D.
DAVE
1 A boy called It (1999)
2 The lost boy (2000)
3 A man called Dave (2000)
  NF Autobiography

PEMBERTON, V.
OUR...
1 Our family (1991)
2 Our street (1993)
3 Our Rose (1994)

PEMBERTON, V.
LONDON SEQUENCE
1 The Londoners (1995)
2 Magnolia Square (1996)
3 Coronation summer (1997)

PENMAN, S. K.
JUSTIN DE QUINCY
1 The Queen's man (1996)
2 Cruel as the grave (1998)
3 Dragon's lair (2004)

PENN, J.
INSPECTOR THORNE AND SGT. ABBOT
1 Notice of death (1982)
2 Deceitful death (1983)
3 Will to kill (1983)
4 Mortal term (1984)
5 A deadly sickness (1985)
6 Unto the grave (1986)
7 Barren revenge (1986)
8 Accident prone (1987)

PENN, J.
DET. CHIEF INSPECTOR TANSEY
1 Outrageous exposures (1988)
2 A feast of death (1989)
3 A killing to hide (1990)
4 A legacy of death (1992)
5 A haven of danger (1993)
6 Widow's end (1993)
7 The guilty party (1994)
8 So many steps to death (1995)
9 Bridal shroud (1996)
10 Sterner stuff (1997)

PENNAC, D.
BENJAMIN MALAUSSENE
1 The scapegoat (1998)
2 Write to kill (1999)

PENTECOST, H.
JULIAN QUIST
1 Don't drop dead tomorrow (1972)
2 The champagne killer (1974)
3 The beautiful dead (1975)
4 The Judas freak (1976)
5 Honeymoon with death (1977)
6 Die after dark (1978)
7 The steel palace (1978)
8 Deadly trap (1979)
9 The homicidal horse (1980)
10 Death mask (1981)
11 Sow death, reap death (1982)
12 Past, present and murder (1983)
13 Murder out of wedlock (1985)
14 The substitute victim (1986)
15 The party killer (1987)
16 Kill and kill again (1988)

PENTECOST, H.
PIERRE CHAMBRUN
1 The cannibal who overate (1963)
2 The shape of fear (1964)
3 The evil that men do (1966)
4 The golden trap (1967)
5 The gilded nightmare (1969)
6 Girl watcher's funeral (1970)
7 The deadly joke (1971)
8 Birthday, deathday (1975)
9 Walking deadman (1975)
10 Bargain with death (1976)
11 Time of terror (1977)
12 The 14 dilemma (1978)
13 Death after breakfast (1979)
14 Random killer (1980)
15 Beware young lovers (1981)
16 Murder in luxury (1981)
17 With intent to kill (1983)
18 Murder in high places (1983)
19 Remember to kill me (1985)
20 Nightmare time (1987)
21 Murder goes round and round (1989)

PENTECOST, H.
UNCLE GEORGE
1 The price of silence (1981)
2 The copycat killers (1984)
3 Death by fire (1991)
4 Murder sweet and sour (1991)
5 Pattern for terror (1992)

PEREIRA, W.
A COTTAGE
1 Cottage in the country (1994)
2 Cottage in the vale (1995)

PERRY, A.
THOMAS AND CHARLOTTE PITT
1 The Cater Street hangman
2 Callander Square (1980)
3 Paragon Walk (1981)
4 Resurrection Row (1981)
5 Rutland Place (1988)
6 Cardington Crescent (1990)
7 Silence in Hanover Close (1989)
8 Death in the Devil's Acre (1991)
9 Bethlehem Road (1991)
10 Bluegate Fields (1992)
11 Highgate Rise (1992)
12 Belgrave Square (1993)
13 Farrier's Lane (1994)
14 The Hyde Park headsman (1994)
15 Traitor's Gate (1996)
16 Pentecost Alley (1997)
17 Ashworth Hall (1998)
18 Brunswick Gardens (1999)
19 Bedford Square (1999)
20 Half Moon Street (2000)
21 The Whitechapel conspiracy (2000)
22 Southampton Row (2002)
23 Seven Dials (2003)

PERRY, A.
WILLIAM MONK
1 A sudden fearful death (1993)
2 The face of a stranger (1994)
3 A dangerous mourning (1994)
4 Sins of the wolf (1994)
5 Defend and betray (1995)
6 Cain his brother (1995)
7 Weighed in the balance (1996)
8 The silent cry (1997)
9 Whited sepulchre (1997)
10 The twisted root (1999)
11 A funeral in blue (2001)
12 Death of a stranger (2002)
13 Ivory and black (2004)

PERRY, S.
THE MATADOR TRILOGY
1 The man who never missed
2 Matadora
3 The Machiavelli interface

PERRY, T.
JANE WHITEFIELD
1 The butcher's boy (1992)
2 Sleeping dogs (1992)

3 Vanishing act (1997)
4 Shadow woman (1998)
5 The facechangers (1999)

PETERS, ELIZABETH
VICKY BLISS
1 Silhouette in scarlet (1984)
2 Street of the Five Moons (1988)
3 Borrower of the night (1974)
4 Trojan gold (1987)
5 Night train to Memphis (1995)

PETERS, ELIZABETH
JACQUELINE KIRBY
1 The murders of Richard III (1989) (1974 in US)
2 Naked once more (1990)

PETERS, ELIZABETH
AMELIA PEABODY EMERSON
1 Crocodile on the sandbank (1976)
2 The curse of the Pharaohs (1982)
3 The mummy case (1986)
4 Lion in the valley (1987)
5 The deeds of the disturber (1989)
6 The last camel died at noon (1991)
7 The snake, the crocodile and the dog (1993)
8 The hippopotamus pool (1995)
9 Seeing a large cat (1995)
10 The ape who guards the balance (1998)
11 The falcon at the portal (1999)
12 Thunder in the sky (2000)
13 Lord of the silent (2001)
14 The golden one (2002)
15 Children of the storm (2003)
16 Guardians of the horizon (2004)

PETERS, ELLIS
BROTHER CADFAEL
1 A morbid taste for bones (1977)
2 One corpse too many (1979)
3 Monk's Wood (1980)
4 St.Peter's Fair (1981)
5 The leper of St. Giles (1981)
6 The virgin in the ice (1982)
7 The sanctuary sparrow (1983)
8 The devil's novice (1983)
9 Dead man's ransom (1984)
10 The pilgrim of hate (1985)
11 An excellent mystery (1985)
12 The raven in the foregate (1986)
13 The rose rent (1986)
14 The hermit of Eyton Forest (1987)
15 The confession of Brother Haluin (1988)
16 The heretic's apprentice (1989)
17 The Potters Field (1989)

18 The summer of the Danes (1991)
19 The holy thief (1992)
20 Brother Cadfael's penance (1994)

PETERS, M.
1 The vinegar seed (1986)
2 The vinegar blossom (1986)
3 The vinegar tree (1987)

PETERS, M.
MALONE FAMILY
1 Tansy (1975)
2 Kate Alanna (1975)
3 A child called Freedom (1976)

PETRIE, G.
MYCROFT HOLMES
1 The Dorking Gap affair (1989)
2 The monstrous regiment (1991)

PEWSEY, E.
MOUNTJOY CHRONICLES
1 Children of chance (1994)
2 Divine comedy (1995)
3 Unholy harmonies (1995)
4 Volcanic airs (1996)
5 Unaccustomed spirits (1997)

PHILBIN, T.
PRECINCT SIBERIA
1 Precinct Siberia
2 Under cover
3 Cop killer

PHINN, G.
1 The other side of the dale (1998)
2 Over hill and dale (2000)
3 Head over heels in the dales (2002)
4 Up and down in the dales (2004)

PICKARD, NANCY
JENNY CAIN
1 Dead crazy
2 Generous death
3 Marriage is murder
4 No body
5 Say no to murder
6 Crossbones (1990)
7 I.O.U. (1991)
8 But I wouldn't want to die there (1993)
9 Confession (1994)

PIERCE, D. M.
VIC DANIEL
1 Down in the valley
2 Hear the wind blow, dear

3 Roses love sunshine
4 Angels in heaven
5 Write me a letter (1992)

PIERCE, M. A.
DARKANGEL TRILOGY
1 The darkangel (1983)
2 A gathering of gargoyles (1984)
3 The pearl of the soul of the world (1990)

PIERCE, M. A.
FIREBRINGER TRILOGY
1 Birth of the firebringer (1985)
2 Dark moon (1992)

PIKE, C.
FINAL FRIENDS
1 The party (1991)
2 The dance (1991)
3 The graduation (1991)

PILCHER, R.
1 The shell seekers (1988)
2 September (1990)

PIRINCCI, A.
FELIDAE
1 Felidae (1993)
2 Felidae on the road (1994)

PLAIDY, J.
PLANTAGENET SAGA
1 Plantagenet prelude (1976)
2 Revolt of the eaglets (1977)
3 Heart of the lion (1977)
4 Prince of darkness (1978)
5 The battle of the Queens (1978)
6 The Queen from Provence (1979)
7 Edward Longshanks (1979)
8 The follies of the King (1980)
9 The vow on the heron (1980)
10 Passage to Pontefract (1981)
11 The star of Lancaster (1981)
12 Epitaph for three women (1981)
13 Red rose of Anjou (1982)
14 The sun in splendour (1982)

PLAIDY, J.
QUEENS OF ENGLAND
1 Myself my enemy (Henrietta Maria)
(1983)
2 Queen of this realm (Elizabeth I) (1984)
3 Victoria victorious (1985)
4 Lady in the Tower (Anne Boleyn) (1986)
5 The courts of love (Eleanor of Aquitaine)
(1987)

6 The Queen's secret (Catherine de Valois)
(1989)
7 Reluctant Queen (Anne Neville) (1990)
9 The pleasures of love (Catherine de
Braganza) (1991)
10 William's wife (Anne) (1992)
11 Rose without a thorn (Catherine
Howard) (1993)

PLAIN, B.
1 Evergreen (1984)
2 The golden cup (1986)
3 Tapestry (1988)

PLANTE, D.
FRANCOEUR FAMILY
1 The family (1978)
2 The country (1981)
3 The woods (1982)
4 The native (1987)

PLASS, A.
SACRED DIARIES
1 The sacred diary of Adrian Plass, aged
37and3/4 (1987)
2 The horizontal epistles of Andromeda
Veal (1988)
3 The theatrical tapes of Leonard Thynn
(1989)
4 The sacred diaries of Adrian
Andromeda and Leonard (2003)
5 The sacred diary of Adrian Plass on tour
(2004)

PLATER, A.
1 The Beiderbecke affair (1985)
2 The Beiderbecke tapes (1986)
3 The Beiderbecke connection (1987)

POE, E. A.
1 Fall of the House of Usher (1842)
2 Usher's passing by Robert McCammon
(1989)

POHL, F.
SPACE MERCHANTS
1 Space merchants (1985)
2 The merchants' war (1985)

POHL, F.
HEECHEE
1 Gateway (1978)
2 Beyond the Blue Event horizon (1980)
3 Heechee rendezvous (1984)
4 The annals of Heechee (1987)

POLLACK, R.
1 Unquenchable fire (1988)
2 Temporary agency (1994)

POPE, D.
EDWARD YORKE
1 Convoy (1979)
2 Decoy (1983)

POPE, D.
NED YORKE
1 Buccaneer (1981)
2 Admiral (1982)
3 Galleon (1986)
4 Corsair (1987)

POPE, D.
RAMAGE
1 Ramage (1966)
2 Ramage and the drum beat (1967)
3 Ramage and the free-booters (1969)
4 Governor Ramage, RN (1972)
5 Ramage's prize (1974)
6 Ramage and the guillotine (1975)
7 Ramage's diamond (1976)
8 Ramage's mutiny (1977)
9 Ramage and the rebels (1978)
10 The Ramage touch (1979)
11 Ramage's signal (1980)
12 Ramage and the renegades (1981)
13 Ramage's devil (1982)
14 Ramage's trial (1984)
15 Ramage's challenge (1985)
16 Ramage at Trafalgar (1805) (1986)
17 Ramage and the Saracens (1988)
18 Ramage and the Dido (1989)

PORTER, D. C.
WHITE INDIAN
1 White Indian (1992)
2 The renegade (1993)
3 War chief (1994)

PORTER, J.
DET. CHIEF INSPECTOR DOVER
1 Dover one (1964)
2 Dover two (1965)
3 Dover three (1965)
4 Dover and the unkindest cut of all (1966)
5 Dover goes to Pott (1968)
6 Dover strikes again (1970)
7 It's murder with Dover (1973)
8 Dover and the claret tappers (1977)
9 Dead easy for Dover (1978)
10 Dover beats the band (1980)

POSEY, C. A.
STEVEN BORG
1 Kiev footprint (1983)
2 Prospero drill (1984)

POTTER, C.
WITCH
1 The witch (1996)
2 The witch's son (1997)

POURNELLE, J.
JANISSARIES
1 Janissaries
2 Clan and crown
3 Storms of victory

POWELL, D.
HOLLIS CARPENTER
1 Bayou city secrets (1992)
2 Houston Town (1992)

POWER, M. S.
CHILDREN OF THE NORTH
1 The killing of yesterday's children (1985)
2 Lonely the man without heroes (1986)
3 Darkness in the eye (1987)

POYER, D.
DAN LENSON
1 The Med (1999)
2 China Sea (2000)

POYER, J.
A TIME OF WAR
1 The transgressors (1984)
2 Come evil days (1985)

PRANTERA, A.
ZOE
1 Proto Zoe (1992)
2 Zoe Trope (1996)

PRATCHETT, T.
DISCWORLD
1 The colour of magic
2 The light fantastic
3 Equal rites (1986)
4 Mort (1987)
5 Sorcery (1988)
6 Wyrd sisters (1988)
7 Pyramids (1989)
8 Guards! Guards! (1989)
9 Eric (1990)
10 Moving pictures (1990)
11 Reaper man (1991)
12 Witches abroad (1991)

13 Small gods (1992)
14 Lords and ladies (1992)
15 Men at arms (1993)
16 Soul music (1994)
17 Interesting times (1994)
18 Maskerade (1995)
19 Feet of clay (1996)
20 Hogfather (1996)
21 Jingo (1997)
22 The last continent (1998)
23 Carpe jugulum (1998)
24 The fifth elephant (1999)
25 The truth (2000)
26 Thief of time (2001)
27 The last hero (2001)
28 Night watch (2002)
29 Monstrous regiment (2003)

PRICE, A.
DR. DAVID AUDLEY
1 44 vintage (1977)
2 A new kind of war (1987)
3 Alamut ambush (1971)
4 Colonel Butler
5 October men (1973)
6 Other paths to glory (1974)
7 Our man in Camelot (1975)
8 War game (1976)
9 Tomorrow's ghost (1979)
10 The Old Vengeful (1982)
11 Gunner Kelly (1983)
12 Sion Crossing (1984)
13 Here be monsters (1985)
14 For the good of the state (1986)
15 The labyrinth makers (1970)
16 A prospect of vengeance (1988)

PRICE, E.
1 Savannah (1986)
2 To see your face again (1987)
3 Before the darkness falls (1988)

PRICE, E.
ST.SIMONS TRILOGY
1 The lighthouse (1972)
2 New moon rising (1973)
3 The beloved invader (1974)

PRICE, R. T.
KENNY MADIGAN
1 Nickers (1998)
2 Grievous (1999)
3 Big deal (2001)

PRICE, REYNOLDS
JOURNEY
1 The surface of earth (1975)

2 The source of light (1982)
3 The promise of rest (1996)

PRIOR, A.
THE OLD MAN
1 The old man and me (1994)
2 The old man and me again (1996)

PRONZINI, B.
THE NAMELESS DETECTIVE
1 The snatch (1974)
2 The vanished (1975)
3 Undercurrent (1975)
4 Blowback (1978)
5 Two spot (1980)
6 Labyrinth (1981)
7 Hoodwink (1981)
8 Scattershot (1982)
9 Dragonfire (1983)
10 Casefile (1983)
11 Bindlestaff (1984)
12 Quicksilver (1984)
13 Nightshades (1986)
14 Jackpot (1991)
15 Breakdown (1991)
16 Quarry (1992)
17 Crazybones (2000)
18 Scenarios: stories (2003)

PRYCE, M.
LOUIE KNIGHT
1 Aberystwyth mon amour (2002)
2 Last tango in Aberystwyth (2003)

PUCKETT, A.
TOM JONES, DEPARTMENT OF
HEALTH INSPECTOR
1 Bloodstains (1987)
2 Bed of nails (1989)
3 Terminus (1990)
4 Bloodhound (1991)
5 Shadows behind a screen (1998)
6 Chilling out (1999)
7 The gift (2000)
8 A life for a life (2000)

PUGH, D.
IRIS THORNE
1 Cold call (1993)
2 Slow squeeze (1994)
3 Pushover (1999)

PURSER, A.
ROUND RINGFORD
1 Pastures new (1994)
2 Spinster of this parish (1995)
3 Orphan lamb (1996)

4 New every morning (1996)
5 Thy neighbour's wife (1997)
6 Mixed doubles (1998)

PURSER, A.
LOIS MEADE MYSTERIES
1 Murder on Monday (2002)
2 Terror on Tuesday (2003)
3 Weeping on Wednesday (2003)

PUZO, M.
DON CORLEONE
1 The Godfather (1969)
2 Godfather II (based on the film script)
3 The Sicilian (1985)
4 Omerta (2000)

QUARTON, M.
AN IRISH CHILDHOOD
1 Breakfast the night before (1991)
2 Saturday's child (1993)
   NF Autobiography

QUEST, E.
DET. CHIEF INSPECTOR KATE
MADDOX
1 Death walk (1989)
2 Cold coffin (1990)
3 Model murder (1991)
4 Deadly deceit (1992)

QUINNELL, A. J.
CREASY
1 Man on fire (1987)
2 The perfect kill (1992)
3 The blue ring (1993)
4 Black horn (1994)
5 Message from hell (1996)

QUINTON, A.
DET. INSPECTOR JAMES ROLAND
1 To mourn a mischief (1989)
2 Death of a dear friend (1990)
3 A fatal end (1992)
4 A little grave (1993)
5 The sleeping and the dead (1994)
6 Some foul play (1996)

QUOGAN, A.
MATTHEW PRIOR
1 The fine art of murder (1989)
2 The touch of a vanished hand (1990)

RADLEY, S.
DET. SUPT. QUANTRILL
1 Death and the maiden (1980)

2 The Chief Inspector
3 A talent for destruction (1982)
4 Blood on the happy highway (1984)
5 Fate worse than death (1985)
6 Who saw him die? (1987)
7 This way out (1989)
8 Cross my heart and hope to die (1992)
9 Fair game (1994)

RANDALL, R.
1 The Drayton legacy (1986)
2 The potter's niece (1987)
3 The rival potters (1990)

RANKIN, I.
DET. INSPECTOR JOHN REBUS
1 Knots and crosses (1990)
2 Hide and seek (1991)
3 Wolfman (1992)
4 A good hanging (short stories) (1992)
5 Strip Jack (1992)
6 The black book (1993)
7 Mortal causes (1997)
8 Let it bleed (1995)
9 Black and blue (1997)
10 The hanging garden (1998)
11 Dead souls (1999)
12 The falls (2000)
13 The resurrection men (2001)
14 Beggar's banquet (short stories) (2002)
15 A question of blood (2003)

RANKIN, R.
BRENTFORD SAGA
1 The anti-Pope
2 The Brentford triangle
3 East of Ealing
4 The sprouts of wrath (1993)
5 Nostradamus ate my hamster (1996)
6 The Brentford chain store massacre
   (1997)

RANKIN, R.
ARMAGEDDON
1 Armageddon (1990)
2 They came and ate us (1991)
3 The suburban book of the dead (1992)
4 The book of ultimate truths (1993)
5 Raiders of the lost car park (1994)
6 The greatest show off earth (1994)

RATHBONE, J.
JAN ARGAND
1 The Eurokillers (1979)
2 Base case (1981)
3 Watching the detectives (1983)

RAVEN, S.
THE FIRST BORN OF EGYPT
1 Morning star (1984)
2 The face of the waters (1985)
3 Before the cock crow (1986)
4 New seed for old (1988)
5 Blood of my bone (1989)
6 In the image of God (1990)
7 The troubadour (1992)

RAVEN, S.
ALMS FOR OBLIVION
1 The rich pay late (1964)
2 Friends in low places (1965)
3 The Sabre squadron (1966)
4 Fielding Gray (1967)
5 The Judas boy (1968)
6 Places where they sing (1970)
7 Sound the retreat (1971)
8 Come like shadows (1972)
9 Bring forth the body (1974)
10 The survivors (1976)

RAWN, M.
DRAGON PRINCE
1 Dragon prince (1989)
2 The star scroll (1990)
3 Sunrunner's file (1993)

RAWN, M.
DRAGON STAR
1 Stronghold (1992)
2 The dragon token (1993)
3 Skybowl (1995)

RAWN, M.
EXILES
1 The ruins of Ambrai (1996)
2 The Mageborn traitor (1997)

RAYMOND, D.
FACTORY SERIES
1 He died with his eyes open (1984)
2 The devil's home on leave (1985)
3 How the dead live (1986)
4 I was Dora Suarez (1990)
5 Dead man upright (1993)
6 Not till the red fog rises (1994)

RAYNER, C.
THE PERFORMERS
1 Gower Street (1973)
2 The Haymarket (1974)
3 Paddington Green (1975)
4 Soho Square (1976)
5 Bedford Row (1977)
6 Long Acre (1978)

7 Charing Cross (1979)
8 The Strand (1980)
9 Chelsea Reach (1982)
10 Shaftesbury Avenue (1983)
11 Piccadilly (1985)
12 Seven Dials (1986)

RAYNER, C.
POPPY CHRONICLES
1 Jubilee (1987)
2 Flanders (1988)
3 Flapper (1989)
4 Blitz (1990)
5 Festival (1991)
6 Sixties (1992)

RAYNER, C.
QUENTIN QUARTET
1 London lodgings (1994)
2 Paying guests (1995)

RAYNER, C.
DR. GEORGE BARNABAS
1 First blood (1993)
2 Second opinion (1994)
3 Third degree (1995)
4 Fourth attempt (1996)
5 Fifth member (1997)

READ, MISS
FAIRACRE
1 Village school (1954)
2 Village diary (1956)
3 Storm in the village (1960)
4 Miss Clare remembers (1962)
5 Over the gate (1964)
6 Village Christmas (1966)
7 Fairacre festival (1969)
8 Tyler's Row (1972)
9 Further afield (1974)
10 No holly for Miss Quinn (1976)
11 Village affairs (1977)
12 The white robin (1979)
13 Village centenary (1980)
14 Summer at Fairacre (1984)
15 Mrs. Pringle (1989)
16 Changes at Fairacre (1991)
17 Farewell to Fairacre (1993)
18 A peaceful retirement (1996)

READ, MISS
THRUSH GREEN
1 Thrush Green (1960)
2 Winter in Thrush Green (1961)
3 News from Thrush Green (1970)
4 Battles at Thrush Green (1975)
5 Return to Thrush Green (1978)

6 Gossip from Thrush Green (1981)
7 Affairs at Thrush Green (1983)
8 At home in Thrush Green (1985)
9 The school at Thrush Green (1987)
10 Friends at Thrush Green (1990)
11 Celebrations at Thrush Green (1992)
12 The year at Thrush Green (1995)
13 Farewell Thrush Green (2000)

REASONER, J.
CIVIL WAR BATTLE SERIES
1 Manassas (2000)
2 Shiloh (2001)
3 Antietam (2001)
4 Chancellorsville (2001)
5 Vicksburg (2002)
6 Chickamauga (2002)
7 Shenendoah (2002)
8 Appomattox (2004)

REAVES, S.
SAM MACLEISH
1 A long cold fall
2 Fear will do it
3 Bury it deep (1993)
4 Get what's coming (1995)

REDFIELD, J.
1 The Celestine prophecy (1994)
2 The tenth insight: holding the vision (1996)

REDMON, A.
BYZANTINE TRILOGY
1 The genius of the sea (1992)
2 The judgement of Solomon (1995)
3 The head of Dionysos (1997)

REEMAN, D.
BLACKWOOD FAMILY
1 Badge of glory (1982)
2 The first to land (1984)
3 The horizon (1993)
4 Dust on the sea (1999)
5 Knife edge (2004)

REEVE, L-D.
ANNE BOLEYN
1 The early years (1980)
2 The royal suitor (1981)

REICHERT, M. Z.
LAST OF THE RENSHAI
1 Last of the Renshai (1993)
2 The Western wizard (1993)
3 Child of thunder (1994)

REICHERT, M. Z.
THE RENSHAI CHRONICLES
1 Beyond Ragnarok (1996)
2 Prince of demons (1997)
3 Children of wrath (1998)

REICHS, K.
TEMPERANCE BRENNAN
1 Deja dead (1998)
2 Death du jour (1999)
3 Deadly decisions (2000)
4 Fatal voyage (2001)
5 Grave secrets (2002)
6 Bare bones (2003)
7 Monday mourning (2004)

REID, M.
FARAH
1 Sex and the single sister (2003)
2 Use me or lose me (2004)

REIMANN, K.
THE TIELMARA CHRONICLES
1 Wind from a foreign sky
2 A tremor in bitter earth

RENAULT, M.
ALEXANDER THE GREAT
1 Fire from heaven (1971)
2 The Persian boy (1972)
3 Funeral games (1981)

RENAULT, M.
THESEUS
1 The King must die (1960)
2 The bull from the sea (1962)

RENDELL, R.
INSPECTOR WEXFORD
1 From Doon with death (1965)
2 A new lease of death (1967)
3 Wolf to the slaughter (1968)
4 The best man to die (1969)
5 A guilty thing surprised (1970)
6 No more dying then (1971)
7 Murder being once done (1972)
8 Some lie and some die (1973)
9 Shake hands for ever (1975)
10 A sleeping life (1978)
11 Put on by cunning (1981)
12 The speaker of Mandarin (1983)
13 An unkindness of ravens (1985)
14 The veiled one (1988)
15 Kissing the gunner's daughter (1992)
16 Simisola (1994)
17 Road rage (1997)

18 Harm done (1999)
19 The babes in the wood (2002)

REUBEN, S.
WYLIE NOLAN AND MAX BRAMBLE
1 Origin and cause (1996)
2 Spent matches (1997)

REYNOLDS, A.
SPACE
1 Revelation space (2000)
2 Chasm city (2001)
3 Absolution gap (2003)

REYNOLDS, W. J.
NEBRASKA
1 Nebraska quotient (1986)
2 Moving targets (1987)
3 Money trouble (1988)
4 Things invisible (1989)
5 Naked eye (1990)

RHEA, NICHOLAS
CONSTABLE
1 Constable on the hill (1979)
2 Constable on the prowl (1980)
3 Constable around the village (1981)
4 Constable across the moors (1982)
5 Constable in the dale (1983)
6 Constable by the sea (1985)
7 Constable along the lane (1986)
9 Constable at the double (1988)
10 Constable in disguise (1989)
11 Constable among the heather (1990)
12 Constable around the green (1993)
13 Constable beneath the trees (1994)
14 Constable about the parish (1996)
15 Constable at the gate (1997)
16 Constable at the dam (1997)
17 Constable over the stile (1998)
18 Constable under the gooseberry bush (1998)
19 Constable in the farmyard (1999)
20 Constable along the highway (2000)
21 Constable over the bridge (2001)
22 Constable along the river bank (2002)
23 Constable in the wilderness (2003)
24 Constable around the park (2004)

RHEA, NICHOLAS
DET. SUPT MARK PEMBERTON
1 False alibi (1991)
2 Grave secrets (1992)
3 Family ties (1994)
4 Suspect (1995)
5 Confession (1997)
6 Death of a princess (1999)

7 Sniper (2001)
8 Dead ends (2003)

RHEA, NICHOLAS
DET. INSPECTOR MONTAGUE PLUKE
1 Omens of death (1997)
2 Superstitious death (1998)
3 The well-pressed shroud (2000)
4 Garland for a dead maiden (2002)

RHINEHART, L.
THE DICE MAN
1 The dice man (1971)
2 Search for the dice man (1993)

RHODES, D.
GUILHELM DE COURDEVAL
1 Next, after Lucifer (1988)
2 Adversary (1989)

RHODES, E.
1 Madeleine (1989)
2 The house of Bonneau (1990)

RICCI, N.
VITTORIO INNOCENCE
1 Lives of the saints (1991)
2 In a glass house (1994)
3 Where she has gone (1998)

RICE, A.
CHRONICLES OF THE VAMPIRES
1 Interview with the vampires (1985)
2 The vampire Lestat (1987)
3 The Queen of the damned (1989)
4 Tale of the bodythief (1993)
5 Memnoch the devil (1995)
6 The vampire Armand (1998)
7 Merrick (2000)
8 Blood and gold (2001)
9 Blackwood Farm (2002)
10 Blood canticle (2003)

RICE, A.
MAYFAIR FAMILY
1 The witching hour (1991)
2 Lasher (1993)
3 Taltos (1994)

RICE, A.
NEW TALES OF THE VAMPIRES
1 Pandora (1998)
2 Vittorio the vampire (1999)

RICE, A.
BEAUTY
1 Beauty's punishment
2 The claiming of Sleeping Beauty
3 Beauty's release

RICHARDS, D. A.
WELSH TRILOGY
1 Nights below Station Street (1988)
2 Evening snow will bring such peace (1990)
3 For those who hunt the wounded down (1993)

RICHARDSON, R.
AUGUSTUS MALTRAVERS
1 The Latimer Mercy (1987)
2 Bellringer Street (1988)
3 The book of the dead (1989)
4 The dying of the light (1990)
5 Sleeping in the blood (1991)
6 The Lazarus tree (1992)

RICHTER, C.
AMERICAN PIONEER TRILOGY
1 The trees (1940)
2 The fields (1946)
3 The town (1950)

RILEY, J. M.
MARGARET OF ASHBURY
1 A vision of light (1990)
2 In pursuit of the green lion (1991)

RILEY, P.
JAMES SINCLAIR AND JERRY WEINBERG
1 Serious misconduct (1993)
2 Serious intent (1994)
3 Serious abuse (1995)

RILEY, S.
CIVIL WAR SERIES
1 The black Madonna (1992)
2 Garland of straw (1993)

RIOLS, N.
ARDNAKI CHRONICLES
1 Katherine
2 To live again
3 Before the dawn

RIPLEY, A.
CHARLESTON
1 Charleston

2 Return to Charleston
3 On leaving Charleston

RIPLEY, M.
FITZROY MACLEAN ANGEL
1 Just another angel (1988)
2 Angel touch (1989)
3 Angel hunt (1990)
4 Angels in arms (1991)
5 Angel city (1994)
6 Angel confidential (1995)
7 Family of Angels (1996)
8 That Angel look (1997)
9 Bootlegged Angel (1999)
10 Lights, camera, Angel (2001)
11 Angel underground (2002)
12 Angel on the inside (2003)

RIPPON, M.
INSPECTOR YGREC
1 Behold the druid weeps (1972)
2 The ninth tentacle
3 The hand of Solange (1985)

RIVERS, C.
1 Virgins (1984)
2 Girls forever brave and true (1986)

RIVKIN, J. F.
SILVERGLASS
1 Silverglass
2 Web of wind

RIX, B.
1 My farce from my elbow (1974)
2 Farce about face (1989)
   NF Autobiography

ROBB, C.
OWEN ARCHER
1 The apothecary rose (1994)
2 The Lady Chapel (1994)
3 The nun's tale (1995)
4 The King's bishop (1996)
5 The riddle of St.Leonards (1997)
6 A gift of sanctuary (1998)
7 A spy for the redeemer (1999)
8 The cross-legged knight (2001)

ROBB, J. D.
EVE DALLAS
1 Naked in death (1996)
2 Glory in death (1996)
3 Immortal in death (1997)
4 Rapture in death (1997)
5 Ceremony in death (1998)

6 Vengeance in death (1998)
7 Loyalty in death (1999)
8 Divided in death (2004)
9 Witness in death (2004)
10 Holiday in death (2004)
11 Judgment in death (2004)
12 Conspiracy in death (2004)
13 Betrayal in death (2004)
14 Seduction to death (2004)
15 Visions in death (2004)

ROBBINS, H.
1 The Betsy (1971)
2 The stallion (1996)

ROBBINS, H.
HOLLYWOOD
1 The dream merchants (1951)
2 The carpetbaggers (1956)
3 The inheritors (1964)
4 The raiders (1995)

ROBBINS, H.
JERRY COOPER
1 The predators (1998)
2 The secret (2001)

ROBERSON, J.
CHRONICLES OF THE CHEYSULI
1 Shapechangers
2 The song of Homana
3 Legacy of the sword
4 Track of the white wolf
5 A pride of princes
6 Daughter of the lion

ROBERTS, A. V.
1 Louisa Elliott (1989)
2 Liam's story (1991)

ROBERTS, BARRIE
CHRIS TYROLL & SHEILA MCKENNA
1 The victory snapshot (1997)
2 Robbery with malice (1999)
3 Bad penny blues (2000)
4 Crowner and justice (2002)

ROBERTS, C. S.
HERITAGE COAST
1 The running tide (1987)
2 Upon stormy downs (1988)
3 A wind from the sea (1989)
4 A seagull crying (1989)
5 The savage shore (1993)
6 An end to summer (1994)

ROBERTS, D.
LORD EDWARD CORINTH AND
VERITY BROWNE
1 Sweet poison (2000)
2 Bones of the buried (2002)
3 Hollow crown (2002)
4 Dangerous sea (2003)

ROBERTS, N.
BORN
1 Born in fire (1998)
2 Born in ice (1998)
3 Born in flame (1999)

ROBERTS, N.
THE DREAM
1 Daring to dream
2 Holding the dream
3 Finding the dream

ROBERTS, N.
THREE SISTERS ISLAND
1 Dance upon the air (2000)
2 Heaven and earth (2001)

ROBERTS, N.
QUINN FAMILY
1 Rising tides (1998)
2 Inner harbour (1999)
3 Seaswept (2000)

ROBERTSON, D.
BELGATE TRILOGY
1 The land of lost content (1985)
2 A year of winter (1987)
3 Blue remembered hills (1987)

ROBERTSON, D.
BELOVED PEOPLE
1 The beloved people (1992)
2 Strength for the morning (1993)
3 Towards Jerusalem (1993)

ROBERTSON, J.
ANY FOOL
1 Any fool can be a pig farmer (1975)
2 Any fool can be a dairy farmer (1980)
3 Any fool can be a countryman (1983)
4 Any fool can be a villager (1984)
5 Any fool can be a yokel (1985)
6 Any fool can be a country lover (1986)
7 Any fool can keep a secret (1987)
8 Any fool can see a vision (1988)
9 Any fool can be independent (1989)

ROBERTSON, W.
PRIORTON
1 Riches of the earth (1992)
2 Under a brighter sky (1993)
3 Land of your possession (1994)
4 Dark light shining (1995)
5 Kitty Rainbow (1996)
6 Children of the storm (1997)
7 A thirsting land (1998)

ROBINSON, D.
1 The Eldorado network (1986)
2 Artillery of lies (1991)

ROBINSON, K. S.
MARS TRILOGY
1 Red Mars (1992)
2 Green Mars (1993)
3 Blue Mars (1996)

ROBINSON, PETER
INSPECTOR BANKS
1 Gallows view (1988)
2 A dedicated man (1989)
3 A necessary end (1989)
4 The hanging valley (1990)
5 Past reason hated (1991)
6 Dry bones that dream (1995)
7 Wednesday's child (1996)
8 Innocent graves (1997)
9 Dead right (1997)
10 In a dry season (2000)
11 Cold is the grave (2001)
12 Aftermath (2002)
13 The summer that never was (2003)
14 Playing with fire (2004)

ROCHE, E.
FORTUNE AND POWER
1 The Berg family fortune (1985)
2 New money (1986)

ROCK, P.
1 Passing bells (1981)
2 Circles of time (1982)
3 A future arrived (1985)

ROE, C. F.
DR. JEAN MONTROSE
1 The Lumsden baby (1989)
2 Death by fire (1990)
3 Bad blood (A classy touch of murder) (1991)
4 Deadly partnership (1991)
5 Fatal fever (1992)
6 A death in the family (1993)

ROHAN, M. S.
THE WINTER OF THE WORLD
1 The anvil of ice (1986)
2 The forge in the forest (1987)
3 The hammer of the sun (1988)
4 The castle of the winds (1998)
5 The singer and the sea (2000)
6 Shadow of the seer (2001)

ROHAN, M. S.
THE SPIRAL
1 Chase the morning (1990)
2 The gates of noon (1992)

ROLPH, C. H.
1 London particulars (1980)
2 Further particulars (1987)
   NF Autobiography

ROOME, A.
CHRIS MARTIN
1 A real shot in the arm (1989)
2 A second shot in the arm (1990)
3 Bad Monday (1997)
4 Deceptive relations (1999)

ROOSEVELT, E.
WHITE HOUSE MYSTERIES
1 Murder and the First Lady (1984)
2 The Hyde Park murder (1985)
3 Murder at the Palace (1987)
4 The White House pantry murder (1987)
5 Murder in the Oval Office (1990)
6 Murder in the West Wing (1994)
7 A Royal murder (1994)
8 The White House murder (1995)
9 Murder in the Map Room (1998)

ROSEN, R.
HARVEY BLISSBERG
1 Strike three, you're dead (1985)
2 Fadeaway
3 Saturday night dead (1989)

ROSENBERG, J.
GUARDIANS OF THE FLAME
1 The sleeping dragon
2 The sword and the chain
3 The silver crown
4 The heir apparent
5 The warrior lives

ROSENBERG, NANCY
D.A.JOANNE KUHLMAN
1 Mitigating circumstances (2000)

2 Buried evidence (2001)
3 Conflict of interest (2002)

ROSS, A.
MARK FARROW
1 The Manchester thing (1970)
2 The Huddersfield job (1971)
3 The London assignment (1972)
4 The Dunfermline affair (1973)
5 The Bradford business (1974)
6 The Amsterdam diversion (1974)
7 The Leeds fiasco (1975)
8 The Edinburgh exercise (1975)
9 The Ampurias exchange (1976)
10 The Aberdeen conundrum (1977)
11 The Burgos contract (1978)
12 The Congleton lark (1979)
13 The Hamburg switch (1980)
14 The Menwith tangle (1982)
15 The Darlington jaunt (1985)
16 The Tyneside ultimatum (1988)

ROSS, ANNIE
BEL CARSON
1 Moving image (1995)
2 Shot in the dark (1996)
3 Double vision (1997)

ROSS, CAMERON
ALISTAIR DUNCAN
1 Case for compensation (1980)
2 Villa plot, counterplot (1981)
3 The scaffold (1981)

ROSS, D. F.
WAGONS WEST
1 Independence
2 Nebraska
3 Wyoming
4 Oregon
5 Texas
6 California
7 Colorado
8 Nevada
9 Washington
10 Montana
11 Dakota
12 Utah
13 Idaho
14 Missouri
15 Mississippi
16 Louisiana
17 Tennessee
18 Illinois
19 Wisconsin
20 Kentucky
21 Arizona

22 New Mexico
23 Oklahoma
24 Celebration

ROSS, D. F.
THE HOLTS
2 Oklahoma pride
3 Carolina courage
4 California glory
5 Hawaii heritage
6 Sierra triumph
7 Yukon justice
8 Pacific destiny
9 Homecoming

ROSS, I.
PAUL SHAW
1 Rocking the boat (1990)
2 Beverley Hills butler (1991)
3 How green was my valet (1992)

ROSS, JONATHAN
CHIEF INSPECTOR ROGERS
1 The blood running cold (1968)
2 Diminished by death (1968)
3 Dead at first hand (1969)
4 The deadest thing you ever saw (1969)
5 Here lies Nancy Frail (1970)
6 The burning of Billy Topper (1974)
7 I know what it's like (1976)
8 A rattling of old bones (1978)
9 Dark blue and dangerous (1981)
10 Death's head (1982)
11 Dead eye (1983)
12 Dropped dead (1984)
13 Burial deferred (1985)
14 Fate accomplished (1987)
15 Sudden departures (1988)
16 A time for dying (1989)
17 Daphne dead and done for (1990)
18 Murder be hanged (1992)
19 The body of a woman (1994)
20 Murder! murder! burning bright (1996)
21 This too, too sullied flesh (1997)

ROSS, K.
JULIAN KESTREL
1 Cut to the quick (1993)
2 A broken vessel (1994)
3 Whom the gods love (1995)
4 The devil in music (1997)

ROTH, H.
MERCY OF A RUDE STREAM
1 A star shines over M T Morris Park (1994)
2 A diving rock on the Hudson (1995)

3 From bondage (1996)
4 Requiem for Harlem (1998)

ROTH, P.
ZUCKERMANN
1 The ghost writer (1979)
2 Zuckermann unbound (1981)
3 The anatomy lesson (1984)
4 The Prague orgy (1985)
5 The counterlife (1987)
6 American pastoral (1997)
7 I married a Communist (1998)

ROUAUD, J.
WAR SERIES
1 Fields of glory (1992)
2 Of illustrious men (1995)
3 The world more or less (1998)

ROWE, R.
LIBERTUS
1 The Germanicus mosaic (1999)
2 A pattern of blood (2000)
3 Murder in the Forum (2001)
4 The chariots of Calyx (2002)
5 The Legatus mystery (2003)

ROWLAND, L. R.
SANIO ICHIRO
1 Shinju (1995)
2 Bundori (1996)
3 The Samurai's wife (2000)
4 Black lotus (2001)
5 The pillow book of Lady Wisteria (2002)
6 Dragon King's palace (2003)

ROWLANDS, B.
MELISSA CRAIG
1 A little gentle sleuthing (1990)
2 Finishing touch (1991)
3 Over the edge (1992)
4 Exhaustive enquiries (1993)
5 Malice poetic (1995)
6 Deadly legacy (1995)
7 Smiling at death (1996)
8 The cherry pickers (1998)
9 The man at the window (2000)
10 The fourth suspect (2001)
11 No laughing matter (2003)
12 Sweet venom (2004)

ROYCE, K.
SPIDER SCOTT AND INSPECTOR
BULMAN
1 The XYY man (1970)
2 The concrete boot (1971)
3 The miniatures frame (1972)

4 Spider underground (1974)
5 Trap Spider (1974)
6 The crypto man (1984)
7 The Mosley receipt (1985)
8 No way back (1986)
9 The Ambassador's son (1994)
10 Shadows (1996)
11 The Judas trail (1996)

RUSCH, K. K.
THE FEY
1 Sacrifice (1995)
2 Changeling (1996)
3 Rival (1997)

RUSSELL, D.
THE TAMARISK TREE
1 My quest for liberty and love (1975)
2 My school and the years of war (1980)
3 Challenge to the Cold War (1985)
NF Autobiography

RUSSELL, R.
DR. STEVEN RUSHTON
1 Go on, I'm listening (1983)
2 While you're here, Doctor (1985)

RUSSELL, S.
THE SWAN'S WAR
1 The one kingdom (2001)
2 The isle of battle (2002)

RUSSO, R.
1 Mohawk (1986)
2 The risk pool (1989)

RYAN, F.
DET. INSPECTOR SANDY WORDINGS
1 Sweet summer (1987)
2 Tiger, tiger (1988)
3 Goodbye, baby blue (1990)

RYBAKOV, A.
ARBAT TRILOGY
1 Children of the Arbat (1988)
2 Fear (1993)
3 Dust and ashes (1996)

SABERHAGEN, F.
BERSERKER
1 Berserker man
2 Brother Berserker
3 Berserker's planet
4 Berserker blue death
5 Shiva in steel

SABERHAGEN, F.
BOOK OF SWORDS
1 The first book of swords
2 The second book of swaords
3 The third book of swords
4 The first book of lost
   swords:Woundhealer's story
5 The second book of lost
   swords:Sightbinder's story
6 The third book of lost
   swords:Stonecutter's story

SADLER, B.
CASCA
1 The eternal mercenary
2 God of death
3 The war lord

SALISBURY, R.
1 Close the door behind you (1982)
2 When the boys came out to play (1984)
3 Birds of the air (1988)
4 Sweet Thursday (1990)

SALLIS, S.
RISING FAMILY
1 A scattering of daisies (1985)
2 The daffodils of Newent (1985)
3 Bluebell windows (1987)
4 Rosemary for remembrance (1987)

SALVATORE, R. A.
NIGHT
1 Starless nights
2 Siege of darkness
3 Passage to dawn

SALVATORE, R. A.
DARK ELF TRILOGY
1 Homeland (1990)
2 Exile (1991)
3 Sojourn (1991)

SALVATORE, R. A.
ICEWIND DALE TRILOGY
1 The crystal shard
2 Streams of silver
3 The halfling's gem

SALVATORE, R. A.
THE CLERIC QUINTET
1 Canticle
2 In sylvan shadow
3 Night masks
4 The fallen fortress
5 The chaos curse

SALVATORE, R. A.
THE SPEARWIELDER TALES
1 The woods out back
2 The dragon's dagger
3 Dragonslayer's return

SALVATORE, R. A.
THE CRIMSON SHADOW
1 The sword of Bedwyr
2 Luthien's gamble

SALVATORE, R. A.
DRIZZT D'UNDE
1 The silent blade
2 Sea of swords

SAMPSON, F.
DAUGHTERS OF TINTAGEL
1 Wise woman's telling (1989)
2 White nun's telling (1989)
3 Black Smith's telling (1990)
4 Taliesin's telling (1991)
5 Herself (1992)

SANDERS, L.
PETER TANGENT
1 Tangent objective (1977)
2 Tangent factor (1978)

SANDERS, L.
TIMOTHY CONE
1 The Timothy files (1987)
2 Timothy's game (1988)

SANDERS, L.
ARCHY MCNALLY
1 McNally's secret (1991)
2 McNally's luck (1992)
3 McNally'srisk (1993)
4 McNally's caper (1994)
5 McNally's trial (1995)
6 McNally's puzzle (1996)
7 McNally's gamble (1997)
8 McNally's dilemma (1999)
9 McNally's folly (2000)
10 McNally's chance, by V.Lardo (2001)

SANDFORD, J.
LUCAS DAVENPORT
1 Rules of prey (1989)
2 Shadow prey (1990)
3 Eyes of prey (1991)
4 Silent prey (1992)
5 Night prey (1994)
6 Mind prey (1996)
7 Sudden prey (1996)

8 Secret prey (1998)
9 Certain prey (1999)
10 Easy prey (2000)
11 Chosen prey (2002)
12 Mortal prey (2003)
13 Naked prey (2003)
14 Hidden prey (2004)

SANDS, M.
1 Sky knife (1998)
2 Serpent and storm (1999)

SATTERTHWAIT, W.
JOSHUA CROFT
1 At ease with the dead (1991)
2 A flower in the desert (1992)
3 The death card (1994)

SAVAGE, A.
BARRINGTON FAMILY
1 The eight banners (1992)
2 The last bannerman (1993)

SAVAGE, A.
ELEANOR
1 Eleanor of Aquitaine (1995)
2 Queen of love (1995)

SAVAGE, A.
THE COMMANDO
1 Commando (1999)
2 The cause (2000)
3 The tiger (2000)

SAVAGE, A.
THE SWORD
1 The sword and the scalpel (1996)
2 The sword and the jungle (1997)
3 The sword and the prison (1997)
4 Stop Rommel! (1998)
5 The Afrika Korps (1999)
6 The traitor within (1999)

SAVARIN, J. J.
GORDON GALLAGHER
1 Waterhole (1983)
2 Wolf run (1984)
3 Windshear (1985)
4 Naja (1986)
5 The Quiraing list (1988)
6 The Queensland file (1999)
7 Villiger (2000)

SAVARIN, J. J.
LEMMUS
1 Waiters on the dance (1972)

2 Children of the Lemmus (1972)
3 Beyond the Outer Mirr (1973)

SAVILLE, A.
BERGERAC
1 Bergerac and the fatal weakness
2 Bergerac and the Jersey Rose
3 Bergerac and the moving fever
4 Bergerac and the traitor's child

SAXTON, J.
NEYLER FAMILY
1 The pride (1983)
2 The glory (1983)
3 The splendour (1984)
4 Full circle (1985)

SAYERS, D. L.
LORD PETER WIMSEY
1 Whose body? (1923)
2 Unnatural death (1927)
3 Clouds of witness (1927)
4 The unpleasantness at the Bellona Club (1928)
5 Lord Peter views the body (short stories) (1929)
6 Strong poison (1930)
7 Five red herrings (1931)
8 Have his carcase (1932)
9 Murder must advertise (1933)
10 Hangman's holiday (short stories) (1933)
11 The Nine Tailors (1934)
12 Gaudy night (1935)
13 Busman's honeymoon (1937)
14 In the teeth of the evidence (1939)
15 Thrones, dominations (completed by J.Paton Walsh) (1998)
16 A presumption of death, by Jill Paton-Walsh (2002)

SAYLOR, S.
GORDIANUS
1 Murder on the Appian Way (1990)
2 Arms of Nemesis (1990)
3 Roman blood (1991)
4 Catalina's riddle (1997)
5 The Venus throw (1998)
6 Rubicon (1999)
7 Last seen in Massilia (2000)
9 A mist of prophecies (2002)
10 The judgement of Caesar (2004)

SCANLAN, P.
THE CITY
1 City woman (1998)
2 City girls (1999)

SCANNELL, D.
DOLLY
1 Mother knew best (1976)
2 Dolly's war (1976)
3 Dolly's mixture (1977)

SCANNELL, D.
BRIGHT FAMILY
1 Polly Bright (1984)
2 Jet Bright (1985)

SCANNELL, V.
1 The tiger and the rose (1971)
2 Argument of kings (1987)
3 Drums of morning (1992)

SCARBOROUGH, E.
ARGONIAN SERIES
1 The song of sorcery
2 The unicorn creed
3 Bronwyn's bane

SCHMIDT, D.
TWILIGHT OF THE GODS
1 The first name
2 Groa's other eye
3 Three trumps sounding

SCHOLEFIELD, A.
ANNE VERNON
1 Burn out (1994)
2 Buried treasure (1995)
3 Bad timing (1997)

SCHOLEFIELD, A.
DET. SUPT. GEORGE MACRAE AND
DET. SGT. LEOPOLD SILVER
1 Dirty weekend (1990)
2 Thief taker (1991)
3 Never die in January (1992)
4 Threats and menaces (1993)
5 Don't be a nice girl (1994)
6 Night moves (1996)

SCOPPETONE, S.
LAUREN LAURANO
1 Everything you have is mine (1993)
2 I'll be leaving you always (1994)
3 My sweet untraceable you (1996)
4 Let's face the music and die (1997)

SCOTT, A.
1 Scott free (1986)
2 Scott goes south (1988)

SCOTT, D.
1 Typhoon pilot
2 One more hour (1989)

SCOTT, J.
DET. INSPECTOR ROSHER
1 The poor old lady
2 A better class of business (1976)
3 A shallow grave (1977)
4 A clutch of vipers (1979)
5 The gospel lamb (1980)
6 A distant view of death (1981)
7 An uprush of mayhem (1982)
8 The local lads (1982)
9 A death in Irish Town (1983)
10 All the pretty people (1983)
11 A knife between the ribs (1986)

SCOTT, JUSTIN
BEN ABBOT
1 Hardscape (1994)
2 Stonedust (1995)
3 Frostline (1997)

SCOTT, MICHAEL
TALES OF THE BARD
1 Magician's law
2 Demon's law
3 Death's law

SCOTTOLINE, L.
BENNIE ROSATO
1 Everywhere that Mary went (1994)
2 Final appeal (1995)
3 Running from the law (1996)
4 Mistaken identity (1999)
5 Moment of truth (2000)
6 The vendetta defence (2001)
7 Courting trouble (2002)
8 Dead ringer (2003)
9 Killer smile (2004)

SCYOC, S. J.
1 Darkchild
2 Bluesong
3 Starsilk

SECOMBE, F.
THE VICAR
1 How green was my curate (1988)
2 A curate for all seasons (1990)
3 Goodbye curate (1992)
4 Hello vicar (1993)
5 A comedy of clerical errors (1994)
6 Pastures new (1996)
NF Autobiography

SEDLEY, K.
ROGER THE CHAPMAN
1 Death and the Chapman (1991)
2 The Plymouth cloak (1992)
3 The hanged man (1993)
4 The holy innocents (1994)
5 The eve of St. Hyacinth (1995)
6 The wicked winter (1996)
7 The Brothers of Glastonbury (1997)
8 The weaver's inheritance (1998)
9 The Saint John's fern (1999)
10 The goldsmith's daughter (2001)
11 The Lammas feast (2002)
12 Nine men dancing (2003)
13 The midsummer rose (2004)

SEGER, M.
1 Sarah (1988)
2 Elizabeth (1989)
3 Catherine (1989)

SELLERS, M.
CALOSTE FISHER
1 Leonardo and others (1980)
2 From eternity to here (1981)
3 Cache on the rocks (1982)

SELVON, S.
THE LONELY LONDONERS
1 The lonely Londoners (1956)
2 Moses ascending (1975)
3 Moses imagrating (1983)

SELWYN, F.
SERGEANT VERITY
1 Cracksman on velvet (1974)
2 Sgt.Verity and the Imperial diamond (1975)
3 Sgt.Verity presents his compliments (1977)
4 Sgt.Verity and the blood royal (1979)
5 Sgt.Verity and the swell mob (1981)
6 The hangman's child (2000)

SERAFIN, D.
SUPT. LUIS BERNAL
1 Saturday of glory (1979)
2 Madrid underground (1982)
3 Christmas rising (1982)
4 The body in Cadiz Bay (1985)
5 Port of light (1987)
6 The angel of Torremolinos (1988)

SERLING, R.
1 The President's plane is missing (1978)
2 Air Force One is haunted (1986)

SETTLE, M. L.
BEULAH QUINTET
1 The long road to Paradise [Prisons] (1974)
2 O Beulah land (1956)
3 Know nothing (1960)
4 The scapegoat (1980)
5 The killing ground (1983)

SEWART, A.
DET. INSPECTOR EVANS
1 Loop current (1980)
2 The turn up (1981)

SEWART, A.
DET. SGT. CHAMBERLAYNE
1 In that rich earth (1981)
2 A romp in green heat (1981)
3 Smoker's cough (1982)
4 Drink! for once dead (1983)
5 Dead man drifting (1984)

SEYMOUR, A.
1 The sins of Rebeccah Russell (1988)
2 The end of the family (1990)

SHADBOLT, M.
FERDINAND WILDBLOOD
1 Season of the Jew (1986)
2 Monday's warrior (1990)
3 The house of strife (1993)

SHAH, D. K.
PARIS CHANDLER
1 As crime goes by (1991)
2 Dying cheek to cheek (1992)

SHAKESPEARE, L. M.
JAMES ROSS-GILBERT
1 Utmost good faith (1988)
2 The gentlemen's Mafia (1989)

SHAMES, L.
FLORIDA CAPERS
1 Florida straits (1994)
2 Scavenger reef (1994)
3 Mangrove squeeze (1998)

SHANNON, D.
LUIS MENDOZA
1 Extra kill (1962)
2 The ace of spades (1963)
3 Knave of hearts (1963)
4 Death of a busybody (1963)
5 Double bluff (1964)
6 Case pending (1964)

7 Mark of murder (1965)
8 Root of all evil (1966)
9 The death-bringers (1966)
10 Death by inches (1967)
11 Coffin corner (1967)
12 With a vengeance (1968)
13 Chance to kill (1969)
14 Rain with violence (1969)
15 Kill with kindness (1969)
16 Schooled to kill (1970)
17 Crime on their hands (1970)
18 Unexpected death (1971)
19 Whim to kill (1971)
20 The ringer (1972)
21 Murder with love (1972)
22 With intent to kill (1973)
23 No holiday for crime (1974)
24 Spring of violence (1974)
25 Crime file (1975)
26 Deuces wild (1976)
27 Streets of death (1977)
28 Cold trail (1978)
29 Felony at random (1979)
30 Felony file (1980)
31 Murder most strange (1981)
32 The motive on record (1982)
33 Exploit of death (1983)
34 Destiny of death (1985)
35 Chaos of crime (1986)
36 Blood count (1987)

SHANNON, DORIS
ROBERT FORSYTH
1 Death for a doctor (1986)
2 Death for a dancer (1987)
3 Death for a dreamer (1991)
4 Death for a double (1992)
5 Death for a dietician
6 Death for a darling
7 Death for a dilettante

SHANNON, J.
JACK LIFFEY
1 The cracked earth (1999)
2 The orange curtain (2002)
3 Streets on fire (2002)

SHARAM, N.
WHITE DOG TRILOGY
1 The white earth (1986)
2 The white arrow (1987)
3 White rage (1988)

SHARPE, T.
PORTERHOUSE CHRONICLES
1 Porterhouse Blue (1974)
2 Grantchester grind (1995)

SHARPE, T.
WILT
1 Wilt (1977)
2 The Wilt alternative (1979)
3 Wilt on high (1984)

SHATNER, W.
JAKE CARDIGAN
1 Tekwar (1990)
2 Teklords (1991)
3 Teklab (1992)
4 Tek vengeance (1993)

SHATNER, W.
QUEST FOR TOMORROW
1 Delta search (2000)
2 In alien hands (2000)
3 Step into chaos (2000)
4 Beyond the stars (2000)

SHAW, B.
ORBITSVILLE
1 Orbitsville
2 Orbitsville departure (1983)
3 Orbitsville judgement (1990)

SHAW, B.
ASTRONAUTS
1 The ragged astronauts (1986)
2 The wooden spaceships (1988)

SHAW, I.
JORDACHE FAMILY
1 Rich man, poor man (1970)
2 Beggarman, thief (1977)

SHAW, R.
BARLEYBRIDGE VETS
1 A country affair (2001)
2 Country wives (2002)
3 Country lovers (2003)

SHAW, R.
TALES OF TURNHAM MALPAS
1 The new rector (1994)
2 Talk of the village (1995)
3 Village matters (1996)
4 The village show (1997)
5 Village secrets (1998)
6 Scandal in the village (1999)
7 Village gossip (1999)
8 Trouble in the village (2000)
9 A village dilemma (2002)
10 Intrigue in the village (2003)

SHAW, S.
PHILIP FLETCHER
1 Murder out of tune (1989)
2 Bloody instructions (1991)
3 Dead for a ducat (1992)
4 The villain of the earth (1994)
5 The company of knaves (1996)
6 Act of darkness (1997)

SHEA, K.
THE SARACEN
1 Land of the infidel
2 The Holy War

SHEA, R.
SHIKE
1 Time of the dragons (1981)
2 Last of the Zinja (1982)

SHEA, R. & WILSON R.T.
ILLUMINATUS
1 Eye of the pyramid
2 The golden apple
3 Leviathan

SHEARS, S.
FRANKLIN FAMILY
1 The village (1984)
2 Family fortunes (1985)
3 The young generation (1986)
4 Return to Russets (1990)

SHEARS, S.
THE NEIGHBOURS
1 The neighbours (1982)
2 The neighbours' children (1983)

SHEARS, S.
THOMAS
1 The sisters (1988)
2 Thomas (1989)
3 Son of Thomas (1991)

SHEARS, S.
LOUISE
1 Louise (1975)
2 Louise's daughters (1976)
3 Louise's inheritance (1977)

SHEARS, S.
ANNIE PARSONS
1 Annie Parsons (1978)
2 Annie's boys (1979)
3 Annie's kingdom (1980)

SHECKLEY, R.
HUNT
1 Victim prime (1987)
2 Tenth victim (1966)
3 Hunter/victim (1988)

SHEFFIELD, C.
HERITAGE UNIVERSE
1 Summertide (1990)
2 Divergance (1991)
3 Transcendance (1992)

SHELDON, S.
1 The other side of midnight (1975)
2 Memories of midnight (1990)

SHELLEY, M.
FRANKENSTEIN
1 Frankenstein (1818)
2 Frankenstein's bride, by H.Bailey (1994)

SHELYNN, J.
SAM CLAYTON
1 The affair at Cralla Voe (1978)
2 A fall of snow (1980)
3 Epilogue for Selena (1980)

SHELYNN, J.
NED PARKER
1 A place called Purgatory (1978)
2 The night marches (1978)
3 The Cuoto snatch (1979)
4 For a girl called Isiah (1979)
5 The Judas factor (1980)
6 Joker in a stacked deck (1981)

SHEPHERD, S.
DET. INSPECTOR RICHARD
MONTGOMERY
1 Thinner than blood (1991)
2 A lethal fixation (1993)
3 Nurse Dawes is dead (1994)
4 Embers of death (1996)

SHERWOOD, JOHN
CELIA GRANT
1 Green trigger fingers (1984)
2 A botanist at bay (1985)
3 The mantrap garden (1986)
4 Flowers of evil (1987)
5 Menacing groves (1988)
6 A bouquet of thorns (1989)
7 The sunflower plot (1990)
8 The hanging garden (1992)
9 Creeping Jenny (1993)

10 Bones gather no moss (1994)
11 Shady borders (1996)

SHERWOOD, V.
LOVESONG
1 The beauty and the English lord (1987)
2 The beauty and the buccaneer (1987)

SHERWOOD, V.
THIS TOWERING PASSION
1 The lovers (1991)
2 The mistress (1991)
3 Her shining splendour (1994)

SHIPLEY, R.
MILLARD FAMILY
1 Wychwood (1989)
2 Echoes of Wychwood (1991)

SHIPWAY, G.
AGAMEMNON
1 Warrior in bronze (1977)
2 King in splendour (1979)

SHONE, A.
ULYSSES F. DONAGHUE
1 Come away death (1994)
2 Secrets in stones (1996)

SHORT, A.
CHRISTIE FAMILY
1 The first fair wind (1984)
2 The running tide (1986)
3 The dragon seas (1988)

SHORT, A.
SILVERCAIRNS
1 Silvercairns (1990)
2 Rainbow Hill (1991)
3 Willowbrae (1992)

SHUPP, M.
DESTINY MAKERS
1 With fate conspire
2 Morning of creation
3 Soldier of another fortune
4 Death's grey land

SHUSTERMAN, N.
STAR SHARDS TRILOGY
1 Scorpion shards (1997)
2 Thief of souls (1999)

SHWARTZ, S.
HEIRS TO BYZANTIUM
1 Byzantium's crown
2 The woman of flowers
3 Queensblade

SIEGEL, J.
FERN CAPEL
1 Prospero's children (1999)
2 The dragon charmer (2000)

SIEGEL, S.
MIKE DALEY
1 Special circumstances (2000)
2 Incriminating evidence (2001)

SILKE, J. R.
DEATH DEALER
1 Prisoner of the horned helmet
2 Lords of destruction
3 Tooth and claw
4 Plague of knives

SILLIPHANT, S.
JOHN LOCKE
1 Steel tiger (1986)
2 Bronze bell (1987)

SILLITOE, A.
MICHAEL CULLEN
1 A start in life (1970) (rev. ed. 1979) (1970)
2 Life goes on (1986)

SILLITOE, A.
SEATON FAMILY
1 The open door (1990)
2 The key to the door (1961)
3 Saturday night and Sunday morning (1953)
4 Birthday (1999)

SILVA, D.
MICHAEL OSBORNE
1 The mark of the assassin (1998)
2 The marching season (1999)

SILVERBERG, R.
MAJIPOOR
1 Lord Valentine's castle (1981)
2 Majipoor chronicles (1982)
3 Valentine Pontifex (1984)
4 The mountains of Majipoor (1995)
5 Sorcerers of Majipoor (1997)
6 Lord Prestimion (1999)
7 The King of dreams (2002)

SILVERBERG, R.
NEW SPRINGTIME
1 At winter's end (1988)
2 The Queen of springtime (1989)

SILVERMAN, D.
JOHN MUNG
1 The fall of the Shogun (1986)
2 The black dragon (1988)
3 Shishi (1989)
4 Tairo: the great elder (1990)

SIMMONS, D.
1 Hyperion (1990)
2 The fall of Hyperion (1991)

SIMONS, P.
TATIANA AND ALEXANDER
1 The bronze horseman (2001)
2 The bridge to Holy Cross (2003)
3 Tatiana and Alexander (2003)

SIMPSON, D.
INSPECTOR LUKE THANET
1 The night she died (1980)
2 Six feet under (1982)
3 Puppet for a corpse (1983)
4 Close her eyes (1984)
5 Last seen alive (1985)
6 Dead on arrival (1986)
7 Element of doubt (1987)
8 Suspicious death (1988)
9 Dead by morning (1989)
10 Doomed to die (1991)
11 Wake the dead (1992)
12 No laughing matter (1993)
13 A day for dying (1995)
14 Once too often (1997)
15 Dead and gone (1999)

SIMPSON, J.
AUTOBIOGRAPHY OF A
MOUNTAINEER
1 Touching the void (1988)
2 This game of ghosts (1993)
3 The beckoning silence (2002)

SIMPSON, M.
MAYAN STEVENSON
1 Anywhere but here (1990)
2 The lost father (1992)

SINCLAIR, A.
BUMBO
1 The breaking of Bumbo (1959)
2 Beau Bumbo (1985)

SINCLAIR, A.
ALBION TRYPTYCH
1 Gog (1967)
2 Magog (1972)
3 King Ludd (1988)

SINCLAIR, A.
EMPIRE QUARTET
1 The far corners of the earth (1991)
2 The strength of the hills (1992)

SINDEN, D.
1 A touch of the memoirs (1982)
2 Laughter in the second act (1985)
  NF Autobiography

SKELTON, C. L.
HARDACRE FAMILY
1 Hardacres
2 Hardacres luck (1985)

SKIDMORE, I.
1 Island fling (1981)
2 The magnificent Evan

SKVORECKY, J.
DANNY SMIRICKY
1 The engineer of human souls
2 The miracle game (1991)

SKVORECKY, J.
LIEUTENANT BORUVKA
1 The mournful demeanour of Lt. Boruvka
  (1988)
2 Sind for Father Knox (1989)
3 The end of Lieutenant Boruvka (1990)
4 The return of Lieutenant Boruvka (1990)

SLADE, M.
SPECIAL X UNIT
1 Headhunter (1992)
2 Cutthroat (1993)
3 Ghoul (1993)
4 Ripper (1994)
5 Zombie (1996)
6 Shrink (1998)

SLOVO, G.
KATE BEIER
1 Morbid symptoms (1984)
2 Death by analysis (1986)
3 Death comes staccato (1987)
4 Catnap (1994)
5 Close call (1995)

SMITH, D. W.
DET. CHIEF INSPECTOR HARRY
FATHERS
1 Father's law (1986)
2 Serious crimes (1987)
3 The fourth crow (1989)

SMITH, E. E. (DOC)
FAMILY D'ALEMBERT
1 The Imperial stars
2 Strangler's moon
3 The clockwork traitor
4 Getaway world
5 The bloodstar conspiracy
6 The purity plot
7 Plant of treachery
8 Eclipsing boundaries
9 The Omicron invasion

SMITH, E. E. (DOC)
LENSMAN
1 Triplanetary (1955)
2 First lensman (1957)
3 Galactic patrol (1971)
4 Grey lensman (1971)
5 Second stage lensman (1972)
6 Children of the lens (1972)
7 Masters of the vortex (1972)
8 Dragon lensman by D.E.Kyle
9 Lensman from Rigel, by D.E.Kyle

SMITH, E. E. (DOC)
LORD TEDRIC
1 Lord Tedric
2 The space pirates
3 The Black Knights of the Iron Sphere
4 Alien realms

SMITH, E. E. (DOC)
SKYLARK
1 The Skylark of space
2 Skylark three
3 The Skylark of Valeron
4 Skylark Duquesne

SMITH, E. E. (DOC)
SUBSPACE
1 Subspace explorers
2 Subspace encounter

SMITH, EVELYN E.
SUSAN MELVILLE
1 Miss Melvile regrets (1987)
2 Miss Melvile returns (1988)
3 Miss Melvile rides a tiger (1992)

SMITH, F. E
1 Rage of the innocent (1987)
2 In presence of my foes (1988)

SMITH, F. E
633 SQUADRON
1 633 Squadron (1956)
2 Operation Rhine Maiden (1975)
3 Operation Crucible (1977)
4 Operation Valkyrie (1978)
5 Operation Cobra (1981)
6 Operation Titan (1982)
7 Operation crisis (1990)
8 Operation Thor (1994)
9 Operation defiant (1995)

SMITH, F. E
SAFFRON
1 Saffron's war
2 Saffron's army
3 Saffron trials

SMITH, F. E
STARS
1 A meeting of stars (1986)
2 A clash of stars (1987)
3 Years of the fury (1989)

SMITH, F. M.
1 Surgery at Aberffrwd (1981)
2 A GP's progress to the Black Country
(1984)
NF Autobiography of a doctor

SMITH, G. N.
SABAT
1 The graveyard vulture
2 The blood merchants
3 Cannibal cult
4 The druid connection

SMITH, G. N.
THIRST
1 The thirst
2 The plague

SMITH, JOAN
LORETTA LAWSON
1 A masculine ending (1987)
2 Why aren't they screaming (1988)
3 Don't leave me this way (1992)
4 What men say (1993)
5 Full stop (1995)

SMITH, M. A.
JEREMIAH
1 Terrorist prophet (1998)
2 New America (1999)
3 The inheritors (2000)

SMITH, M. C.
ARKADY RENKO
1 Gorky Park (1981)
2 Polar star (1989)
3 Red Square (1992)
4 Havana Bay (1999)

SMITH, S.
NOREEN SPINKS
1 Flies (1990)
2 Dosh (1991)

SMITH, SYLVIA
LIFE STORY
1 Misadventure (2000)
2 Appleby House (2002)

SMITH, W.
BALLANTYNE FAMILY
1 A falcon flies (1980)
2 Men of men (1981)
3 The angels weep (1982)

SMITH, W.
COURTNEY FAMILY
1 The burning shore (1985)
2 Power of the sword (1986)
3 Rage (1987)
4 A time to die (1989)
5 Golden fox (1990)
6 Monsoon (1999)
7 Blue horizon (2003)

SMITH, W.
SEAN COURTNEY
1 When the lion feeds (1965)
2 The sound of thunder (1966)
3 A sparrow falls (1977)

SMITH, W.
THE NILE
1 River God (1993)
2 The seventh scroll (1995)

SNYDER, M.
THE QUEEN'S QUARTER
1 New moon
2 Sadar's keep

SOLOMITA, S.
STANLEY WOODROW
1 Force of nature (1990)
2 Last chance for glory (1994)
3 Good day to die (1994)
4 Damaged goods (1997)

SOLZHENITSYN, A.
RUSSIAN REVOLUTION
1 August 1917 (1972)
2 Lenin in Zurich (1976)

SOLZHENITSYN, A.
THE RED WHEEL
1 August 1914 (1998)
2 November 1916 (1999)

SOMERS, J. [D. LESSING]
1 Diary of a good neighbour (1983)
2 If the old could (1984)

SOMTOW, S. P.
TIMMY VALENTINE
1 Vampire junction (1991)
2 Valentine (1992)

SOMTOW, S. P.
VAMPIRES
1 Rivverrun (1993)
2 Armorica (1994)

SORIANO, O.
1 A funny dirty little war (1983)
2 Winter quarters (1989)

SOYINKA, W.
1 Ake:years of childhood (1985)
2 Isara:a voyage round Essay (1990)

SPEDDING, A.
A WALK IN THE DARK
1 The road and the hills (1988)
2 A cloud over water
3 The streets of the city

SPENCER, CHARLES
WILL BENSON
1 I nearly died (1994)
2 Full personal service (1996)
3 Under the influence (2001)

SPENCER, S.
TAYLOR FAMILY AND BECKY
WORRALL
1 Salt of the earth (1993)

2 Up our street (1994)
3 Old Father Thames (1995)
4 Those golden days (1995)
5 South of the river (1997)

SPENCER, SALLY
DET. CHIEF INSPECTOR WOODEND
1 Murder at Swann's Lake (1999)
2 Death of a cave dweller (2000)
3 The Golden Mile to murder (2001)
4 Dead on cue (2001)
5 The red herring (2002)
6 Death of an innocent (2002)
7 The enemy within (2003)
8 The witch maker (2004)

SPICER, M.
LADY JANE HILDRETH
1 Cotswold manners (1990)
2 The Cotswold murders (1991)
3 The Cotswold mistress (1992)

SPRAGUE DE CAMP, L.
THE RELUCTANT KING
1 The goblin tower
2 The clocks of Iraz
3 The unbeheaded king

SPRAGUE DE CAMP, L.
THE ENCHANTER
1 The incompleat enchanter
2 The castle of iron
3 The enchanter compleated

SPRIDGEON, G.
GREEN BOATERS
1 Eight green boaters (1995)
2 The return of the green boaters (1996)

SPRING, M.
LAURA PRINCIPAL
1 Every breath you take (1994)
2 Running for shelter (1995)
3 Standing in the shadows (1998)
4 Nights in white satin (1999)
5 Into the midnight hour (2001)

SPRINGER, N.
THE BOOK OF ISLE
1 The white hart (1984)
2 The silver sun (1984)
3 The sable moon (1985)
4 The black beast (1985)
5 The golden swan (1985)

SPRINGER, N.
SEA KING TRILOGY
1 Madbond
2 Mindbond

SPURLING, H.
1 Ivy when young (1974)
2 Secrets of a woman's heart (1984)
   NF Biography of Ivy Compton Burnett

ST.AUBYN, E.
PATRICK MELROSE
1 Never mind (1992)
2 Bad news (1992)
3 Some hope (1994)

STABENOW, K.
KATE SHUGAK
1 Midnight come again (2000)
2 The singing of the dead (2001)

STABLEFORD, B.
ASGARD TRILOGY
1 Journey to the centre
2 Invaders fromthe centre
3 The centre almost told

STABLEFORD, B.
GENESYS
1 Serpent's blood (1995)
2 Salamander's fire (1996)
3 Chimera's cradle (1997)

STABLEFORD, B.
HOODED SWAN
1 Halcyon drift (1973)
2 Rhapsody in black (1974)
3 Promised land (1975)

STABLEFORD, B.
THE DAEDALUS MISSION
1 The Florians
2 Critical threshold
3 Wildeblood's empire
4 City of the sun

STABLEFORD, B.
WEREWOLVES
1 The werewolves of London (1990)
2 The angel of pain (1991)

STABLEFORD, B.
FUTURE HISTORY
1 Inherit the earth
2 Architects of emortality
3 The fountains of youth

4 The Cassandra complex
5 Dark Ararat (2003)

STACKPOLE, M. A.
THE WARRIOR TRILOGY
1 En garde
2 Riposte

STACY, R.
DOOMSDAY WARRIOR
1 Doomsday warrior
2 Red America
3 The last American
4 Bloody America
5 America's last declaration
6 American rebellion
7 American defiance
8 American glory

STAINCLIFFE, C.
SAL KILKENNY
1 Looking for trouble (1996)
2 Go not gently (1997)
3 Dead wrong (1999)
4 Stone cold, red hot (2001)
5 Towers of silence (2002)
6 Bitter blue (2003)

STALL, M.
DANIEL LACEY
1 The killing mask (1981)
2 The wet job (1982)

STALLMAN, R.
THE BEAST
1 The orphan
2 The captive
3 The book of the beast

STALLWOOD, V.
KATE IVORY
1 Death and the Oxford box (1993)
2 Oxford exit (1994)
3 Oxford mourning (1995)
4 Oxford fall (1996)
5 Oxford knot (1998)
6 Oxford blue (1998)
7 Oxford shift (1999)
8 Oxford shadows (2000)
9 Oxford proof (2002)
10 Oxford remains (2004)

STAMP.T.
1 Stamp album (1987)

2 Coming attractions (1988)
3 Double feature (1989)
   NF Autobiography

STANDIFORD, L.
JOHN DEAL
1 Done Deal (1995)
2 Raw Deal (1996)
3 Deal to die for (1997)

STANLEY, G.
ARAKI
1 A death in Tokyo (1990)
2 The ivory seal (1991)

STAPLES, M. J.
ADAMS FAMILY
1 Down Lambeth way (1988)
2 Our Emily (1989)
3 King of Camberwell (1990)
4 On Mother Brown's doorstep (1991)
5 A family affair (1992)
6 Missing person (1993)
7 Pride of Walworth (1994)
8 Echoes of yesterday (1995)
9 The Camberwell raid (1996)
10 The last summer (1996)
11 Fire over London (1998)
12 The family at war (1998)
13 Bright day, dark night (1998)
14 Churchill's people (1999)
15 Tomorrow is another day (2000)
16 The way ahead (2000)
17 Year of victory (2001)
18 The homecoming (2001)
19 Sons and daughters (2002)
20 Appointment at the Palace (2002)
21 Changing times (2003)
22 Spreading wings (2003)
23 Family fortunes (2004)

STAR TREK
MY BROTHERS KEEPER
1 Republic
2 Constitution
3 Enterprise

STAR TREK
Q
1 Q-squared
2 I, Q
3 Q in law

STAR TREK
THE Q CONTINUUM
1 Q-space

2 Q-zone
3 Q-strike

STAR TREK
INVASION
1 First strike, by D.Carey
2 The soldiers of fear, by D.W. Smith
3 Time's enemy, by L.A.Graf
4 Final fury, by D.ab Hugh

STAR TREK
DAY OF HONOR
1 Ancient blood, by D.Carey
2 Armageddon sky, by L.A.Graf
3 Her Klingon soul, by M.J.Friedman
4 Treaty's law, by D.W.Smith

STAR TREK
THE DOMINION WAR
1 Behind enemy lines, by J.Vornholt
2 Call to arms, by D.Carey
3 Tunnel through the stars, by J.Vornholt
4 Sacrifice of angels, by D.Carey

STAR TREK
THE CAPTAINS TABLE
1 War dragon s, by L.A.Graf
2 Dujonian's board, by M.J.Friedman
3 The mist, by D.W.Smith
4 Fire ship, by D.Carey
5 Once burned, by P.David
6 Where sea meets sky, by J.Oltion

STAR TREK
NEW EARTH
1 Wagon trail to the stars, by D.Carey
2 Belle terre, by D.W.Smith
3 Rough trails, by L.A.Graf
4 The flaming arrow, by J.Oltion

STAR TREK
ERRAND OF VENGEANCE
1 The edge of the sword, by J.Oltion
2 Killing blow, by J.Oltion
3 River of blood, by J.Oltion

STAR TREK
THE JANUS GATE
1 Present tense, by L.A.Graf
2 Future imperfect, by L.A.Graf
3 Past prologue, by L.A.Graf

STAR TREK, DEEP SPACE NINE
MILLENNIUM
1 The fall of Terok Nor

2 The war of the prophets
3 Inferno

STAR TREK, DEEP SPACE NINE
REBELS
1 The conquered
2 The courageous
3 The liberated
4 Unity

STAR TREK, DEEP SPACE NINE
MISSION GAMMA
1 Twilight, by D.R.George
2 This gray spirit, by H.Jarman
3 Cathedral, by A.Mangels
4 Lesser evil, by R.Simpson

STAR TREK, THE NEXT GENERATION
DOUBLE HELIX
1 Infection, by J.G.Betancourt
2 Vectors, by D.W.Smith
3 Red sector, by D.Carey
4 Quarantine, by J.Vornholt
5 Double or nothing, by P.David
6 The first virtue, by M.J.Friedman

STAR WARS
THE BOUNTY HUNTER WARS
1 The Mandalorian armour, by K.W.Jeter
2 Slave ship, by K.W.Jeter
3 Hard merchandise, by K.W.Jeter

STAR WARS
BLACK FLEET TRILOGY
1 Before the storm
2 Shield of lies
3 Tyrant's test

STAR WARS
CANTINA TRILOGY
1 Tales from the Mos Eisley cantina
2 Tales from the Jabba's palace
3 Tales of the bounty hunters

STAR WARS
HAN SOLO TRILOGY
1 The paradise snare
2 The Hutt gambit
3 Rebel dawn

STAR WARS
CORELLIAN TRILOGY
1 Ambush at Corellia
2 Assault at Selonia
3 Showdown at Centerpoint

STAR WARS
JEDI ACADEMY
1 Jedi search
2 Dark apprentice
3 Champions of the Force
4 Leviathan

STAR WARS
NEW JEDI ORDER
1 Vector prime, by R.A.Salvatore
2 Jedi eclipse, by J Lucerno
3 Balance point, by K.Tyers
4 Destiny's way, by H.J.Williams

STAR WARS
AGENTS OF CHAOS
1 Hero's trial, by J. Lucerno
2 The unifying force, by J.Lucerno
3 The Cestus deception, by S.Barnes

STAR WARS
DARK TIDE
1 Onshaught, by M.A.Stackpole
2 Ruin, by M.A.Stackpole

STAR WARS
X WING
1 Rogue squadron
2 Wedge's gamble
3 The Kryptos trap
4 The Bacta war
5 Rogues unbound
6 Iron fist
7 Solo command
8 Isand's revenge
9 Starfighters of Aduma
10 The warrior princess

STARK, R.
PARKER
1 The score (retitled Point blank) (1985)
2 The hunter
3 The man with the getaway face (The steel hit) (1985)
4 The outfit (1988)
5 The mourner (Killtown) (1987)
6 The jugger (Made in the USA) (1986)
7 The seventh (The split) (1966)
8 The handle (Run lethal) (1986)
9 The rare coin score (1967)
10 The green eagle score (1987)
11 The black ice score (1986)
12 The sour lemon score (1985)
13 Deadly edge
14 Slayground (1969)
15 Plunder squad (1972)
16 Butcher's moon (1977)

17 Comeback (1997)
18 Backflash (2001)
19 Firebreak (2001)
20 Flashfire (2002)
21 Breakout (2003)

STARLING, J.
1 Alice in reflection (1987)
2 Emily in waiting (1988)

STASHEFF, C.
A WIZARD IN RHYME
1 Her Majesty's wizard
2 The oathbound wizard
3 The witch doctor

STASHELT, C.
COSMIC WARLOCK
1 A warlock in spite of himself
2 A wizard in Bedlam
3 King Kobold

STATHAM, F. P.
1 The Roswell women (1989)
2 Roswell legacy (1990)

STAYNES, J. & STOREY, M.
DET. SUPT. BONE
1 Goodbye, Nanny Gray (1987)
2 A knife at the opera (1988)
3 Body of opinion (1988)
4 Grave words (1991)
5 The late lady (1991)
6 Bone idle (1993)
7 Dead serious (1995)
9 Quarry (1999)

STEED, N.
PETER MARKLIN
1 Tin-plate (1986)
2 Die-cast (1987)
3 Chipped (1988)
4 Wind up (1990)
5 Boxed-in (1991)
6 Dead cold (1992)

STEED, N.
JOHNNY BLACK
1 Black eye (1989)
2 Black mail (1990)

STEIN, A. M.
MATT ERRIDGE
1 Never need an enemy
2 Home and murder
3 Blood on the stars

4 I fear the Greeks
5 Faces of death
6 Deadly delight
7 Executioner's rest
8 Snare Andalucia
9 Kill is a four-letter word
10 Alp murder
11 The finger
12 Lock and key
13 Coffin country
14 Lend me your ear
15 Body search
16 Nowhere?
17 The rolling heads
18 One dip dead
19 The cheating butcher
20 A nose for it
21 A body for a buddy (1981)
22 Hangman
23 The bombing run (1983)
24 The garbage collector (1986)

STEIN, M.
MARK ROSSETTI
1 Marked man (1995)
2 Red card (1996)
3 White lines (1997)

STEIN, S.
GEORGE THOMASSY
1 The magician (1983)
2 Other people (1984)
3 The touch of treason (1985)

STEPHENS, K.
STONEMOOR
1 Stonemoor House (1995)
2 Heir to Stonemoor (1995)
3 Return to Stonemoor (1998)

STEPHENS.R.
BREW GINNY
1 The man who killed his brother (1980)
2 The man who risked his partner (1985)
3 The man who tried to get away (1990)

STEVENS, G.
DAVE HASLAM
1 Provo (1993)
2 Kennedy's ghost (1994)

STEVENSON, J.
1 Astraea
2 The pretender
3 The Emperor of the last days

STEVENSON, R. L.
TREASURE ISLAND
1 Treasure Island (1883)
2 The adventures of Long John Silver (1977)
3 Return to Treasure Island, by D.Judd (1977)
4 The adventures of Ben Gunn, by R.F.Delderfield
5 Silver's revenge, by R.Leeson (1978)
6 Jim Hawkins and the curse of Treasure Island, by F.Bryan (2002)

STEWART, MARY
MERLIN AND ARTHUR
1 The crystal cave (1972)
2 The hollow hills (1973)
3 The last enchantment (1979)
4 The savage day (1984)

STIRLING, JESSICA
HOLLY BECKMAN
1 Deep well at noon (1979)
2 Blue evening gone (1981)
3 The gates of midnight (1983)

STIRLING, JESSICA
PATTERSON FAMILY
1 Treasures on earth (1985)
2 Creature comforts (1986)
3 Hearts of gold (1987)

STIRLING, JESSICA
NICHOLSON FAMILY
1 The good provider (1988)
2 The asking price (1989)
3 The wise child (1990)
4 The welcome light (1991)

STIRLING, JESSICA
CLARE KELSO
1 Lantern for the dark (1992)
2 Shadows on the shore (1993)

STIRLING, JESSICA
STALKER FAMILY
1 The spoiled earth (1975)
2 The hiring fair (1976)
3 The dark pasture (1978)

STIRLING, JESSICA
CAMPBELL FAMILY
1 The island wife (1997)
2 The wind from the hills (1998)
3 The strawberry season (2000)

STOCKLEY, G.
GIDEON PAGE
1 Expert testimony
2 Probable cause
3 Blind judgment

STOCKWIN, J.
KYDD
1 Kydd (2001)
2 Artemis (2002)
3 Seaflower (2003)
4 Mutiny (2003)

STOKER, B.
DRACULA
1 Dracula (1897)
2 The Dracula archives, by R.Rudorff (1971)
3 Dracula's diary, by M.Geare & M. Corby (1982)
4 Dracula, my love, by P.Tremayne (1983)
5 Dracula's children, by R.Chetwynd-Hayes (1987)
6 House of Dracula, by R.Chetwynd-Hayes (1987)
7 Dracula unbound, by B.Aldiss (1991)
8 Anno Dracula, by K.Newman (1992)
9 Covenant with the vampire, by J.Kalogridis (1994)
10 The secret life of Laszlo, Count Dracula, by R.Anscombe (1996)
11 Dracula the undead, by F.Warrington (1997)
12 Count Dracula, by H.Slawkberg (1998)
13 Dracula cha cha cha, by K.Newman (2000)

STOKES, D.
1 Voices in my ear (1980)
2 More voices in my ear (1981)
3 Innocent voices in my ear (1983)
4 Whispering voices in my ear (1985)
   NF Autobiography of a medium

STOREY, J.
JOYCE
1 Our Joyce (1987)
2 Joyce's war (1990)
3 Joyce's dream:the post war years (1995)

STOTT, M.
1 Forgetting's no excuse (1973)
2 Before I go (1985)
   NF Reminiscences

STRAITON, E.
1 Animals are my life (1979)

2 A vet at large (1982)
3 Positively vetted (1983)
4 A vet on the set (1985)

STRALEY, J.
CECIL YOUNGER ALASKAN MYSTERIES
1 The woman who married a bear (1995)
2 The curious eat themselves (1996)
3 The music of what happens (1997)
4 Death and the language of happiness (1998)
5 The angels will not care (1999)

STRANGER, J.
DOG SERIES
1 Three's a pack (1980)
2 Two for joy (1982)
3 A dog in a million (1984)
4 Dog days (1986)

STREET, PAMELA
1 The millrace (1983)
2 The way of the river (1984)
3 Many waters (1985)
4 Unto the fourth generation (1985)

STRESHINSKY, S.
1 Hers the kingdom (1981)
2 Gift of the golden mountain (1989)

STRONG, T.
SAS
1 Whisper who dares (1983)
2 The fifth hostage (1984)

STUART, I.
DAVID GRIERSON
1 Death from disclosure (1979)
2 End on the rocks (1981)
3 The garb of truth (1982)
4 Thrilling sweet and rotten (1983)
5 A growing concern (1987)

STUART, V.
THE AUSTRALIANS
1 The exiles (1981)
2 The settlers (1981)
3 The traitors (1982)
4 The explorers (1983)
5 The adventurers (1983)
6 The colonists (1984)
7 The gold-seekers (1985)
8 The patriots (1986)
9 The Empire builders (1987)
10 The seafarers (1988)

11 The nationalists (1989)
12 The imperialists (1990)

STUBBS, J.
BRIEF CHRONICLES
1 Kit's Hill (1979)
2 The ironmaster (1981)
3 The Vivian inheritance (1982)
4 The Northern correspondent (1984)

STURROCK, J.
THE BOW STREET RUNNER
1 Village of rogues (1972)
2 A wicked way to die (1973)
3 The wilful lady (1975)
4 A conspiracy of poisons (1977)
5 Suicide most foul (1981)
6 Captain Bolton's corpse (1982)
7 The Pangersbourne murders (1984)

STYLES, S.
MR. FITTON
1 A sword for Mr. Fitton (1975)
2 Mr. Fitton's commission (1977)
3 Baltic convoy (1979)
4 The quarterdeck ladder (1982)
5 The lee shore (1986)
6 Gun-brig captain (1987)
7 H.M.S. Cracker (1988)
8 A ship for Mr. Fitton (1992)
9 The independent cruise (1992)
10 Mr. Fitton's prize (1993)
11 Mr. Fitton and the Black Legion (1994)
12 Mr. Fitton in command (1995)
13 The 12 gun cutter (1996)
14 Lieutenant Fitton (1997)
15 Mr. Fitton at the helm (1998)
16 The Martinique mission (1999)
17 Mr. Fitton's hurricane (2000)

SUCHET, J.
LUDWIG VAN BEETHOVEN
1 The last master; passion and anger
  (1996)
2 Passion and pain (1997)
3 Passion and glory (1998)

SUGERMAN, D.
1 No-one gets out of here alive (1980)
2 Wonderland Avenue (1989)

SULITZER, P. L.
1 Hannah (1988)
2 The empress (1989)

SUMMERS, R.
KILLIGREW FAMILY
1 Killigrew clay (1986)
2 Clay country (1987)
3 Family ties (1988)
4 Family shadows (1995)
5 Primmy's daughter (1998)
6 White rivers (1998)
7 September morning (1999)
8 A brighter tomorrow (2000)

SUNLEY, M.
1 The quiet earth (1990)
2 Fields inthe sun (1991)

SUTHREN, V.
EDWARD MAINWARING
1 Royal Yankee (1987)
2 The golden galleon (1989)
3 Admiral of fear (1991)
4 Captain Monsoon (1993)

SUTHREN, V.
PAUL GALLANT
1 The black cockade (1979)
2 A King's ransom (1980)

SUTTON, J.
BEL AIR GENERAL
1 Bel Air General (1987)
2 The price of life (1988)
3 Masks and faces (1988)
4 Vital signs
5 Critical condition

SWANSON, D. J.
JACK FLIPPO
1 Big town (1994)
2 Dreamboat (1995)
3 96 tears (1997)

SWITHIN, A.
THE PERILOUS QUEST FOR LYONESSE
1 Princes of Sandastre
2 The lords of the stony mountains
3 The winds of the wastelands
4 The nine gods of Safaddne

SYLVESTER, M.
WILLIAM WARNE
1 A dangerous age (1986)
2 A lethal vintage (1988)

SYMONS, J.
SHERIDAN HAYNES
1 The Blackheath poisonings (1978)

2 Sweet Adelaide (1980)
3 The Detling murders (1982)
4 A three-pipe problem
5 The Kentish Manor murders (1988)

TALBOT, M.
AUSTRALIAN SAGA
1 To the ends of the earth (1987)
2 A wilful woman (1989)

TAN, M.
JANE NICHOLS
1 Aka Jane (1999)
2 Run, Jane, run (1999)

TANENBAUM, R.
BUTCH KARP
1 Enemy within (2001)
2 Absolute rage (2002)

TANGYE, D.
MINACK CHRONICLES
1 A gull on the roof (1964)
2 A cat in the window (1965)
3 A drake at the door (1966)
4 A donkey in the meadow (1967)
5 Lama (1969)
6 Cornish summer (1971)
7 Cottage on a cliff (1973)
8 A cat affair (1975)
9 The way to Minack (1975)
10 Sun on the lintel (1976)
11 Somewhere a cat is waiting (1977)
12 The winding lane (1978)
13 When the winds blow (1980)
14 The Ambrose rock (1982)
15 A quiet year (1984)
16 The cherry tree (1986)
17 The world of Minack (1991)
   NF Life on a Cornish farm

TANNAHILL, R.
1 The world, the flesh and the devil
   (1400s) (1985)
2 Camerons of Kinveil (1800s) (1988)

TANNER, J.
HILLSBRIDGE
1 The black mountains (1983)
2 The emerald valley (1985)
3 The hills and the valley (1988)

TAPPLY, W. G.
BRADY COYNE
1 Death at Charity's Point (1984)
2 The Dutch Blue error (1985)

3 Follow the sharks (1986)
4 A rodent of doubt (1987)
5 Dead meat (1987)
6 The vulgar boatman (1988)
7 A void in hearts (1989)
8 Dead winter (1990)
9 Client privilege (1991)
10 The spotted cats (1992)
11 Tight lines (1993)
12 The snake eater (1994)

TARR, J.
THE HOUND AND THE FALCON
1 The Isle of Glass (1986)
2 The golden horn (1986)
3 The hounds of God (1987)

TARR, J.
THE AVARYAN RISING
1 The hall of the mountain king
2 The lady of Han-Gilen
3 A fall of princes

TAYLOR, A. G.
NORTH WALES POLICE SERIES
1 Simeon's bride (1995)
2 In guilty night (1996)

TAYLOR, ALICE
RURAL IRELAND
1 To school through the fields (1990)
2 Quench the lamp (1991)

TAYLOR, ALISON J.
DET. SUPT. MICHAEL MCKENNA
1 Unsafe convictions (1999)
2 The house of women (2000)
3 Child's play (2001)

TAYLOR, ANDREW
WILLIAM DOUGAL
1 Caroline Miniscule (1983)
2 Waiting for the end of the world (1984)
3 Our fathers
4 An old school tie (1986)
5 Freelance death (1987)
6 Blood relation (1990)
7 The sleeping policeman (1992)
8 Odd man out (1993)

TAYLOR, ANDREW
LYDMOUTH MYSTERIES
1 The air that kills (1994)
2 The mortal sickness (1995)
3 The lover of the grave (1997)
4 The suffocating night (1999)

5 Where roses fade (2000)
6 Death's own door (2001)

TAYLOR, ANDREW
THE ROTH TRILOGY
1 The four last things (1997)
2 The judgment of strangers (1998)
3 The office of the dead (1999)

TAYLOR, DAVID
1 Zoo vet (1976)
2 Doctor in the zoo (1978)
3 Going wild (1980)
4 Next panda, please (1982)
5 The wandering whale (1984)
6 Dragon doctor (1986)
   NF Experiences of a vet

TAYLOR, F.
1 The kinder garden (1991)
2 The peacebrokers (1992)

TAYLOR, K.
BARD
1 Bard
2 The first long ship
3 The wild sea
4 Raven's gathering
5 Felimid's homecoming

TAYLOR, R.
CHRONICLES OF HAWKLAN
1 The call of the sword
2 The fall of Fyorland
3 The waking of Orthlund
4 Into Narsindal
5 The return of the sword

TAYLOR, R.
NIGHTFALL
1 Farnor (1992)
2 Valderen (1993)

TELEP, P.
SQUIRE
1 Squire (1995)
2 Squire's blood (1995)
3 Squire's honor (1996)

TELL, D.
POPPY DILLWORTH
1 Murder at Red Rock Ranch (1990)
2 The Hallelujah murders (1991)

TELUSHKIN, J.
RABBI DANIEL WINTER
1 The unorthodox murder of Rabbi Moss (1987)
2 The final analysis of Dr. Stark (1988)
3 An eye for an eye (1990)

TEMPLETON, A.
DET. SGT. DIANE BRAITHWAITE
1 Last act of all (1995)
2 Past praying for (1996)
3 The trumpet shall sound (1997)
4 Shades of death (2001)

TENNANT, E.
1 A house of hospitalities (1987)
2 A wedding of cousins (1988)

TEPPER, S. S.
PETER
1 King's blood four
2 Necromancer nine
3 Wizard's eleven

TEPPER, S. S.
JINIAN FOOTSEER
1 Jinian Footseer
2 Dervish daughter
3 Jinian Stareye

TEPPER, S. S.
MARVIN MANYSHAPED
1 The song of Marvin Manyshaped
2 The flight of Marvin Manyshaped
3 The search of Marvin Manyshaped

TERRY, C.
1 King of diamonds (1983)
2 The fortune seekers (1985)

TETTMAR, E.
THORNMERE
1 House of birds (1994)
2 The years between (1994)
3 The scarlet landscape (1995)

TEVIS, W.
FAST EDDY
1 The hustler (1960)
2 The colour of money (1985)

TEY, J.
DET. INSPECTOR ALAN GRANT
1 The man in the queue (1927)
2 A shilling for candles (1936)
3 The Franchise affair (1948)

4 To love and be wise (1950)
5 The daughter of time (1951)
6 The singing sands (1952)

THEROUX, P.
1 The consul's file (1981)
2 The London embassy (1982)

THEW, L. M.
1 The pit village and the store (1985)
2 From store to war (1987)
   NF *Life in the South Yorkshire coalfields*

THOMAS, CHRISTINE
O NEILL FAMILY
1 Bridie (1989)
2 April (1990)
3 Hannah (1991)

THOMAS, CRAIG
FIREFOX
1 Firefox (1977)
2 Firefox down (1983)
3 Winter hawk (1987)
4 A different war (1997)

THOMAS, CRAIG
KENNETH AUBREY
1 The bear's tears (1985)
2 All the grey cats (1988)
3 The last raven (1990)
4 A hooded crow (1992)
5 Playing with cobras (1993)

THOMAS, D. M.
SERGEI ROZANOV
1 Ararat (1983)
2 Swallow (1984)
3 Sphinx (1986)
4 Summit (1987)
5 Lying together (1990)

THOMAS, DONALD
INSPECTOR SWANN
1 Belladonna (1984)
2 The Ripper's apprentice (1986)
3 Jekyll, alias Hyde (1988)

THOMAS, GORDON
DAVID MORTON
1 Deadly perfume (1991)
2 Godless icon (1992)
3 Voices in the silence (1993)
4 Organ hunters (1994)
5 Poisoned sky (1995)

THOMAS, H.
1 As it was (1926)
2 World without end (1931)
3 Time and again (1978)
4 Under storm's wing (1988)
   NF *Autobiography*

THOMAS, LESLIE
1 This time next week (1974)
2 In my wildest dreams (1984)

THOMAS, LESLIE
DANGEROUS DAVIES
1 Dangerous Davies (1976)
2 Dangerous in love (1987)
3 Dangerous by moonlight (1993)
4 Dangerous Davies and the lonely heart (1999)

THOMAS, LESLIE
THE VIRGIN SOLDIERS
1 The virgin soldiers (1966)
2 Onward, virgin soldiers (1971)
3 Stand up, virgin soldiers (1975)

THOMAS, R.
WUDU, LTD.
1 Out on the rim (1988)
2 Chinaman's chance (1978)
3 Voodoo, Ltd. (1993)

THOMAS, S.
LILY PASQUALE
1 Dead clever (1999)
2 Seaside (1999)

THOMPSON, E. V.
NATHAN JAGO
1 The restless sea (1983)
2 Polrudden (1985)
3 Mistress of Polrudden (1993)

THOMPSON, E. V.
RETALLICK FAMILY
1 Ben Reatallick (1980)
2 Chase the wind (1977)
3 Harvest of the sun (1978)
4 Singing spears (1982)
5 The stricken land (1986)
6 Lottie Trago (1990)
7 Ruddlemoor (1995)
8 Fires of evening (1998)

THOMPSON, E. V.
BECKY
1 Becky (1988)
2 Lewin's Mead (1996)

THOMPSON, G.
DADE COOLEY
1 Murder mystery (1981)
2 Nobody cared for Kate (1983)
3 A cup of death (1988)

THOMPSON, GRACE
VALLEY SERIES
1 A welcome in the valley (1989)
2 Valley affairs (1990)
3 The changing valley (1990)
4 Valley in bloom (1993)

THOMPSON, GRACE
HOLIDAYS AT HOME
1 Wait till summer (2000)
2 Swingboats on the sand (2001)
3 Waiting for yesterday (2001)
4 Day trippers (2002)

THOMPSON, GRACE
PENDRAGON ISLAND
1 Corner of a small town (1996)
2 The Weston women (1996)
3 Unlocking the past (1997)
4 Maisie's way (1998)
5 A shop in the High Street (1998)
6 Sophie Street (1999)
7 Unwise promises (2002)
8 Street parties (2003)

THOMPSON, N.
1 At their departing (1986)
2 On their return (1987)

THOMSON, DAVID
1 Nairn in darkness and light (1987)
2 Woodbrook (1974)
   NF *Memories of a Scots childhood*

THOMSON, J.
CHIEF INSPECTOR FINCH
1 Not one of us (1972)
2 Death cap (1973)
3 The long revenge (1974)
4 Case closed (1977)
5 A question of identity (1978)
6 Deadly relations (1979)
7 Alibi in time (1980)
8 Shadow of a doubt (1981)
9 To make a killing (1982)

10 Sound evidence (1984)
11 A dying fall (1985)
12 The dark stream (1986)
13 No flowers, by request (1987)
14 Rosemary for remembrance (1988)
15 The spoils of time (1989)
16 Past reckoning (1990)
17 Foul play (1991)
18 Burden of innocence (1996)
19 The unquiet grave (2001)

THORNDYKE, R.
DOCTOR SYN
1 Doctor Syn on the high seas (1936)
2 Doctor Syn returns (1935)
3 Further adventures of Doctor Syn (1936)
4 Courageous exploits of Doctor Syn (1936)
5 The amazing quest of Doctor Syn (1938)
6 The shadow of Doctor Syn (1944)
7 Doctor Syn (1915)

THORNE, B.
ZION COVENANT
1 Vienna prelude (1992)
2 Prague counterpoint
3 Munich signature
4 Jerusalem interlude
5 Danzig passage
6 Warsaw requiem

THORNE, B.
ZION CHRONICLES
1 Gates of Zion (1995)
2 Daughter of Zion (1996)
3 Return to Zion (1997)
4 Light in Zion (1998)
5 Key to Zion (1998)

THORNE, B. & B.
SAGA OF THE SIERRAS
1 Sequoia scout (1991)
2 The year of the grizzly (1992)

THORNE, N.
ASKHAM CHRONICLES
1 Never such innocence (1985)
2 Yesterday's promises (1986)
3 Bright morning (1986)
4 A place in the sun (1987)

THORNE, N.
CHAMPAGNE
1 Champagne (1991)
2 Champagne gold (1992)

THORNE, N.
PEG HALLAM
1 The broken bough (2000)
2 The blackbird's song (2001)
3 The water's edge (2002)

THORNE, N.
PEOPLE OF THE PARISH
1 People of this parish (1991)
2 The rector's daughter (1992)
3 Rules of engagement (1997)
4 Old money (1997)
5 Past love (1999)
6 In time of war (2000)

THURLEY, J.
1 Household gods (1988)
2 Tenements of clay (1989)

TILLEY, P.
AMTRAK WARS
1 Cloud warrior (1984)
2 The first family (1985)
3 Iron master
4 Blood river
5 Death bringer
6 Earth-thunder

TIMLETT, P. V.
1 Seedbearers
2 Power of the serpent
3 Twilight of the serpent

TIMLIN, M.
NICK SHARMAN
1 A good year for the roses (1988)
2 Gun street girl (1990)
3 Romeo's tune (1990)
4 The turnaround (1991)
5 Take the A-train (1991)
6 Zip gun boogie (1992)
7 Hearts of stone (1992)
8 Pretend we're dead (1994)
9 Paint it black (1995)
10 Find my way home (1996)
11 A street that rhymed at 3am (1997)
12 Dead flowers (1998)
13 Quick before they catch us (1999)
14 All the empty places (2000)

TIMPSON, J.
1 Paper trail (1990)
2 Sound track (1991)

TINNISWOOD, P.
THE BRIGADIER
1 Tales from a long room (1981)
2 More tales from a long room (1982)
3 The Brigadier down under (1983)
4 The Brigadier in season (1984)
5 Tales from Witney Scrotum (1987)

TINNISWOOD, P.
BRANDON FAMILY
1 A touch of Daniel (1969)
2 I didn't know you cared (1973)
3 Except you're a bird (1974)
4 Call it a canary (1985)
5 Uncle Mort's North Country (1986)
6 Uncle Mort's South Country (1990)

TINNISWOOD, P.
WINSTON
1 Hayballs (1989)
2 Winston (1991)

TOD, M.
WOODSTOCK SAGA
1 The silver tide (1994)
2 The second wave (1994)
3 The golden flight (1995)

TODD, C.
INSPECTOR IAN RUTLEDGE
1 A test of wills (1997)
2 Wings of fire (1998)
3 Search the dark (1999)

TODD, M.
CLAUDIA SEFERIUS
1 Claudia (1995)
2 Virgin territory (1996)
3 Man eater (1997)
4 Wolf whistle (1998)
5 Jail bait (1999)
6 Black salamander (2000)
7 Dream boat (2002)
8 Second act (2003)

TOER, P. A.
1 This earth of mankind (1979)
2 Child of all nations (1980)

TOLKIEN, J. R. R.
HISTORY OF MIDDLE EARTH
1 The book of lost tales 1 (1983)
2 The book of lost tales 2 (1984)
3 The lays of Beleriad (1985)
4 The shaping of Middle Earth (1986)
5 The lost road (1987)

6 The return of the shadow (1988)
7 The treason of Eisengard (1989)
8 The war of the ring (1990)
9 Sauron defeated (1992)
10 Morgoth's ring (1993)
11 The war of the jewels (1994)
12 The peoples of Middle Earth (1996)

TOLKIEN, J. R. R.
THE LORD OF THE RINGS
1 The Hobbit (1950)
2 The Silmarillion (1978)
3 The fellowship of the ring (1952)
4 The two towers (1954)
5 The return of the King (1955)

TONKIN, P.
TOM MUSGROVE
1 The point of death (2002)
2 One head too many (2002)
3 The hound of the borders (2003)

TOPE, R.
DET. CONSTABLE DEN COOPER
1 A dirty death (1999)
2 Death of a friend (2000)
3 A death to record (2001)

TOPE, R.
DREW SLOCOMBE
1 Dark undertakings (1997)
2 Grave concerns (2000)
3 The sting of death (2002)
4 A market for murder (2003)

TOURNEY, L.
MATTHEW STOCK
1 The players
2 Low treason (1984)
3 Familiar spirits (1985)
4 The Bartholomew Fair murders (1987)

TOVEY, D.
1 Cats in the belfry (1958)
2 Donkey work (1962)
3 Cats in May (1959)
4 Life with Grandma (1964)
5 Raining cats and donkeys (1966)
6 The new boy (1970)
7 Double trouble (1972)
8 Making the horse laugh (1974)
9 The coming of Saska (1977)
10 A comfort of cats (1979)
11 Roses round the door (1984)
12 Waiting in the wings (1986)
   NF *The story of the author's cats*

TOWNLEY, P.
1 The stone maiden (1986)
2 Nearest of kin (1988)

TOWNSEND, P.
1 Duel of eagles (1970)
2 Duel in the dark (1986)

TOWNSEND, S.
ADRIAN MOLE
1 The secret diary of Adrian Mole, aged 1 3/4 (1982)
2 The growing pains of Adrian Mole (1985)
3 Adrian Mole: the wilderness years (1993)
4 Adrian Mole: the cappuccino years (1998)

TOYE, J.
THE ARCHERS
1 Family ties, 1951-67 (1998)
2 Looking for love, 1968-86 (1999)

TRANTER, N.
1 Macbeth the King (1978)
2 Margaret the Queen (1979)
3 David the Prince (1980)
4 True Thomas (1981)
5 The Wallace (1975)

TRANTER, N.
JAMES V TRILOGY
1 The riven realm (1984)
2 James, by the grace of God (1985)
3 Rough wooing (1986)

TRANTER, N.
MASTER OF GRAY
1 The Master of Gray (1961)
2 The courtesan (1963)
3 Past Master (1965)
4 Mail Royal (1989)

TRANTER, N.
JAMES GRAHAM, EARL OF MONTROSE
1 The young Montrose (1972)
2 Montrose the Captain-General (1973)

TRANTER, N.
MARY STEWART
1 Price of a princess (1994)
2 Lord in waiting (1994)

RANTER, N.
MCGREGOR TRILOGY
1 McGregor's gathering (1975)
2 The clansmen (1953)
3 Gold for Prince Charlie (1962)

RANTER, N.
ROBERT THE BRUCE
1 The steps to an empty throne (1969)
2 The path of the hero king (1969)
3 The price of the King's peace (1971)

RANTER, N.
THE HOUSE OF STEWART
1 Lords of Misrule (1976)
2 Folly of princes (1977)
3 The captive crown (1977)
4 Warden of the Queen's March (1989)
5 Lion let loose (1967)
6 The Unicorn rampant (1984)

RAVEN, B.
THE JUNGLE NOVELS
1 Government (1971)
2 The carreta (1970)
3 March to Caobaland (1961)
4 Trozas
5 The rebellion of the hanged (1952)
6 General from the jungle

REHERNE, J.
DR. JAMES YEO
1 The trap (1985)
2 Mangrove chronicles (1986)

REMAYNE, K.
LOVEDAY FAMILY
1 The Loveday fortunes (2001)
2 The Loveday trials (2002)
3 The Loveday scandals (2002)
4 Loveday honour (2004)

REMAYNE, P.
LANKERNE
1 The fires of Lankerne (1979)
2 The destroyers of Lankerne (1982)
3 Buccaneers of Lankerne (1983)

REMAYNE, P.
SISTER FIDELMA
1 Absolution by murder (1994)
2 Shroud for the Archbishop (1995)
3 Suffer little children (1995)
4 The subtle serpent (1996)
5 The spider's web (1997)
6 Valley of the shadow (1998)

7 The monk who vanished (1998)
8 Act of mercy (1999)
9 Hemlock at Vespers (2000)
10 Our Lady of darkness (2000)
11 Smoke in the wind (2001)
12 The haunted Abbot (2002)
13 Badger's moon (2003)
14 Whispers of the dead: short stories (2004)

TRENHAILE, J.
STEPAN POVIN
1 A view from the square (1983)
2 Nocturne for the general (1985)

TRESILLIAN, R.
BONDMASTER
1 Bondmaster (1977)
2 Bondmaster Buck (1984)
3 Blood of the Bondmaster (1978)
4 Bondmaster breed (1979)
5 Bondmaster fury (1982)
6 Bondmaster's revenge (1983)

TRESILLIAN, R.
BLOODHEART
1 Bloodheart (1986)
2 Bloodheart royal (1986)
3 Bloodheart feud (1987)

TREVELYAN, R.
PENDRAGON
1 Pendragon - late of Prince Albert's Own (1975)
2 His Highness commands Pendragon (1976)
3 Pendragon and the Montenegran plot (1977)
4 Pendragon and the seeds of mutiny (1979)

TREVOR, J.
DET. CHIEF INSPECTOR CHRIS SIMON
1 A gathering of dust (1995)
2 The same corruption there (1996)
3 Time to die (1999)
4 A fine and private place (2002)
5 A deadly deceit (2004)

TREVOR, M.
LUXEMBOURG
1 The fugitives (1973)
2 The marked man (1974)
3 The enemy at home (1974)
4 The forgotten country (1975)
5 The treacherous paths (1976)
6 The civil prisoner (1977)

7 The fortunes of peace (1978)
8 Wanton fires (1979)

TRIPP, M.
JOHN SAMSON
1 Obsession (1973)
2 The once a year man (1977)
3 Cruel victim (1979)
4 The wife smuggler (1978)
5 A woman in bed (1976)
6 Going solo (1981)
7 One love too many (1983)
8 Death of a man-tamer (1987)
9 The frightened wife (1987)
10 The cords of vanity (1989)
11 Video vengeance (1990)
12 A woman of conscience (1994)
13 Samson and the Greek Delilah (1995)
14 The suitcase killings (1997)
15 Deadly ordeal (1999)

TROCHECK, K. H.
CALLAGHAN GARRITY
1 Homemade sin (1994)
2 Happy never after (1995)
3 Every crooked nanny (1995)
4 To live and die in Dixie (1995)
5 Heart trouble (1996)
6 Strange brew (1999)
7 Midnight clear (2000)
8 Irish eyes (2001)

TROW, M. J.
INSPECTOR LESTRADE
1 The adventures of Inspector Lestrade (1985)
2 Brigade (1986)
3 Lestrade and the hallowed house (1986)
4 Lestrade and the Leviathan (1987)
5 Lestrade and the brother of death (1987)
6 Lestrade and the Ripper (1988)
7 Lestrade and the guardian angel (1990)
8 Lestarde and the deadly game (1990)
9 Lestrade and the gift of the prince (1991)
10 Lestrade and the dead man's hand (1992)
11 Lestrade and the sign of nine (1992)
12 Lestrade and the sawdust ring (1993)
13 Lestrade and the mirror of murder (1993)
14 Lestrade and the kiss of Horus (1995)
15 Lestrade and the devil's own (1996)

TROW, M. J.
PETER MAXWELL
1 Maxwell's house (1994)
2 Maxwell's flame (1995)

3 Maxwell's movie (1998)
4 Maxwell's war (1999)
5 Maxwell's ride (2000)
6 Maxwell's curse (2000)
7 Maxwell's reunion (2001)
8 Maxwell's match (2002)
9 Maxwell's inspection (2003)

TROYAT, H.
SYLVIE
1 Sylvie (1982)
2 Sylvie; her teenage years (1987)
3 Happiness (1989)

TRUMAN, M.
MAC AND ANNABEL SMITH
1 Murder in Washington (1989)
2 Murder at the Kennedy Centre (1990)
3 Murder at the National Cathedral (1991)
4 Murder at the Pentagon (1993)
5 Murder in the CIA (1994)
6 Murder on the Potomac (1995)
7 Murder at the FBI (1996)

TRUMP, I.
KATINKA KOVAR
1 For love alone (1992)
2 Free to love (1993)

TS'AO CHAN HSUEH CHIN
THE STORY OF THE STONE
1 The golden days (1973)
2 The crab-flower club (1977)
3 The warning voice (1980)
4 The debt of tears (1982)
5 The dreamer wakes (1986)

TUBB, E. C.
DUMAREST SAGA
1 Winds of Gath
2 Derai
3 Toyman
4 Kalin
5 The jester at Scar
6 Lallia
7 Technos
8 Veruchia
9 Mayenne
10 Jendelle
11 Zenya
12 The eye of the Zodiac
13 Eloise
14 Jack of swords
15 Spectrum of a forgotten sun
16 Haven of darkness
17 Prison of night
18 Incident on Ath

19 The Quillian sector
20 Web of sand
21 Iduna
22 The terra data
23 World of promise
24 Nectar of heaven
25 The Terridae
26 The coming event
27 Earth is heaven
28 Melome
29 Angado
30 Symbol of Terra
31 The temple of truth

TURNBULL, P.
GLASGOW POLICE DIVISION
1 Deep and crisp and even (1981)
2 Dead knock (1982)
3 Fair Friday (1983)
4 Big money (1984)
5 Condition purple (1989)
6 Two way cut (1988)
7 And did murder him (1991)
8 Long day Monday (1991)
9 The killing floor (1994)
10 The man with no face (1998)

TURNBULL, P.
CHIEF INSPECTOR HENNESSEY
1 Deathtrap (1999)
2 Perils and dangers (2000)
3 The return (2001)
4 After the flood (2002)
5 Dark secrets (2002)
6 Treasure trove (2003)

TURNER, GEORGE
1 Beloved son (1978)
2 Vaneglory (1981)
3 Yesterday

TURNER, J.
HAISBY
1 The arcade (1990)
2 Harbour Hill (1991)

TUROW, S.
"SANDY" STERN
1 Presumed innocent (1988)
2 Burden of proof (1990)
3 Pleading guilty (1993)

TUROW, S.
SONIA KLONSKY
1 The burden of proof (1990)
2 The laws of our fathers (1996)

TURTLEDOVE, H.
THE VIDESSOS CYCLE
1 The misplaced legion
2 An Emperor for the Legion
3 The Legion of Videssos
4 Swords of the Legion

TURTLEDOVE, H.
COLONIZATION
1 Second contact (1999)
2 Down to earth (2000)
3 Aftershocks (2001)

TURTLEDOVE, H.
DARKNESS
1 Into the darkness (1999)
2 Darkness descending (2000)
3 Through the darkness (2001)

TURTLEDOVE, H.
THE GREAT WAR
1 American front (1998)
2 Walk in hell (1999)
3 Breakthrough (2001)

TURTLEDOVE, H.
THE TALE OF CRISPOS
1 Krispos rising
2 Krispos of Videssos

TURTLEDOVE, H.
WORLD WAR
1 In the balance (1994)
2 Tilting the balance (1995)
3 Upsetting the balance (1996)
4 Striking the balance (1996)

TURTLEDOVE, H.
THE AMERICAN EMPIRE
1 Blood and iron (2001)
2 The centre cannot hold (2002)
3 The victorious opposition (2003)

TWAIN, M.
TOM SAWYER AND HUCKLEBERRY FINN
1 Adventures of Tom Sawyer
2 Adventures of Huckleberry Finn
3 Ton Sawyer abroad
4 Tom Sawyer, detective
5 Tom Sawyer grows up, by C.Wood
6 Further adventures of Huck Finn, by G.Matthews (1982)

UNDERWOOD, M.
NICK ATTWELL
1 The juror (1975)
2 The fatal trip (1977)
3 Murder with malice (1977)
4 Crooked wood (1978)

UNDERWOOD, M.
ROSA EPTON
1 A pinch of snuff (1974)
2 Anything but the truth (1978)
3 Smooth justice (1979)
4 Victim of circumstance (1980)
5 Crime upon crime (1981)
6 Double jeopardy (1981)
7 Goddess of death (1982)
8 A party to murder (1984)
9 Death in camera (1985)
10 The hidden man (1985)
11 Death at Deepwood Grange (1986)
12 The uninvited corpse (1987)
13 The injudicious judge (1987)
14 Dual enigma (1988)
15 A compelling case (1989)
16 Rosa's dilemma (1990)
17 Dangerous business (1990)
18 The seeds of murder (1991)
19 Guilty conscience (1992)

UPDIKE, J.
BECH
1 Bech:a book (1970)
2 Bech is back (1983)
3 Bech at bay (1998)

UPDIKE, J.
HARRY (RABBIT) ANGSTROM
1 Rabbit, run (1961)
2 Rabbit redux (1972)
3 Rabbit is rich (1982)
4 Rabbit at rest (1990)
5 Rabbit remembered (in Licks of Love) (2001)

UPWARD, E.
EDWARD SEBRILL
1 In the thirties (1968)
2 The rotten elements (1969)
3 No home but the struggle (1977)

URIS, L.
IRISH SERIES
1 Trinity (1976)
2 Redemption (1995)

VACHSS, A.
BURKE
1 Flood
2 Strega
3 Blue Belle (1990)
4 Hard candy (1990)
5 Blossom (1991)
6 Sacrifice (1992)
7 Shella (1993)
8 Down in the zero (1995)

VALENTINE, D.
KEVIN BRYCE
1 Unorthodox methods (1988)
2 A collector of photographs (1989)
3 Fine distinctions (1991)

VALIN, J.
HARRY STONER
1 The lime pit (1980)
2 Final notice (1981)
3 Dead letter (1982)
4 Day of wrath (1983)
5 Natural causes (1984)
6 Life's work (1988)
7 Fire lake (1989)
8 The music lovers (1993)

VAN GREENAWAY, P.
INSPECTOR CHERRY
1 The Medusa touch (1973)
2 Doppelganger (1975)
3 The destiny man (1977)
4 "Cassandra" Bell (1981)
5 The Lazarus lie (1982)
6 The killing cup (1987)

VAN SLYKE, H.
1 The heart listens (1974)
2 The mixed blessing (1975)

VAN VOGT, A. E.
NULL-A
1 The worlds of Null-A (1968)
2 The players of Null-A (1970)

VAN VOGT, A. E.
WEAPONS
1 The weapon shops of Isher
2 The weapon makers

VAN WORMER, L.
ALEXANDRA WARING
1 Riverside Drive (1989)
2 West End (1991)

VANCE, J.
DEMON PRINCES
1 Star king (1968)
2 The killing machine
3 Palace of love
4 The face (1980)
5 The book of dreams (1982)

VANCE, J.
LYONESSE
1 Lyonesse
2 The green pearl
3 Madouc (1990)

VANCE, J.
CADWAL CHRONICLES
1 Araminta Station (1988)
2 Ecce and Old Earth (1992)
3 Throy (1993)

VANCE, J.
PLANET OF ADVENTURE
1 City of Chasch (1974)
2 Servant of the Wankh (1974)
3 The Dirdir (1975)
4 The Pnume (1975)

VANDERGRIFF, A.
DAUGHTERS OF THE SOUTH WIND
1 Daughters of the wild country
2 Daughters of the opal skies
3 Daughters of the far islands
4 Daughters of the misty isles

VANNER, L.
1 Rannoch Chase
2 Guardian of Rannoch (1986)

VARDEMAN, R. E.
THE WAR OF POWERS
1 The war of powers
2 Istu awakened

VARDEMAN, R. E.
SWORDS OF RAEMLLYN
1 Swords of Raemllyn
2 Death's acolyte
3 The beasts of the mist
4 For crown and kingdom

VARLEY, J.
GAE TRILOGY
1 Titon
2 Wizard (1981)
3 Demon (1984)

VAUGHAN, A.
1 Signalman's morning (1981)
2 Signalman's twilight (1983)
3 Signalman's nightmare (1987)
   NF Memoirs of a railwayman

VENTERS, A.
GIL KENNEDY
1 Kennedy
2 Blood on the rocks (1983)

VERNON, F.
1 Gentlemen and players (1984)
2 Privileged children (1982)
3 A desirable husband (1987)

VERNON, T.
FAT MAN
1 Fat man on a bicycle (1981)
2 Fat man on a Roman road (1983)
3 Fat man in the kitchen (1986)
4 Fat man in Argentina (1990)
   NF Travel

VICKERS, B.
1 Fed up to the top attic (1984)
2 Life golden in time (1985)
   NF Life in Victorian Bridlington

VIDAL, G.
MYRA
1 Myra Breckinridge (1968)
2 Myron (1975)

VIDAL, G.
WASHINGTON TRILOGY
1 Burr (1973)
2 1876 (1976)
3 Washington DC (1967)

VINCENZI, P.
SPOILS OF TIME TRILOGY
1 No angel (2000)
2 Something dangerous (2001)
3 Into temptation (2002)

VINGE, J.
1 The snow queen (1980)
2 The summer queen (1992)

VINGE, V.
1 The peace war
2 Marooned in real time

VITES, C.
THE NORTHRON FOLK
1 The Northron folk (1993)
2 Passing shadows (1996)
3 Class of '39 (1997)

VIVIS, A.
STRATHANNAN
1 Daughters of Strathannan (1992)
2 The Lennox women (1993)
3 The rowan tree (1994)
4 The provost's woman (1996)
5 The heather loft (1997)

VOINOVICH, V.
1 Life and adventures of Private Ivan
  Chomkin (1978)
2 Pretender to the throne (1981)

VOLLMANN, W. T.
SEVEN DREAMS
1 The ice shirt (1990)
2 Fathers and crows (1992)
3 The rifles (1994)

WAIN, J.
1 Where the rivers meet (1988)
2 Comedies (1990)
3 Hungry generations (1994)

WAINWRIGHT, J.
DAVIS
1 Davis doesn't live here any more (1970)
2 The pig got up and slowly walked away
  (1971)
3 My word you should have seen us
  (1972)
4 My God how the money rolls in (1972)
5 The devil you don't (1974)

WAINWRIGHT, J.
YORKSHIRE POLICE SERIES
1 Death in a sleeping city (1966)
2 Ten steps to the gallows (1966)
3 Evil intent (1966)
4 The crystallised carbon pig (1967)
5 Talent for murder (1967)
6 The worms must wait (1968)
7 Web of silence (1968)
8 Edge of extinction (1968)
9 The darkening glass (1969)
10 The takeover men (1969)
11 The big tickle (1969)
12 Prynter's devil (1970)
13 Freeze thy blood less coldly (1970)
14 The last buccaneer (1971)
15 Dig the grave and let him die (1971)

16 Night is a time to die (1972)
17 Requiem for a loser (1972)
18 A pride of pigs (1973)
19 High class kill (1973)
20 A touch of malice (1973)
21 Kill the girls and make them cry (1974)
22 The hard hit (1974)
23 Square dance (1974)
24 Death of a big man (1975)
25 Landscape with violence (1975)
26 Coppers don't cry (1975)
27 Acquittal (1976)
28 Walther P.38 (1976)
29 Who goes next? (1976)
30 The bastard (1976)
31 Pool of tears (1977)
32 A nest of rats (1977)
33 The day of the peppercorn kill (1977)
34 The jury people (1978)
35 Thief of time (1978)
36 Death certificate (1978)
37 A ripple of murders (1978)
38 Brainwash (1979)
39 Tension (1979)
40 Duty elsewhere (1979)
41 Take murder (1979)
42 The eye of the beholder (1980)
43 Dominoes (1980)
44 A kill of small consequences (1980)
45 Venus fly trap (1980)
46 The tainted man (1980)
47 All on a summer's day (1981)
48 An urge for justice (1981)
49 Anatomy of a riot (1982)
50 Blayde RIP (1982)
51 Distaff factor (1982)
52 Their evil ways (1983)
53 Spiral staircase (1983)
54 All through the night (1985)
55 Clouds of guilt (1985)
56 Forgotten murders (1987)
57 A very parochial murder (1988)
58 The man who wasn't there (1989)

WAITE, E.
EAST END SERIES
1 Cockney waif (1994)
2 Cockney family (1995)

WALKER, A.
MISS CELIE AND MISS SHUG
1 The color purple (1983)
2 The temple of my familiar (1987)
3 Possessing the secret of joy (1992)

WALKER, M. W.
MOLLY CATES
1 The red scream (1994)

2 Under the beetle's cellar (1995)
3 All the dead lie down (1998)

WALKER, P. N.
CARNABY-KING
1 Carnaby and the hi-jackers (1967)
2 Carnaby and the jail breakers (1968)
3 Carnaby and the assassins (1968)
4 Carnaby and the conspirators (1969)
5 Carnaby and the saboteurs (1970)
6 Carnaby and the eliminators (1971)
7 Carnaby and the demonstrators (1972)
8 Carnaby and the infiltrators (1974)
9 Carnaby and the kidnappers (1976)
10 Carnaby and the counterfeiters (1980)
11 Carnaby and the campaigners (1984)

WALKER, P. N.
PANDA ONE
1 Panda One on duty (1977)
2 Panda One investigates (1978)
3 Witchcraft for Panda One (1979)
4 Siege for Panda One (1980)

WALKER, R. W.
DR. JESSICA COREN
1 Killer instinct (1992)
2 Fatal instinct (1993)
3 Primal instinct (1994)
4 Pure instinct (1995)
5 Darkest instinct (1996)

WALLACE, R.
ESSINGTON HOLT
1 To catch a forger (1988)
2 An axe to grind (1989)
3 Paint out (1990)
4 Finger play (1991)

WALLER, L.
WOODS PALMER
1 The banker (1968)
2 The family (1969)
3 The American (1972)
4 The Swiss account (1976)
5 Game plan (1983)
6 Embassy (1987)
7 Deadly sins (1992)

WALSH, B.
1 Live bait (1981)
2 Cheat (1982)

WALSH, J.PATON
IMOGEN QUY
1 The Wyndham case (1993)
2 A piece of justice (1995)

WALTON, E.
MONA
1 Prince of Annwynn
2 The children of Llyr
3 The song of Rhiannon
4 The island of the mighty

WALTON, J.
TIR TANAGIRI
1 The King's peace (2001)
2 The King's name (2002)

WARE, P.
VINH
1 Flight of the Mariner (1997)
2 Beyond freedom (1998)

WARREN, C. H.
1 Happy countryman (1939)
2 England is a village (1940)
3 The land is yours (1943)
4 Miles from anywhere (1944)
5 Adam was a ploughman (1947)
6 Scythe in the apple tree (1953)
7 Content with what I have (1967)
   NF Country life

WARRINGTON, F.
BLACKBIRD SERIES
1 A blackbird in silver
2 A blackbird in darkness
3 A blackbird in amber
4 A blackbird in twlight

WARRINGTON, F.
VAMPIRE SERIES
1 A taste of blood wine (1993)
2 A dance in blood velvet (1994)
3 The dark blood of poppies (1995)

WATERHOUSE, K.
BILLY LIAR
1 Billy Liar (1961)
2 Billy Liar on the moon (1975)

WATSON, CLARISSA
PERSIS WILLUM
1 The fourth stage of Gainsborough Brown (1978)
2 The bishop in the back seat (1981)
3 Runaway (1986)

WATSON, I.
1 The book of the river (1983)
2 The book of the stars (1984)
3 The book of being (1985)

WATSON, I.
MANA
1 Lucky's harvest (1994)
2 The fallen moon (1994)

WATSON, I.
INQUISITION WAR TRILOGY
1 Inquisitor
2 Harlequin
3 Chaos child

WATSON, J.
DIPLOMATS
1 Russian salad (1994)
2 American pie (1995)

WATSON, L.
MONTANA
1 Justice (1997)
2 Montana (1948)
3 White crosses (1997)

WATT-EVANS, L.
LORDS OF DUS
1 Lure of the basilisk
2 The seven altars of Dusarra
3 The sword of Bheleu
4 The book of silence

WAUGH, H.
SIMON KAYE
1 The Glenna Powers case (1981)
2 The Doria Rafe case (1982)
3 The Billy Cantrell case (1982)
4 The Nerissa Claire case (1983)
5 The Veronica Dean case (1984)
6 The Priscilla Copperthwaite case (1986)

WEALE, A.
LONGWARDEN SERIES
1 All my wordly goods (1988)
2 Time and chance (1989)

WEBER, D.
HONOR HARRINGTON
1 Honor among enemies (1997)
2 Mutineers moon (1997)
3 The Honor of the Queen (1998)
4 Echoes of Honor (1998)
5 Field of dishonor (1998)
6 Worlds of Honor (1999)

WEBSTER, E.
BENNI SOLDANO
1 Cossack hide-out (1981)
2 Red alert (1982)
3 The Venetian spy-glass (1982)
4 Madonna of the black market (1983)
5 Million dollar stand-in (1983)
6 The Verratoli inheritance (1983)

WEBSTER, JACK
1 A grain of truth (1981)
2 Another grain of truth (1988)
   NF Autobiography of a journalist

WEINSTEIN, H. & CRISPIN, A. C.
V
1 V (1984)
2 East coast crisis (1985)
3 The alien swordmaster (1986)
4 Prisoners and pawns (1988)

WEIR, M.
MOLLIE
1 Shoes were for Sunday (1969)
2 Best foot forward (1972)
3 A toe on the ladder (1973)
4 Stepping into the spotlight (1975)
5 Walking into the Lyon's den (1977)
6 One small footprint (1980)
7 Spinning like a peerie (1986)
8 A gangin' fits aye getting (1988)
   NF Autobiography

WEIS, M.
STAR OF THE GUARDIANS
1 The lost king (1991)
2 King's jest (1992)
3 King's sacrifice (1992)
4 The Knights of the Black Earth (1995)
5 Robot blues (1996)

WEIS, M.
THE SOVEREIGN STONE TRILOGY
1 Well of darkness
2 Guardians of the lost

WEIS, M. & HICKMAN, T.
DRAGONLANCE LEGENDS
1 Time of the twins
2 War of the twins
3 Test of the twins

WEIS, M. & HICKMAN, T.
DRAGONLANCE TALES
1 The magic of Krynn

2 Kender, gully dwarves and gnomes
3 Love and war

WEIS, M. & HICKMAN, T.
THE DARKSWORD TRILOGY
1 Forging the darksword
2 Doom of the darksword
3 Triumph of the darksword

WEIS, M. & HICKMAN, T.
ROSE OF THE PROPHET
1 The will of the wanderer
2 The paladin of the night
3 The prophet of Akhran

WEIS, M. & HICKMAN, T.
THE DEATH GATE CYCLE
1 Dragon wing (1990)
2 Elven star (1991)
3 Fire sea (1991)
4 Serpent mage (1992)
5 The hand of chaos (1993)
6 Into the labyrinth (1994)

WEIS, M. & HICKMAN, T.
DRAGONLANCE CHRONICLES
1 The soulforge
2 Dragons of autumn twlight
3 Dragons of winter night
4 Dragons of spring dawning
5 Dragons of a fallen sun

WEIS, M. & HICKMAN, T.
STARSHIELD
1 The mantle of Kendis-Dai
2 Nightsword

WELCH, J.
THE RUNESPELL TRILOGY
1 The runes of war (1995)
2 The lost runes (1996)
3 The runes of sorcery (1997)

WELCH, J.
THE BOOK OF OND
1 The lament of Abalone
2 The bard of Castagard
3 The Lord of Necronal

WELCH, J.
THE BOOK OF MAN
1 Dawn of a dark age (2001)
2 The broken chalice (2002)
3 The allegiance of man (2003)

WELCH, P.
HELEN BLACK
1 Murder by the book (1990)
2 Still waters (1991)
3 A proper burial (1993)

WELCOME, J.
1 Bellary Bay (1979)
2 A call to arms (1985)

WELLMAN, M. W.
SILVER JOHN
1 Who fears the devil (1975)
2 The old gods waken (1979)
3 After dark (1981)
4 The lost and the lurking (1982)

WELLS, A.
THE BOOKS OF THE KINGDOMS
1 The wrath of Ashar
2 The usurper
3 The way beneath

WELLS, A.
EXILES
1 Exile's children (1995)
2 Exile's challenge (1996)

WELLS, A.
GODWARS
1 Forbidden magic
2 Dark magic
3 Wild magic

WELLS, M.
THE EXPATRIATES
1 The expatriates (1987)
2 The silk king (1987)
3 The tycoon (1988)

WELSH, I.
LEITH
1 Trainspotting (1993)
2 Porno (2002)

WENDORF, P.
THE PATTERAN TRILOGY
1 Larksleve (1985)
2 Blanche (1986)
3 Bye bye blackbird (1987)

WENDORF, P.
TOLL HOUSE
1 The Toll House (1997)
2 The marriage menders (1999)

WENSBY-SCOTT, C.
THE PERCY TRILOGY
1 Lion of Alnwick (1980)
2 Lion dormant (1983)
3 Lion invincible (1984)

WENTWORTH, P.
MISS MAUD SILVER
1 Grey mask (1928)
2 The case is closed (1937)
3 Lonesome road (1939)
4 Danger point (1942)
5 The Chinese shawl (1943)
6 Miss Silver intervenes (1944)
7 The clock strikes twelve (1945)
8 The key (1946)
9 The traveller returns (1948)
10 Pilgrim's Rest (1948)
11 Latter End (1949)
12 Spotlight (1949)
13 The eternity ring (1950)
14 The case of William Smith (1950)
15 Miss Silver comes to stay (1951)
16 The catherine wheel (1952)
17 The Brading collection (1952)
18 Through the wall (1952)
19 The ivory dagger (1953)
20 Anna, where are you? (1953)
21 The watersplash (1953)
22 Ladies' Bane (1954)
23 Out of the past (1955)
24 Vanishing point (1955)
25 The silent pool (1955)
26 The Benevent treasure (1956)
27 Poison in the pen (1956)
28 The listening eye (1957)
29 The gazebo (1957)
30 The fingerprint (1958)
31 The Alington inheritance (1959)
32 The girl in the cellar (1960)
33 Miss Silver detects (1961)

WESLEY, V. W.
TAMARA HAYLE
1 When death comes stealing (1994)
2 Devil's gonna get him (1995)
3 Where evil sleeps (1996)
4 No hiding place (1997)
5 Easier to kill (2000)
6 The devil riding (2001)

WESSEL, J.
HARDING
1 This far, no further (1997)
2 Pretty ballerina (1998)
3 Kiss it goodbye (2001)

WEST, C.
PAUL CROOK
1 Funnel web (1988)
2 Stonefish (1990)
3 Little ripper (1991)
4 Stage fright (1993)

WEST, CHRISTOPHER
INSPECTOR WANG
1 Death of a blue lantern (1994)
2 Death on Black Dragon River (1995)

WEST, J.
JESS AND ELIZA BIRDWELL
1 The friendly persuasion (1946)
2 Except for thee and me (1969)

WEST, M.
VATICAN TRILOGY
1 The shoes of the fisherman (1963)
2 Clowns of God (1983)
3 Lazarus (1990)

WEST, R.
AUBREY FAMILY
1 The fountain overflows (1957)
2 This real night (1984)
3 Cousin Rosamund (1985)

WESTLAKE, D. E.
JOHN DORTMUNDER
1 Hot rock (1969)
2 Bank shot (1972)
3 Jimmy the kid (1975)
4 Nobody's perfect (1978)
5 Why me?
6 Good behaviour (1987)
7 Bad news (2002)

WETERING, J VAN DE
ADJUTANT GRIJPSTRA AND SGT. DE GIER
1 Outsider in Amsterdam (1976)
2 Tumbleweed (1976)
3 Corpse on the dyke (1977)
4 Death of a hawker (1977)
5 The Japanese corpse (1978)
6 The blond baboon (1978)
7 The Maine massacre (1979)
8 The mind murders (1981)
9 The streetbird (1984)
10 The rattle-rat (1986)
11 Hard rain (1987)
12 The Adjutant's cat and other stories (1988)

WHALLEY, P.
HARRY SOMMERS
1 Robbers (1986)
2 Bandits (1986)
3 Villains (1987)

WHEATLEY, D.
DUC DE RICHLIEU
1 Three inquisitive people (1931)
2 The forbidden territory (1933)
3 The devil rides out (1935)
4 The golden Spaniard (1938)
5 Strange conflict (1941)
6 Code-word Golden Fleece (1946)
7 The second seal (1944)
8 Dangerous inheritance (1965)
9 Gateway to hell (1970)

WHEATLEY, D.
GREGORY SALLUST
1 The scarlet impostor (1942)
2 Faked passports (1943)
3 The black baroness (1944)
4 V for vengeance (1946)
5 Come into my parlour (1947)
6 The island where time stands still (1954)
7 Traitor's gate (1958)
8 They used dark forces (1964)
9 The white witch of the South Seas (1967)

WHEATLEY, D.
JULIAN DAY
1 The quest of Julian day (1939)
2 The sword of fate (1944)
3 Bill for the use of a body (1964)

WHEATLEY, D.
ROGER BROOK
1 The launching of Roger Brook (1947)
2 The shadow of Tyburn Tree (1948)
3 The rising storm (1952)
4 The man who killed the king (1953)
5 The dark secret of Josephine (1958)
6 The rape of Venice (1959)
7 The Sultan's daughter (1963)
8 The wanton princess (1966)
9 Evil in a mask (1969)
10 The ravishing of Lady Mary Weare (1970)
11 The Irish witch (1973)
12 Desperate measures (1974)

WHEATLEY, D.
THE TIME HAS COME...
1 The young man said (1978)

2 Drink and ink (1979)
3 My secret war (1980)
NF Autobiography

WHEELER, R. S.
SAM FLINT
1 Flint's gold
2 Flint's truth

WHITBOURN, J.
1 A dangerous energy (1994)
2 To build Jerusalem (1995)

WHITE, A.
AYSGILL FAMILY
1 Ravenswyke (1979)
2 The homeward tide (1981)
3 The vanishing land (1982)
4 The years of change (1983)

WHITE, EDMUND
1 A boy's own story (1985)
2 The beautiful room is empty (1988)

WHITE, J.
BEN ESCOBIE
1 The Persian oven (1987)
2 California exit (1987)

WHITE, J. D.
SEBASTIAN KETTLE
1 The Leipzig affair (1974)
2 The Salzburg affair (1977)
3 The Brandenburg affair (1979)

WHITE, J. D.
ROGER KELSO
1 Young Mr. Kelso (1963)
2 Brave Captain Kelso (1959)
3 Kelso of the 'Paragon' (1969)
4 Captain of Marine (1960)
5 The Princess of Persia (1961)
6 Commodore Kelso (1967)
7 Fair wind to Malabar (1978)
8 A wind in the rigging (1973)
9 A spread of sail (1975)

WHITE, JAMES
SECTOR GENERAL
1 Ambulance ship (1986)
2 Star surgeon (1987)
3 Hospital station (1987)
4 Sector General (1988)
5 Star healer (1989)
6 Futures past (1989)
7 Code blue emergency (1990)

WHITE, STEPHEN
DR. ALAN GREGORY
1 Privileged information (1992)
2 Private practices (1993)

WHITEHEAD, B.
YORK CYCLE OF MYSTERIES
1 Playing God (1988)
2 The girl with red suspenders (1990)
3 The Dean it was that died (1991)
4 Sweet death, come softly (1992)
5 The killings at Barley Hall (1995)
6 Secrets of the dead (1996)
7 Death at the Dutch House (1997)
8 Dolls don't choose (1998)

WHITELAW, S.
JORDAN LACEY
1 Pray and die (2000)
2 Wave and die (2001)
3 Spin and die (2002)
4 Hide and die (2003)
5 Jest and die (2004)

WHITING, C.
MAJOR JOHN BOLD
1 Bugles at dawn (1990)
2 Sabres in the sun (1991)

WHITING, C.
COMMON SMITH, V. C.
1 The Baltic run (1993)
2 In Turkish waters (1994)
3 Death on the Rhine (1994)
4 Passage to Petrograd (1995)
5 The Japanese princess (1996)
6 Death trap (1996)
7 Hell's angels (1997)

WHITTAKER, J.
1 The raking of the embers (1982)
2 The flame in the morning (1984)

WHYTE, B.
1 Yellow on the broom (1979)
2 Red rowans and wild honey (1990)

WHYTE, J.
THE CAMULOD CHRONICLES
1 The skystone (1996)
2 The singing sword (1996)
3 The eagle's brood (1997)
4 The Saxon shore (1998)
5 The fort at river's bend (1999)
6 The sorcerer (1999)
7 Uther (2001)

WIAT, P.
EDWARD III TRILOGY
1 Queen gold (1985)
2 The grey goose-wing (1986)
3 The whyte swan (1986)

WIAT, P.
GREY FAMILY
1 Five gold rings (1981)
2 Children of the spring (1983)

WIAT, P.
CHARLTON MEAD
1 The mistletoe bough (1981)
2 Bride of darkness (1982)
3 Wychwood (1982)

WIAT, P.
HOWARD SAGA
1 Maid of gold (1971)
2 Like as the roaring waves (1972)
3 Wear a green kirtle (1987)
4 The Queen's fourth husband (1976)
5 Lion without claws (1976)
6 Yet a lion (1978)

WIAT, P.
GRAVE
1 Headstone (1994)
2 Archangel (1995)

WIAT, P.
PLANTAGENETS
1 The hammer and the sword (1992)
2 The lovers (1993)

WIAT, P.
WYATT SAGA
1 Master of Blandeston Hall (1973)
2 The heir of Alington (1973)
3 Sound now the passing bell (1973)
4 Knight of Alington (1974)
5 Rebel of Alington (1977)
6 My lute be still (1977)

WIDEMAN, J. E.
1 Damballah (1984)
2 Hiding place (1984)
3 Sent for you yesterday (1984)

WILBORNE, D.
YORKSHIRE VICAR
1 A vicar's diary (1998)
2 A summer's diary (1999)

WILCOX, C.
LIEUT. FRANK HASTINGS
1 The lonely hunter (1971)
2 The disappearance (1972)
3 Dead aim (1972)
4 Hiding place (1973)
5 Long day down (1974)
6 Aftershock (1974)
7 The watcher (1977)
8 Power plays (1981)
9 Mankiller (1982)
10 Victims (1986)
1 Swallow's fall (1987)

WILCOX, J.
1 Modern Baptists (1984)
2 North Gladiola (1985)
3 Miss Undine's living room (1987)

WILDE, O.
DORIAN GRAY
1 The picture of Dorian Gray (1891)
2 Dorian, by J.Reed (1997)

WILHELM, K.
CHARLIE MEIKLEJOHN &
CONSTANCE LEIDL
1 The Hamlet trap (1987)
2 Smart house (1989)
3 The dark door (1990)
4 Sweet, sweet poison (1991)

WILHELM, K.
BARBARA HOLLOWAY
1 The best defence (1996)
2 For the defence (1997)

WILLEFORD, C.
HOKE MOSELEY
1 Miami blues (1985)
2 New hope for the dead
3 Sideswipe (1988)

WILLETT, M.
THE CHADWICK FAMILY
CHRONICLES
1 Looking forward (1998)
2 Holding on (1999)
3 Winning through (2001)

WILLIAM, S.
EVERGENCE
1 The prodigal sun
2 The dying light
3 The dark imbalance

WILLIAMS, D.
FIGHTER
1 Bluebirds over (1982)
2 Vendetta (1982)

WILLIAMS, D.
MARK TREASURE
1 Unholy writ (1974)
2 Treasure by degrees (1977)
3 Treasure up in smoke (1978)
4 Murder for Treasure (1979)
5 Copper, gold and Treasure (1982)
6 Treasure preserved (1983)
7 Advertise for Treasure (1984)
8 Wedding Treasure (1985)
9 Murder in Advent (1985)
10 Treasure in roubles (1986)
11 Divided Treasure (1987)
12 Treasure in Oxford (1988)
13 Holy Treasure! (1989)
14 Prescription for murder (1990)
15 Treasure by post (1991)
16 Planning on murder (1992)
17 Banking on murder (1993)

WILLIAMS, D.
TANK
1 Tank (1985)
2 Fortress Eagle (1986)
3 Sugar sugar (1987)

WILLIAMS, D.
DET. CHIEF INSPECTOR MERLIN
PARRY
1 Last seen breathing (1994)
2 Death of a prodigal (1995)
3 Dead in the market (1996)
4 A terminal case (1997)
5 Suicide intended (1999)
6 Practise to deceive (2003)

WILLIAMS, G.
AMAZING CHRONICLES OF THE
MICRONAUTS
1 Micronaut world
2 Revolt of the Micronauts

WILLIAMS, GERARD
DR. MORTIMER
1 Dr. Mortimer and the Aldgate mystery
   (2001)
2 Dr. Mortimer and the barking man
   mystery (2003)
3 Dr. Mortimer and the carved head
   mystery (2003)

WILLIAMS, L.
LEGENDARY MURDERS
1 A copper snare (1981)
2 The murder triangle (1982)
3 Images of death (1984)
4 Portrait of the dead (1985)

WILLIAMS, MICHAEL
HAWKENS OF ARCADY
1 Arcady (1996)
2 Allamanda (1997)

WILLIAMS, N.
WIMBLEDON
1 The Wimbledon poisoner (1990)
2 Scenes from a poisoner's life (1994)

WILLIAMS, P. O.
PELBAR
1 The ends of the circle
2 The breaking of North Wall
3 The dome in the forest
4 The fall of the shell

WILLIAMS, R.
PEOPLE OF THE BLACK MOUNTAINS
1 The beginning (1989)
2 Eggs of the eagle (1990)

WILLIAMS, TAD
MEMORY, SORROW AND THORN
1 The dragonbone chair (1989)
2 Stone of farewell (1990)
3 To green angel tower (1993)

WILLIAMS, TAD
OTHERLAND
1 City of golden shadow (1998)
2 River of blue fire (1999)
3 Mountain of black glass (1999)
4 Sea of silver light (2001)

WILLIAMS, TIMOTHY
COMMISSARIO TROTTI
1 Converging parallels (1982)
2 The puppeteer (1985)
3 Persona non grata (1987)
4 Black August (1992)
5 Big Italy (1996)

WILLIAMSON, HENRY
A CHRONICLE OF ANCIENT
SUNLIGHT
1 Dark lantern (1951)
2 Donkey boy (1952)
3 Young Philip Maddison (1953)
4 How dear is life (1954)
5 A fox under my cloak (1957)
6 The golden virgin (1957)
7 Love and the loveless (1958)
8 A test of destruction (1960)
9 The innocent moon (1961)
10 It was the nightingale (1962)
11 The power of the dead (1963)
12 The phoenix generation (1965)
13 A solitary war (1966)
14 Lucifer before sunrise (1967)
15 The gate of the world (1969)

WILLIAMSON, P. G.
1 The orb and the sceptre (1996)
2 Orbus's world (1997)
3 The soul of the orb (1998)

WILLIAMSON, P. G.
FIRSTWORLD CHRONICLES
1 Dinbig of Khimmur (1991)
2 The legend of Shadd's torment (1993)
3 From enchantery (1993)
4 Heart of shadows (1994)
5 Citadel (1995)

WILLIS, T., LORD
ROSIE CARR
1 Spring at the "Winged Horse" (1983)
2 The green leaves of summer (1988)
3 The bells of Autumn (1991)

WILLSHER, A.
A LEICESTERSHIRE CHRONICLE
1 Inherit the earth (1996)
2 So shall you reap (1997)
3 The fruitful vine (1998)
4 The sower went forth (1999)

WILMOTT, P.
1 Growing up in a London village (1979)
2 Green girl (1983)
  NF Autobiography

WILSON, A. N.
LAMPITT PAPERS
1 Incline our hearts (1989)
2 Bottle in the smoke (1990)
3 Daughters of Albion (1991)
4 Hearing voices (1995)
5 A watch in the night (1996)

WILSON, ANNE
SARA KINGSLEY
1 Truth or dare (1997)
2 Governing body (1997)

WILSON, B.
PAM NILSEN
1 Murder in the collective (1986)
2 Sisters of the road (1987)
3 The dog collar murders (1989)

WILSON, B.
CASSANDRA REILLY
1 Gaudi afternoon (1992)
2 Trouble in Transylvania (1993)

WILSON, C.
CHIEF INSPECTOR GREGORY
SALTFLEET
1 The schoolgirl murder case (1974)
2 The Janus murder case (1984)

WILSON, C.
SPIDER WORLD
1 The tower (1987)
2 The delta (1987)
3 The magician (1992)
4 Shadowland (2002)

WILSON, C.
GERALD SORME
1 Ritual in the dark (1960)
2 Man without a shadow (1963)
3 The god of the labyrinth (1970)

WILSON, D.
ROBERT DUDLEY
1 Bear's whelp (1979)
2 Bear rampant (1981)
3 Sweet Robin (1984)

WILSON, DEREK
KEENE'S REVOLUTION
1 Keene's quest (2000)
2 Keene's terror (2001)

WILSON, DEREK
TIM LACY
1 The triarchs (1993)
2 The Dresden text (1994)
3 The Hellfire papers (1995)
4 The Camargue brotherhood (1995)
5 The Borgia chalice (1996)
6 Cumberland's cradle (1996)

WILSON, E.
1 The lost time cafe (1993)
2 Poisoned hearts (1995)

WILSON, F. P.
NIGHTWORLD
1 The keep (1981)
2 The tomb (1984)
3 The touch (1986)
4 Reborn (1990)
5 Reprisal (1991)
6 Nightworld (1992)

WILSON, R.
SCHRODINGER'S CAT
1 The universe next door
2 The trick top hat
3 Homing pigeons

WILSON, ROBERT
BRUCE MEDWAY
1 Instruments of darkness (1995)
2 The big killing (1996)
3 Blood is dirt (1997)
4 A darkening stain (1998)

WILSON, T. E.
BIG TOM HOLDER
1 The newcomers (1981)
2 Yellow fever (1982)
3 Harvest of gold (1983)

WILSON, T. R.
1 Master of Morholm (1986)
2 The ravished earth (1988)
3 The straw tower (1990)

WILTSE, D.
BECKER
1 A prayer for the dead (1992)
2 Close to the bone (1993)
3 The edge of sleep (1994)

WILTZ, C.
NEAL RAFFERTY
1 The killing circle (1981)
2 A diamond before you die (1988)

WINGFIELD, R. D.
INSPECTOR JACK FROST
1 Frost at Christmas (1989)
2 A touch of Frost (1990)
3 Night Frost (1992)
4 Hard Frost (1995)
5 Winter Frost (1999)

WINGROVE, D.
CHUNG KUO
1 The middle kingdom (1989)
2 Broken wheel (1990)

3 The white mountain (1991)
4 Stone within (1992)
5 Beneath the tree of heaven (1993)
6 White moon, red dragon (1994)
7 Days of bitter strength (1995)
8 The marriage of the living dark (1997)

WINGS, M.
EMMA VICTOR
1 She came too late (1986)
2 She came in a flash (1988)
3 Divine victim (1992)
4 She came to the Castro (1997)
5 She came in drag (1999)

WINSLOW, P. G.
SUPT. MERLIN CAPRICORN
1 Death of an angel (1974)
2 The Brandenburg hotel (1976)
3 The Witch Hill murders (1977)
4 Coppergold (1978)
5 The counsellor heart (1979)
6 The Rockefeller gift (1982)

WINWARD, W.
1 The Canaris fragments (1983)
2 The last and greatest art (1983)

WISHART, D.
CORVINUS
1 Ovid (1996)
2 Germanicus (1997)
3 Sejanus (1998)
4 The Lydian baker (1998)
5 The horse coin (1999)
6 Old bones (2000)
7 Last rites (2001)
8 White murder (2002)
9 A vote for murder (2003)
10 Parthian shot (2004)

WITHALL, M.
EISDALSA ISLAND
1 Beacon on the shore (1995)
2 The gorse in bloom (1996)
3 Where the wild thyme grows (1997)
4 Fields of heather (1998)

WODEHOUSE, P. G.
BLANDINGS CASTLE
1 Something fresh (1915)
2 Leave it to Psmith (1923)
3 Blandings Castle (1935)
4 Summer lightning (1929)
5 Heavy weather (1933)
6 Lord Emsworth and others (1927)
7 Full moon (1947)

8 Pigs have wings (1952)
9 Service with a smile (1962)
10 Galahad at Blandings (1969)
11 A pelican at Blandings (1969)
12 Sunset at Blandings (unfinished) (1977)

WODEHOUSE, P. G.
JEEVES AND WOOSTER
1 My man Jeeves (1915)
2 The inimitable jeeves (1923)
3 Carry on Jeeves (1925)
4 Very good, Jeeves (1930)
5 Thank you Jeeves (1934)
6 Right-ho, Jeeves (1934)
7 Code of the Woosters (1938)
8 Joy in the morning (1946)
9 The mating season (1949)
10 Ring for Jeeves (1953)
11 Jeeves and the feudal spirit (1954)
12 Jeeves in the offing (1960)
13 Stiff upper lip, Jeeves (1963)
14 Jeeves and the tie that binds (1971)
15 Aunts aren't gentlemen (1974)

WOIWODE, L.
1 Beyond the bedroom wall (1987)
2 Born brothers (1990)

WOLF, J.
CAMELOT
1 The road to Avalon (1989)
2 Born of the sun (1990)
3 The edge of light (1991)

WOLFE, G.
THE BOOK OF THE NEW SUN
1 Shadow of the torturer (1980)
2 The claw of the conciliator (1981)
3 The sword of the Lictor (1982)
4 The citadel of the Autarch (1983)
5 The urth of the New Sun (1987)

WOLFE, G.
THE BOOK OF THE LONG SUN
1 Nightside (1993)
2 Lake of the long sun (1994)
3 Calde of the long sun (1994)
4 Wxodus from the long sun (1996)

WOLFE, G.
THE BOOK OF THE SHORT SUN
1 On Blue's waters (2000)
2 In Green's jungles (2001)
3 Return to the whorl (2001)

WOLFE, G.
SOLDIER
1 Soldier of the mist (1986)
2 Soldier of Arete (1990)

WOMACK, S.
HARRY JAMES DENTON
1 Dead folk's blues (1994)
2 Torch town boogie (1995)
3 Way past dead (1995)
4 Chain of fools (1996)

WOMACK, S.
JACK LYNCH TRILOGY
1 Murphy's fault
2 Smash cut
3 The software bomb

WONGAR, B.
1 Walg (1987)
2 Karan (1987)
3 Gabo Djara (1988)

WOOD, B.
1 Minstrel's lute (1987)
2 Satanic lute (1987)

WOOD, B.
DARK AGES
1 Wolf king (1991)
2 The lost prince (1992)

WOOD, CHRISTOPHER
1 Taiwan (1983)
2 A dove against death (1983)

WOOD, R. S.
1 The Riding Officer (1987)
2 The rose of St.Keverne (1989)

WOOD, T.
REID BENNETT
1 Dead in the water (1984)
2 The killing cold (1984)
3 Dead centre (1985)
4 Fool's gold (1986)
5 The killing cold (1987)
6 Corkscrew (1988)
7 When the killing starts (1989)
8 On the inside (1990)
9 Flashback (1992)
10 Snow job (1993)
11 A clean kill (1995)

WOOD, V.
EMILY
1 Emily (1999)
2 Going home (2000)

WOODCRAFT, E.
FRANKIE RICHMOND
1 Good bad woman (2000)
2 Baby-face (2002)

WOODHOUSE, S.
DR. ALEXANDER FRENCH
1 Season of mists (1984)
2 Peacock's feather (1989)
3 Native air (1990)

WOODING, C.
THE BRAIDED PATH
1 The weavers of Saramyr (2003)
2 The skein of lament (2004)

WOODMAN, R.
NATHANIEL DRINKWATER
1 An eye of the fleet (1780) (1981)
2 A King's cutter (1797) (1983)
3 A brig of war (1798) (1983)
4 Bomb vessel (1801) (1984)
5 The corvette (1803) (1985)
6 1805 (1985)
7 Baltic mission (1807) (1986)
8 In distant waters (1812) (1988)
9 A private revenge (1808-9) (1989)
10 Under false colours (1812) (1991)
12 Beneath the aurora (1813) (1995)
13 The shadow of the eagle (1815) (1997)
14 Ebb tide (1843) (1998)

WOODMAN, R.
JAMES DUNBAR
1 The darkening sea (1991)
2 Under sail (1997)

WOODMAN, R.
JAMES ST.JOHN STANIER
1 Captain of the Caryatid (1997)
2 The cruise of the Commissioner (1998)

WOODMAN, R.
WILLIAM KITE
1 The guineaman (1999)
2 The privateersman (2000)
3 The East Indiaman (2001)

WOODRUFF, W.
NAB END
1 The road to Nab End
2 Beyond Nab End

WOODS, STUART
AMANDA ROBERTS & JOE DONELLI
1 Reckless
2 Body and soul
3 Stolen moments (1991)
4 Ties that bind (1991)

WOODS, STUART
STONE BARRINGTON
1 Dirt (1997)
2 The worst fears realised (2000)
3 New York dead (2000)
4 LA dead (2001)
5 The short forever (2001)

WOODS, S.
ANTONY MAITLAND
1 Bloody instructions (1961)
2 Malice domestic (1962)
3 The taste of fears (1963)
4 Error of the moon (1963)
5 Trusted like the fox (1964)
6 This little measure (1964)
7 The windy side of the law (1965)
8 Though I know she lies (1965)
9 Enter certain murderers (1966)
10 Let's choose executioners (1966)
11 The case is altered (1967)
12 And shame the devil (1967)
13 Knives have edges (1968)
14 Past praying for (1968)
15 Tarry to be hanged (1969)
16 An improbable fiction (1970)
17 Serpent's tooth (1971)
18 The knavish crown (1971)
19 They love not poison (1972)
20 Yet she must die (1973)
21 Enter the corpse (1973)
22 Done to death (1974)
23 A show of violence (1975)
24 My life is done (1976)
25 The law's delay (1977)
26 A thief or two (1977)
27 Exit murderer (1978)
28 This fatal writ (1979)
29 Proceed to judgment (1979)
30 They stay for death (1980)
31 Weep for her (1980)
32 Cry guilty (1981)
33 Dearest enemy (1981)
34 Enter a gentlewoman (1982)
35 Villains by necessity (1982)
36 Most grievous murder (1982)

37 Call back yesterday (1983)
38 The lie direct (1983)
39 Where should he die (1983)
40 The bloody book of law (1984)
41 Murder's out of tune (1984)
42 Defy the devil (1984)
43 An obscure grave (1985)
44 Away with them to prison (1985)
45 Put out the light (1985)
46 Most deadly hate (1986)
47 Nor live so long (1986)
48 Naked villainy (1986)

WOOLLEY, P.
GUINEVERE AND ARTHUR
1 Child of the northern spring (1990)
2 Guinevere, Queen of the summer stars (1991)
3 Guinevere, the legend in autumn (1991)

WREDE, P. C.
LYRA
1 Mairelan the magician
2 Dealing with the dragon
3 The raven ring

WREN, M. K.
THE PHOENIX LEGACY
1 Sword of the lamb
2 Shadow of the swan
3 House of the wolf

WRIGHT, A. T.
ISLANDIA
1 Islandia (1942)
2 The Islar, by M. Saxton (1969)
3 The two kingdoms
4 Havoc in Islandia, by M.Saxton (1984)

WRIGHT, D.
THREADED DANCES SEQUENCE
1 The parrot cage (1990)
2 Never such innocence (1991)
3 Dreams of another day (1992)
4 The tightrope walkers (1993)

WRIGHT, E.
CHARLIE SALTER
1 The night the gods smiled (1983)
2 Smoke detector (1984)
3 Death in the old country (1985)
4 A single death (1986)
5 A body surrounded by water (1987)
6 A question of murder (1988)
7 A sensitive case (1989)
8 Final cut (1991)

9 A fine Italian hand (1992)
10 Death by degrees (1993)

WRIGHT, K.
DET. INSPECTOR DAVE STARK
1 One oblique one (1991)
2 Trace and eliminate (1992)
3 Addressed to kill (1993)
4 Fair means or foul? (1994)

WRIGHT, L. R.
KARL ALBERG
1 The suspect
2 Sleep while I sing
3 Chill rain in January (1990)
4 Fall from grace (1992)

WRIGHT, P.
1 I am England (1987)
2 That near and distant place (1988)

WRIGHTSON, P.
THE BOOK OF WIRRUN
1 The ice is coming (1977)
2 The dark bright water (1979)
3 Behind the wind (1981)

WURTS, J.
CYCLE OF FIRE
1 Stormwarden (1989)
2 Keeper of the keys (1989)
3 Shadowfane (1990)

WURTS, J.
WARS OF LIGHT AND SHADOWS
1 The curse of the Mistwraith (1993)
2 The ships of Merior (1994)
3 Warhost of Vastmark (1995)

WURTS, J.
ALLIANCE OF LIGHT
1 The fugitive prince (1997)
2 Grand conspiracy (1999)
3 Peril's gate (2001)

WYLIE, J.
SERVANTS OF ARK
1 The first named
2 Centre of the circle
3 The mage-born child

WYLIE, J.
THE UNBALANCED EARTH
1 Dreams of stone
2 The lightless kingdom
3 The age of chaos

WYLIE, J.
ISLAND AND EMPIRE
1 Dark fire
2 Echoes of flame
3 The last augury

WYNDHAM, JOAN
1 Love is blue (1986)
2 Love lessons (1984)
3 Anything once (1992)
NF Autobiography

WYNDHAM, JOHN
TRIFFIDS
1 The day of the triffids (1951)
2 The night of the triffids, by S.Clark (2001)

YEH, CHUN-CHAN
QUIET ARE THE MOUNTAINS
1 The mountain village (1988)
2 The open fields (1988)
3 A distant journey (1989)

YORK, A.
MUNROE TALLENT
1 Tallent for trouble (1976)
2 Tallent for disaster (1978)
3 Tallent for terror (1995)
4 Tallent for democracy (1996)

YORKE, K.
1 A woman's place (1983)
2 The pair bond (1984)

YOSHIKAWA, E.
MUSASHI
1 The way of the Samurai
2 The art of war
3 The way of the sword
4 The Bushido code
5 The way of life and death

YOUNG, GAVIN
1 Slow boats to China (1981)
2 Slow boats home (1985)
NF Travel

YOUNG, L.
1 Baby love (1997)
2 Desiring Cairo (1999)

ZETTELL, S.
ISAVALTA
1 A sorcerer's treason (2001)

2 The usurper's crown (2002)
3 The firebird's vengeance (2004)

ZINDELL, D.
EA CYCLE
1 The lightstone (2001)
2 The red dragon (2002)

ZUBRO, M. R.
TOM MASON
1 Are you nuts? (1999)
2 One dead drag queen (2001)

INDEX OF SERIES AND CHARACTERS

Titles of the most popular series and names of leading characters are listed alphabetically in this index. It is by no means comprehensive, but it may prove useful in identifying fictional characters or the titles of series. Details of individual items in a series are to be found in the main text, under the author's name.

Title/character	Author	Title/character	Author
Castang, Henri	Freeling, N.	Death merchants	Rosenberger, J.
Casteel family	Andrews, V.	Decker, Pete	Kellerman, F.
Castle Rising	Cradock, F.	Deene, Carolus	Bruce, L.
Catherine	Benzoni, J.	Delancy, Richard	Parkinson, J.N.
Chambrun, Pierre	Pentecost, J.	Delaware, Alex	Kellerman, J.
Changewinds	Chalker, J.H.	Derain family	Thompson, K.
Chazalet Chronicles	Howard, E.J.	Desert Commandos	Landsborough, C.
Chee, Jim	Hillerman, T.		
Chelmarsh, Dorian		Destiny of Eagles	Carnegie, S.
Fairweather	Hardwick, M.	Devlin, Brock	Mitchell, S.
Children of the North	Powers, M.S.	Devlin, Harry	Edwards, M.
Children of violence	Lessing, D.	Devlin, Sean	Higgins, J.
Chronicles of an age of		Didier, Auguste	Myers, A.
Darkness	Cook, H.	Dillon, Sean	Higgins, J.
Chronicles of ancient		Discworld	Pratchett, T.
sunlight	Williamson, H.	Dobie, Professor	Cory, D.
Chronicles of Hawklan	Taylor, R.	Dollengager family	Andrews, V.
Clachan series	Armstrong, S.	Dominions of Irth	Attanasio, A.
Claudia Seferina	Todd, M.	Doomsday Books	Marston, A.E.
Claudia series	Franken, R.	Dorsai	Dickson, C.R.
Cluster	Anthony, P.	Dowling, Father	McInerny, R.
Cody	Brierley, D.	Dragon series	McCaffrey, A.
Coffin, *Inspector*	Butler, C.	Dragon Prince	Rawn, M.
Conan the Barbarian	Howard, R.	Dragonard	Gilchrist, R.
Corbett, Hugh	Doherty, P.C.	Drenai saga	Gemmel, D.
Cordwainers	Gower, I.	Drinkwater, Nathaniel	Woodman, R.
Cornelius, Jerry	Moorcock, M.	Duddleswell, Father	Boyd, N.
Colorado, Kat	Kijiewski, K.	Duffy	Kavanagh, D.
Corvinus	Wishart, D.	Dumarest saga	Tubb, E.C.
Courage series	Shears, S.	Duncton chronicles	Horwood, W.
Courtney family	Smith, W.	Dune	Herbert, F.
Coyne, Brady	Tapply, W.C.	East Enders	Miller, H.
Craddocks of		Eddathorpe Mysteries	Flynn, R.
Shallowford	Delderfield, R.F.	Eightyseventh Precinct	McBain, E.
Craigallan family	Barclay, T.	Elsengrin trilogy	Davies, R.
Crawford of Lymond	Dunnett, D.	Elenium	Eddings, D.
Cribb, *Sergeant*	Lovesey, P.	Eliot family	Goudge, E.
Crichton, Tessa	Morice, A.	Ender Wiggins	Card, O. S.
Croft, D.I. Mike	Adams, J.	Epton, Rosa	Underwood, M.
Crook, Paul	West, C.	Erridge, Matt	Stein, A.M.
Crow, Inspector	Lewis, R.	Everard, Nick	Fullerton, A.
Crowner John	Knight, B.	Fairfax, Robert	March, H.
Cunningham, John	Hammond, C.	Fairacre series	Miss Read
Dalgleish, Adam	James, P.D.	Fairlyden	Kirkwood, C.
Dalrymple Daisy	Dunn, C.	Falco	Davis, L.
Dalrymple, Quint	Johnson, P.	Falcon family	Darby, C.
Dalziel, Supt.	Hill, R.	Falcon series	Benzoni, J.
Dancers at the end of		Falconhurst	Onstott, K.
time	Moorcock, M.	Falkenstein, Jesse	Egan, L
Dancing Gods	Chalker, J.L.	Family d'Alambert	Smith, E.E.
Dando	Clive, W.	Fansler, Kate	Cross, A.
Daniels, Charmtan	Melville, J.	Faro, Jeremy	Knight, A.
Darkover series	Bradley, M.Z.	Farrow, Mark	Ross, A.
Davenport, Lucas	Sandford, J.	Fell, Gideon	Carr, J.D.
Dawlish, Patrick	Creasey, I.	Fen, Gervase	Crispin, E.
Daughters of England	Carr, P.	Fethering mysteries	Brett, S.
Death Gate Cycle	Weis, M.	Finch, Inspector	Thomson, J.

Title/character	Author	Title/character	Author
Lavender Road	Carey, H.	McGarr, Ch. Inspector	Gill, B.
Lavette family	Fast, H.	Men at war	Baldwin, A.
Lawson, Loretta	Smith, I.	Mendoza, Luis	Shannon, D.
Leaphorn, Joe	Hillerman, T.	Merivale, *Sir* Henry	Carr, J.D.
Lensman series	Smith, E.E.	Miami Vice	Grave, S.
Lestrade, *Inspector*	Trow, M.J.	Middleton-Brown, David	Charles, K.
Levant trilogy	Manning, 0.	Millhone, Kinsey	Grafton, S.
Lewker, Abercrombie	Carr, I.C.	Minder	Masters, A.
Lightbringer trilogy	Lee, T.	Mission Earth	Hubbard, L.R.
Lisle, Darina	Laurence, J.	Mitchell & Markby	Granger, A.
Lloyd, *Inspector*	McGown, J.	Mongo mysteries	Chesbro, G.C.
Logan family	Andrews, V.	Monk, William	Perry, A.
Lomax, Jacob	Allegretto, M.	Montgomery family	Deveraux, J.
Lorimer family	Melville, A.	Montrose, Dr. Jean	Roe, C.F.
Louise	Shears, S.	Morrissey, Det.Ch.Insp.	Mitchell, K.
Love, Jason	Leasor, J.	Morgan, Rain	Grant-
Lovejoy	Gash, J.		Adamson, L.
Lubbock, John	Cooper, B.	Morse, Det. Chief	
Lucia	Benson, E.F.	Inspector	Dexter, C.
Ludlow, Harry	Donachie, D.	Mortdecai, Charlie	Bonfiglioli, K.
Lugh the Harper	Finney, P.	Mosley, *Detective*	
Lydmouth mysteries	Taylor, A.	*Inspector*	Greenwood, J.
Lynley, Thomas	George, E.	Mountjoy Chronicles	Pewsey, E.
McAllister	Chisholm, M.	Muffin, Charlie	Freemantle, B.
McCone, Sharon	Muller, M.	Mulcahaney, Norah	O'Donnell, L
McGarr, *Chief Inspector*	Gill, B.	Music of Time, The	Powell, A.
McGee, Travis	Macdonald, J.D.	Myth	Asprin, R.
McGuire, Kelly	Hennessey, M.	Necroscope	Lumley, B.
McPherson, Elizabeth	McCrumb, S.	Neighbours	Ruhan, C.
M.A.S.H.	Hooker, R.	Neylor family	Saxton, J.
Maddox, *Sergeant*	Blaisdell, A.	Niccolo, House of	Dunnett, D.
Maddox, Kate	Quest, E.	November Man	Granger, B.
Maguire, Trish	Cooper, N.	Nugent family	Burton, B.
Maigret, *Inspector*	Simenon, G.	Oakes, Blackford	Buckley, W.F.
Maitland, Antony	Woods, S.	Oakes, Boysie	Gardner, J.
Majipoor	Silverberg, R.	Ogilvie, James	McNeil, D.
Mallen family	Cookson, C.	Omaran saga	Cole, A.
Mallett, Dan	Parrish, F.	Omen	Howard, J.
Mallin & Coe	Ormerod, R.	Onedin Line	Abrahams, C.
Malloreon	Eddings, D.	Otani, *Superintendent*	Melville, J.
Malone, Scobie	Cleary, J.	Palfrey, Dr.	Creasey, J.
Mamur Zapt	Pearce, M.	Palmer-Jones, George	Cleeves, A.
Margery family	Bassett, R.	Pamplemousse M.	Bond, M.
Marianne	Benzoni, J.	Panda One	Walker, P.N.
Marlowe, Philip	Chandler, R.	Panzer Platoon	Lutz, G.
Marple, Miss	Christie, A.	Pargeter, Mrs.	Brett, S.
Martian series	Burroughs, E.R.	Paris, Charles	Brett, S.
Mary Ann Shaughnessy	Cookson, C.	Parker	Stark, R.
Mason, Perry	Gardner, E.S.	Parsons, Annie	Shears, S.
Masters, *Chief Inspector*	Clark, D.	Pascoe, *Inspector*	Hill, R.
Masuto, Masao	Cunningham,	Paton, Crispin	Draper, A.
	E.V.	Peabody, Amelia	Peters, E.
Matthew and Son	Kenworthy, C.	Peace, D.C. Charlie	Barnard, R.
Maxim, Harry	Lyall, C.	Peacock series	Gordon, K.
Maxwell, Peter	Trow, M.	Peckover, Harry	Kenyon, M.
Mayo, Det. Ch. Insp.	Eccles, M.	Pel, *Inspector*	Hebden, M.
McGann family	Nicole, C.	Pellucidar series	Burroughs, E.R.

Title/character	Author	Title/character	Author
Pendragon	Trevelyan, R.	Rawlins, Easy	Mosley, W.
Pendragon Cycle	Lawhead, S.	Reacher, Jack	Child, L.
Pengarron	Cook, G.	Reachfar series	Duncan, J.
Penhaligon series	White, A.	Rebus, John	Rankin, I.
Pentecost family	Malpass, E.	Recluce	Modessitt L.E.
Percy trilogy	Wensby-Scott,	Red Dwarf	Naylor, G.
	C.	Redmayne, Christopher	Marston, E.
Performers	Rayner, C.	Resnick, Charlie	Harvey, J.
Pern	McCaffrey, A.	Rhodenbarr, Bernie	Block, L.
Peroni, *Inspector*	Holme, T.	Richlieu, Duc de	Wheatley, D.
Perrin, Reginald	Nobbs, D.	Riftwar saga	Feist, R.
Peters, Toby	Kaminsky, S.	Rigantes	Gemmell, D.
Peterson, D.S. Wes	Ellis, K.	Ripley	Highsmith, P.
Philis	Perry, R.	Rivers, Sophie	Cutler, J.
Pink, Melissa	Moffat, G.	Riverworld saga	Farmer, PJ.
Pink Panther	Waldman, F.	Robicheaux, Dave	Burke, J. L.
Pitt, Charlotte and		Roger the Chapman	Sedley, K.
Thomas	Perry, A.	Rogers, *Chief Inspector*	Ross, J.
Pitt, Dirk	Cussler, C.	Roper, *Det. Superintendent*	Hart, IL
Plantagenet saga	Plaidy, J.	Roper, Ian	Bolitho, J.
Plantagenets	Dymoke, J.	Roselynde chronicles	Gellis, R.
Plum, Stephanie	Evanovitch, J.	Rostnikov, Porfiry	Kaminsky, S.
Poirot, Hercule	Christie, A.	Round Ringford	Purser, A.
Poldark series	Graham, W.	Rowan series	Darby, C.
Pollard, Det.		Rumpole	Mortimer, J.
Superintendent	Lemarchand E.	Runestaff series	Moorcock, M.
Pollifax, Mrs.	Gilman, D.	Russell, Charles	Haggard, W.
Poppy chronicles	Rayner, C.	Ryan, Father 'Blackie'	Greeley, AN.
Porridge	Clement, D.	Ryan, Jack	Clancy, T.
Potter, Brock	Maling, A.	Sabre series	Darby, C.
Power, D.S. Kate	Cutler, J.	Sackett	L'Amour, L.
Powers, Georgina	Danks, D.	Saint, The	Charteris, L.
Pratt, Henry	Nobbs, D.	Sallust, Gregory	Wheatley, D.
Preston, Mark	Chambers, P.	Salter, Charlie	Wright, E.
Priest, Det.Insp.	Pawson, S.	Samson, Bernard	Deighton, L
Principal, Laura	Spring, M.	Savage family	Masters, J.
Pringle, Mr.	Livingston, N.	Savage, Mark	Payne, L.
Prism Pentad	Denning, T.	Sawyer, Pete	Albert, M.
Probyn, Julia	Bridge, A.	Scarpetta, Kay	Cornwell, P.D.
Pym, Mrs. Morland, N.		School for Manners	Chesney, M.
Quantrill, Det.		Scudder, Matthew	Block, L.
Superintendent	Radley, S.	Scully	Bleasdale, A.
Quatermass	Kneale, N.	Seaton family	Sillitoe, A.
Quiller	Hall, A.	Sector General	White, J.
Quinn, Kit	French, N.	Secret Army	Brason, J.
Quist, Julian	Pentecost, H.	Seeton, Miss	Carvic, H.
Rackstraw	Hardwick, M.	Seddall, Harry	Mayo, J.K.
Rainwood family	Bromige, I.	Sensual life	Croft-Cooke, R.
Raj quartet	Scott, P.	Shadow on the Crown	Carter, N.
Rama	Clarke, A.C.	Sidhe legends	Flint, K.C.
Ramage	Pope, D.	Shaft	Tidyman, E.
Rambo	Morrell, D.	Shallott, Sir Roger	Clynes, M.
Ramsay, *Inspector*	Cleeves, A.	Shanara	Brooks, T.
Ramses	Jacq, C.	Shapiro, Frank	Bannister, J.
Raven	Mackenzie, D.	Shard, Simon	McCutchan, P.
Raven, Richard	Griffin, J.	Sharman, Nick	Timlin, M.
Rawlings, John	Lake, D.	Sharpe, Richard	Cornwell, B.

Title/character	Author	Title/character	Author
Shaw, Commander	McCutchan, P.	Thatcher, John Putnam	Lathen, E.
Sheridan, Alex	Stuart, V.	Thomas Covenant	Donaldson, S.R.
Shore, Jemilna	Fraser, A.	Thongor	Carter, L.
Sidel, Isaac	Charyn, J.	Thorne, *Inspector*	Penn, J.
Sigismondo	Eyre, E.	Thrush Green	Miss Read
Silver, Maud	Wentworth, P.	Tibbett, Henry	Moyes, P.
Sipstrassi tales	Gemmell, D.	Tibbs, Virgil	Ball, J.
Sister Agnes	Joseph, A.	Tildy Crawford	Fraser, S.
Sister Fidelma	Tremayne, P.	Todd, "Sweeney"	Palmer, F.
633 Squadron	Smith, F.E.	Tramont series	Barclay, T.
Skinner, ACC	Jardine, Q.	Travers, Ludovic	Bush, C.
Skylark series	Smith, E.E.	Treasure, Mark	Williams, D.
Slade, Anthony	Gribble, L.	Trethowan, Perry	Barnard, R.
Slider, Bill	Harrod-Eagles, C.	Trevelyan, Rose	Bolitho, J.
		Trotter, Tilly	Cookson, C.
Sloan, *Inspector*	Aird, C.	Turner, Sam	Baker, J.
Small, Rabbi	Kemelman, H.	Tweed	Forbes, C.
Smiley, George	Le Carre, J.	Unwin, Miss	Hervey, E.
Smith, Grace	Evans, L.	Urgent, Mark	Forde, N.
Soul Rider	Chalker, J.H.	Urquhart, Francis	Dobbs, M.
Spenser	Parker, R.B.	Valentine, Claudia	Day, M.
Squadron	Holden, M.	Van der Valk, Piet	Freeling, N.
Stahl, Otto	Kessler, L.	Varallo, Vic	Egan, L.
Stainless Steel Rat	Harrison, H.	Virginian series	Fletcher, I.
Stainton, Alec	Murray, S.	Walker, Amos	Estleman, L.D.
Starbuck, Nathaniel	Cornwell, B.	Wanawake, Penny	Moody, S.
Star Lord saga	Buffery, J.	Ward, Eric	Lewis, R.
Star requiem	Cole A.	Webb, *Chief Inspector*	Fraser, A.
Star Trek see title		Weavers	Baker, D.
Star Wars see title		Wellworld saga	Chalker, J.L.
Starsky and Hutch	Franklin, M.	Wentworth, Lyon	Forrest, R.
Stephanie	Gobineau, M.	West, Helen	Fyfield, F.
Stevenson family	Macdonald, M.	Wexford, *Chief Inspector*	Rendell, R.
Stoner, Harry	Valin, J.	Wheel of Time	Jordan, R.
Storm Troop series	Kessler, L.	Whiteoaks	De la Roche, M.
Strathannan	Vivis, A.	Williamsburg series	Thane, B.
Summer wine chronicles	Clarke, R.	Willing, Basil	McCloy, H.
Sutton Place	Lampitt, D.	Willows and Parker	Gough, L
Swann, Cassie	Moody, A.	Wimsey, Peter	Sayers, D.L
Swann saga	Delderfield, R.F.	Windmill Hill	Evans, S.
Sweyneseye	Cower, I.	Wings of gold	Cruise, T.F.
Sword of Truth	Goodkind, T.	Wintercombe	Belle, P.
Syn, Doctor	Thorndike, R.	Winter King's war	Dexter, S.
Tales of Turnham Malpas	Shaw, R.	Winter, *Lieut.* Jason	Gaston, B.
Tallentire family	Bragg, M.	Witchworld	Norton, A.
Tallon, Jack	Ball, J.	Wolfe, Nero	Stout, R.
Tamuli	Eddings, D.	World of the Alfar	Boyer, E.H.
Tanner, Alex	Donald, A.	Wotan Panzer series	Kessler, L.
Tanner, Evan	Block, L	Wyatt saga	Wiat, P.
Tanner, John	Greenleaf, S.	Wycliffe, *Det. Superintendent*	Burley, WJ.
Tansey, *Det. Chief Inspector*	Penn, J.	Xanth	Anthony, P.
Tarzan	Burroughs, E.R.	Yellowthread Street	Marshall, W.L
Tedric, Lord	Smith, E.E.	York Cycle of Mysteries	Whitehead, B.
Temple, Paul	Durbridge, F.	Yorke, Edward	Pope, D.
Thane and Moss	Knox, B.	Yorke, Ned	Pope, D.
Thanet, Luke	Simpson, D.	Zen, Aureilo	Dibdin, M.